D0405958

My assistant's desk

The legendary Excalibur!! It's just a spoon stuck in a jar.

樋口大輔

Words are difficult. A single word can make me feel so happy it can bring tears to my eyes, while another can make me feel too depressed to even stand up. Words can be frightening. A casually spoken word can deeply hurt a person. It is indeed very difficult to accurately express what's on your mind to someone. If we could communicate via telepathy and understand one another that way, I suppose all misunderstandings and disputes would disappear. But in a way, that would be kind of sad. Mankind continues to use imperfect words to communicate and be closer to one another. The fact that we do this despite the risk of hurting each other is what makes us human. That's why I don't need telepathy.

— Daisuke Higuchi

Daisuke Higuchi's manga career began in 1992 when the artist was honored with third prize in the 43rd Osamu Tezuka Award. In that same year, Higuchi debuted as creator of a romantic action story titled **Itaru**. In 1998, **Weekly Shonen Jump** began serializing **Whistle!** Higuchi's realistic soccer manga became an instant hit with readers and eventually inspired an anime series, debuting on Japanese TV in May of 2002.

1964

WHISTLE!
VOL. 7: STEP BY STEP

The SHONEN JUMP Graphic Novel Edition

STORY AND ART BY
DAISUKE HIGUCHI

English Adaptation/Drew Williams
Translation/Naomi Kokubo
Touch-up Art & Lettering/Jim Keefe
Cover, Graphics & Layout/Sean Lee
Editor/Megan Bates

Managing Editor/Elizabeth Kawasaki
Director of Production/Noboru Watanabe
Vice President of Publishing/Alvin Lu
Vice President & Editor in Chief/ Yumi Hoashi
Sr. Director of Acquisitions/Rika Inouye
Vice President of Sales & Marketing/Liza Coppola
Publisher/Hyoe Narita

Printed in the U.S.A.

Published by VIZ Media, LLC
P.O. Box 77010
San Francisco, CA 94107

SHONEN JUMP Graphic Novel Edition
10 9 8 7 6 5 4 3 2 1
First printing, August 2005

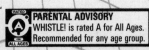

PARENTAL ADVISORY
WHISTLE! is rated A for All Ages.
Recommended for any age group.

THE WORLD'S
MOST POPULAR MANGA

www.viz.com
www.shonenjump.com

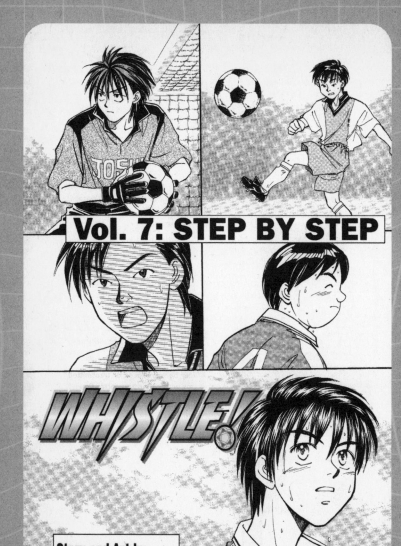

Vol. 7: STEP BY STEP

WHISTLE!

Story and Art by
Daisuke Higuchi

SHŌ
KAZAMATSURI

● **JOSUI JUNIOR HIGH SOCCER TEAM FORWARD**

KŌ
KAZAMATSURI

YŪKO
KATORI

TATSUYA
MIZUNO

● **JOSUI JUNIOR HIGH SOCCER TEAM MIDDLE FIELDER**

CHARACTERS

SOUJŪ MATSUSHITA

FORMER JAPAN LEAGUE PLAYER

JOSUI JUNIOR HIGH COACH

SHIGEKI SATŌ

JOSUI JUNIOR HIGH SOCCER TEAM

FORWARD

HIROYOSHI NORO

JOSUI JUNIOR HIGH SOCCER TEAM

DEFENSE

S T O R Y

TO REALIZE HIS DREAM, SHŌ KAZAMATSURI, A BENCHWARMER AT SOCCER POWERHOUSE MUSASHINOMORI, TRANSFERRED TO JOSUI JUNIOR HIGH SO HE COULD PLAY THE GAME HE LOVES.

SOON AFTER SHO'S ARRIVAL, SOUJŪ MATSUSHITA, A FORMER JAPAN LEAGUE PLAYER, BECAME THE TEAM'S COACH, AND THE TEAM GEARED UP FOR THE SUMMER CHAMPIONSHIP.

THEIR FIRST OPPONENT IN THE PRELIMINARY MATCHES WAS POWERFUL WAKISAKA FIRST JUNIOR HIGH. NOBODY GAVE JOSUI MUCH OF A CHANCE, BUT THE PERENNIAL LOSERS WON THE GAME 6-0, AND MADE IT THROUGH THE REMAINING TWO GAMES.

AS JOSUI PREPARES TO ENTER THE TOURNAMENT, TEAMWORK ISSUES HAVE CROPPED UP BETWEEN THE KEEPER AND THE DEFENDERS. WITH ONLY ONE WEEK LEFT BEFORE THE BIG GAME, CAN THEY SOLVE THEIR PROBLEMS IN TIME?

WHISTLE!

**Vol. 7
STEP BY STEP**

STAGE.54
Keeper's Job
7

STAGE.55
Weakness
28

STAGE.56
Everlasting Passion (STEP BY STEP)
48

STAGE.57
Key Is Locked
67

STAGE.58
Nightmare of the Last Five Minutes
87

STAGE.59
What It Means to Be a Teammate
105

STAGE.60
On Happiness
127

STAGE.61
Time to Go
149

STAGE.62
Stoppage Time
171

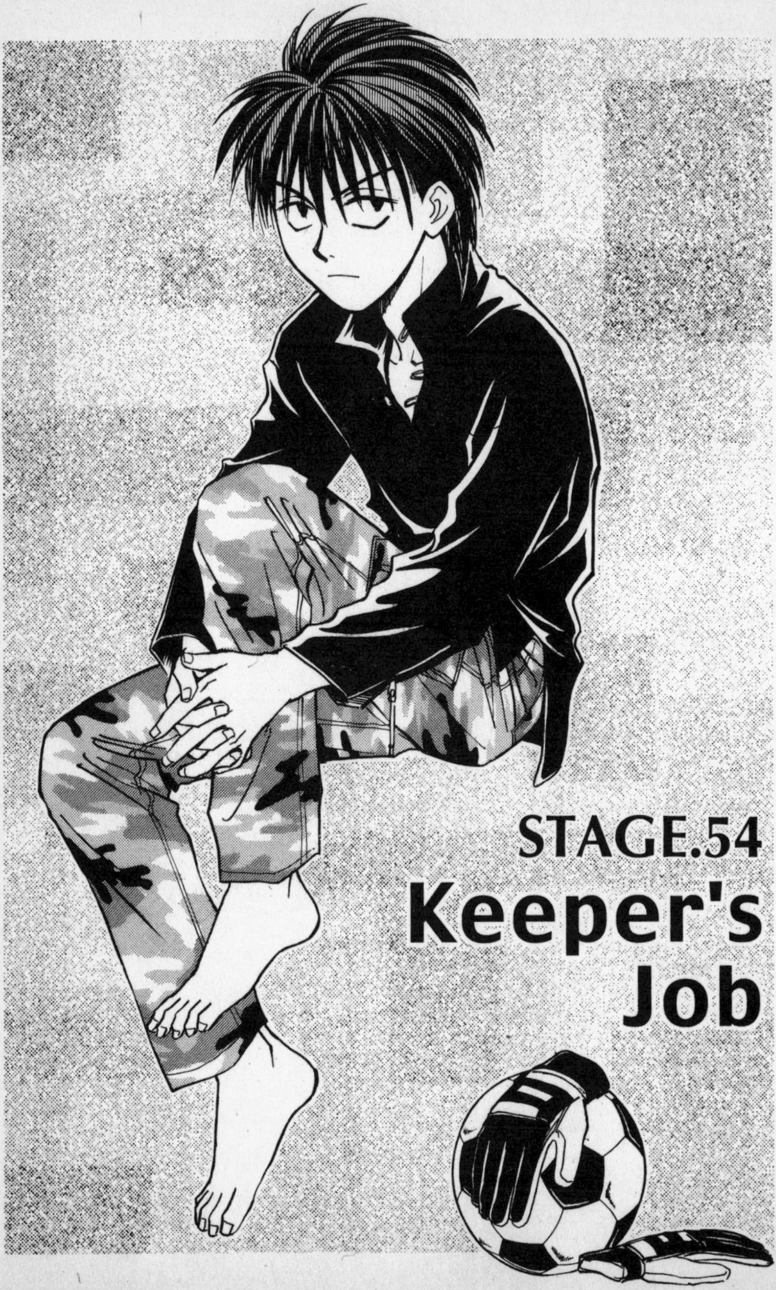

STAGE.54
Keeper's Job

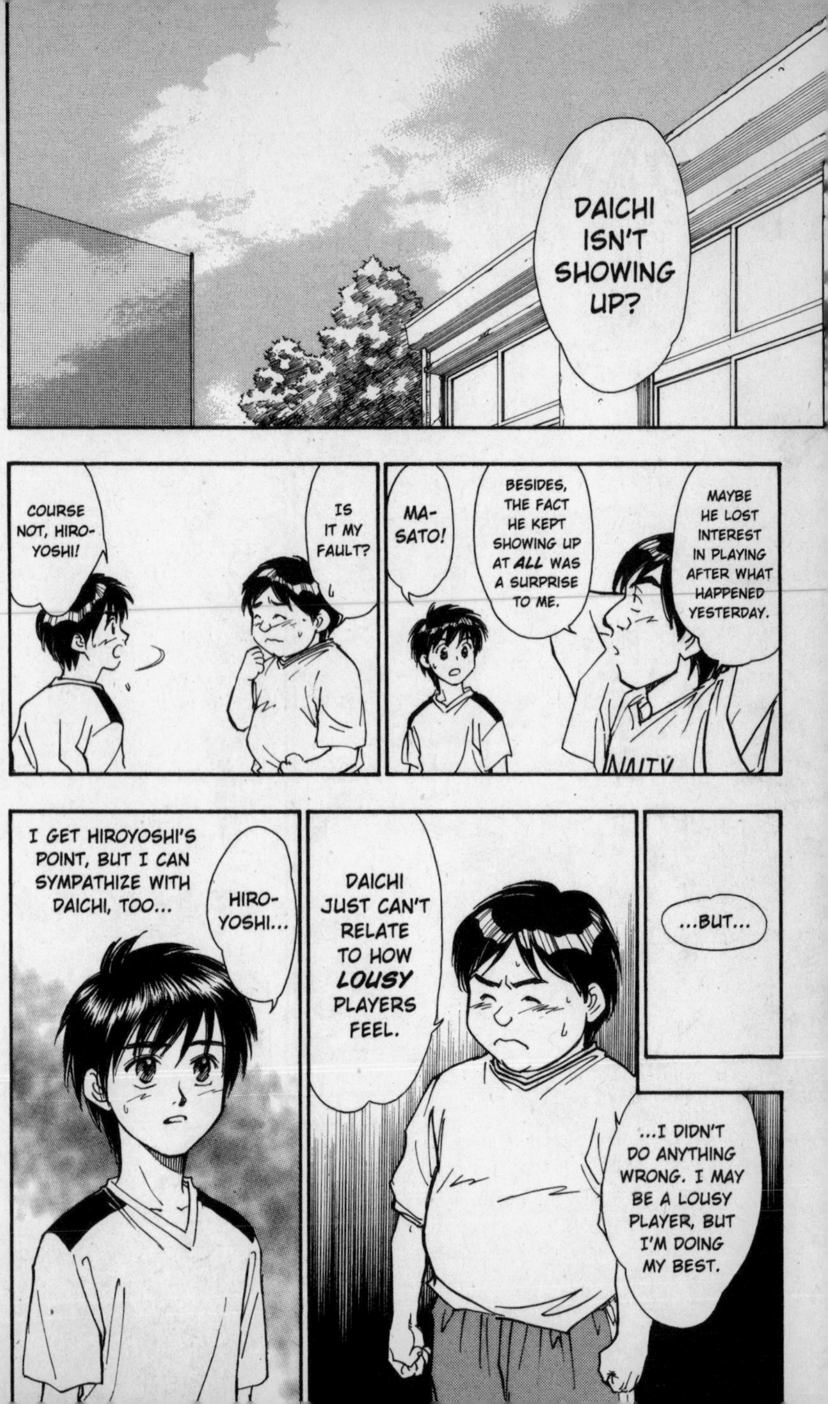
DAICHI ISN'T SHOWING UP?
MAYBE HE LOST INTEREST IN PLAYING AFTER WHAT HAPPENED YESTERDAY.
BESIDES, THE FACT HE KEPT SHOWING UP AT ALL WAS A SURPRISE TO ME.
MA-SATO!
IS IT MY FAULT?
COURSE NOT, HIRO-YOSHI!
...BUT...
...I DIDN'T DO ANYTHING WRONG. I MAY BE A LOUSY PLAYER, BUT I'M DOING MY BEST.
DAICHI JUST CAN'T RELATE TO HOW LOUSY PLAYERS FEEL.
HIRO-YOSHI...
I GET HIROYOSHI'S POINT, BUT I CAN SYMPATHIZE WITH DAICHI, TOO...

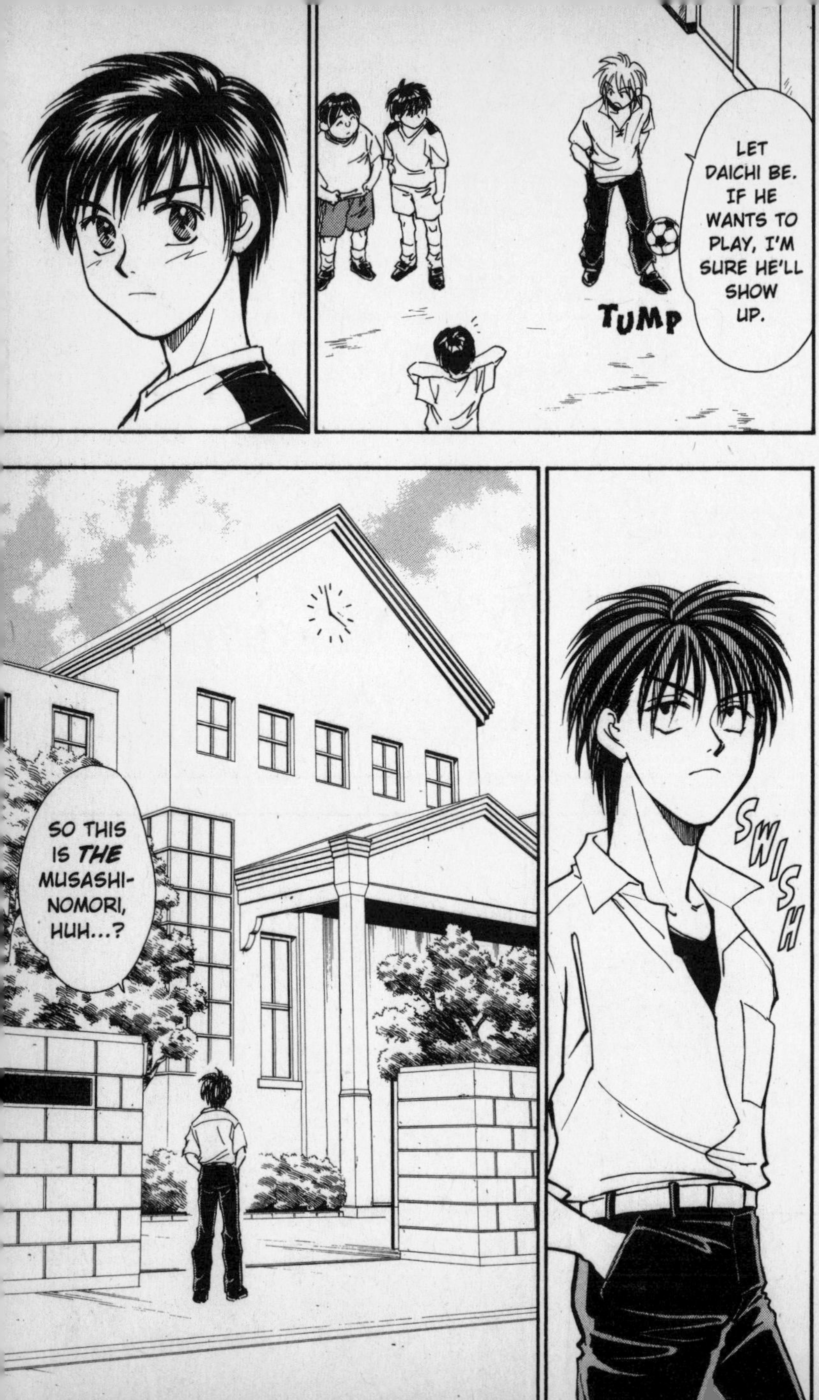
LET DAICHI BE. IF HE WANTS TO PLAY, I'M SURE HE'LL SHOW UP.
TUMP
SWISH
SO THIS IS *THE* MUSASHI-NOMORI, HUH...?

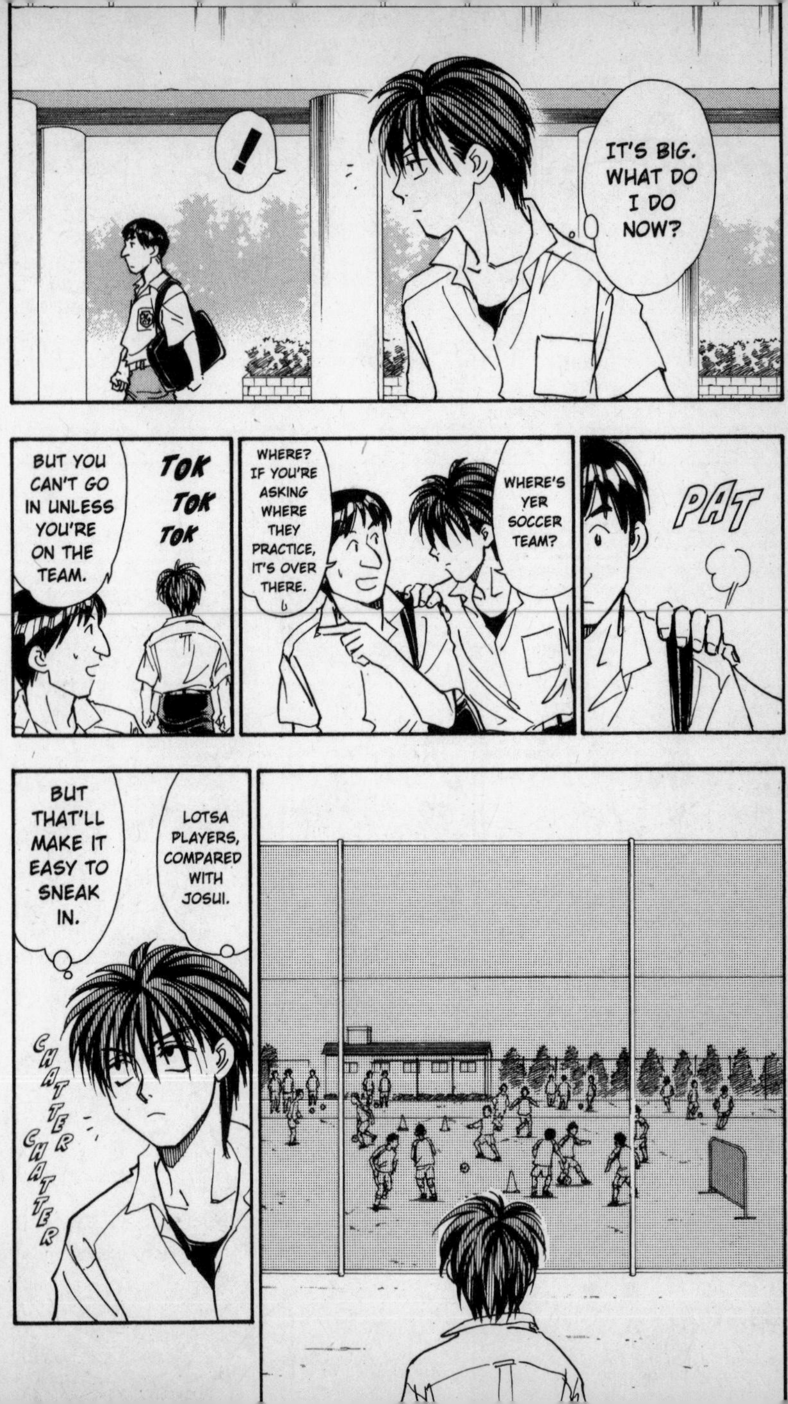
IT'S BIG. WHAT DO I DO NOW?
!
PAT
WHERE'S YER SOCCER TEAM?
WHERE? IF YOU'RE ASKING WHERE THEY PRACTICE, IT'S OVER THERE.
TOK TOK TOK
BUT YOU CAN'T GO IN UNLESS YOU'RE ON THE TEAM.
LOTSA PLAYERS, COMPARED WITH JOSUI.
BUT THAT'LL MAKE IT EASY TO SNEAK IN.
CHATTER CHATTER

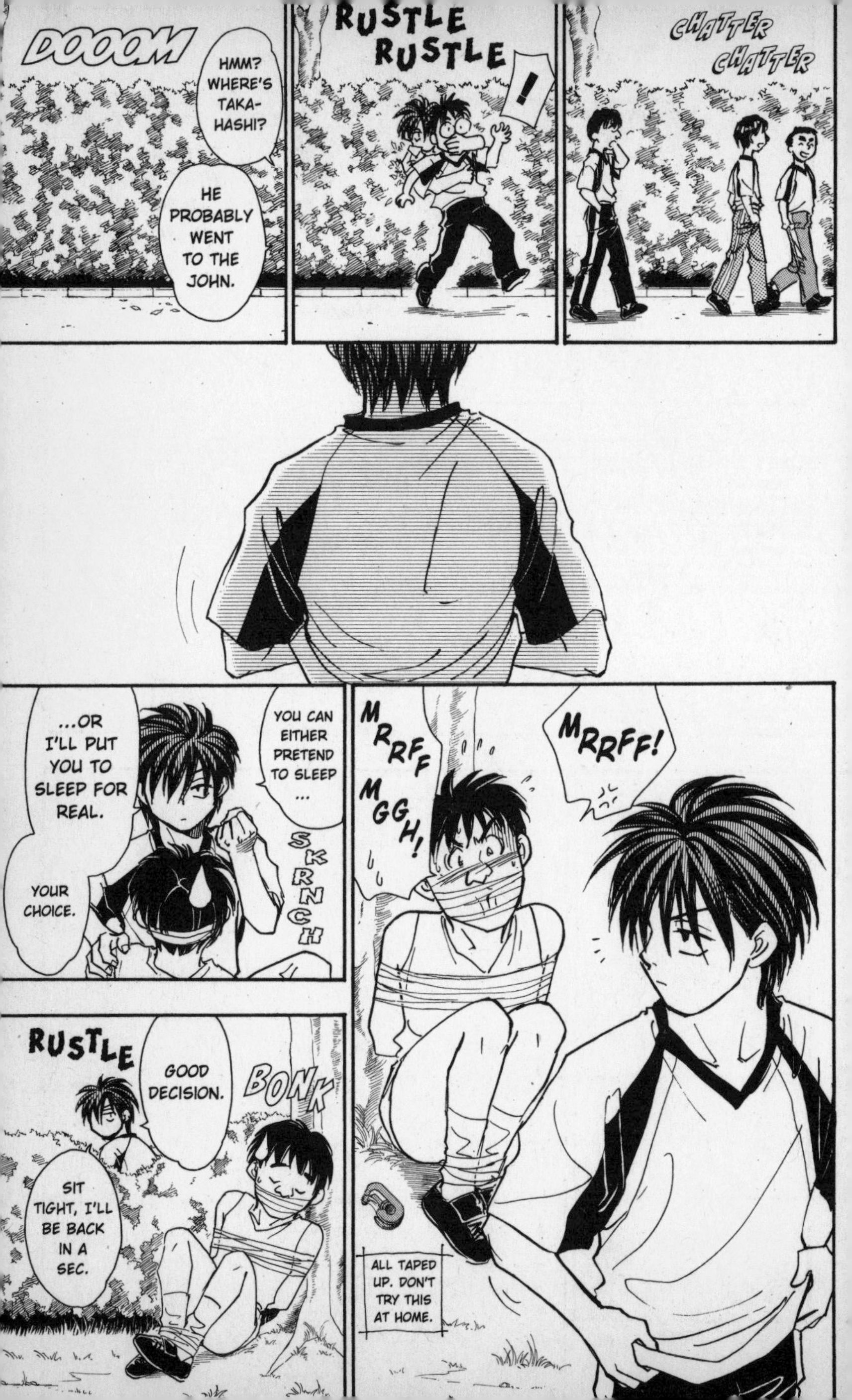
CHATTER CHATTER
RUSTLE RUSTLE
!
DOOOM
HMM? WHERE'S TAKA-HASHI?
HE PROBABLY WENT TO THE JOHN.
...
MRRFF!
MRRFF MGGH!
ALL TAPED UP. DON'T TRY THIS AT HOME.
YOU CAN EITHER PRETEND TO SLEEP ...
SKRNCH
...OR I'LL PUT YOU TO SLEEP FOR REAL.
YOUR CHOICE.
BONK
GOOD DECISION.
RUSTLE
SIT TIGHT, I'LL BE BACK IN A SEC.

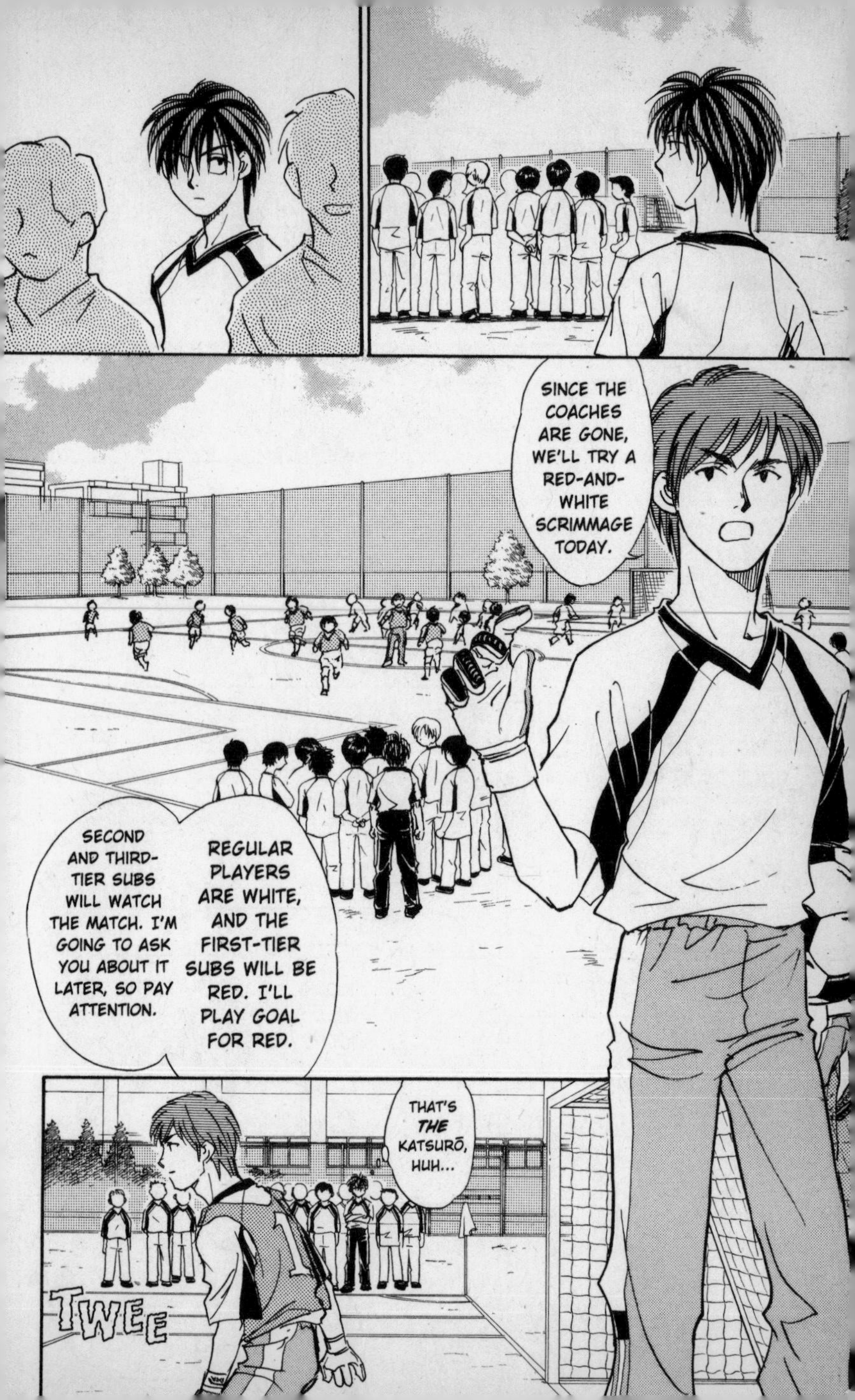
SINCE THE COACHES ARE GONE, WE'LL TRY A RED-AND-WHITE SCRIMMAGE TODAY.
REGULAR PLAYERS ARE WHITE, AND THE FIRST-TIER SUBS WILL BE RED. I'LL PLAY GOAL FOR RED.
SECOND AND THIRD-TIER SUBS WILL WATCH THE MATCH. I'M GOING TO ASK YOU ABOUT IT LATER, SO PAY ATTENTION.
THAT'S *THE* KATSURŌ, HUH...
TWEE

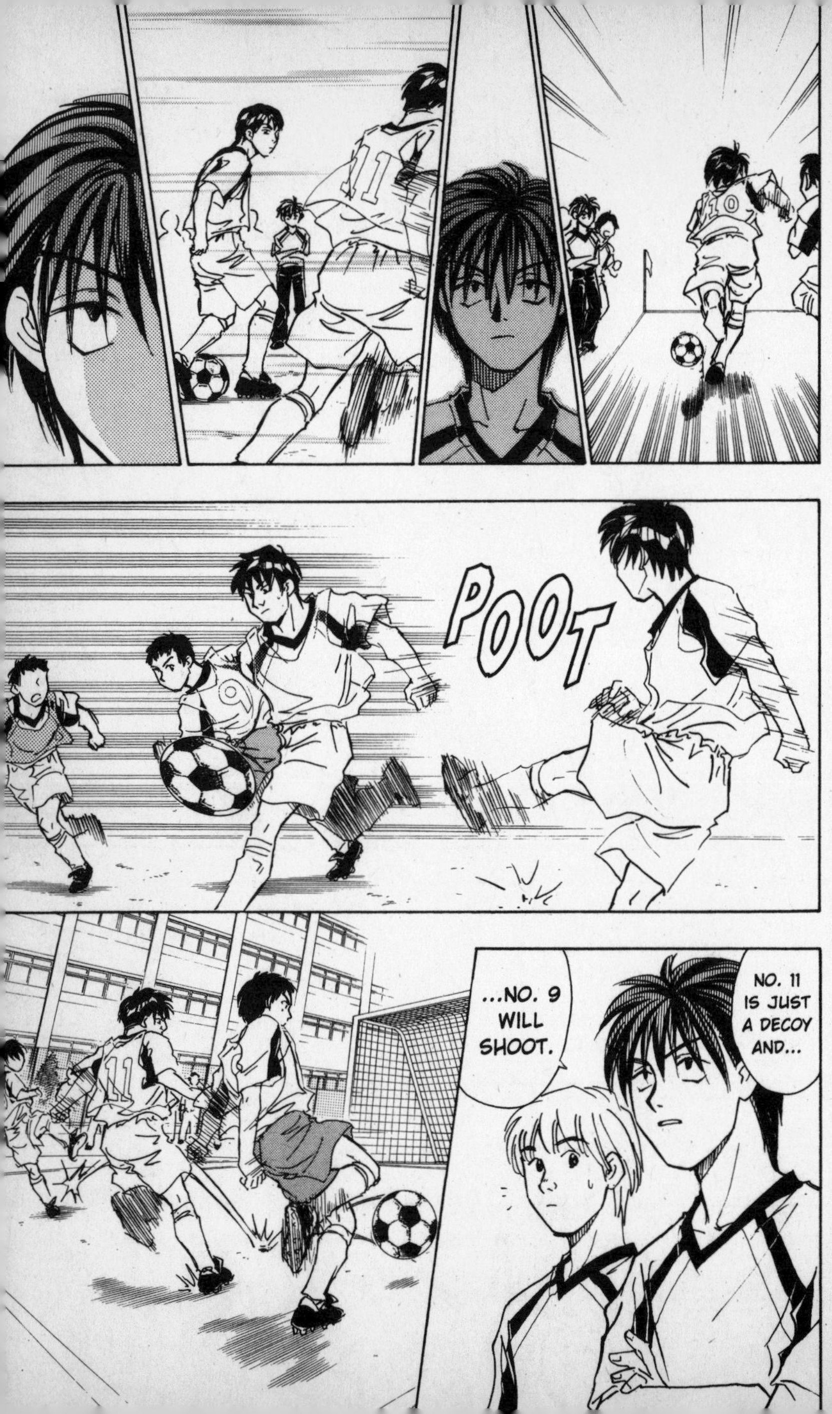
POOT
NO. 11 IS JUST A DECOY AND...
...NO. 9 WILL SHOOT.

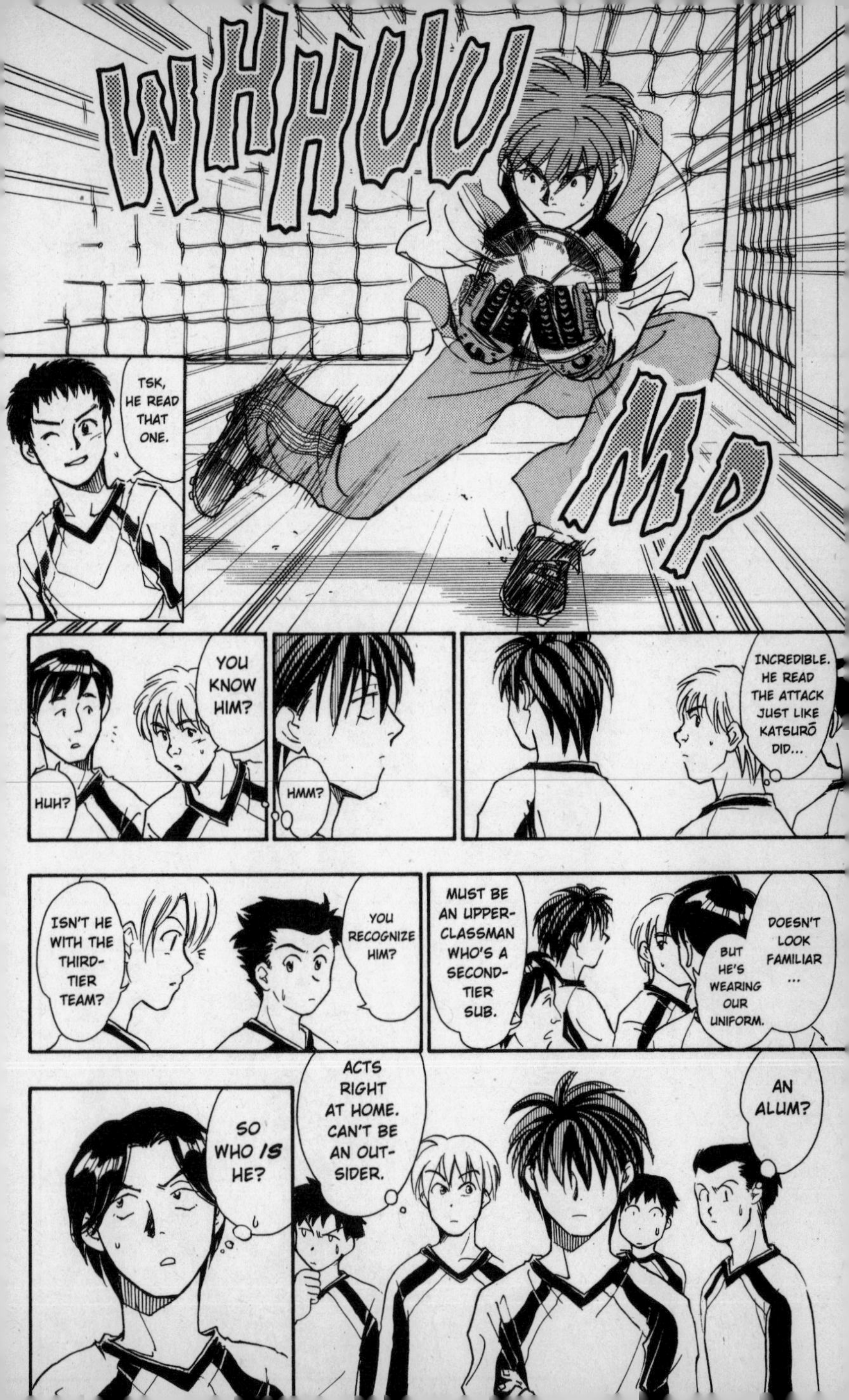
WHHUU
MP
TSK, HE READ THAT ONE.
INCREDIBLE. HE READ THE ATTACK JUST LIKE KATSURŌ DID...
HMM?
YOU KNOW HIM?
HUH?
DOESN'T LOOK FAMILIAR ...
BUT HE'S WEARING OUR UNIFORM.
MUST BE AN UPPER-CLASSMAN WHO'S A SECOND-TIER SUB.
YOU RECOGNIZE HIM?
ISN'T HE WITH THE THIRD-TIER TEAM?
AN ALUM?
ACTS RIGHT AT HOME. CAN'T BE AN OUT-SIDER.
SO WHO *IS* HE?

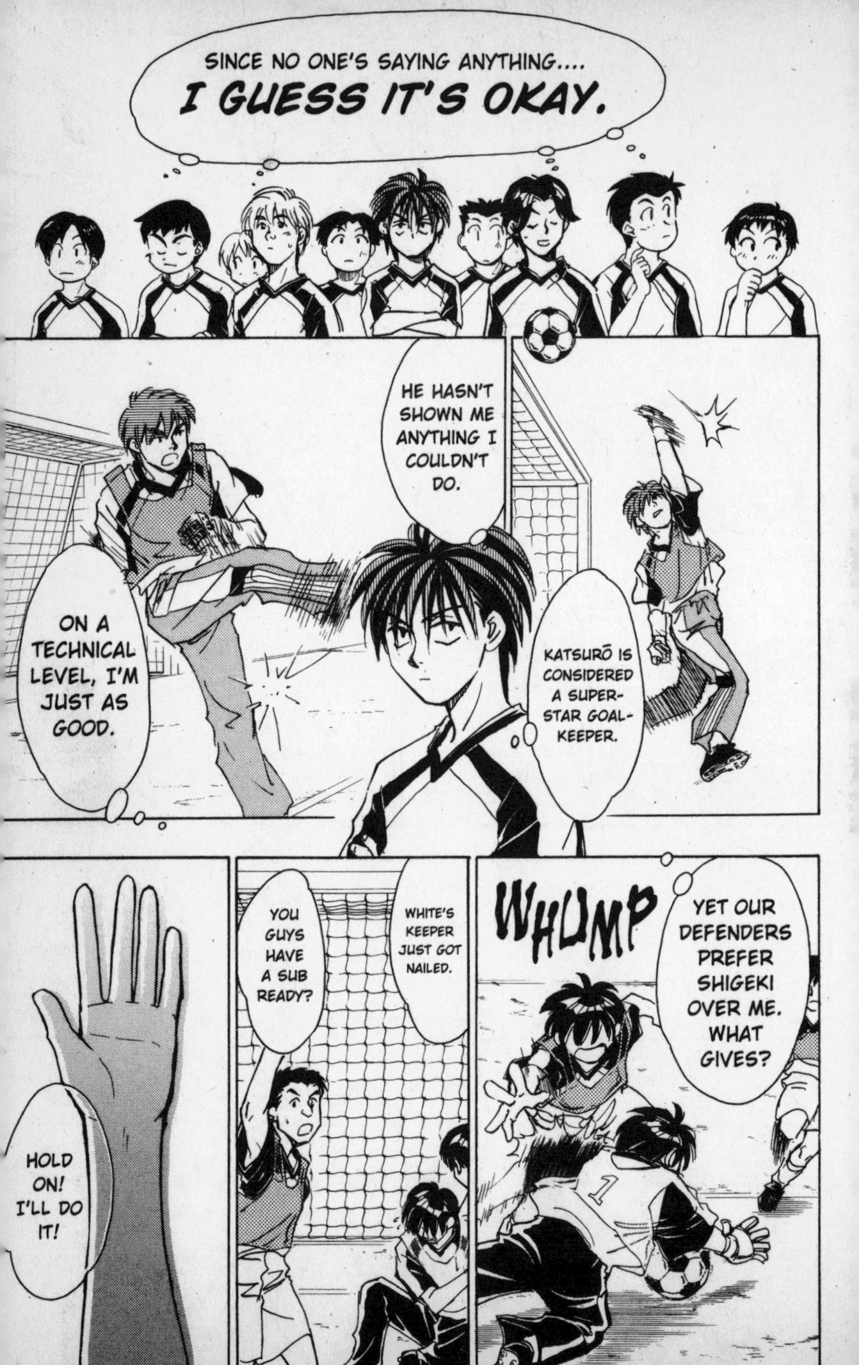
SINCE NO ONE'S SAYING ANYTHING....
I GUESS IT'S OKAY.
KATSURŌ IS CONSIDERED A SUPER-STAR GOAL-KEEPER.
HE HASN'T SHOWN ME ANYTHING I COULDN'T DO.
ON A TECHNICAL LEVEL, I'M JUST AS GOOD.
WHUMP
YET OUR DEFENDERS PREFER SHIGEKI OVER ME. WHAT GIVES?
WHITE'S KEEPER JUST GOT NAILED.
YOU GUYS HAVE A SUB READY?
HOLD ON! I'LL DO IT!

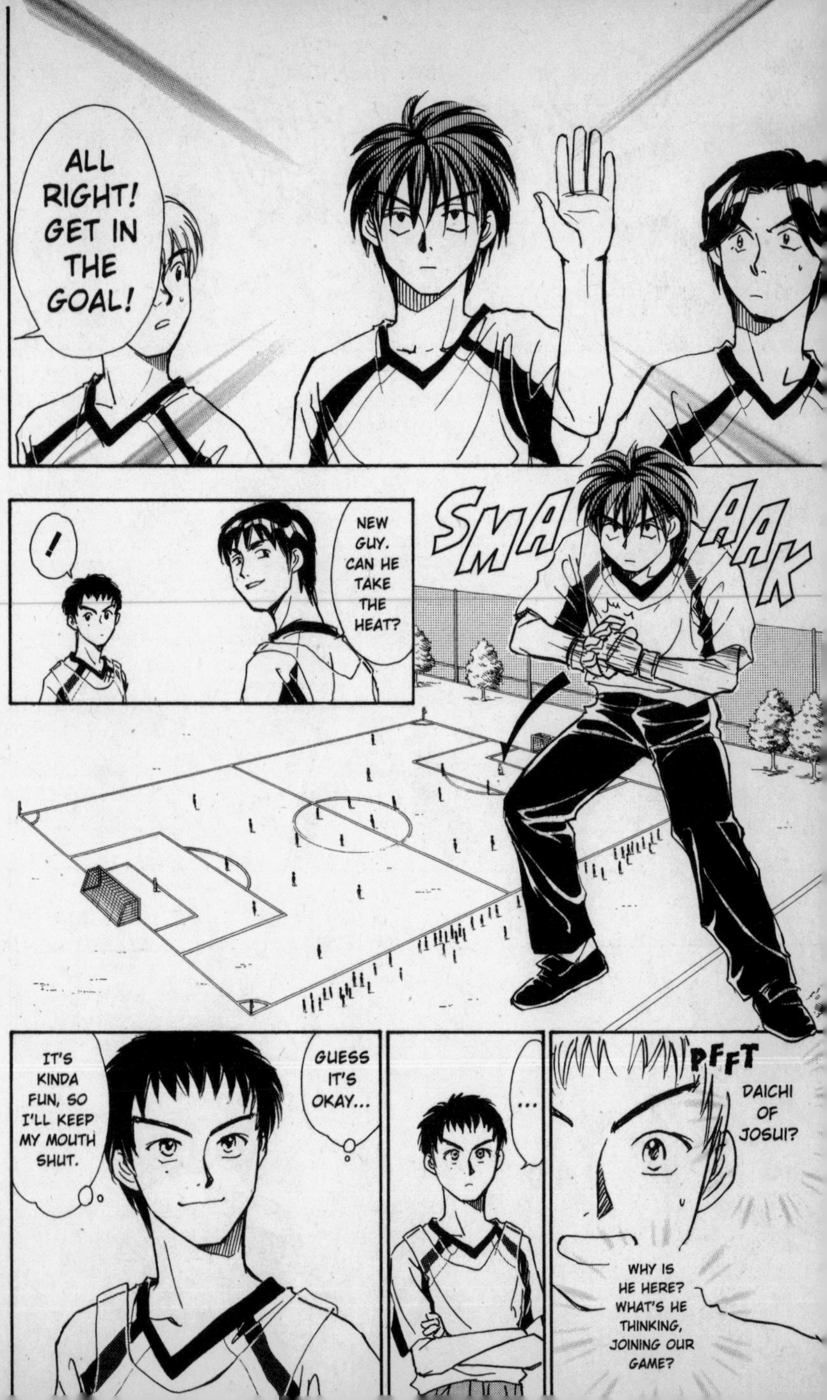
ALL RIGHT! GET IN THE GOAL!
SMAAAK
NEW GUY. CAN HE TAKE THE HEAT?
!
PFFT
DAICHI OF JOSUI?
WHY IS HE HERE? WHAT'S HE THINKING, JOINING OUR GAME?
...
GUESS IT'S OKAY...
IT'S KINDA FUN, SO I'LL KEEP MY MOUTH SHUT.

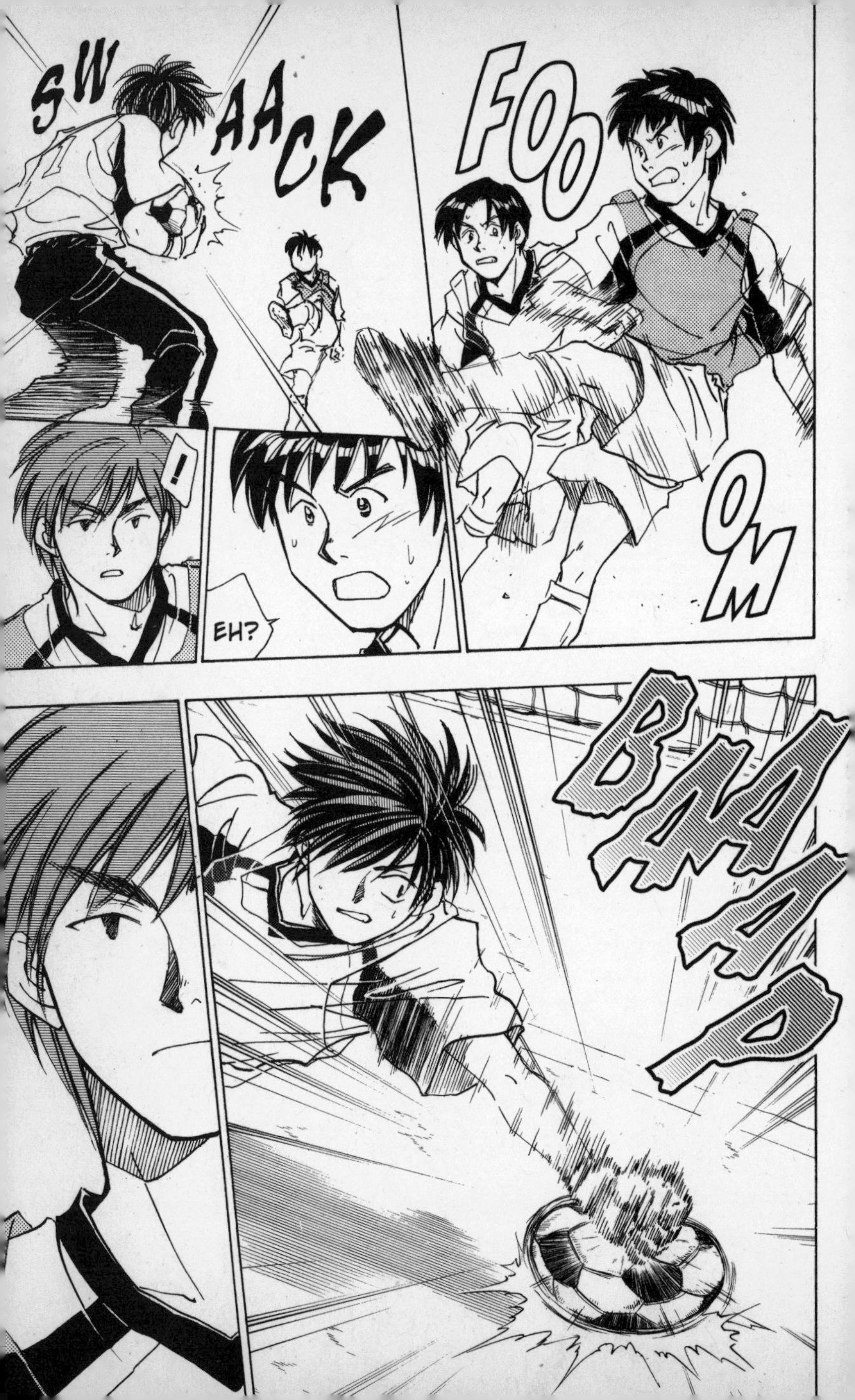
FOOO
OM
SWAACK
EH?
!
BAMP

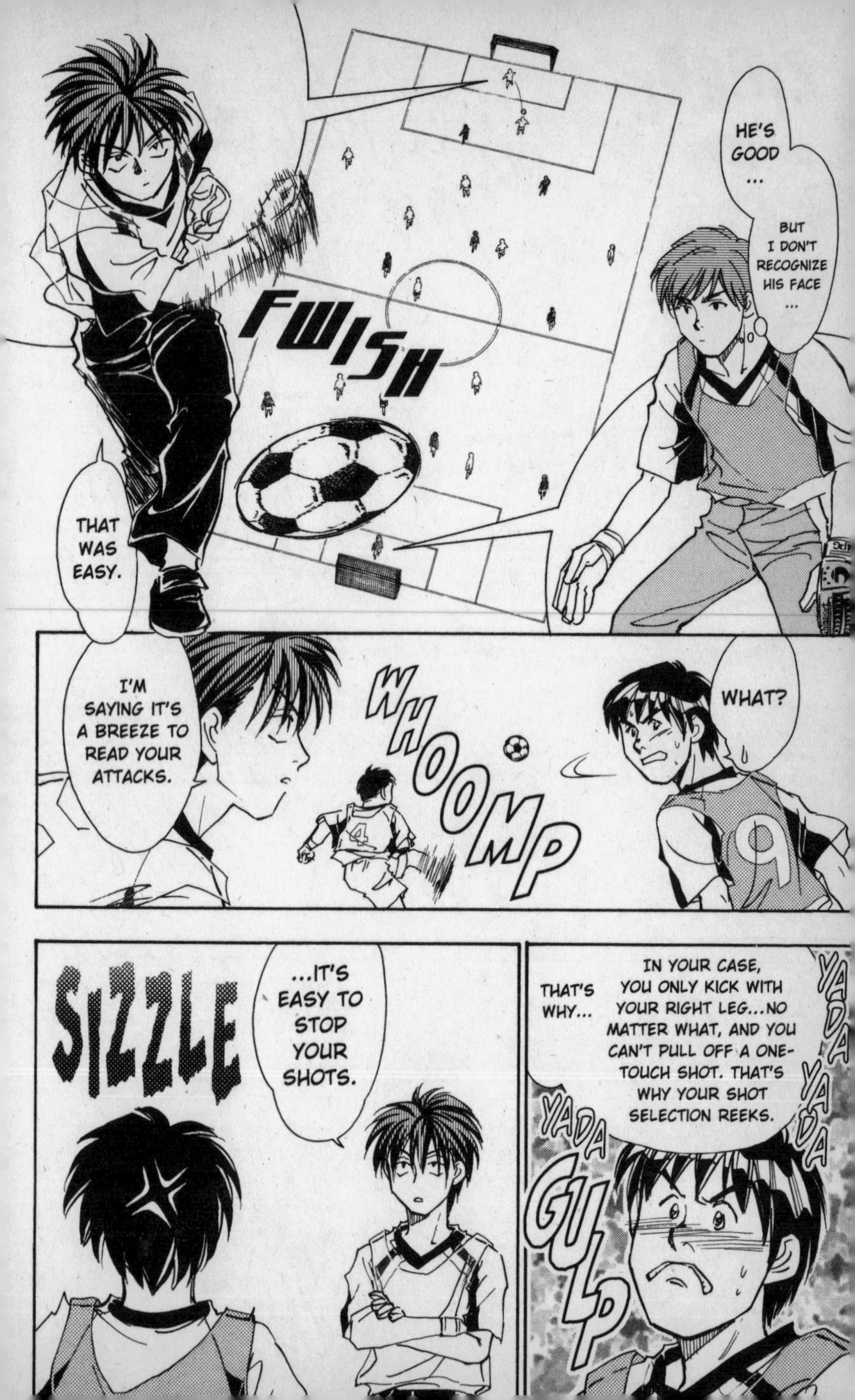
HE'S GOOD ...
BUT I DON'T RECOGNIZE HIS FACE ...
FWISH
THAT WAS EASY.
WHAT?
WHOOMP
I'M SAYING IT'S A BREEZE TO READ YOUR ATTACKS.
YADA YADA YADA YADA
IN YOUR CASE, YOU ONLY KICK WITH YOUR RIGHT LEG...NO MATTER WHAT, AND YOU CAN'T PULL OFF A ONE-TOUCH SHOT. THAT'S WHY YOUR SHOT SELECTION REEKS.
THAT'S WHY...
GULP
SIZZLE
...IT'S EASY TO STOP YOUR SHOTS.

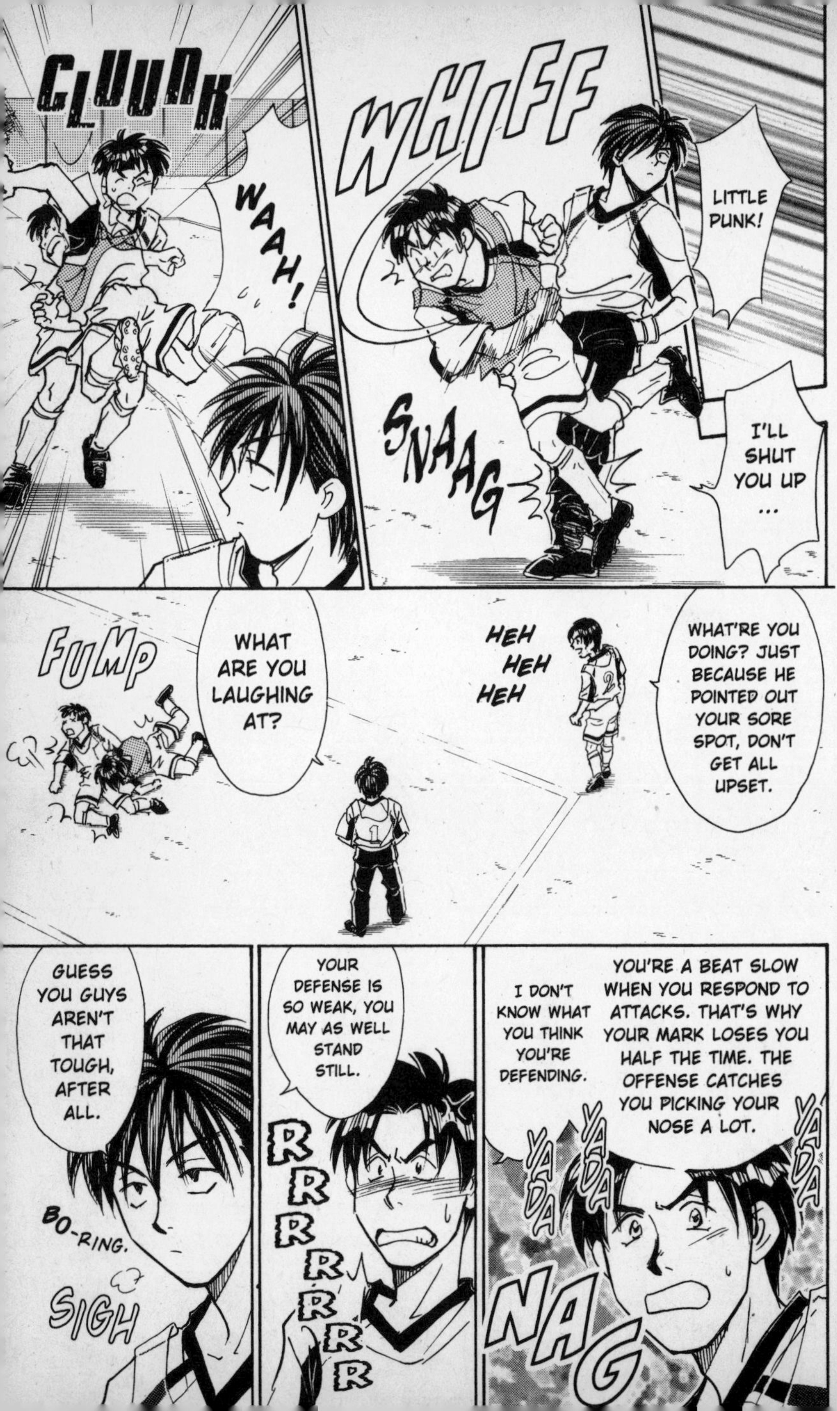
LITTLE PUNK!
I'LL SHUT YOU UP ...
WHIFF
SNAAG
CLUUNK
WAAAH!
WHAT'RE YOU DOING? JUST BECAUSE HE POINTED OUT YOUR SORE SPOT, DON'T GET ALL UPSET.
HEH HEH HEH
WHAT ARE YOU LAUGHING AT?
FUMP
YOU'RE A BEAT SLOW WHEN YOU RESPOND TO ATTACKS. THAT'S WHY YOUR MARK LOSES YOU HALF THE TIME. THE OFFENSE CATCHES YOU PICKING YOUR NOSE A LOT.
I DON'T KNOW WHAT YOU THINK YOU'RE DEFENDING.
YADA
YADA
YADA
NAG
YOUR DEFENSE IS SO WEAK, YOU MAY AS WELL STAND STILL.
RRRRRRRR
GUESS YOU GUYS AREN'T THAT TOUGH, AFTER ALL.
BO-RING.
SIGH

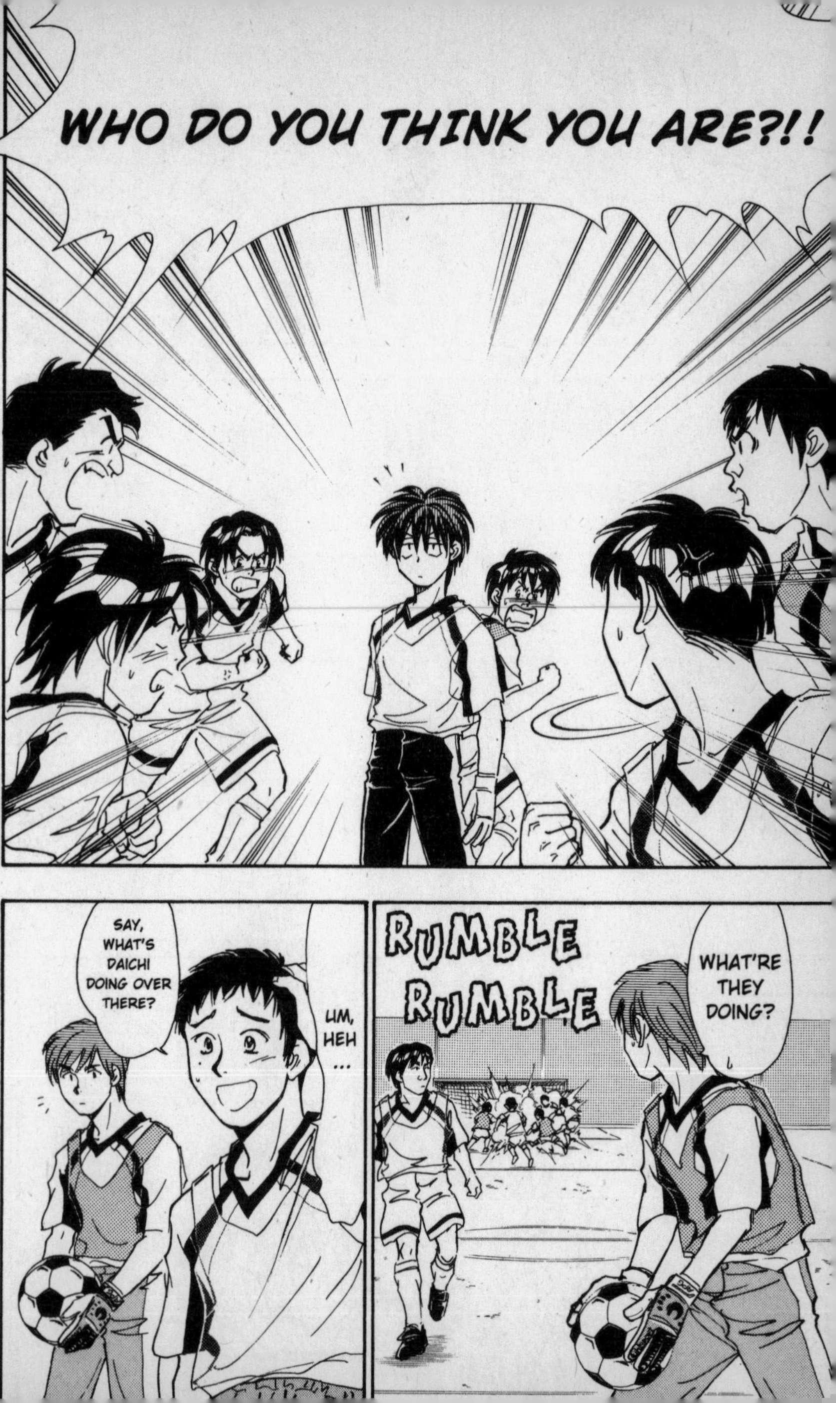
WHO DO YOU THINK YOU ARE?!!
WHAT'RE THEY DOING?
RUMBLE RUMBLE
SAY, WHAT'S DAICHI DOING OVER THERE?
UM, HEH ...

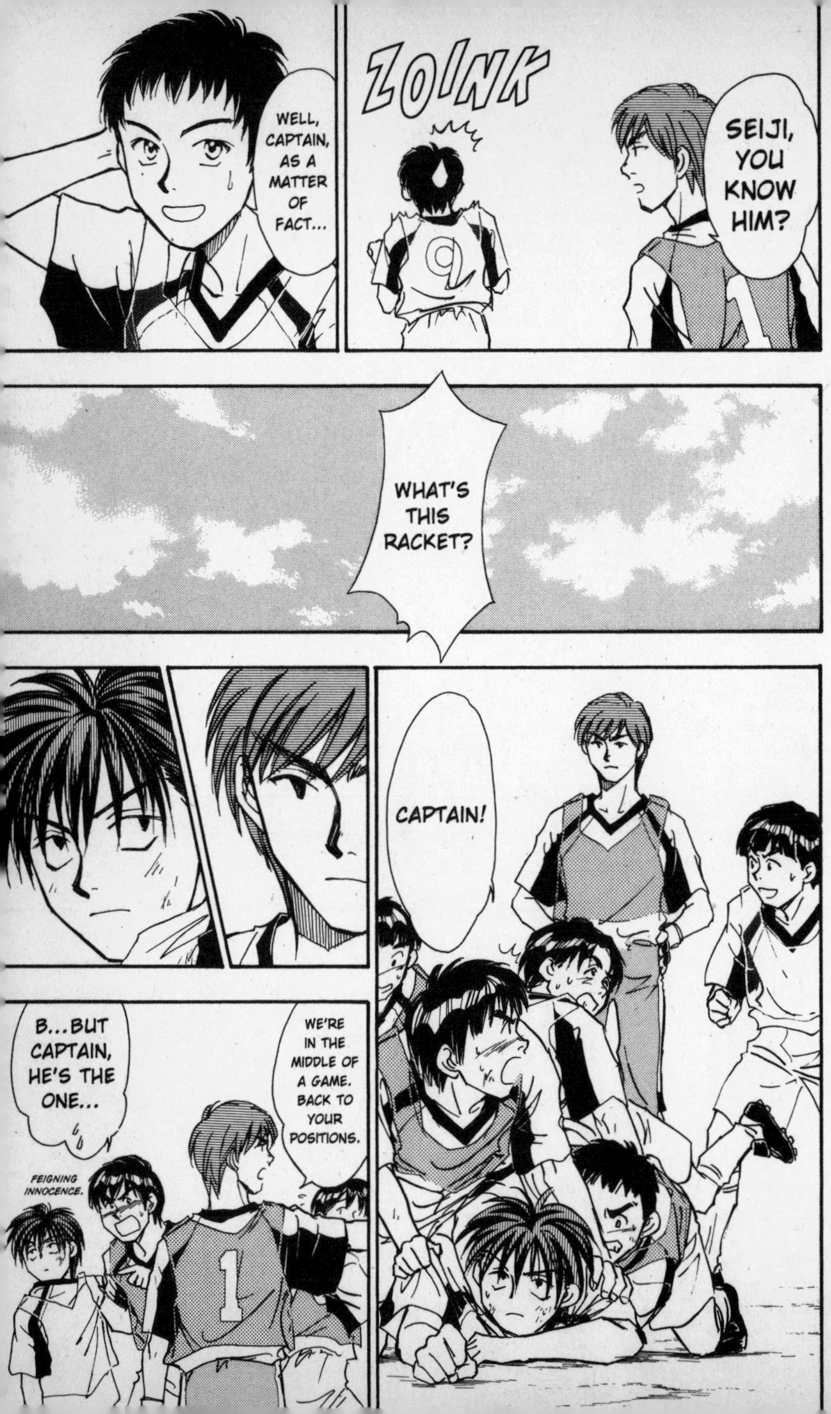
SEIJI, YOU KNOW HIM?
ZOINK
WELL, CAPTAIN, AS A MATTER OF FACT...
WHAT'S THIS RACKET?
CAPTAIN!
WE'RE IN THE MIDDLE OF A GAME. BACK TO YOUR POSITIONS.
B...BUT CAPTAIN, HE'S THE ONE...
FEIGNING INNOCENCE.

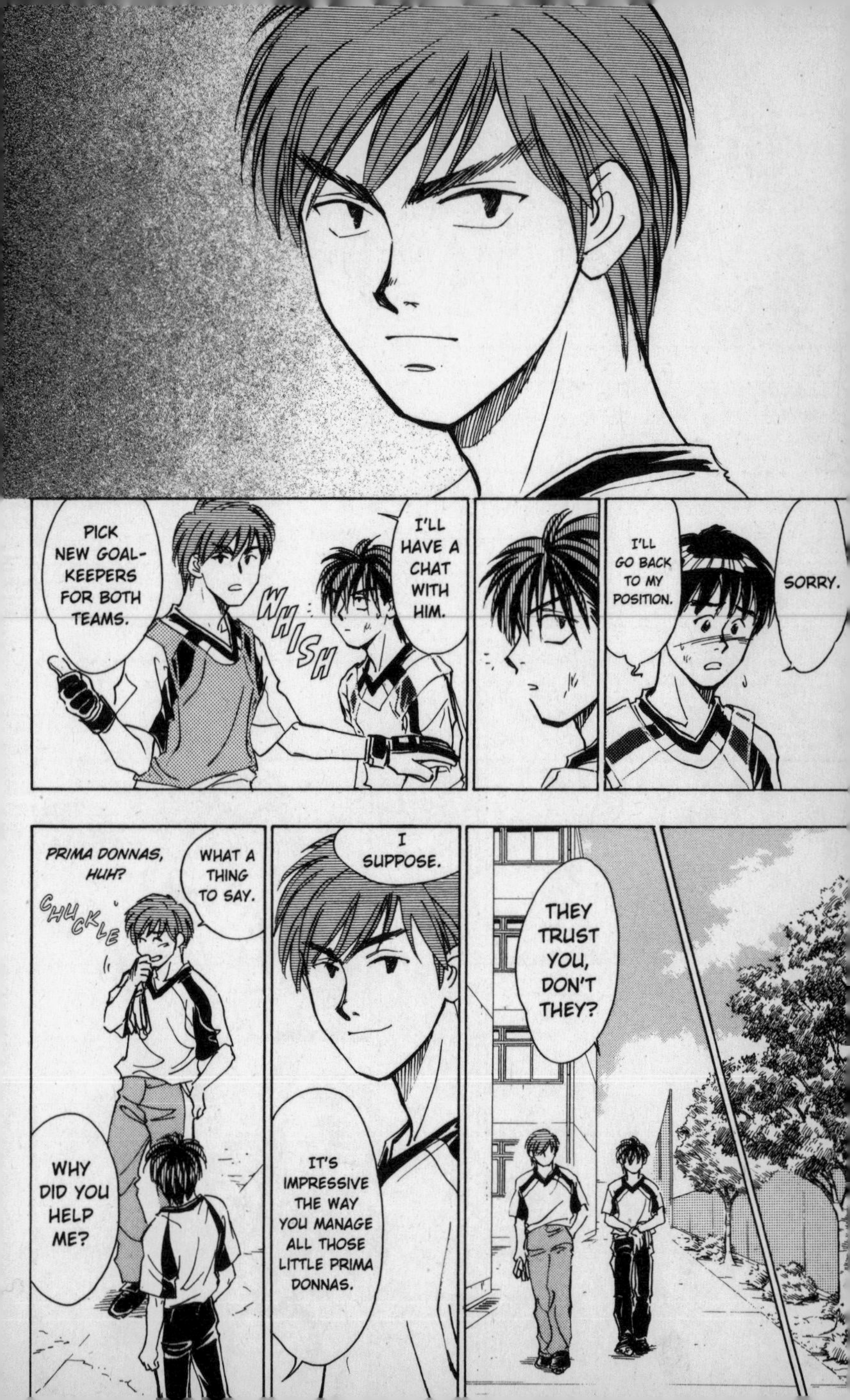
SORRY.
I'LL GO BACK TO MY POSITION.
I'LL HAVE A CHAT WITH HIM.
WHISH
PICK NEW GOAL-KEEPERS FOR BOTH TEAMS.
THEY TRUST YOU, DON'T THEY?
I SUPPOSE.
IT'S IMPRESSIVE THE WAY YOU MANAGE ALL THOSE LITTLE PRIMA DONNAS.
WHAT A THING TO SAY.
PRIMA DONNAS, HUH?
CHUCKLE
WHY DID YOU HELP ME?

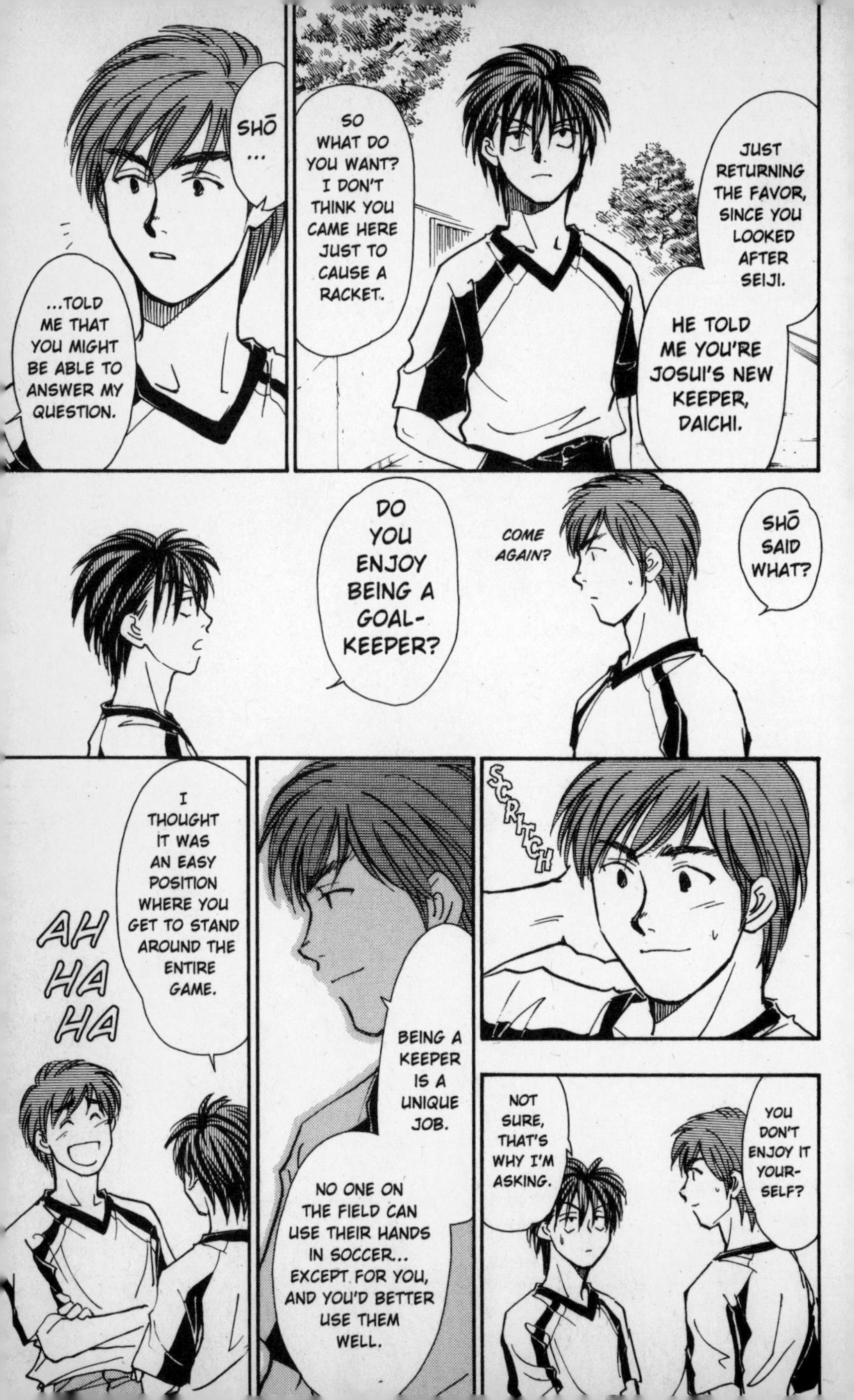
SO WHAT DO YOU WANT? I DON'T THINK YOU CAME HERE JUST TO CAUSE A RACKET.
JUST RETURNING THE FAVOR, SINCE YOU LOOKED AFTER SEIJI.
HE TOLD ME YOU'RE JOSUI'S NEW KEEPER, DAICHI.
SHŌ ...
...TOLD ME THAT YOU MIGHT BE ABLE TO ANSWER MY QUESTION.
SHŌ SAID WHAT?
COME AGAIN?
DO YOU ENJOY BEING A GOAL-KEEPER?
SCRITCH
YOU DON'T ENJOY IT YOUR-SELF?
NOT SURE, THAT'S WHY I'M ASKING.
BEING A KEEPER IS A UNIQUE JOB.
NO ONE ON THE FIELD CAN USE THEIR HANDS IN SOCCER... EXCEPT FOR YOU, AND YOU'D BETTER USE THEM WELL.
I THOUGHT IT WAS AN EASY POSITION WHERE YOU GET TO STAND AROUND THE ENTIRE GAME.
AH HA HA

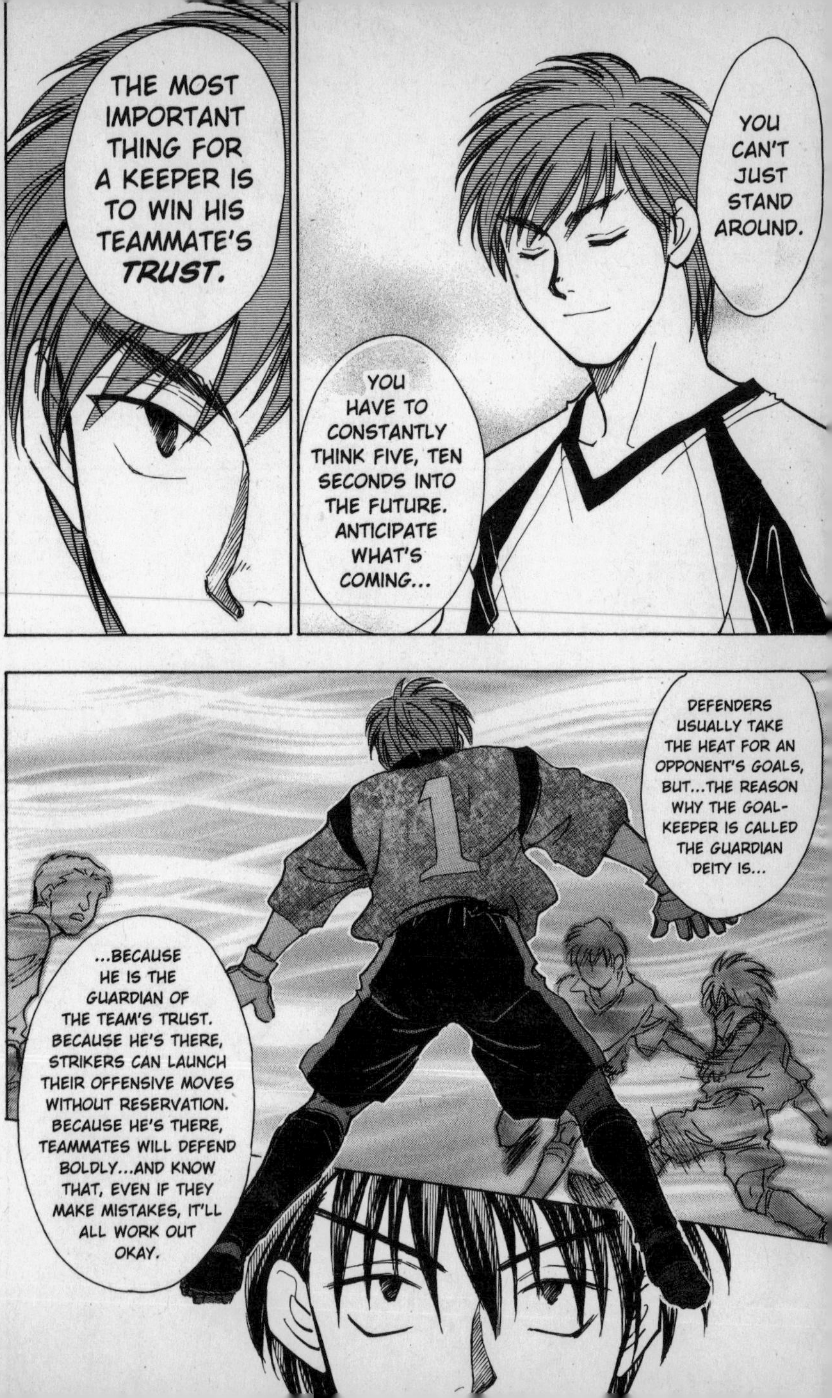
YOU CAN'T JUST STAND AROUND.
YOU HAVE TO CONSTANTLY THINK FIVE, TEN SECONDS INTO THE FUTURE. ANTICIPATE WHAT'S COMING...
THE MOST IMPORTANT THING FOR A KEEPER IS TO WIN HIS TEAMMATE'S TRUST.
DEFENDERS USUALLY TAKE THE HEAT FOR AN OPPONENT'S GOALS, BUT...THE REASON WHY THE GOAL-KEEPER IS CALLED THE GUARDIAN DEITY IS...
...BECAUSE HE IS THE GUARDIAN OF THE TEAM'S TRUST. BECAUSE HE'S THERE, STRIKERS CAN LAUNCH THEIR OFFENSIVE MOVES WITHOUT RESERVATION. BECAUSE HE'S THERE, TEAMMATES WILL DEFEND BOLDLY...AND KNOW THAT, EVEN IF THEY MAKE MISTAKES, IT'LL ALL WORK OUT OKAY.

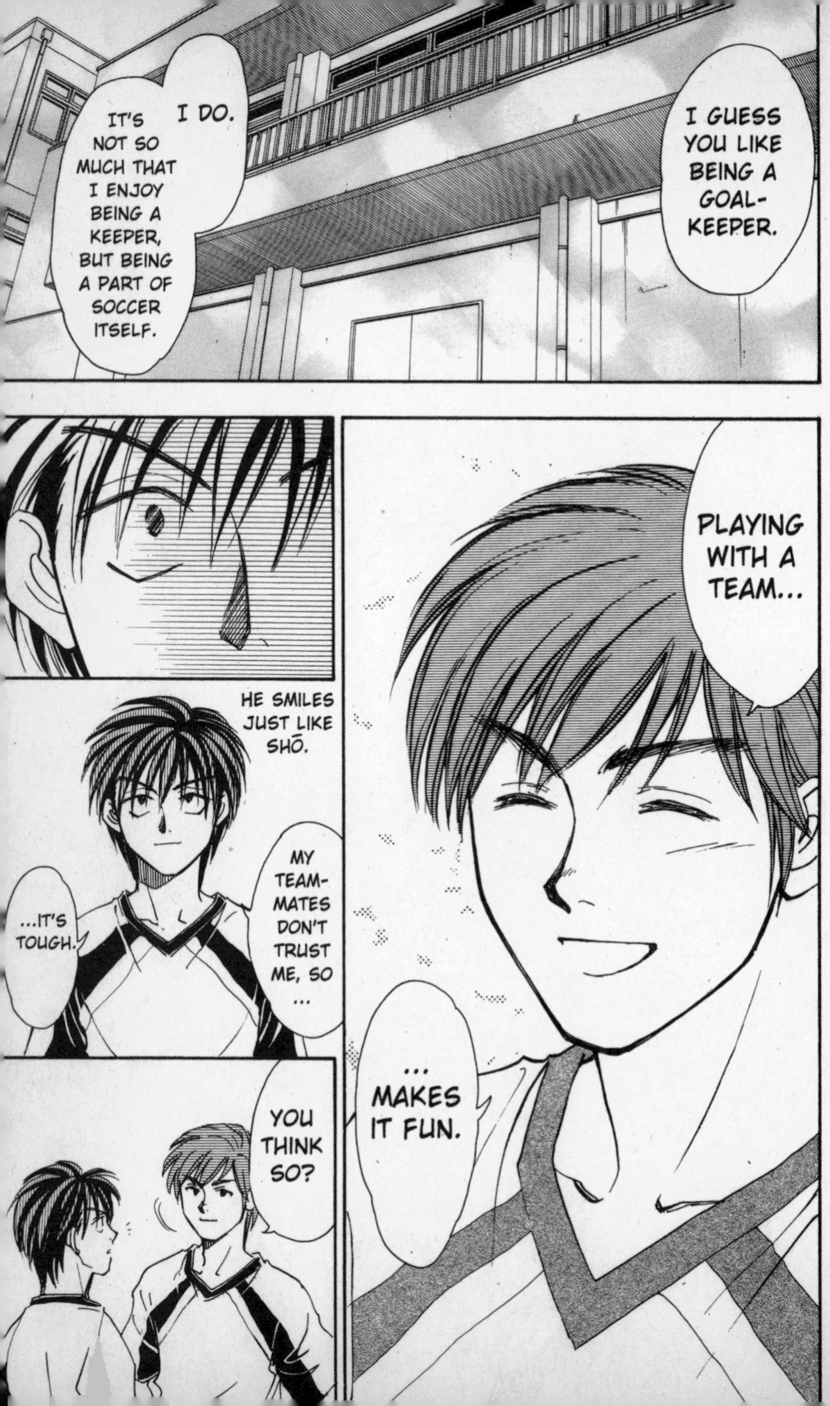
I GUESS YOU LIKE BEING A GOAL-KEEPER.
I DO.
IT'S NOT SO MUCH THAT I ENJOY BEING A KEEPER, BUT BEING A PART OF SOCCER ITSELF.
PLAYING WITH A TEAM...
...MAKES IT FUN.
HE SMILES JUST LIKE SHŌ.
MY TEAM-MATES DON'T TRUST ME, SO ...
...IT'S TOUGH.
YOU THINK SO?

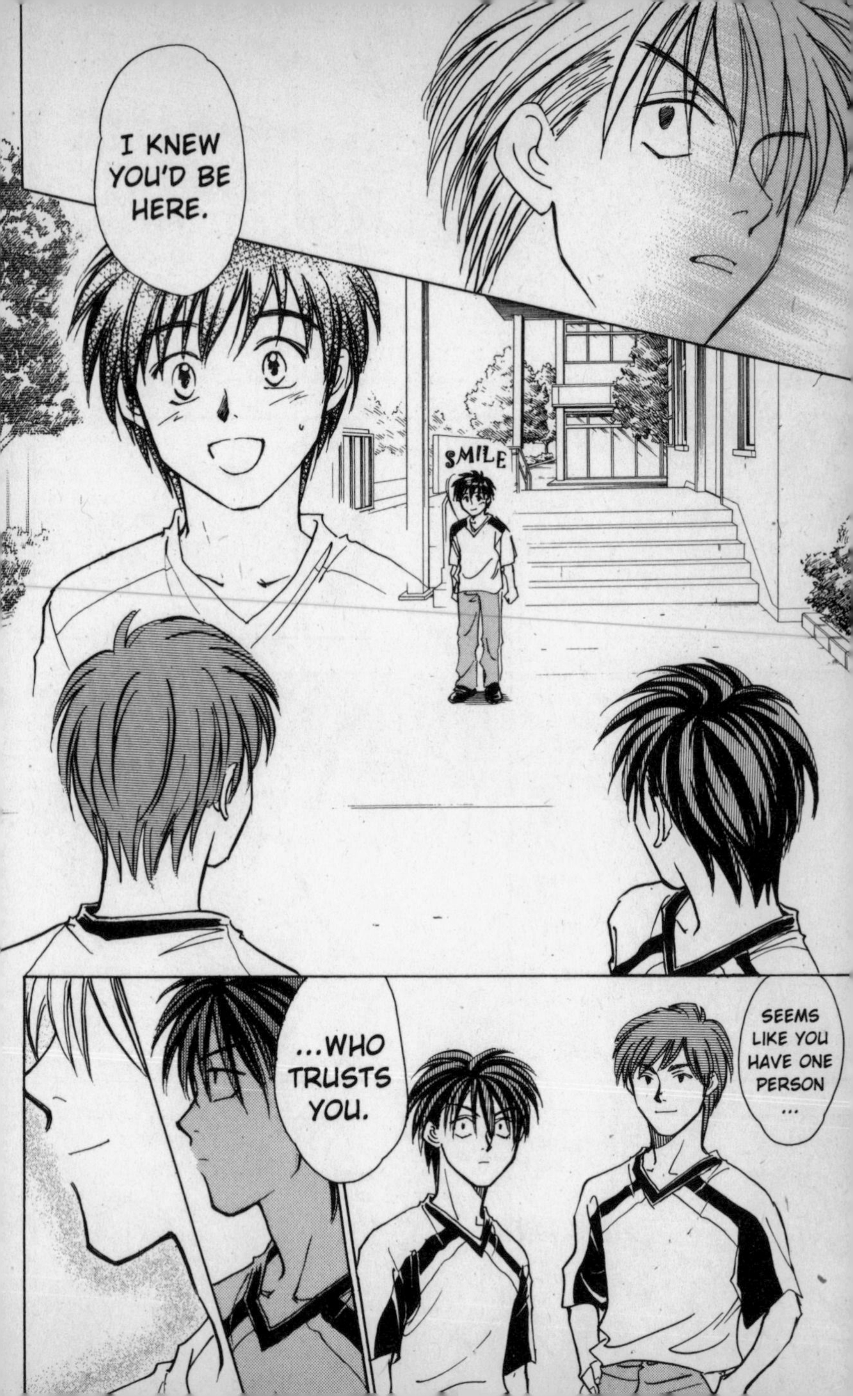
I KNEW YOU'D BE HERE.
SMILE
SEEMS LIKE YOU HAVE ONE PERSON ...
...WHO TRUSTS YOU.

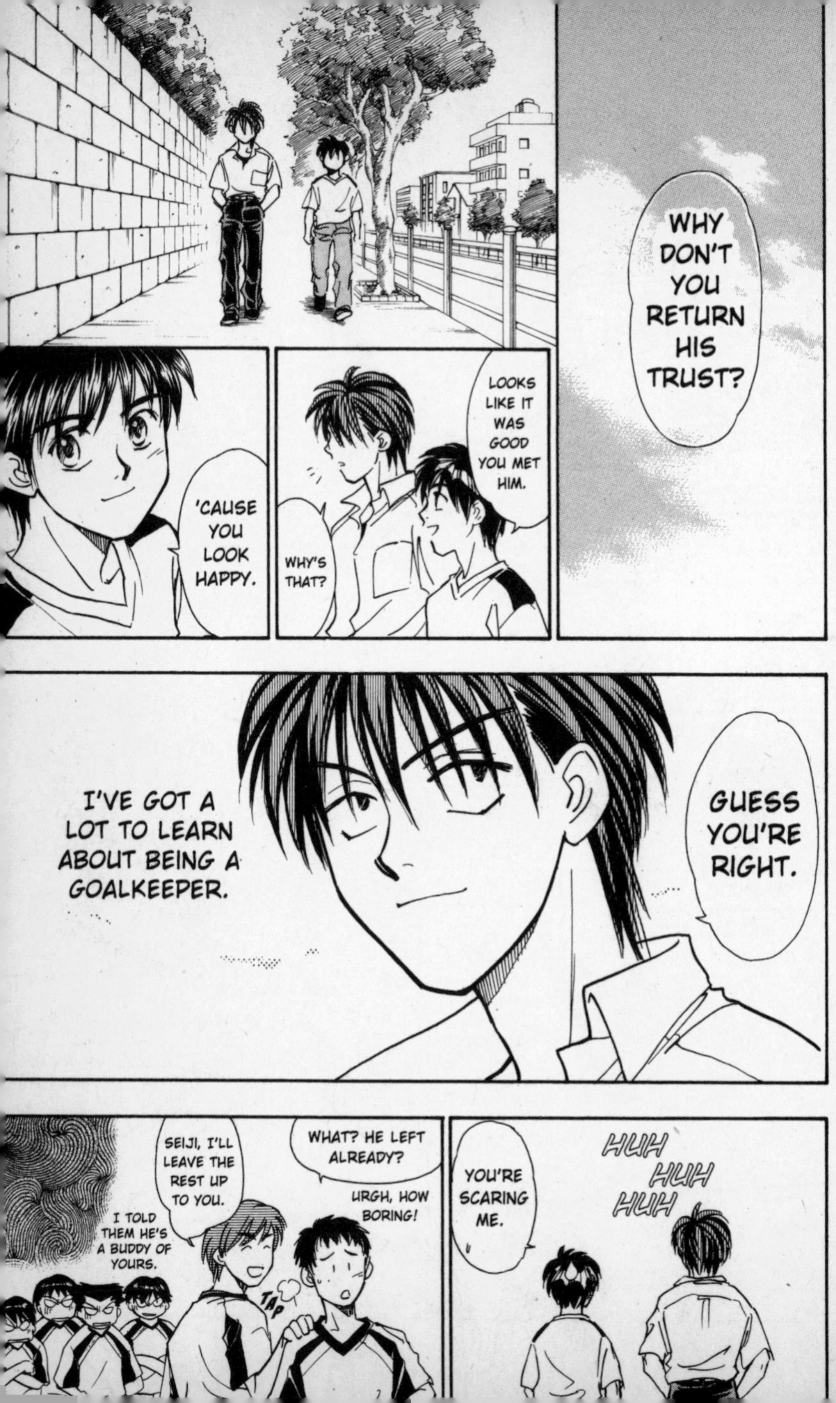
WHY DON'T YOU RETURN HIS TRUST?
LOOKS LIKE IT WAS GOOD YOU MET HIM.
WHY'S THAT?
'CAUSE YOU LOOK HAPPY.
GUESS YOU'RE RIGHT.
I'VE GOT A LOT TO LEARN ABOUT BEING A GOALKEEPER.
HUH HUH HUH
YOU'RE SCARING ME.
WHAT? HE LEFT ALREADY?
URGH, HOW BORING!
SEIJI, I'LL LEAVE THE REST UP TO YOU.
TAP
I TOLD THEM HE'S A BUDDY OF YOURS.

STAGE.55 Weakness

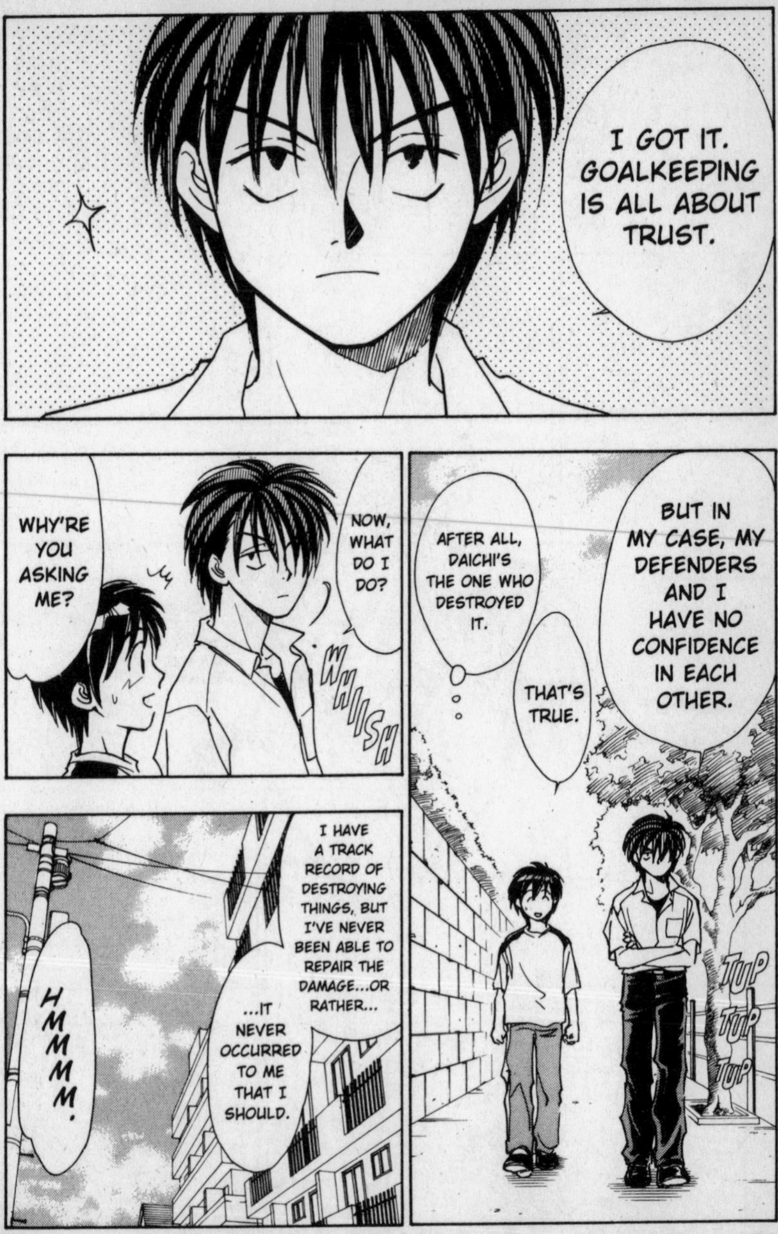
I GOT IT. GOALKEEPING IS ALL ABOUT TRUST.
BUT IN MY CASE, MY DEFENDERS AND I HAVE NO CONFIDENCE IN EACH OTHER.
AFTER ALL, DAICHI'S THE ONE WHO DESTROYED IT.
THAT'S TRUE.
TUP
TUP
TUP
NOW, WHAT DO I DO?
WHISH
WHY'RE YOU ASKING ME?
I HAVE A TRACK RECORD OF DESTROYING THINGS, BUT I'VE NEVER BEEN ABLE TO REPAIR THE DAMAGE...OR RATHER...
...IT NEVER OCCURRED TO ME THAT I SHOULD.
HMMMM.

READ THIS WAY

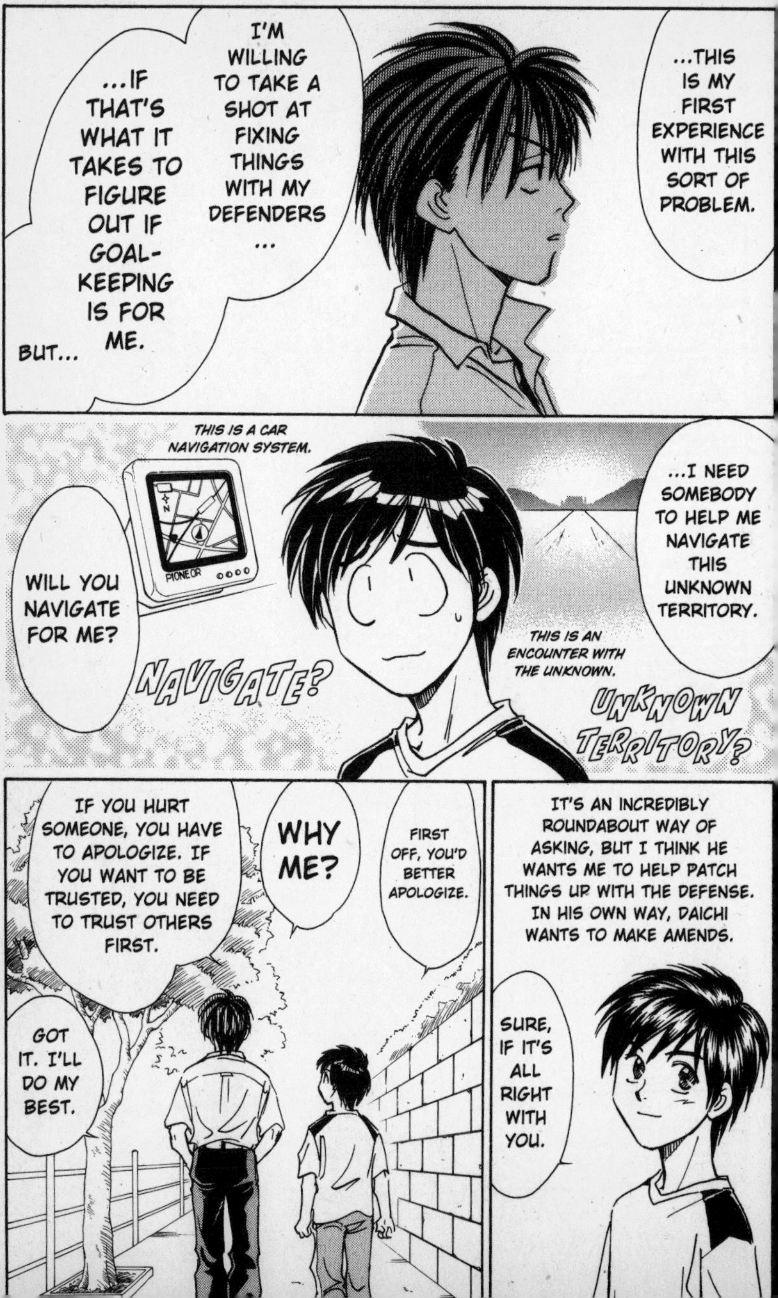

...THIS IS MY FIRST EXPERIENCE WITH THIS SORT OF PROBLEM.
I'M WILLING TO TAKE A SHOT AT FIXING THINGS WITH MY DEFENDERS...
...IF THAT'S WHAT IT TAKES TO FIGURE OUT IF GOAL-KEEPING IS FOR ME.
BUT...
...I NEED SOMEBODY TO HELP ME NAVIGATE THIS UNKNOWN TERRITORY.
UNKNOWN TERRITORY?
THIS IS AN ENCOUNTER WITH THE UNKNOWN.
THIS IS A CAR NAVIGATION SYSTEM.
PIONEOR
WILL YOU NAVIGATE FOR ME?
NAVIGATE?
IT'S AN INCREDIBLY ROUNDABOUT WAY OF ASKING, BUT I THINK HE WANTS ME TO HELP PATCH THINGS UP WITH THE DEFENSE. IN HIS OWN WAY, DAICHI WANTS TO MAKE AMENDS.
SURE, IF IT'S ALL RIGHT WITH YOU.
FIRST OFF, YOU'D BETTER APOLOGIZE.
WHY ME?
IF YOU HURT SOMEONE, YOU HAVE TO APOLOGIZE. IF YOU WANT TO BE TRUSTED, YOU NEED TO TRUST OTHERS FIRST.
GOT IT. I'LL DO MY BEST.

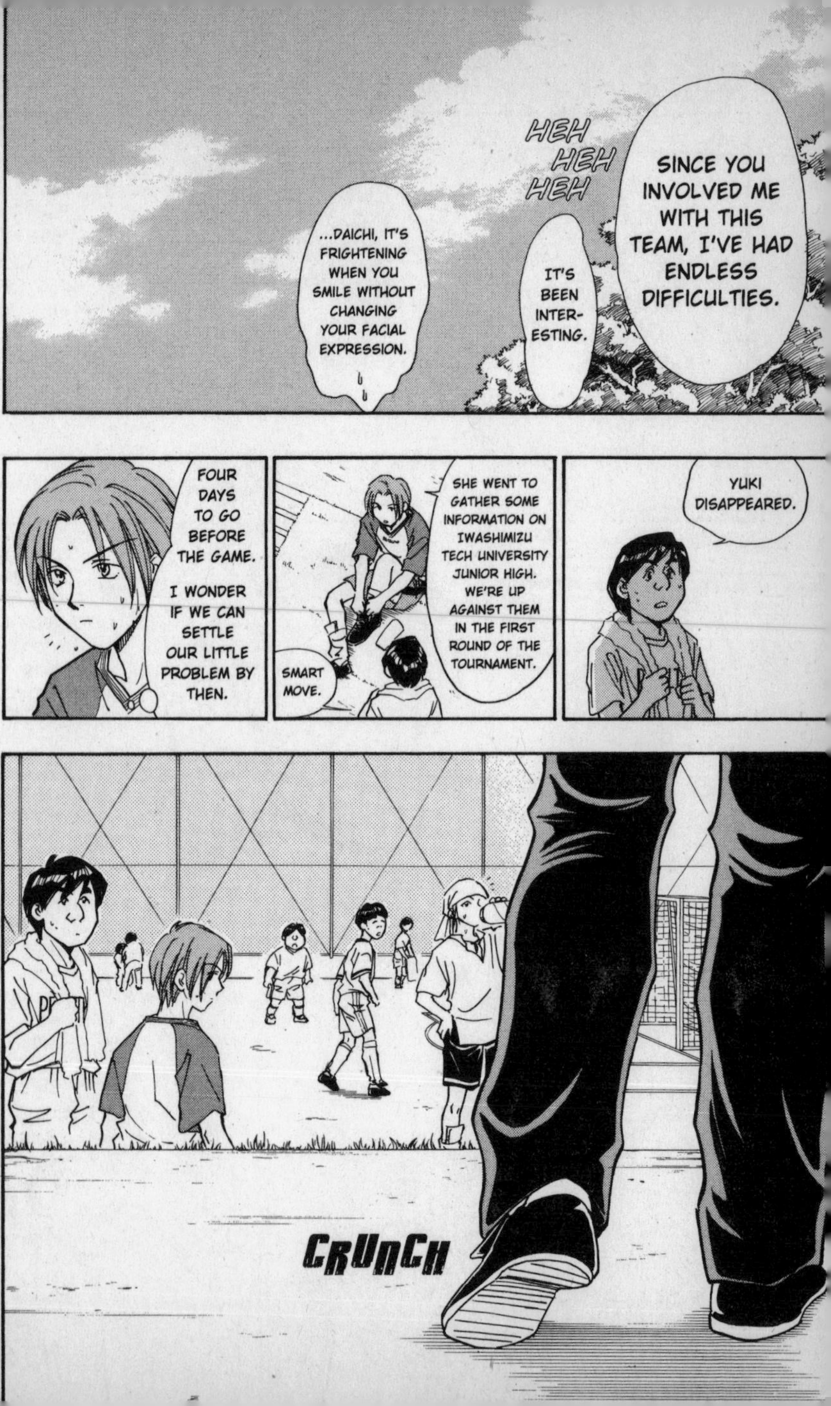
SINCE YOU INVOLVED ME WITH THIS TEAM, I'VE HAD ENDLESS DIFFICULTIES.
HEH HEH HEH
IT'S BEEN INTER-ESTING.
...DAICHI, IT'S FRIGHTENING WHEN YOU SMILE WITHOUT CHANGING YOUR FACIAL EXPRESSION.
YUKI DISAPPEARED.
SHE WENT TO GATHER SOME INFORMATION ON IWASHIMIZU TECH UNIVERSITY JUNIOR HIGH. WE'RE UP AGAINST THEM IN THE FIRST ROUND OF THE TOURNAMENT.
SMART MOVE.
FOUR DAYS TO GO BEFORE THE GAME.
I WONDER IF WE CAN SETTLE OUR LITTLE PROBLEM BY THEN.
CRUNCH

STAGE.55 Weakness

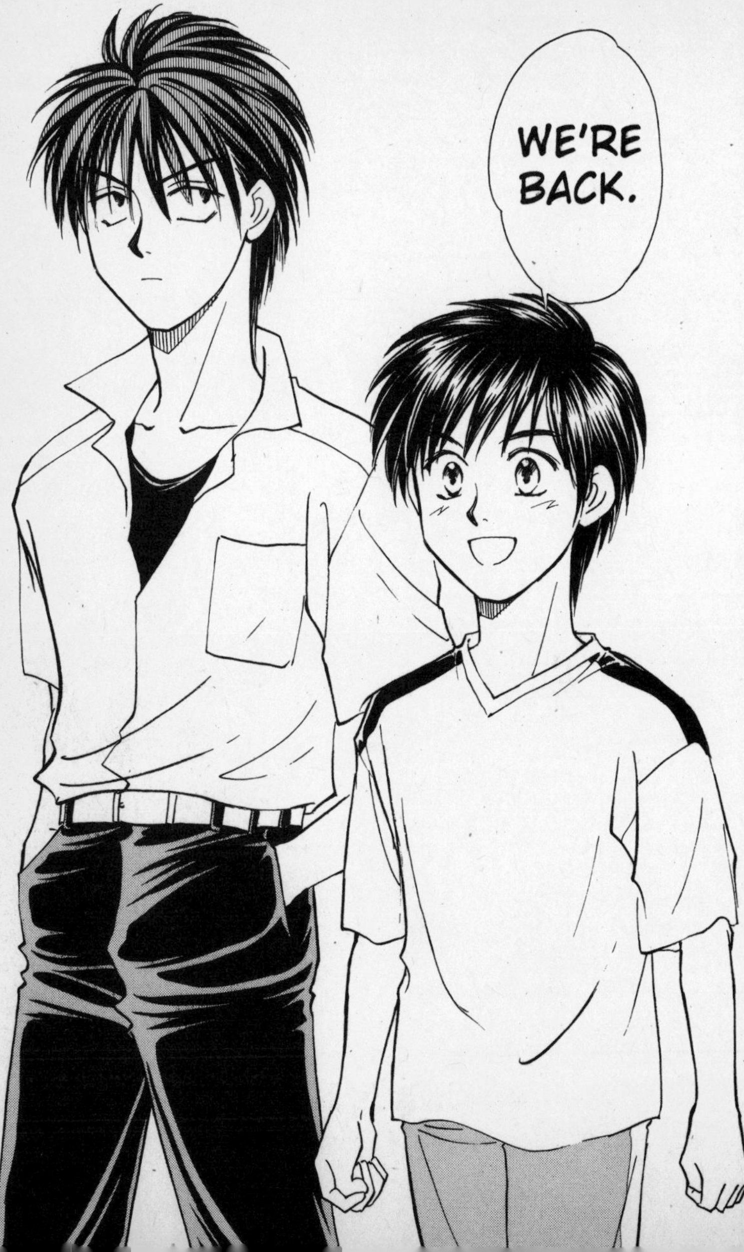
WE'RE BACK.

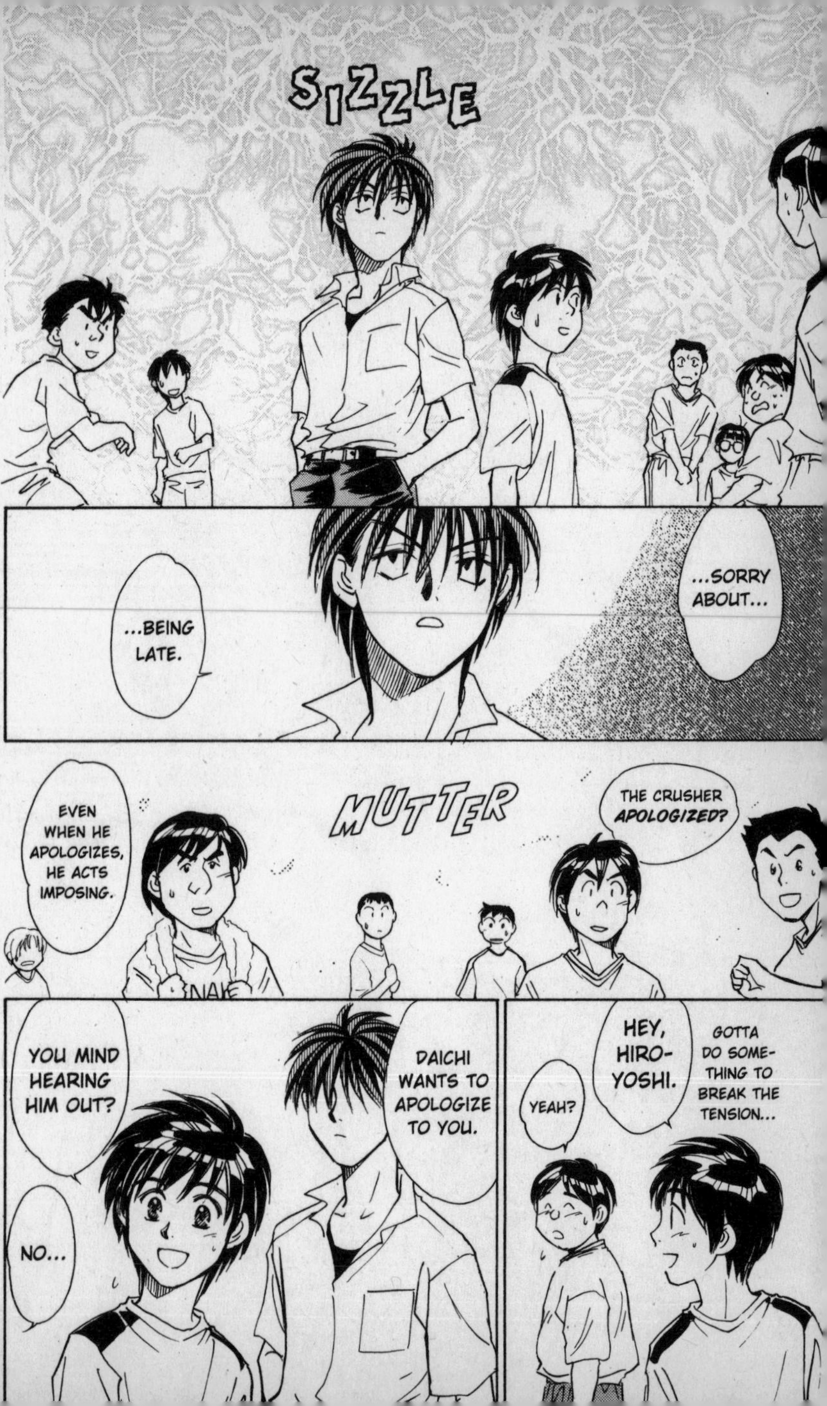
SIZZLE
...SORRY ABOUT...
...BEING LATE.
THE CRUSHER APOLOGIZED?
MUTTER
EVEN WHEN HE APOLOGIZES, HE ACTS IMPOSING.
GOTTA DO SOME-THING TO BREAK THE TENSION...
HEY, HIRO-YOSHI.
YEAH?
DAICHI WANTS TO APOLOGIZE TO YOU.
YOU MIND HEARING HIM OUT?
NO...

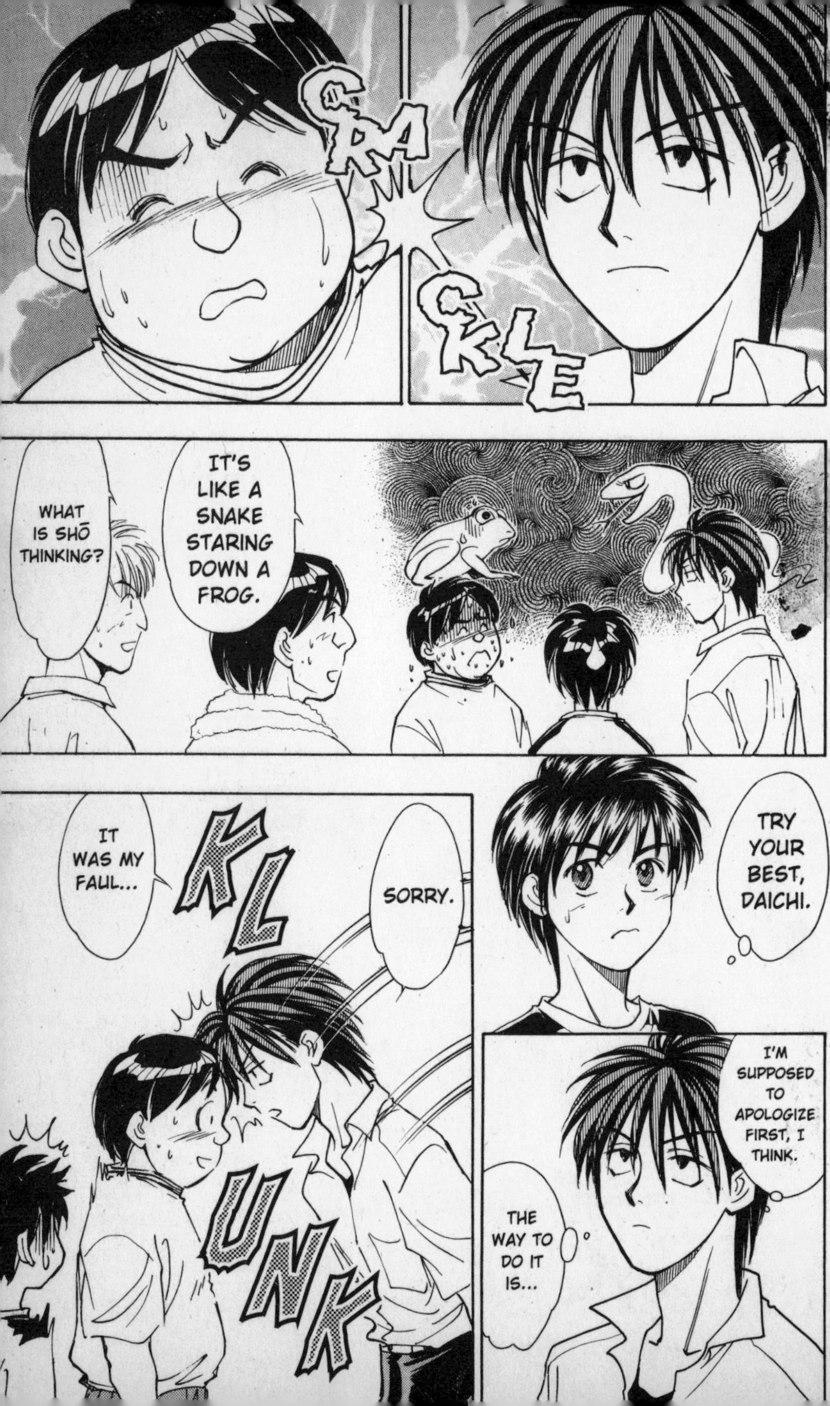
CRACKLE
IT'S LIKE A SNAKE STARING DOWN A FROG.
WHAT IS SHŌ THINKING?
TRY YOUR BEST, DAICHI.
I'M SUPPOSED TO APOLOGIZE FIRST, I THINK.
THE WAY TO DO IT IS...
SORRY.
KLUNK
IT WAS MY FAUL...

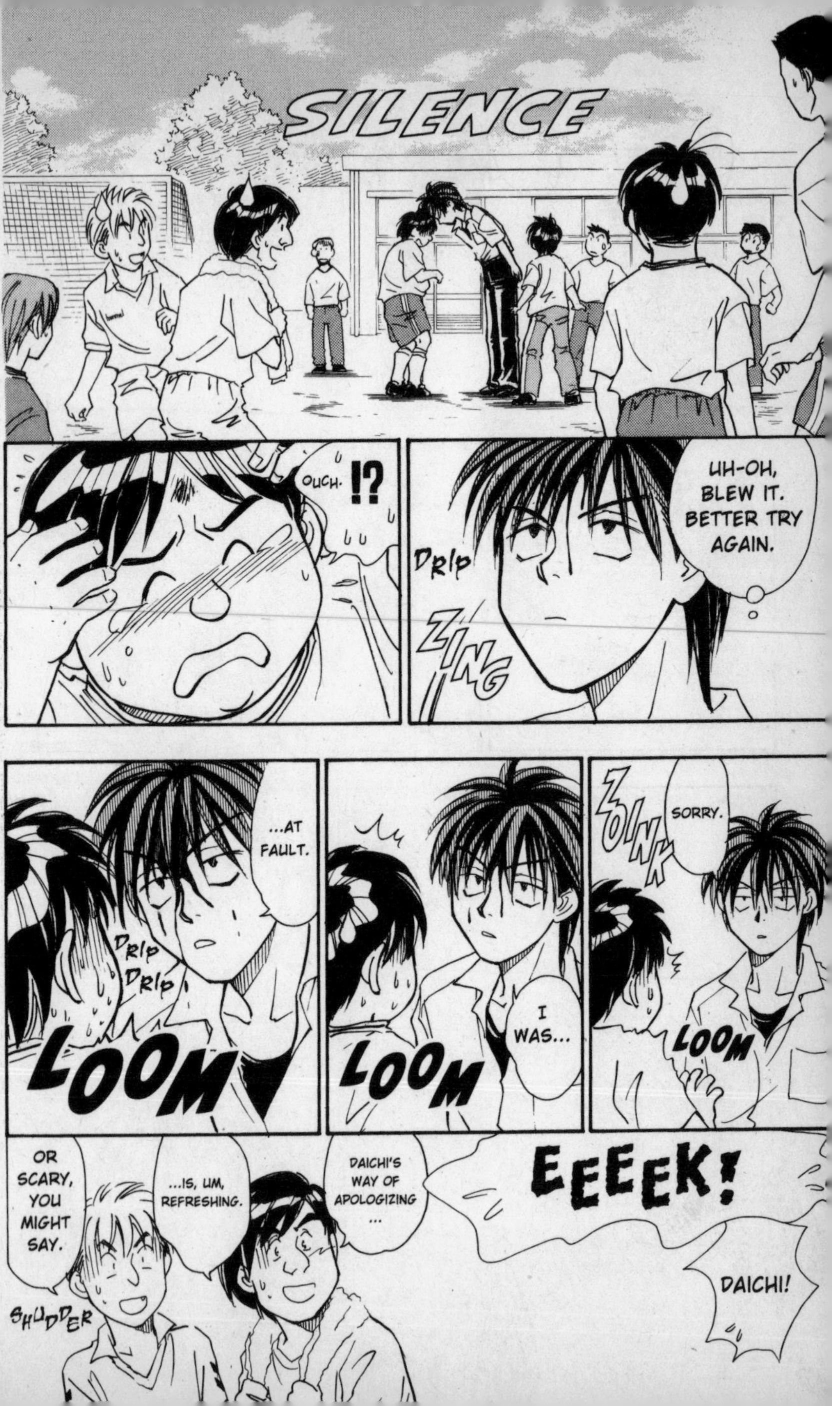
SILENCE
UH-OH, BLEW IT. BETTER TRY AGAIN.
DRIP
ZING
OUCH.
!?
SORRY.
ZOINK
LOOM
I WAS...
LOOM
...AT FAULT.
DRIP DRIP
LOOM
EEEEK!
DAICHI!
DAICHI'S WAY OF APOLOGIZING ...
...IS, UM, REFRESHING.
OR SCARY, YOU MIGHT SAY.
SHUDDER

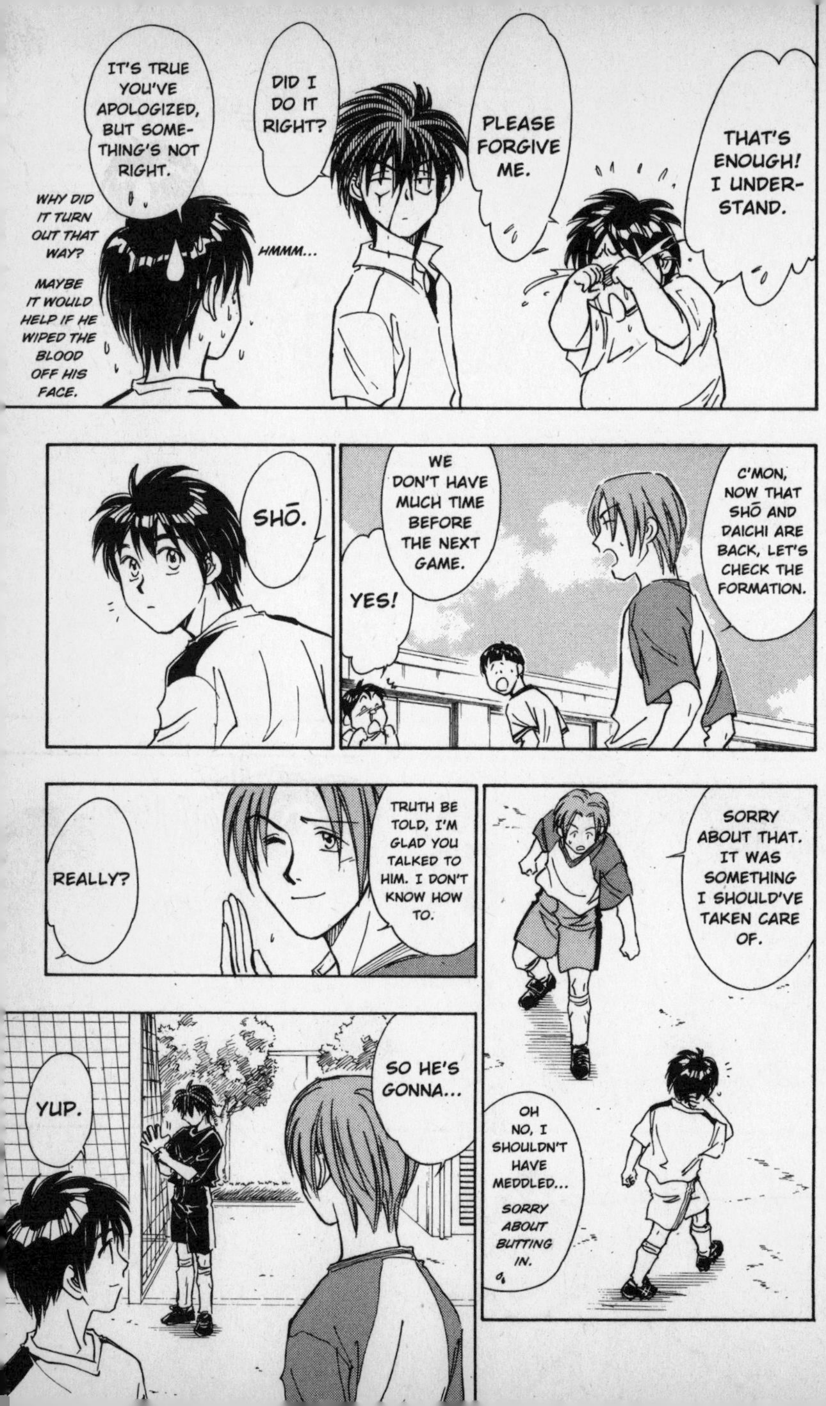
THAT'S ENOUGH! I UNDERSTAND.
PLEASE FORGIVE ME.
DID I DO IT RIGHT?
HMMM...
IT'S TRUE YOU'VE APOLOGIZED, BUT SOMETHING'S NOT RIGHT.
WHY DID IT TURN OUT THAT WAY?
MAYBE IT WOULD HELP IF HE WIPED THE BLOOD OFF HIS FACE.
C'MON, NOW THAT SHŌ AND DAICHI ARE BACK, LET'S CHECK THE FORMATION.
WE DON'T HAVE MUCH TIME BEFORE THE NEXT GAME.
YES!
SHŌ.
SORRY ABOUT THAT. IT WAS SOMETHING I SHOULD'VE TAKEN CARE OF.
OH NO, I SHOULDN'T HAVE MEDDLED...
SORRY ABOUT BUTTING IN.
TRUTH BE TOLD, I'M GLAD YOU TALKED TO HIM. I DON'T KNOW HOW TO.
REALLY?
SO HE'S GONNA...
YUP.

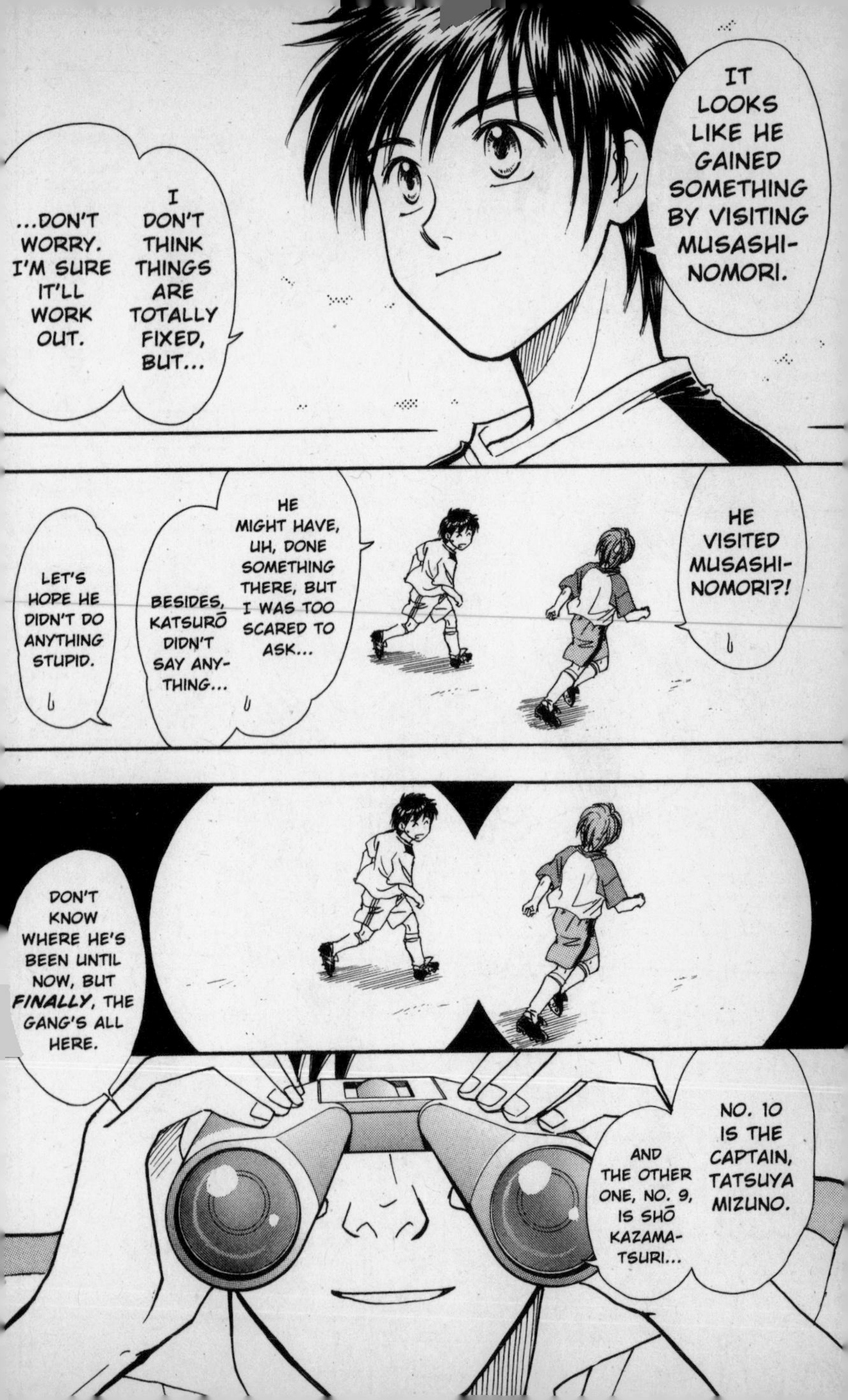
IT LOOKS LIKE HE GAINED SOMETHING BY VISITING MUSASHI-NOMORI.
I DON'T THINK THINGS ARE TOTALLY FIXED, BUT...
...DON'T WORRY. I'M SURE IT'LL WORK OUT.
HE VISITED MUSASHI-NOMORI?!
HE MIGHT HAVE, UH, DONE SOMETHING THERE, BUT I WAS TOO SCARED TO ASK...
BESIDES, KATSURŌ DIDN'T SAY ANYTHING...
LET'S HOPE HE DIDN'T DO ANYTHING STUPID.
DON'T KNOW WHERE HE'S BEEN UNTIL NOW, BUT *FINALLY*, THE GANG'S ALL HERE.
NO. 10 IS THE CAPTAIN, TATSUYA MIZUNO.
AND THE OTHER ONE, NO. 9, IS SHŌ KAZAMATSURI...

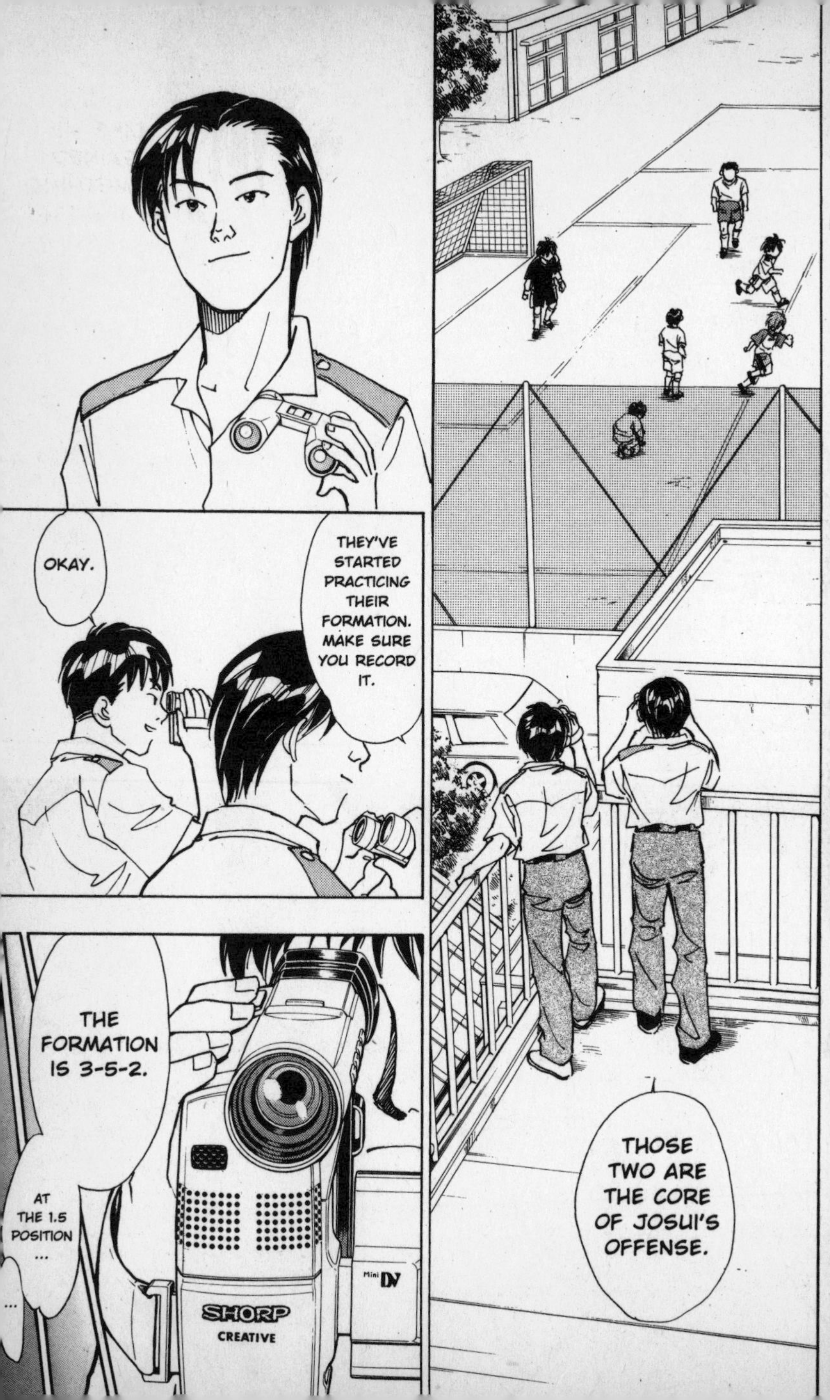
THOSE TWO ARE THE CORE OF JOSUI'S OFFENSE.
THEY'VE STARTED PRACTICING THEIR FORMATION. MAKE SURE YOU RECORD IT.
OKAY.
THE FORMATION IS 3-5-2.
AT THE 1.5 POSITION ...
...
Mini DV
SHORP
CREATIVE

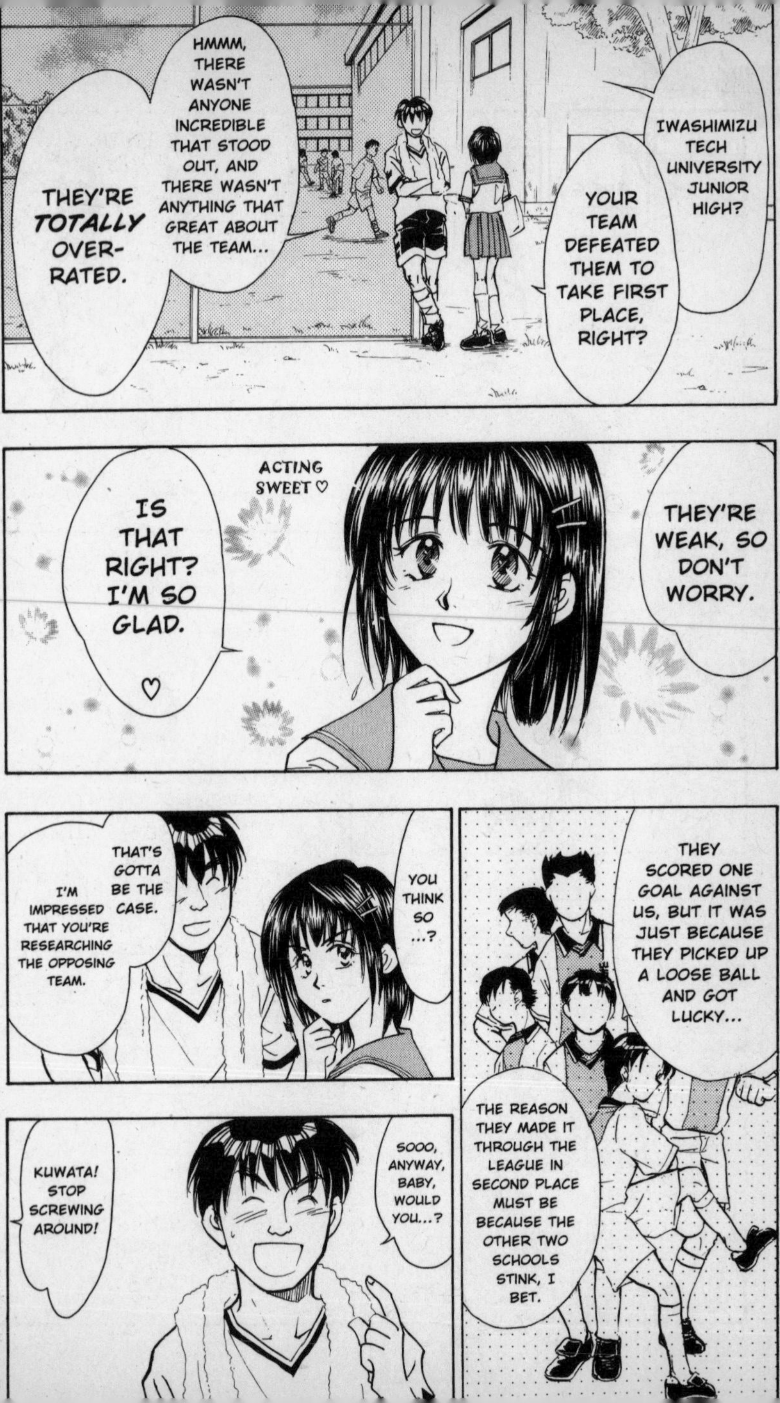
IWASHIMIZU TECH UNIVERSITY JUNIOR HIGH?
YOUR TEAM DEFEATED THEM TO TAKE FIRST PLACE, RIGHT?
HMMM, THERE WASN'T ANYONE INCREDIBLE THAT STOOD OUT, AND THERE WASN'T ANYTHING THAT GREAT ABOUT THE TEAM...
THEY'RE *TOTALLY* OVER-RATED.
THEY'RE WEAK, SO DON'T WORRY.
ACTING SWEET ♡
IS THAT RIGHT? I'M SO GLAD. ♡
THEY SCORED ONE GOAL AGAINST US, BUT IT WAS JUST BECAUSE THEY PICKED UP A LOOSE BALL AND GOT LUCKY...
THE REASON THEY MADE IT THROUGH THE LEAGUE IN SECOND PLACE MUST BE BECAUSE THE OTHER TWO SCHOOLS STINK, I BET.
YOU THINK SO ...?
THAT'S GOTTA BE THE CASE.
I'M IMPRESSED THAT YOU'RE RESEARCHING THE OPPOSING TEAM.
SOOO, ANYWAY, BABY, WOULD YOU...?
KUWATA! STOP SCREWING AROUND!

READ THIS WAY

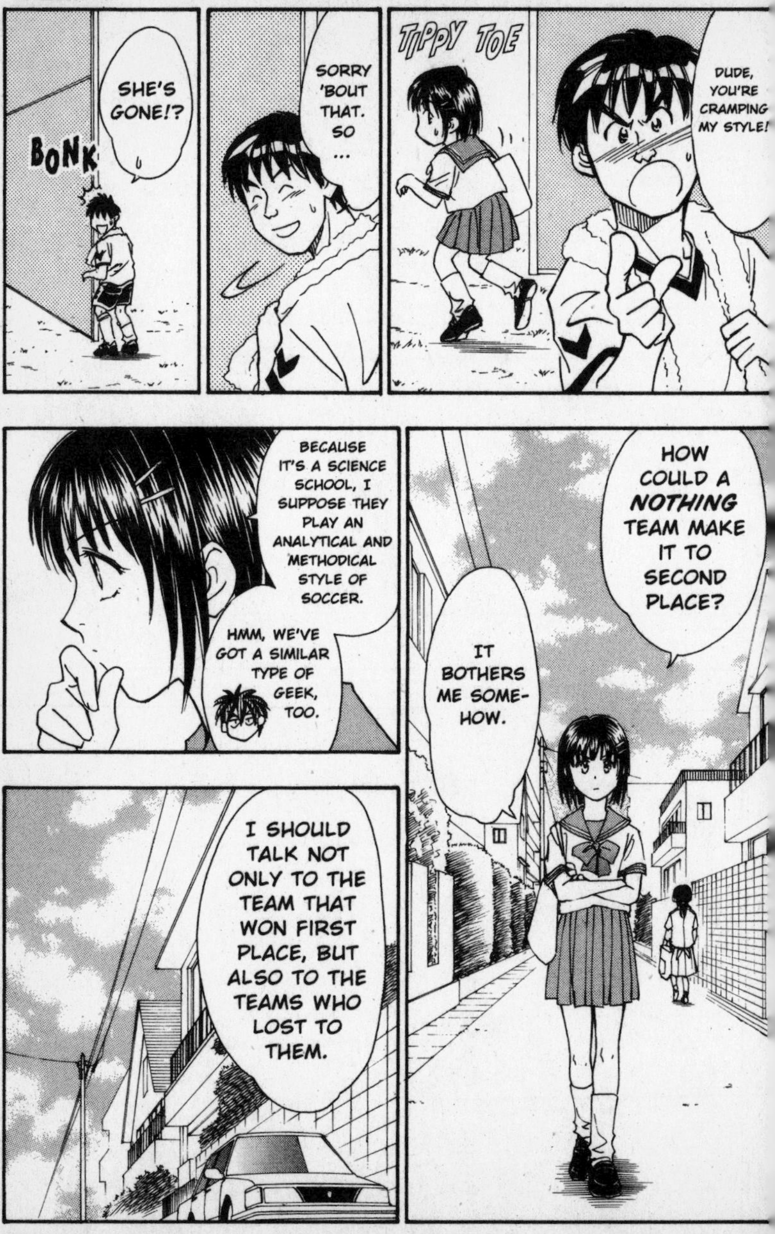
DUDE, YOU'RE CRAMPING MY STYLE!
TIPPY TOE
SORRY 'BOUT THAT. SO ...
SHE'S GONE!?
BONK
HOW COULD A *NOTHING* TEAM MAKE IT TO SECOND PLACE?
IT BOTHERS ME SOME-HOW.
BECAUSE IT'S A SCIENCE SCHOOL, I SUPPOSE THEY PLAY AN ANALYTICAL AND METHODICAL STYLE OF SOCCER.
HMM, WE'VE GOT A SIMILAR TYPE OF GEEK, TOO.
I SHOULD TALK NOT ONLY TO THE TEAM THAT WON FIRST PLACE, BUT ALSO TO THE TEAMS WHO LOST TO THEM.

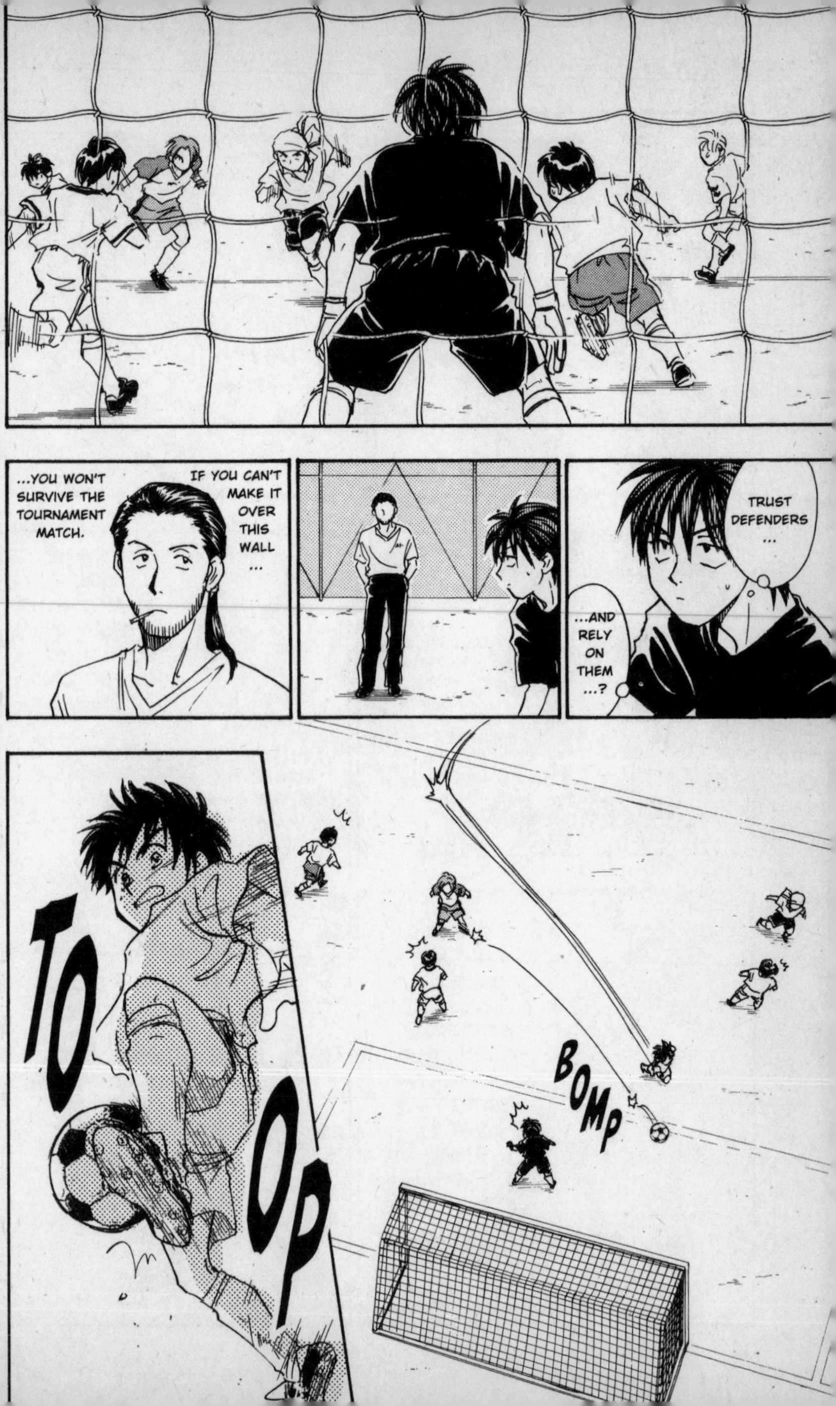
TRUST DEFENDERS ...
...AND RELY ON THEM ...?
IF YOU CAN'T MAKE IT OVER THIS WALL ...
...YOU WON'T SURVIVE THE TOURNAMENT MATCH.
BOMP
TOOP

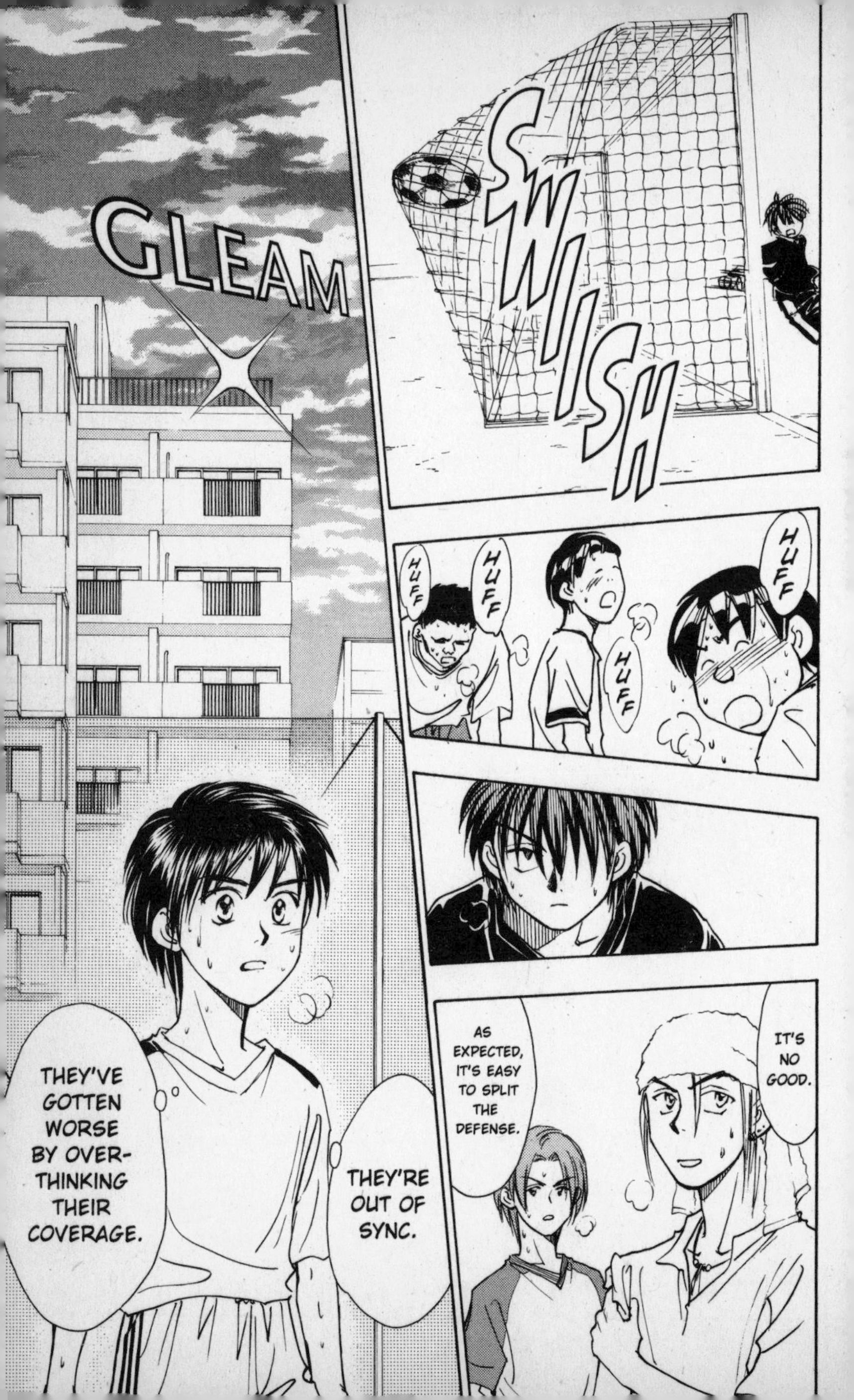
SWISH
HUFF
HUFF
HUFF
HUFF
IT'S NO GOOD.
AS EXPECTED, IT'S EASY TO SPLIT THE DEFENSE.
GLEAM
THEY'RE OUT OF SYNC.
THEY'VE GOTTEN WORSE BY OVER-THINKING THEIR COVERAGE.

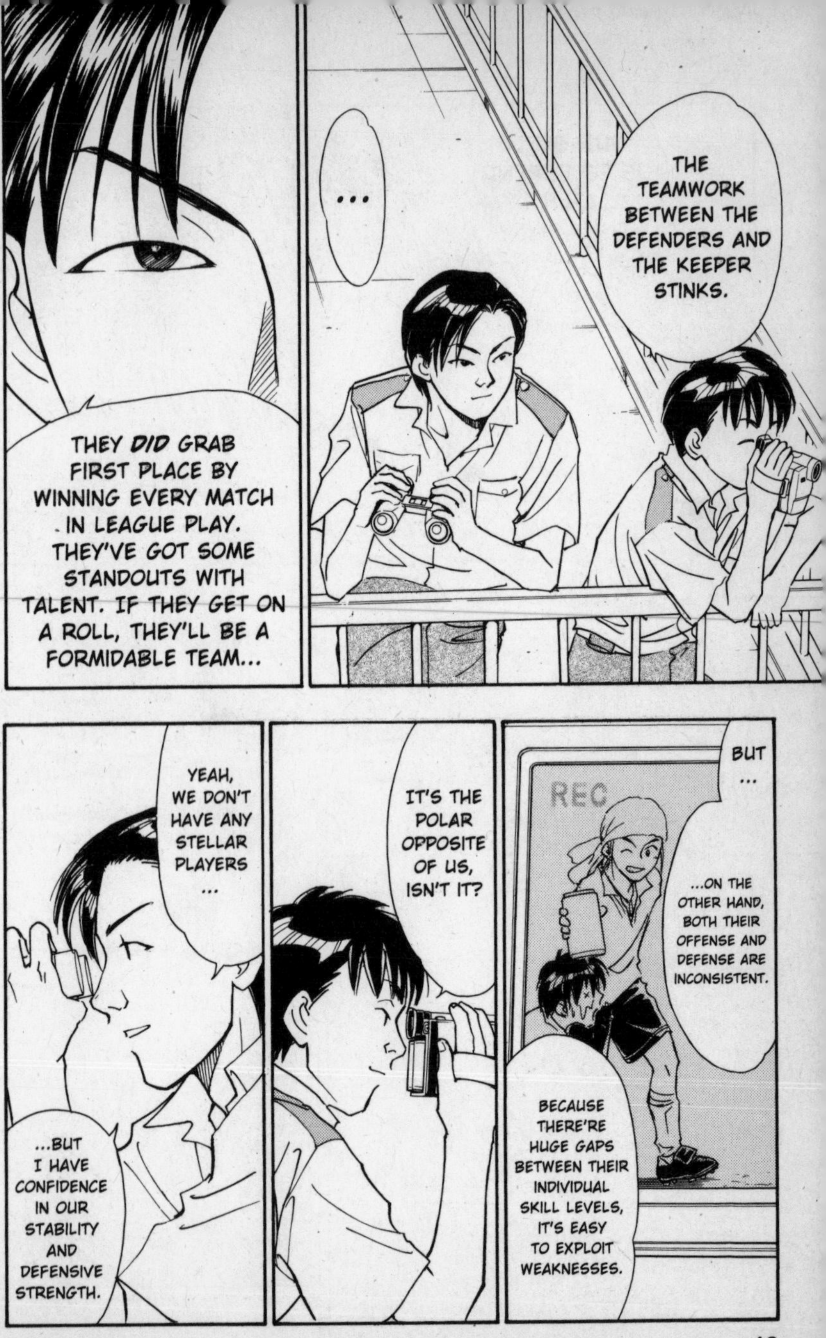
THE TEAMWORK BETWEEN THE DEFENDERS AND THE KEEPER STINKS.
...
THEY *DID* GRAB FIRST PLACE BY WINNING EVERY MATCH IN LEAGUE PLAY. THEY'VE GOT SOME STANDOUTS WITH TALENT. IF THEY GET ON A ROLL, THEY'LL BE A FORMIDABLE TEAM...
BUT ...
REC
...ON THE OTHER HAND, BOTH THEIR OFFENSE AND DEFENSE ARE INCONSISTENT.
BECAUSE THERE'RE HUGE GAPS BETWEEN THEIR INDIVIDUAL SKILL LEVELS, IT'S EASY TO EXPLOIT WEAKNESSES.
IT'S THE POLAR OPPOSITE OF US, ISN'T IT?
YEAH, WE DON'T HAVE ANY STELLAR PLAYERS ...
...BUT I HAVE CONFIDENCE IN OUR STABILITY AND DEFENSIVE STRENGTH.

READ THIS WAY

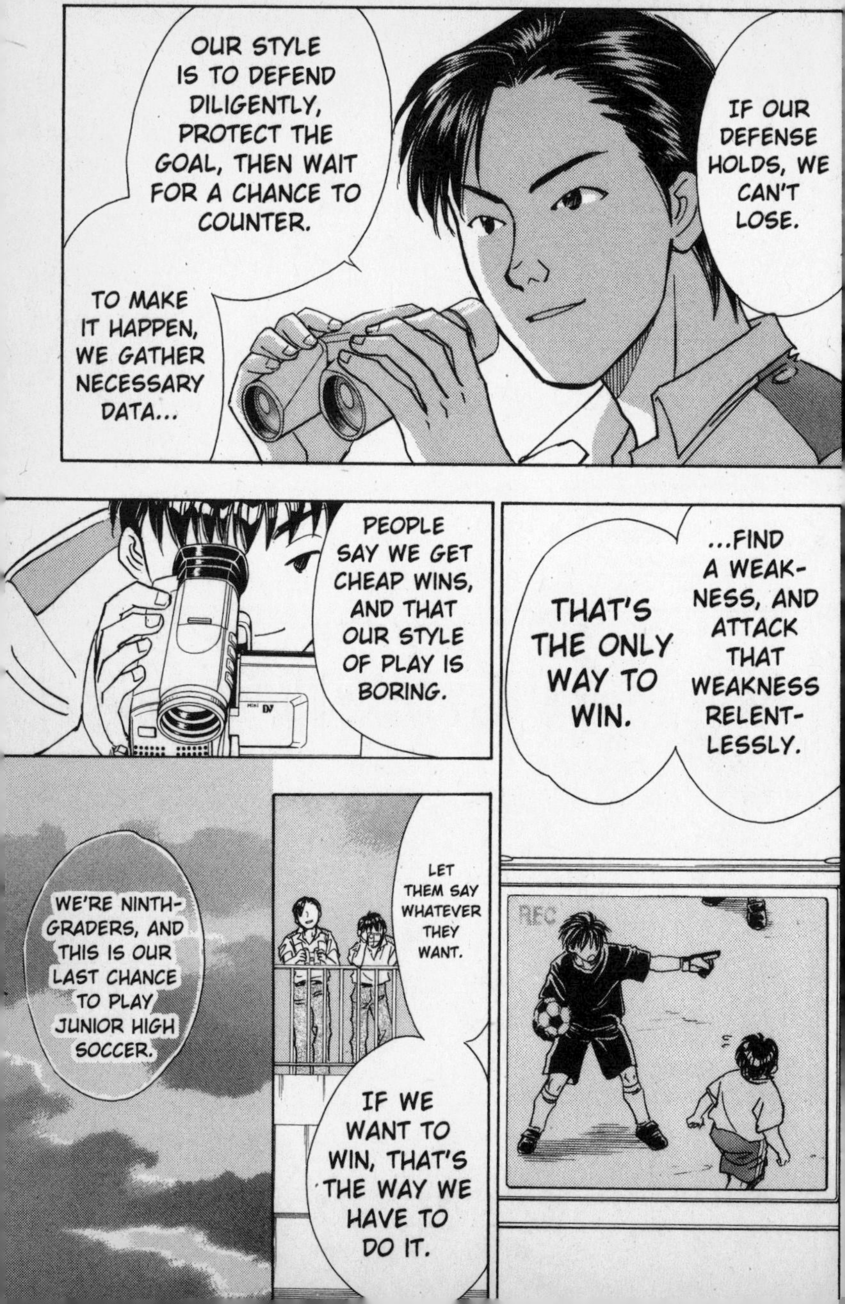
IF OUR DEFENSE HOLDS, WE CAN'T LOSE.
OUR STYLE IS TO DEFEND DILIGENTLY, PROTECT THE GOAL, THEN WAIT FOR A CHANCE TO COUNTER.
TO MAKE IT HAPPEN, WE GATHER NECESSARY DATA...
...FIND A WEAK-NESS, AND ATTACK THAT WEAKNESS RELENT-LESSLY.
THAT'S THE ONLY WAY TO WIN.
PEOPLE SAY WE GET CHEAP WINS, AND THAT OUR STYLE OF PLAY IS BORING.
LET THEM SAY WHATEVER THEY WANT.
IF WE WANT TO WIN, THAT'S THE WAY WE HAVE TO DO IT.
WE'RE NINTH-GRADERS, AND THIS IS OUR LAST CHANCE TO PLAY JUNIOR HIGH SOCCER.
REC

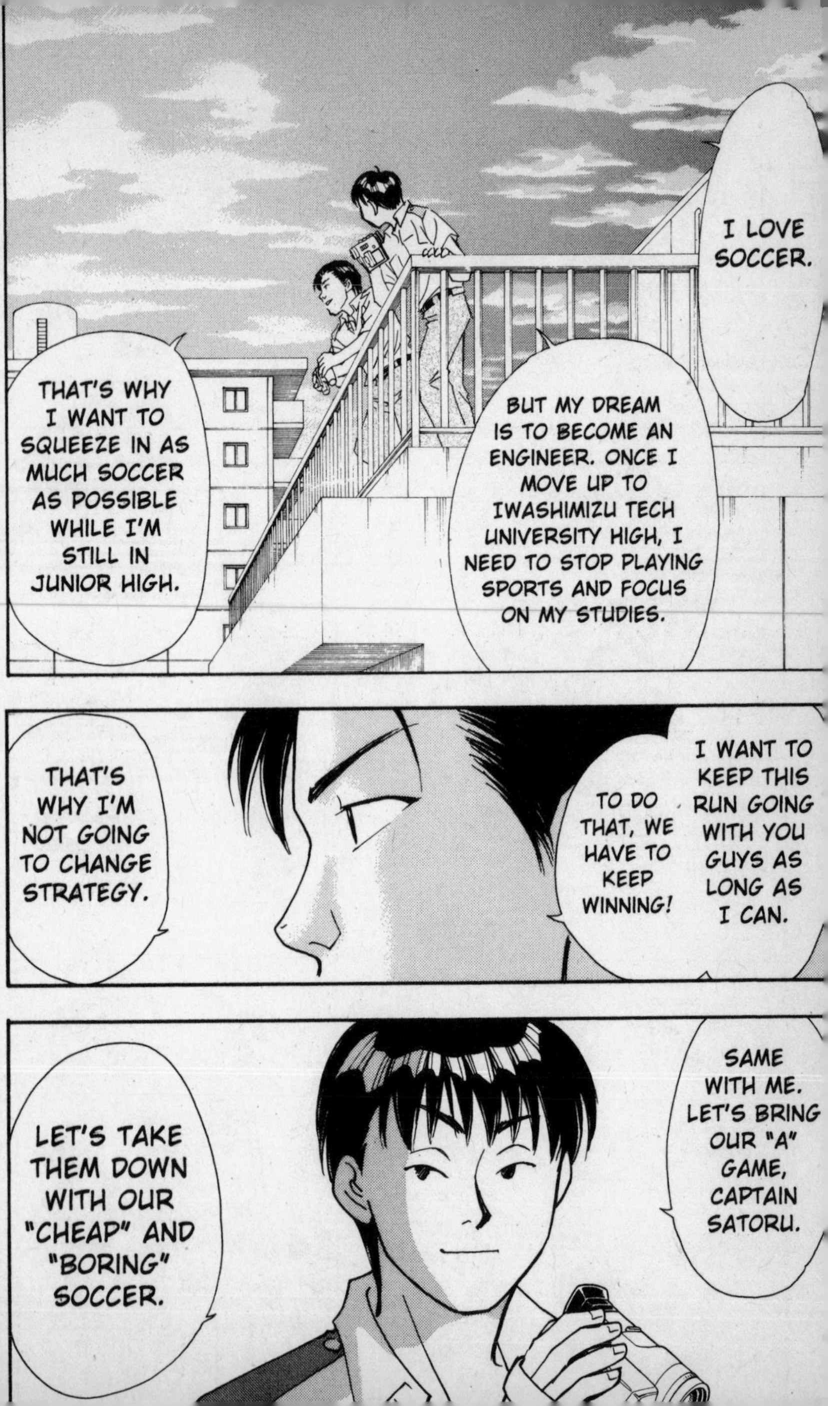
I LOVE SOCCER.
BUT MY DREAM IS TO BECOME AN ENGINEER. ONCE I MOVE UP TO IWASHIMIZU TECH UNIVERSITY HIGH, I NEED TO STOP PLAYING SPORTS AND FOCUS ON MY STUDIES.
THAT'S WHY I WANT TO SQUEEZE IN AS MUCH SOCCER AS POSSIBLE WHILE I'M STILL IN JUNIOR HIGH.
I WANT TO KEEP THIS RUN GOING WITH YOU GUYS AS LONG AS I CAN.
TO DO THAT, WE HAVE TO KEEP WINNING!
THAT'S WHY I'M NOT GOING TO CHANGE STRATEGY.
SAME WITH ME. LET'S BRING OUR "A" GAME, CAPTAIN SATORU.
LET'S TAKE THEM DOWN WITH OUR "CHEAP" AND "BORING" SOCCER.

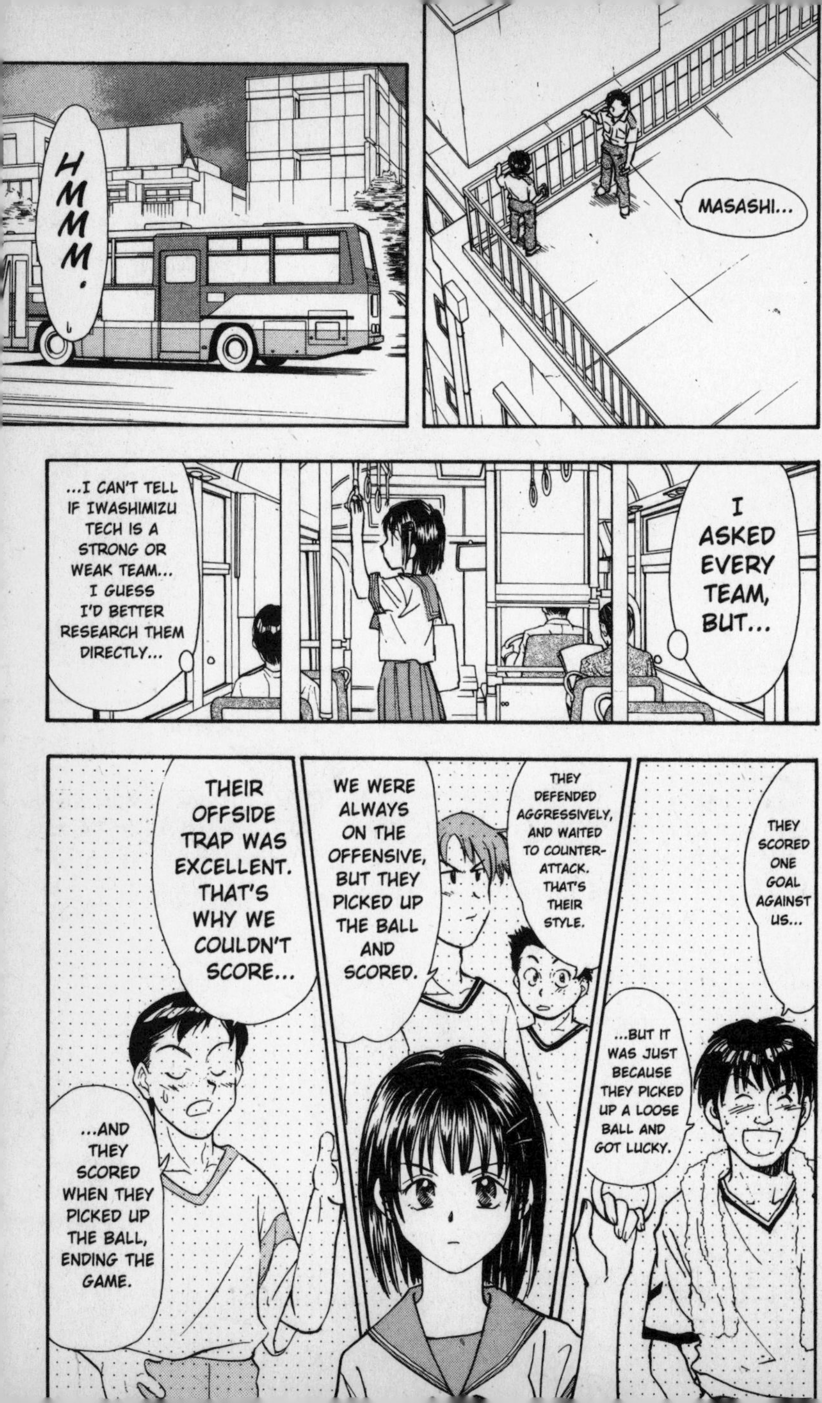
MASASHI...
HMMM.
I ASKED EVERY TEAM, BUT...
...I CAN'T TELL IF IWASHIMIZU TECH IS A STRONG OR WEAK TEAM... I GUESS I'D BETTER RESEARCH THEM DIRECTLY...
THEY SCORED ONE GOAL AGAINST US...
...BUT IT WAS JUST BECAUSE THEY PICKED UP A LOOSE BALL AND GOT LUCKY.
THEY DEFENDED AGGRESSIVELY, AND WAITED TO COUNTER-ATTACK. THAT'S THEIR STYLE.
WE WERE ALWAYS ON THE OFFENSIVE, BUT THEY PICKED UP THE BALL AND SCORED.
THEIR OFFSIDE TRAP WAS EXCELLENT. THAT'S WHY WE COULDN'T SCORE...
...AND THEY SCORED WHEN THEY PICKED UP THE BALL, ENDING THE GAME.

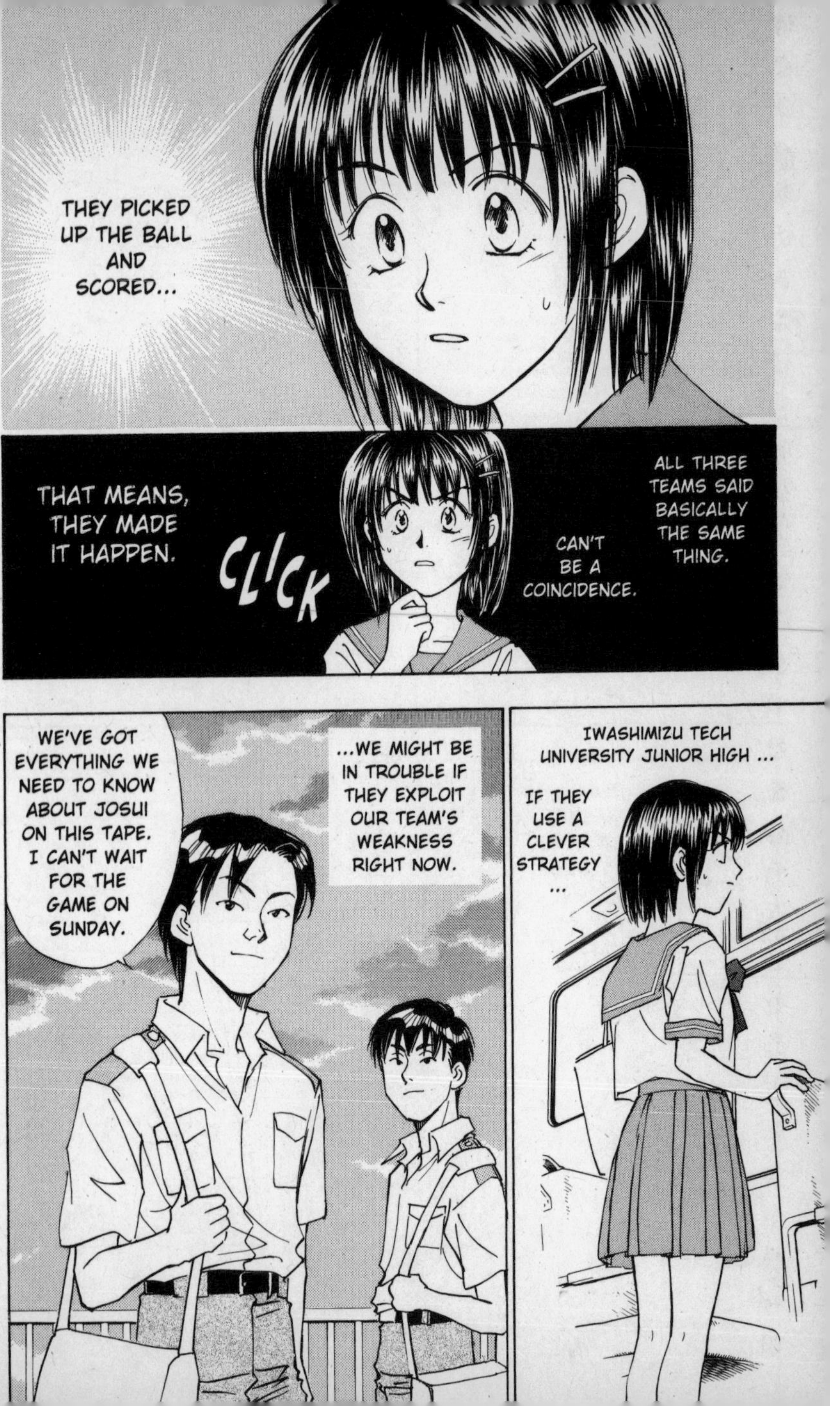
THEY PICKED UP THE BALL AND SCORED...
ALL THREE TEAMS SAID BASICALLY THE SAME THING.
CAN'T BE A COINCIDENCE.
CLICK
THAT MEANS, THEY MADE IT HAPPEN.
IWASHIMIZU TECH UNIVERSITY JUNIOR HIGH ...
IF THEY USE A CLEVER STRATEGY ...
...WE MIGHT BE IN TROUBLE IF THEY EXPLOIT OUR TEAM'S WEAKNESS RIGHT NOW.
WE'VE GOT EVERYTHING WE NEED TO KNOW ABOUT JOSUI ON THIS TAPE. I CAN'T WAIT FOR THE GAME ON SUNDAY.

DAISUKE
NOTE

PERSONAL DATA	
BIRTHDAY:	MARCH 3, 1986
SIZE:	149 cm 58 kg
BLOOD TYPE:	A
FAVORITE FOOD:	PUDDING
WHAT HE DISLIKES:	FRESH APPLES
HOBBY AND SPECIAL SKILLS:	TOY MODEL MAKING & HAVING A FLEXIBLE BODY

HIROYOSHI NORO

SEIYA AMANO

THE MITCHI*
OF MUSASHINO
MORI.

AS A JOKE, I
DREW HIM IN
COSPLAY. IT
SUITS HIM
PERFECTLY.

PERSONAL DATA	
BIRTHDAY:	JUNE 20, 1983
SIZE:	173 cm 57 kg
BLOOD TYPE:	B
FAVORITE FOOD:	CHOCOLATE SUNDAES
WHAT HE DISLIKES:	SCALLIONS, CELERY, ASIAN MINT, NATTO (FERMENTED SOYBEAN)
HOBBY AND SPECIAL SKILLS:	COLLECTING THE SIGNATURES OF FAMOUS SOCCER PLAYERS & SMOOTH TALKING

*MITCHI REFERS TO JAPANESE POP STAR MITSUHIRO OIKAWA.

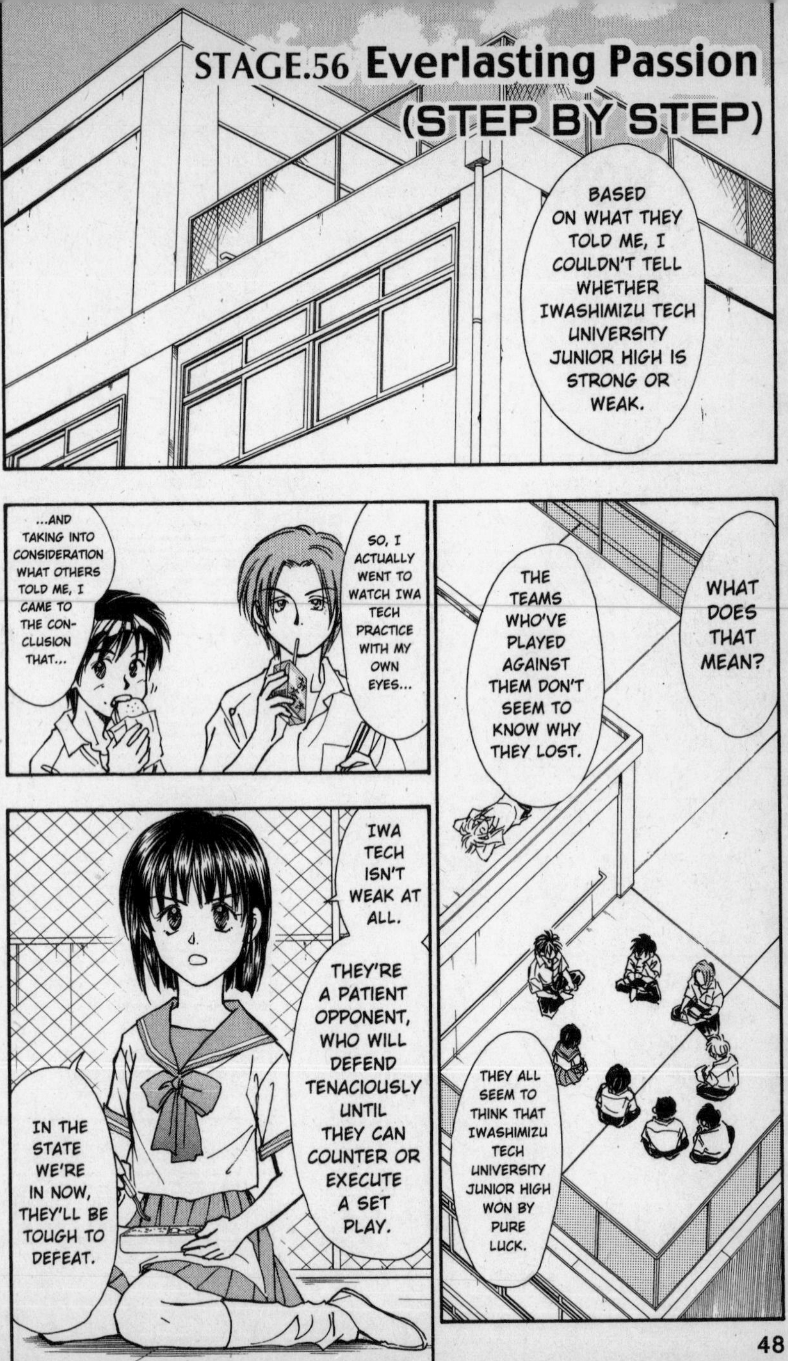
STAGE.56 Everlasting Passion
(STEP BY STEP)
BASED ON WHAT THEY TOLD ME, I COULDN'T TELL WHETHER IWASHIMIZU TECH UNIVERSITY JUNIOR HIGH IS STRONG OR WEAK.
WHAT DOES THAT MEAN?
THE TEAMS WHO'VE PLAYED AGAINST THEM DON'T SEEM TO KNOW WHY THEY LOST.
THEY ALL SEEM TO THINK THAT IWASHIMIZU TECH UNIVERSITY JUNIOR HIGH WON BY PURE LUCK.
SO, I ACTUALLY WENT TO WATCH IWA TECH PRACTICE WITH MY OWN EYES...
...AND TAKING INTO CONSIDERATION WHAT OTHERS TOLD ME, I CAME TO THE CON-CLUSION THAT...
IWA TECH ISN'T WEAK AT ALL.
THEY'RE A PATIENT OPPONENT, WHO WILL DEFEND TENACIOUSLY UNTIL THEY CAN COUNTER OR EXECUTE A SET PLAY.
IN THE STATE WE'RE IN NOW, THEY'LL BE TOUGH TO DEFEAT.

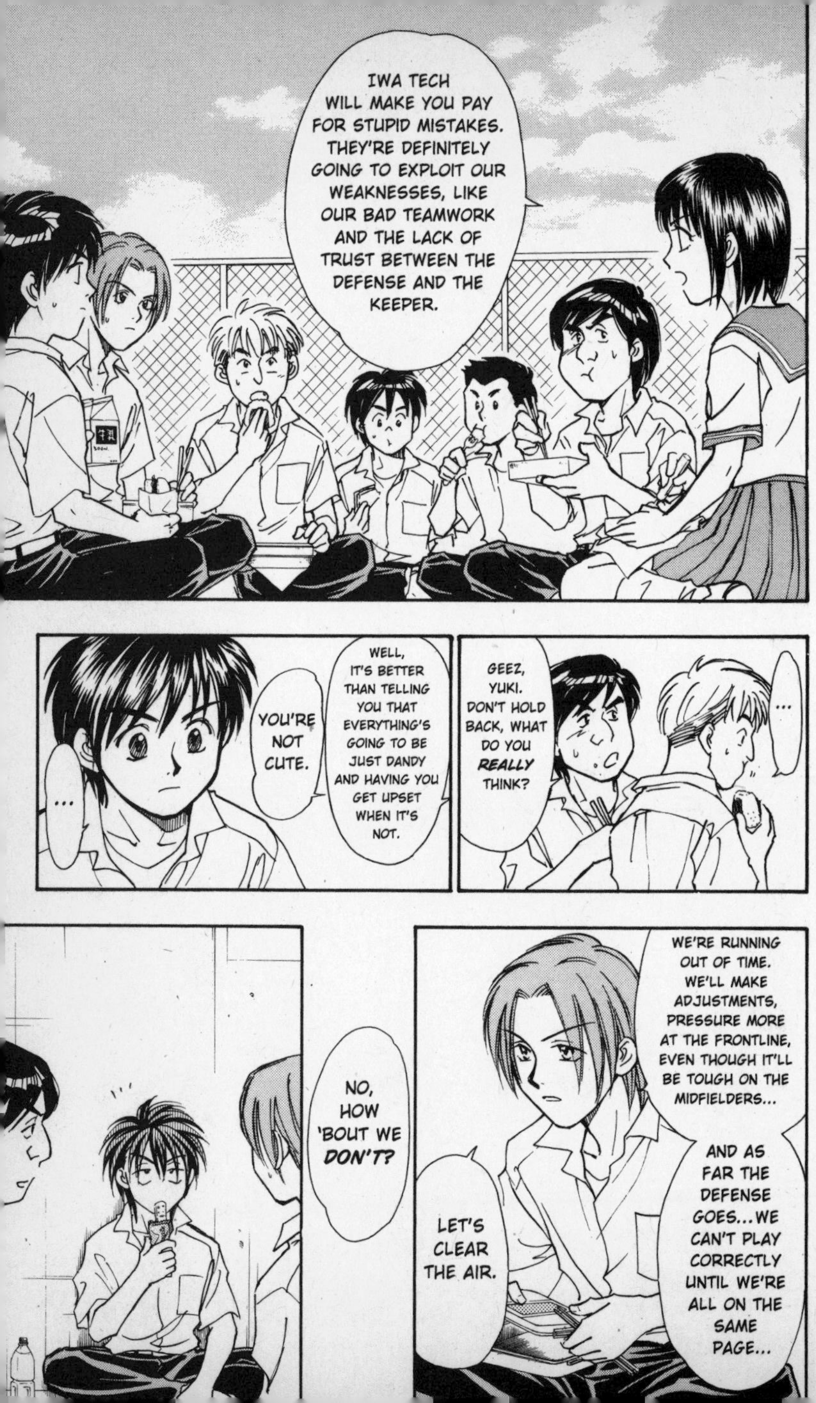
IWA TECH WILL MAKE YOU PAY FOR STUPID MISTAKES. THEY'RE DEFINITELY GOING TO EXPLOIT OUR WEAKNESSES, LIKE OUR BAD TEAMWORK AND THE LACK OF TRUST BETWEEN THE DEFENSE AND THE KEEPER.
...
GEEZ, YUKI. DON'T HOLD BACK, WHAT DO YOU *REALLY* THINK?
WELL, IT'S BETTER THAN TELLING YOU THAT EVERYTHING'S GOING TO BE JUST DANDY AND HAVING YOU GET UPSET WHEN IT'S NOT.
YOU'RE NOT CUTE.
...
WE'RE RUNNING OUT OF TIME. WE'LL MAKE ADJUSTMENTS, PRESSURE MORE AT THE FRONTLINE, EVEN THOUGH IT'LL BE TOUGH ON THE MIDFIELDERS...
AND AS FAR THE DEFENSE GOES...WE CAN'T PLAY CORRECTLY UNTIL WE'RE ALL ON THE SAME PAGE...
LET'S CLEAR THE AIR.
NO, HOW 'BOUT WE *DON'T?*

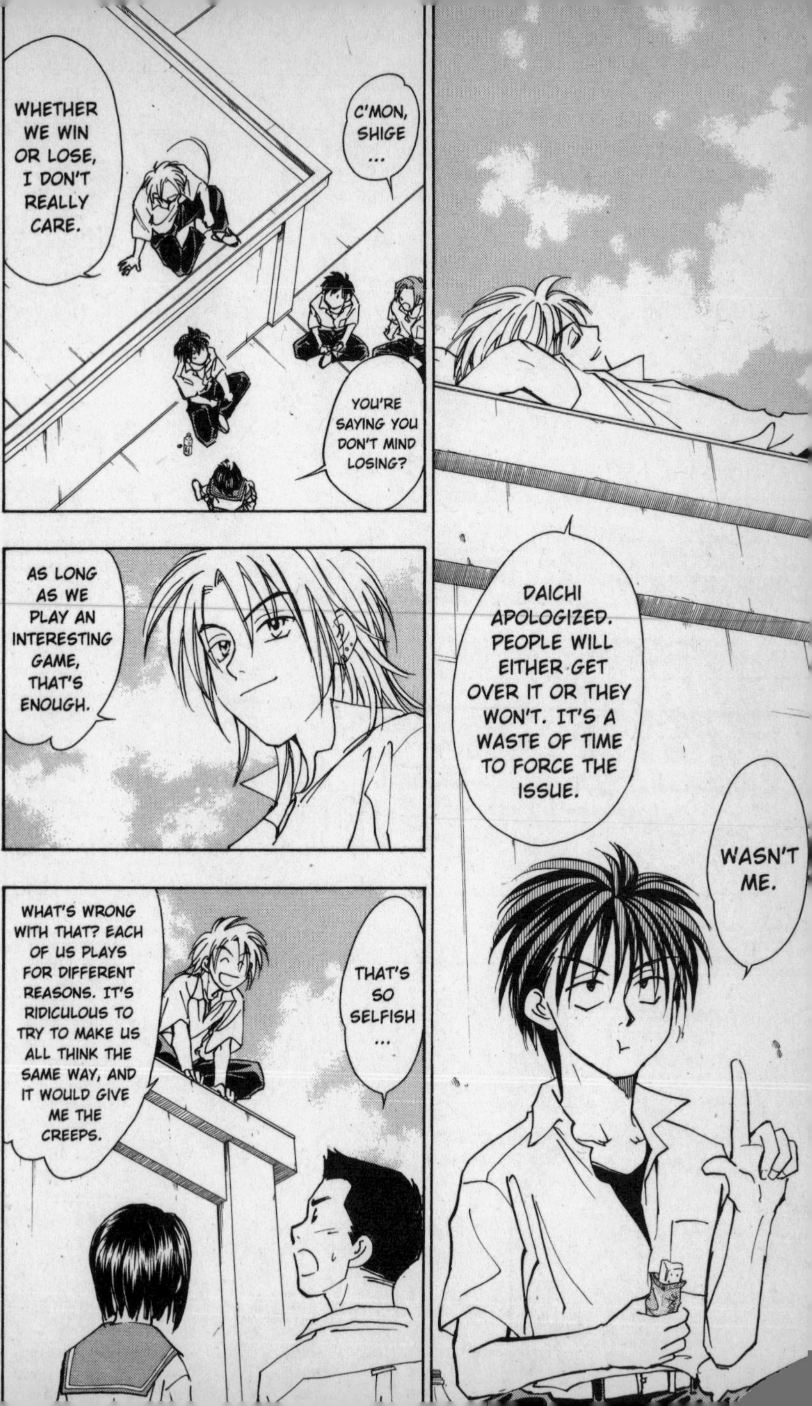
DAICHI APOLOGIZED. PEOPLE WILL EITHER GET OVER IT OR THEY WON'T. IT'S A WASTE OF TIME TO FORCE THE ISSUE.
WASN'T ME.
C'MON, SHIGE ...
WHETHER WE WIN OR LOSE, I DON'T REALLY CARE.
YOU'RE SAYING YOU DON'T MIND LOSING?
AS LONG AS WE PLAY AN INTERESTING GAME, THAT'S ENOUGH.
THAT'S SO SELFISH ...
WHAT'S WRONG WITH THAT? EACH OF US PLAYS FOR DIFFERENT REASONS. IT'S RIDICULOUS TO TRY TO MAKE US ALL THINK THE SAME WAY, AND IT WOULD GIVE ME THE CREEPS.

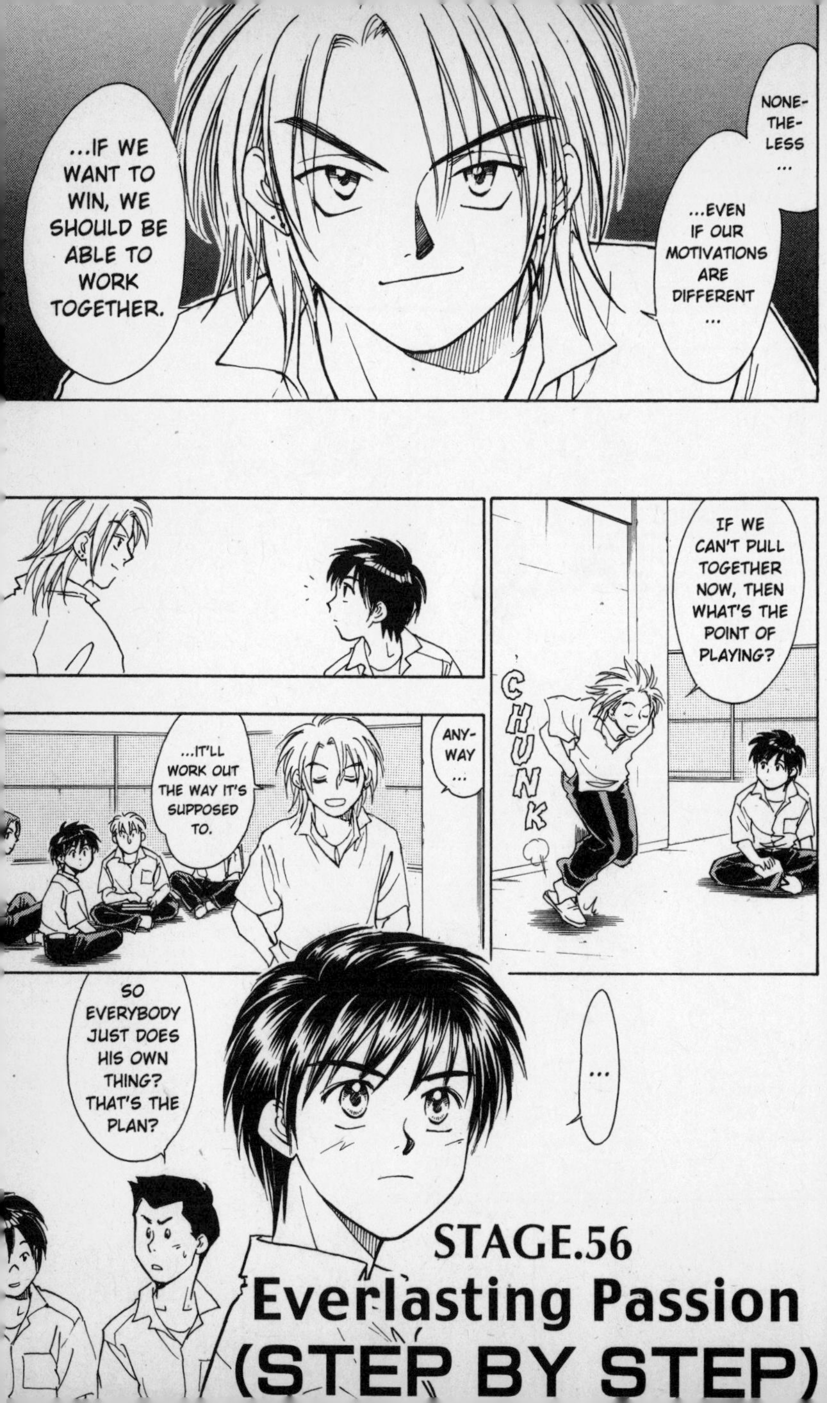
NONE-THE-LESS ...
...EVEN IF OUR MOTIVATIONS ARE DIFFERENT ...
...IF WE WANT TO WIN, WE SHOULD BE ABLE TO WORK TOGETHER.
IF WE CAN'T PULL TOGETHER NOW, THEN WHAT'S THE POINT OF PLAYING?
CHUNK
ANY-WAY ...
...IT'LL WORK OUT THE WAY IT'S SUPPOSED TO.
...
SO EVERYBODY JUST DOES HIS OWN THING? THAT'S THE PLAN?
STAGE.56
Everlasting Passion
(STEP BY STEP)

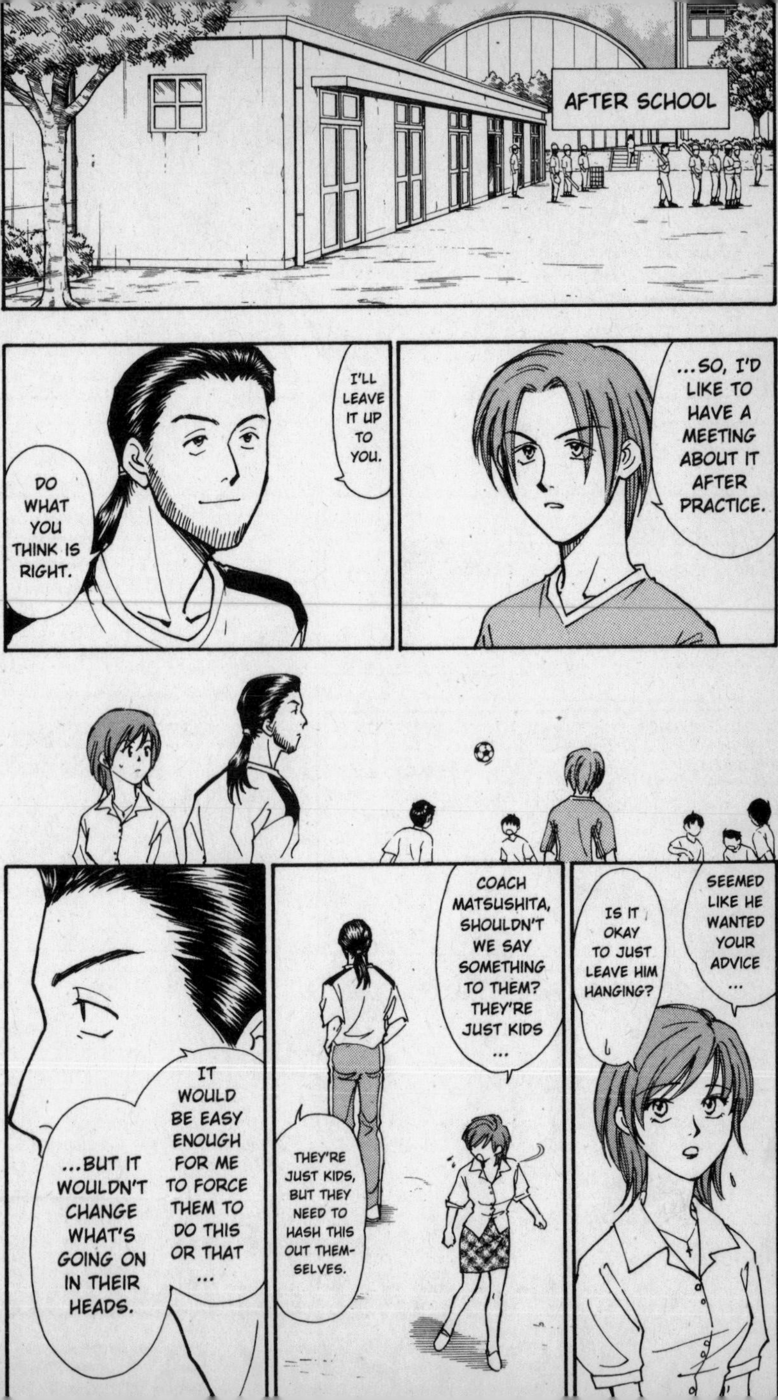
AFTER SCHOOL
...SO, I'D LIKE TO HAVE A MEETING ABOUT IT AFTER PRACTICE.
I'LL LEAVE IT UP TO YOU.
DO WHAT YOU THINK IS RIGHT.
SEEMED LIKE HE WANTED YOUR ADVICE ...
IS IT OKAY TO JUST LEAVE HIM HANGING?
COACH MATSUSHITA, SHOULDN'T WE SAY SOMETHING TO THEM? THEY'RE JUST KIDS ...
THEY'RE JUST KIDS, BUT THEY NEED TO HASH THIS OUT THEM-SELVES.
IT WOULD BE EASY ENOUGH FOR ME TO FORCE THEM TO DO THIS OR THAT ...
...BUT IT WOULDN'T CHANGE WHAT'S GOING ON IN THEIR HEADS.

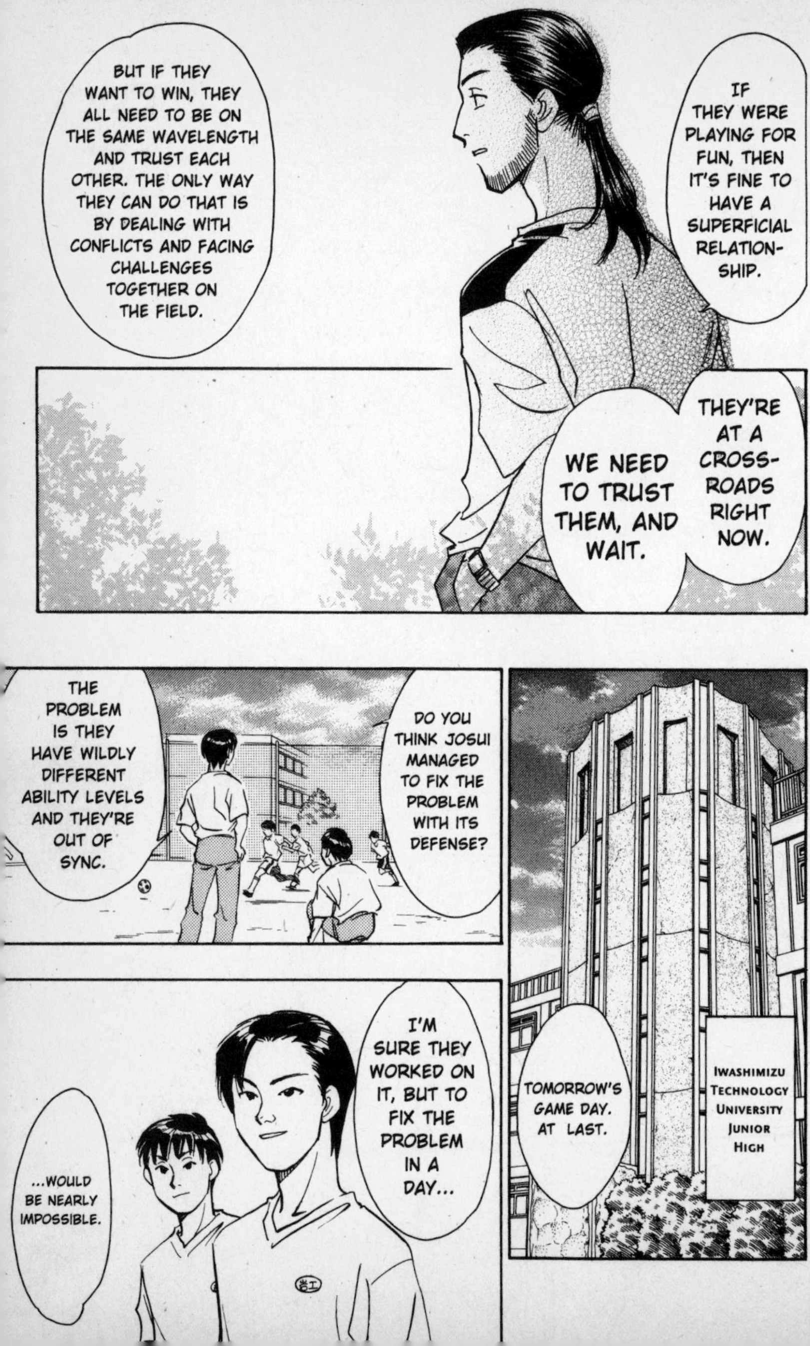
IF THEY WERE PLAYING FOR FUN, THEN IT'S FINE TO HAVE A SUPERFICIAL RELATIONSHIP.
BUT IF THEY WANT TO WIN, THEY ALL NEED TO BE ON THE SAME WAVELENGTH AND TRUST EACH OTHER. THE ONLY WAY THEY CAN DO THAT IS BY DEALING WITH CONFLICTS AND FACING CHALLENGES TOGETHER ON THE FIELD.
THEY'RE AT A CROSSROADS RIGHT NOW.
WE NEED TO TRUST THEM, AND WAIT.
IWASHIMIZU TECHNOLOGY UNIVERSITY JUNIOR HIGH
TOMORROW'S GAME DAY. AT LAST.
DO YOU THINK JOSUI MANAGED TO FIX THE PROBLEM WITH ITS DEFENSE?
THE PROBLEM IS THEY HAVE WILDLY DIFFERENT ABILITY LEVELS AND THEY'RE OUT OF SYNC.
I'M SURE THEY WORKED ON IT, BUT TO FIX THE PROBLEM IN A DAY...
...WOULD BE NEARLY IMPOSSIBLE.

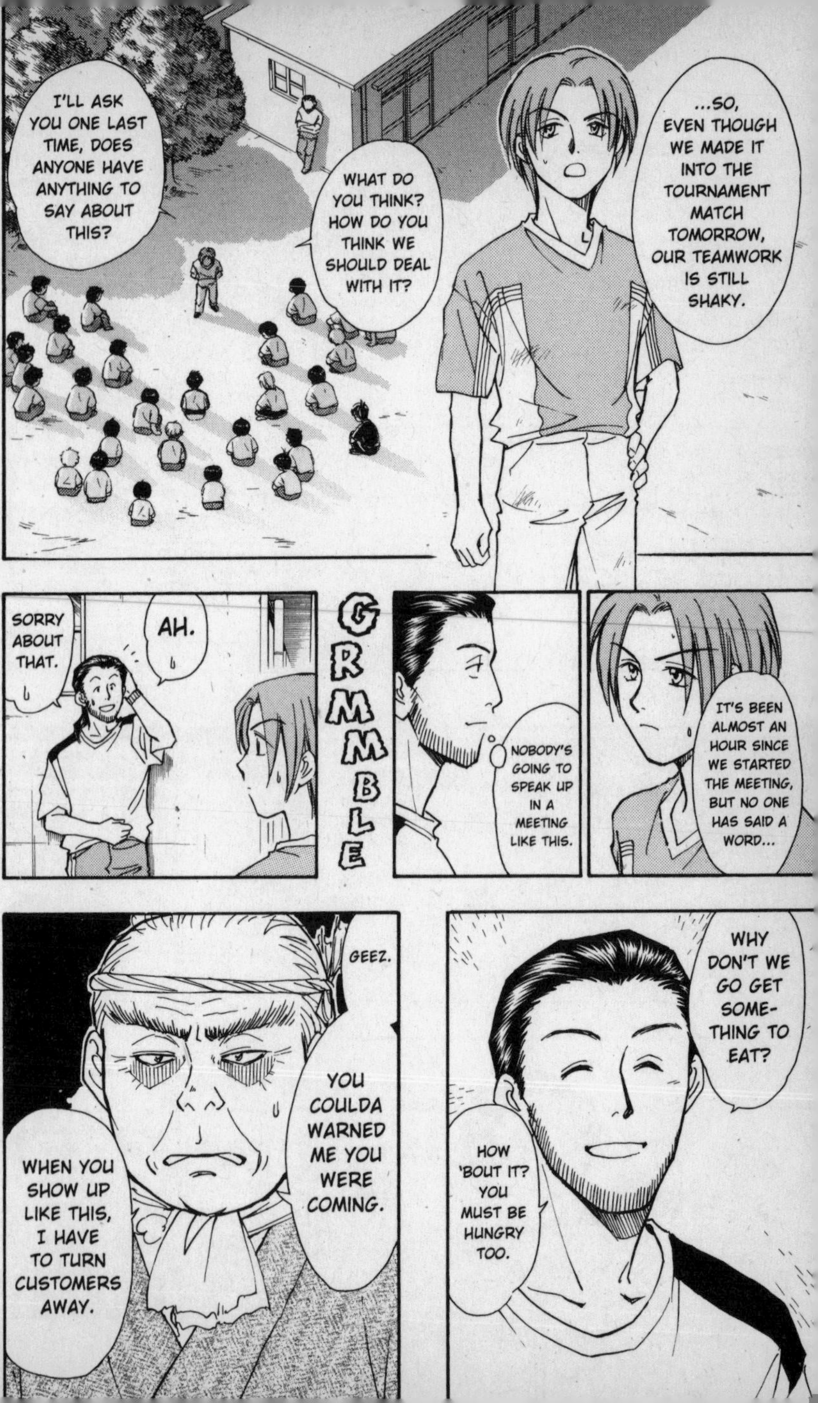
...SO, EVEN THOUGH WE MADE IT INTO THE TOURNAMENT MATCH TOMORROW, OUR TEAMWORK IS STILL SHAKY.
WHAT DO YOU THINK? HOW DO YOU THINK WE SHOULD DEAL WITH IT?
I'LL ASK YOU ONE LAST TIME, DOES ANYONE HAVE ANYTHING TO SAY ABOUT THIS?
IT'S BEEN ALMOST AN HOUR SINCE WE STARTED THE MEETING, BUT NO ONE HAS SAID A WORD...
NOBODY'S GOING TO SPEAK UP IN A MEETING LIKE THIS.
GRMMBLE
AH.
SORRY ABOUT THAT.
WHY DON'T WE GO GET SOME-THING TO EAT?
HOW 'BOUT IT? YOU MUST BE HUNGRY TOO.
GEEZ.
YOU COULDA WARNED ME YOU WERE COMING.
WHEN YOU SHOW UP LIKE THIS, I HAVE TO TURN CUSTOMERS AWAY.

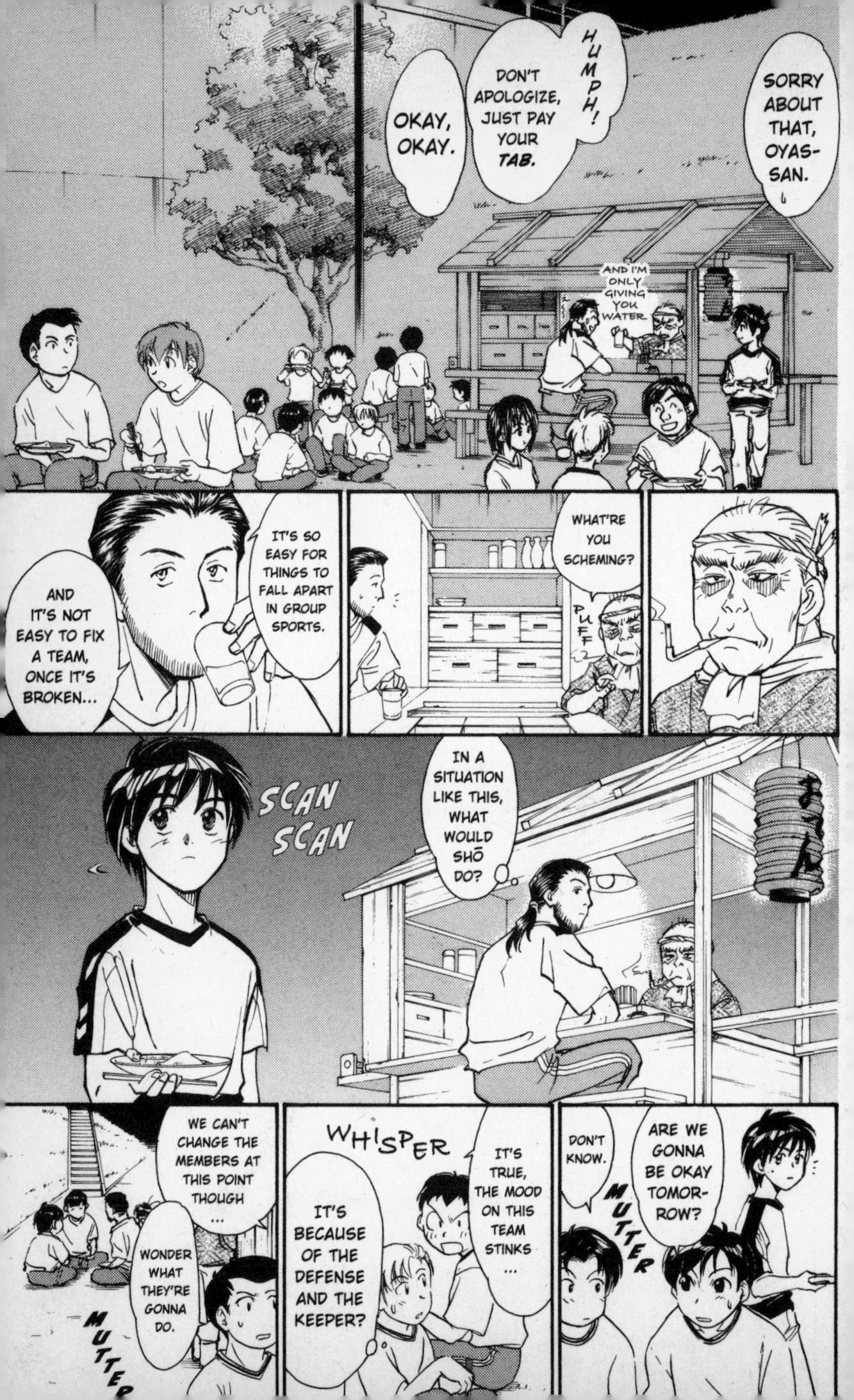
SORRY ABOUT THAT, OYAS-SAN.
HUMPH!
DON'T APOLOGIZE, JUST PAY YOUR TAB.
AND I'M ONLY GIVING YOU WATER
OKAY, OKAY.
WHAT'RE YOU SCHEMING?
PUFF
IT'S SO EASY FOR THINGS TO FALL APART IN GROUP SPORTS.
AND IT'S NOT EASY TO FIX A TEAM, ONCE IT'S BROKEN...
IN A SITUATION LIKE THIS, WHAT WOULD SHŌ DO?
SCAN SCAN
ARE WE GONNA BE OKAY TOMORROW?
DON'T KNOW.
MUTTER
IT'S TRUE, THE MOOD ON THIS TEAM STINKS...
WHISPER
IT'S BECAUSE OF THE DEFENSE AND THE KEEPER?
WE CAN'T CHANGE THE MEMBERS AT THIS POINT THOUGH...
WONDER WHAT THEY'RE GONNA DO.
MUTTER

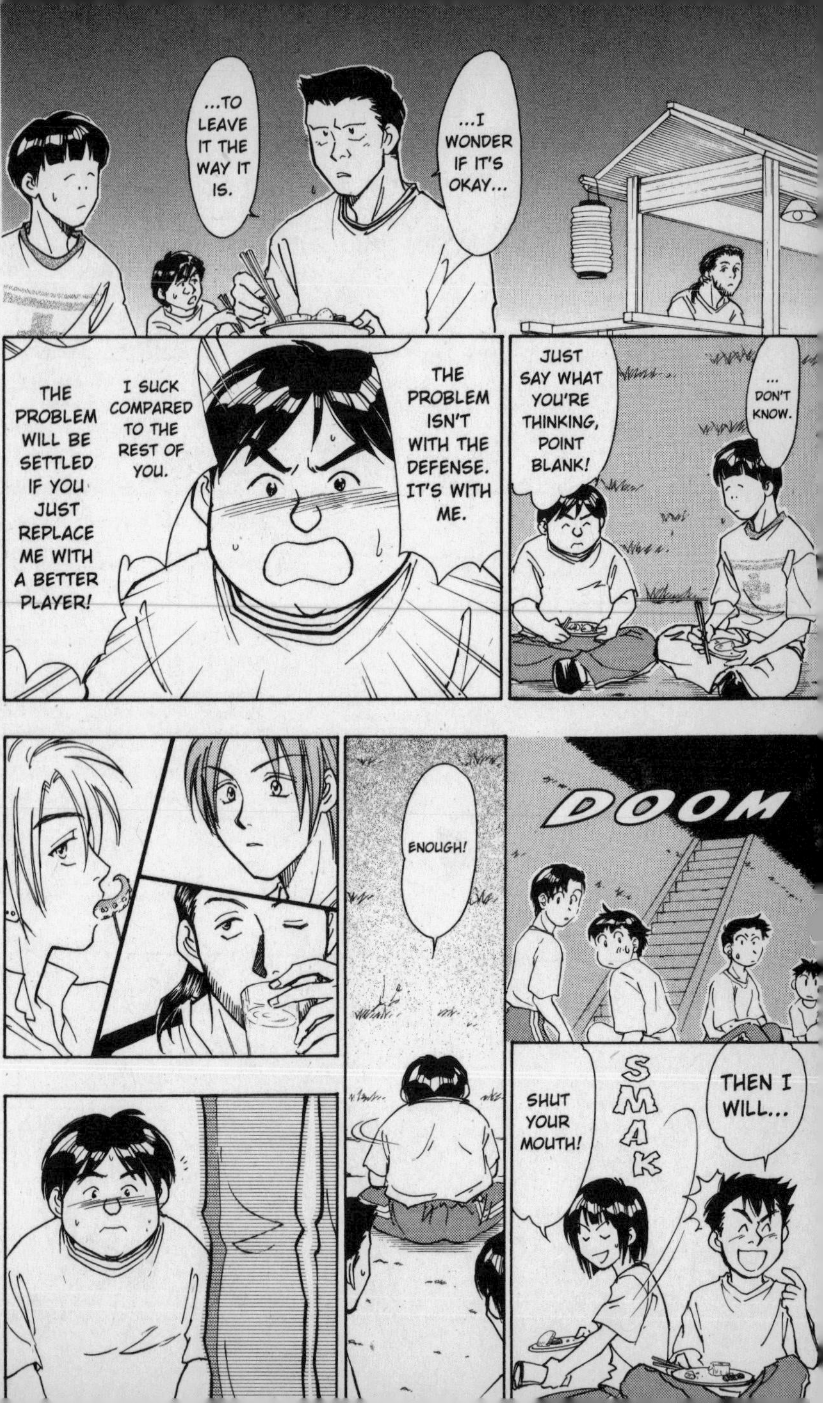
...I WONDER IF IT'S OKAY...
...TO LEAVE IT THE WAY IT IS.
... DON'T KNOW.
JUST SAY WHAT YOU'RE THINKING, POINT BLANK!
THE PROBLEM ISN'T WITH THE DEFENSE. IT'S WITH ME.
I SUCK COMPARED TO THE REST OF YOU.
THE PROBLEM WILL BE SETTLED IF YOU JUST REPLACE ME WITH A BETTER PLAYER!
DOOM
THEN I WILL...
SMAK
SHUT YOUR MOUTH!
ENOUGH!

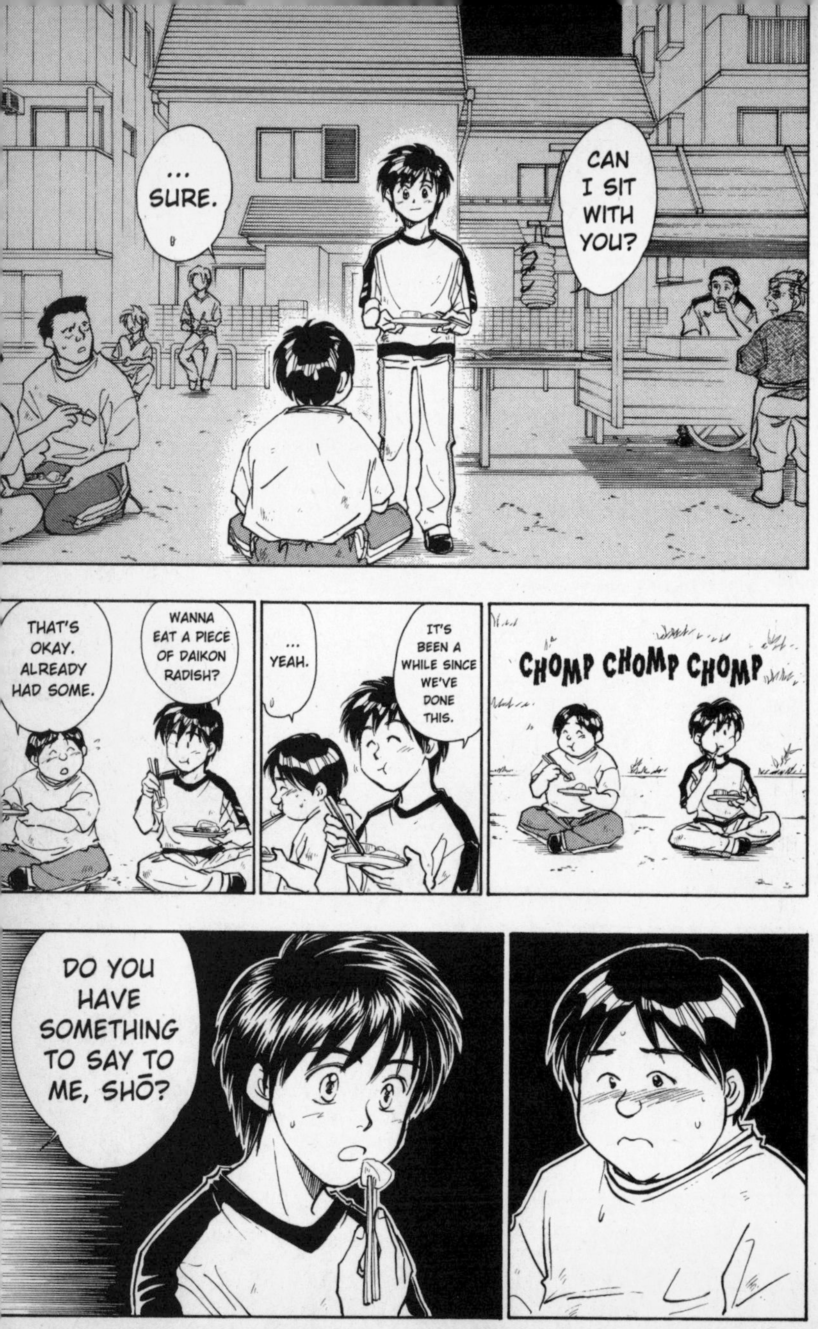
CAN I SIT WITH YOU?
... SURE.
CHOMP CHOMP CHOMP
IT'S BEEN A WHILE SINCE WE'VE DONE THIS.
... YEAH.
WANNA EAT A PIECE OF DAIKON RADISH?
THAT'S OKAY. ALREADY HAD SOME.
DO YOU HAVE SOMETHING TO SAY TO ME, SHŌ?

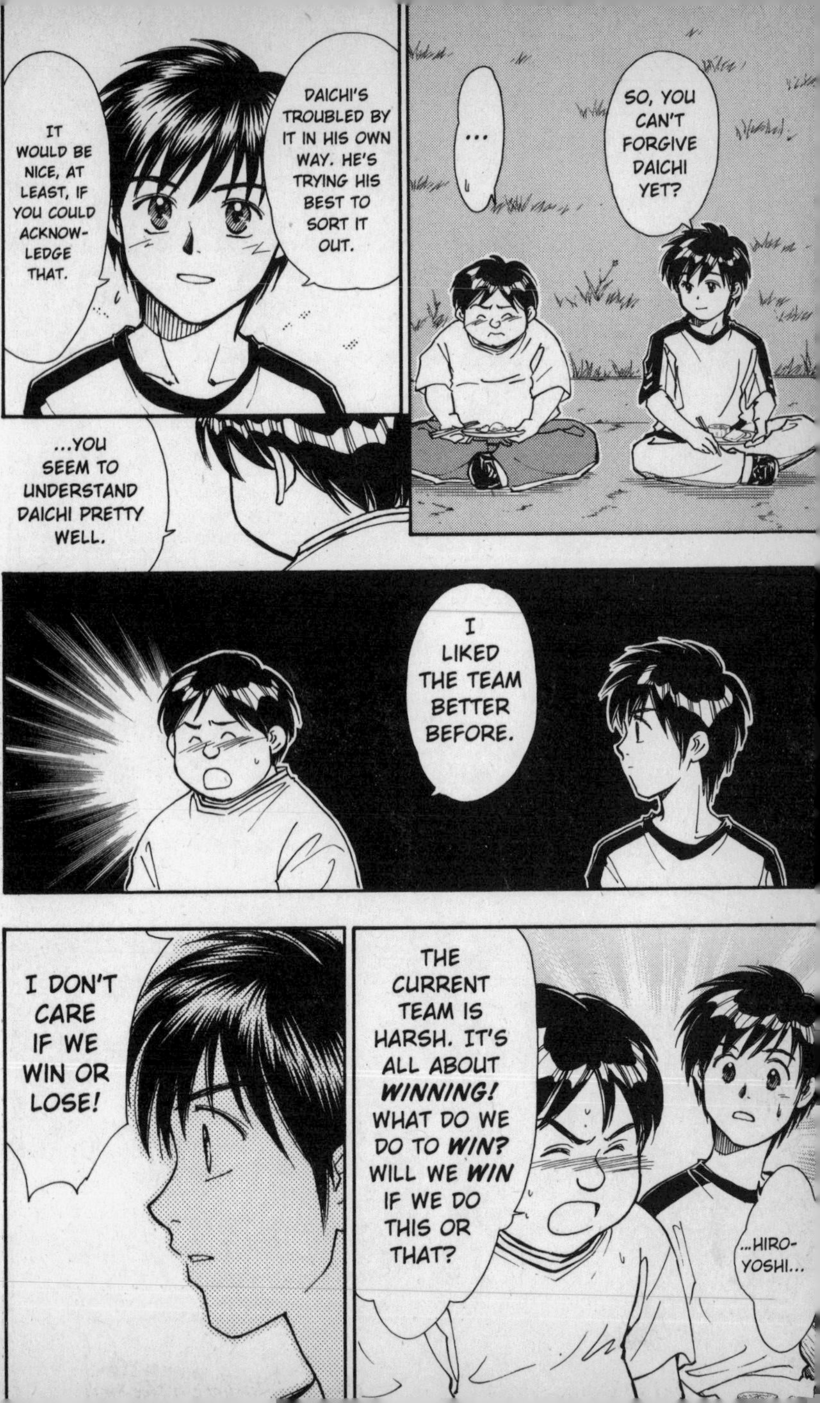

SO, YOU CAN'T FORGIVE DAICHI YET?
...
DAICHI'S TROUBLED BY IT IN HIS OWN WAY. HE'S TRYING HIS BEST TO SORT IT OUT.
IT WOULD BE NICE, AT LEAST, IF YOU COULD ACKNOW-LEDGE THAT.
...YOU SEEM TO UNDERSTAND DAICHI PRETTY WELL.
I LIKED THE TEAM BETTER BEFORE.
THE CURRENT TEAM IS HARSH. IT'S ALL ABOUT *WINNING!* WHAT DO WE DO TO *WIN?* WILL WE *WIN* IF WE DO THIS OR THAT?
...HIRO-YOSHI...
I DON'T CARE IF WE WIN OR LOSE!

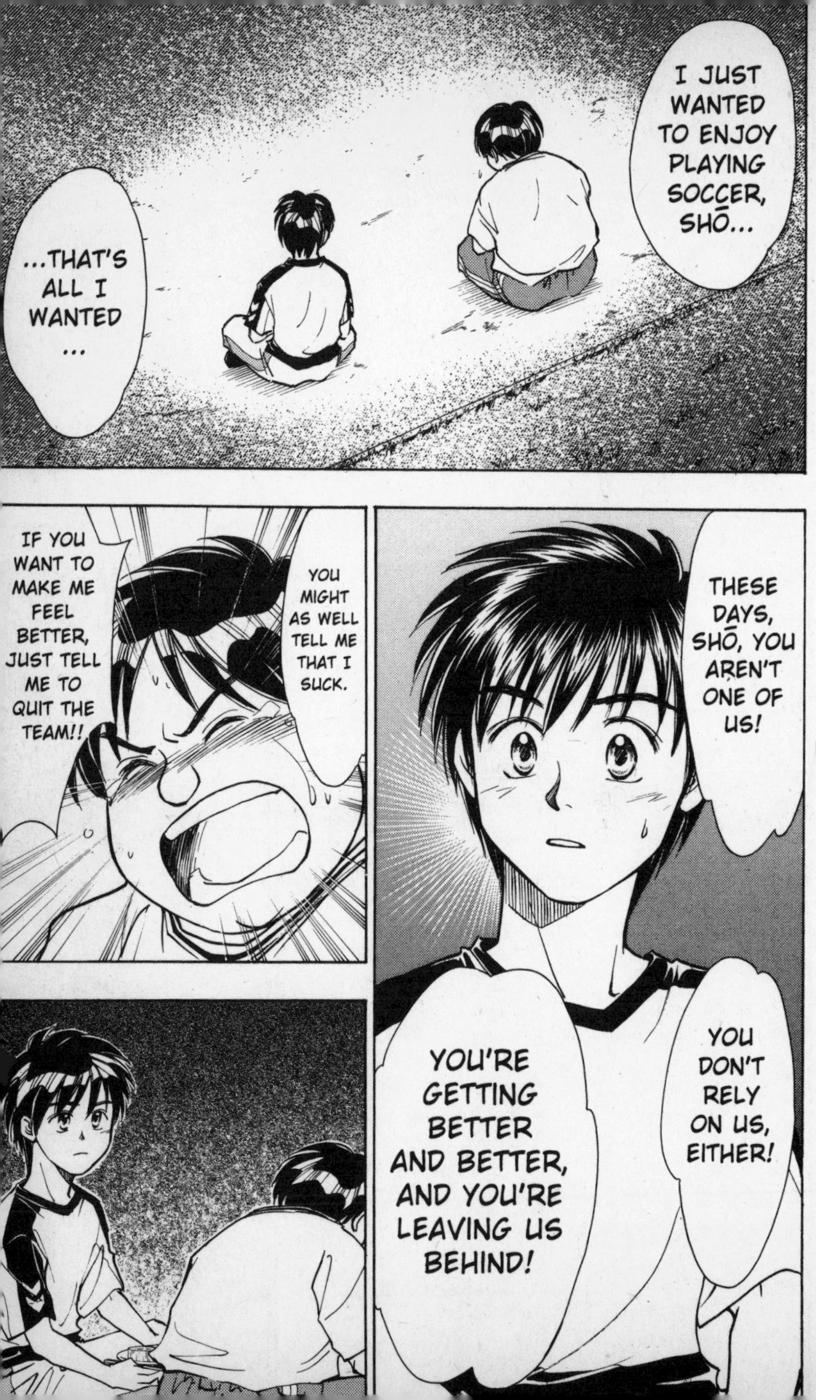
I JUST WANTED TO ENJOY PLAYING SOCCER, SHŌ...
...THAT'S ALL I WANTED ...
THESE DAYS, SHŌ, YOU AREN'T ONE OF US!
YOU DON'T RELY ON US, EITHER!
YOU'RE GETTING BETTER AND BETTER, AND YOU'RE LEAVING US BEHIND!
YOU MIGHT AS WELL TELL ME THAT I SUCK.
IF YOU WANT TO MAKE ME FEEL BETTER, JUST TELL ME TO QUIT THE TEAM!!

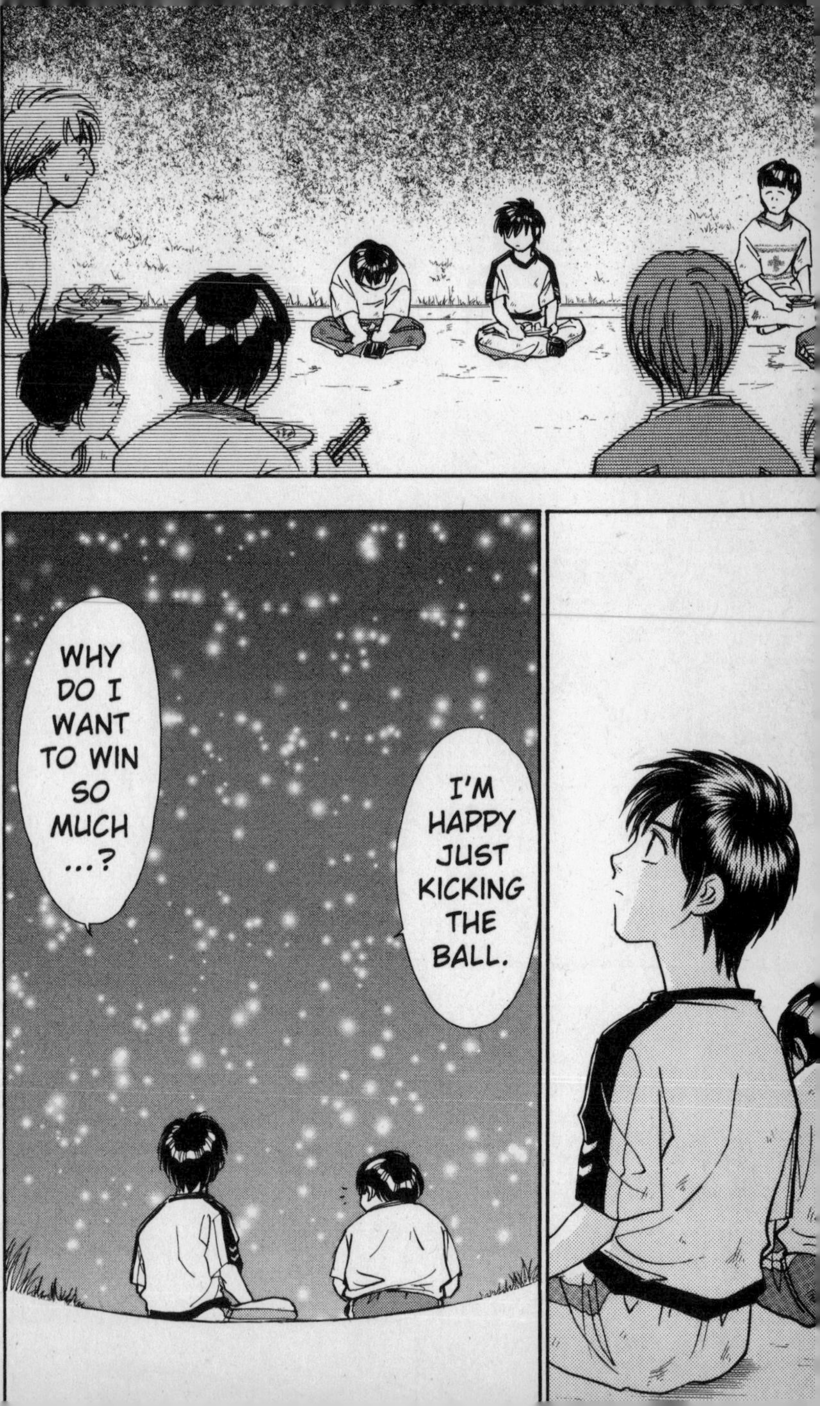
I'M HAPPY JUST KICKING THE BALL.
WHY DO I WANT TO WIN SO MUCH ...?

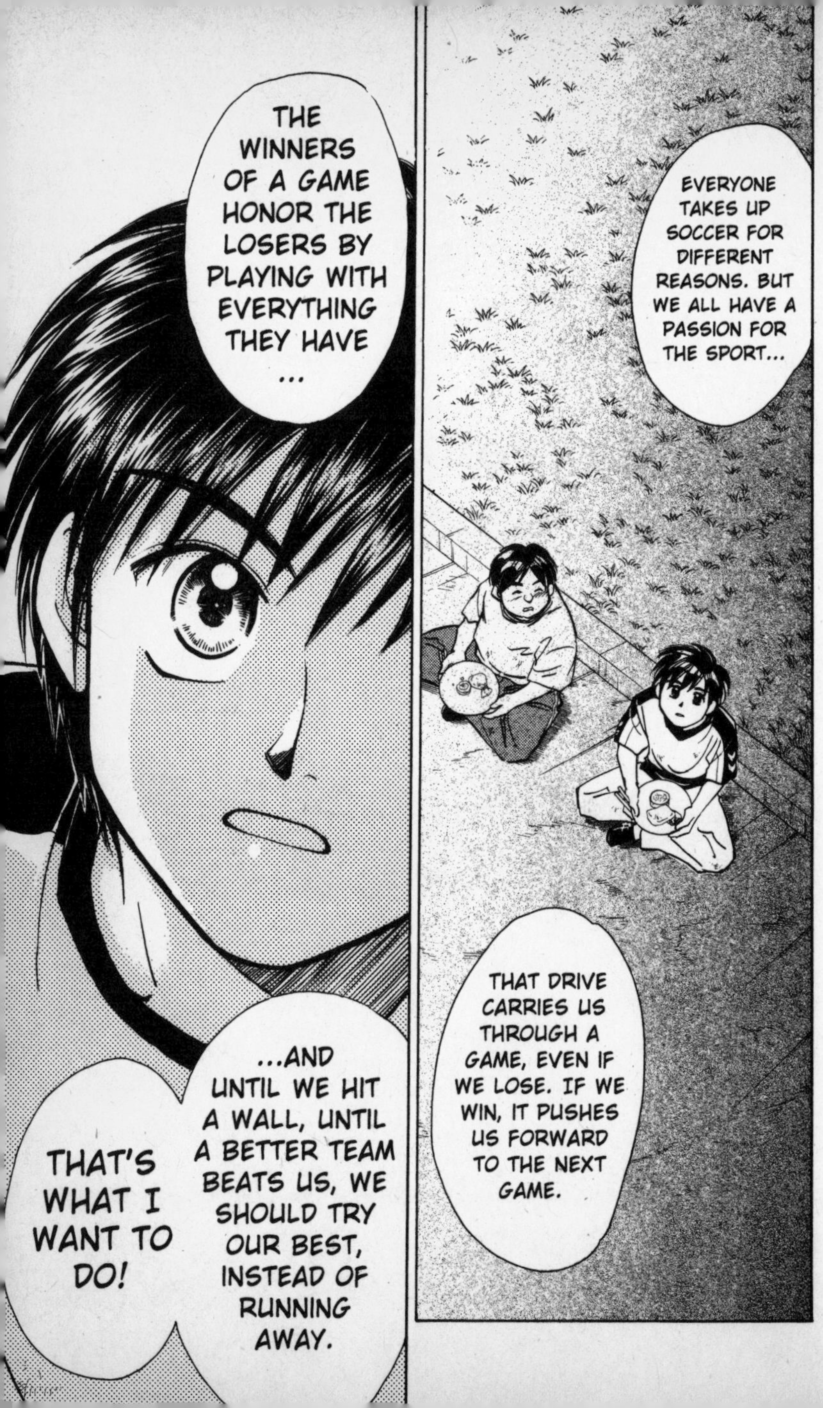
EVERYONE TAKES UP SOCCER FOR DIFFERENT REASONS. BUT WE ALL HAVE A PASSION FOR THE SPORT...
THAT DRIVE CARRIES US THROUGH A GAME, EVEN IF WE LOSE. IF WE WIN, IT PUSHES US FORWARD TO THE NEXT GAME.
THE WINNERS OF A GAME HONOR THE LOSERS BY PLAYING WITH EVERYTHING THEY HAVE ...
...AND UNTIL WE HIT A WALL, UNTIL A BETTER TEAM BEATS US, WE SHOULD TRY OUR BEST, INSTEAD OF RUNNING AWAY.
THAT'S WHAT I WANT TO DO!

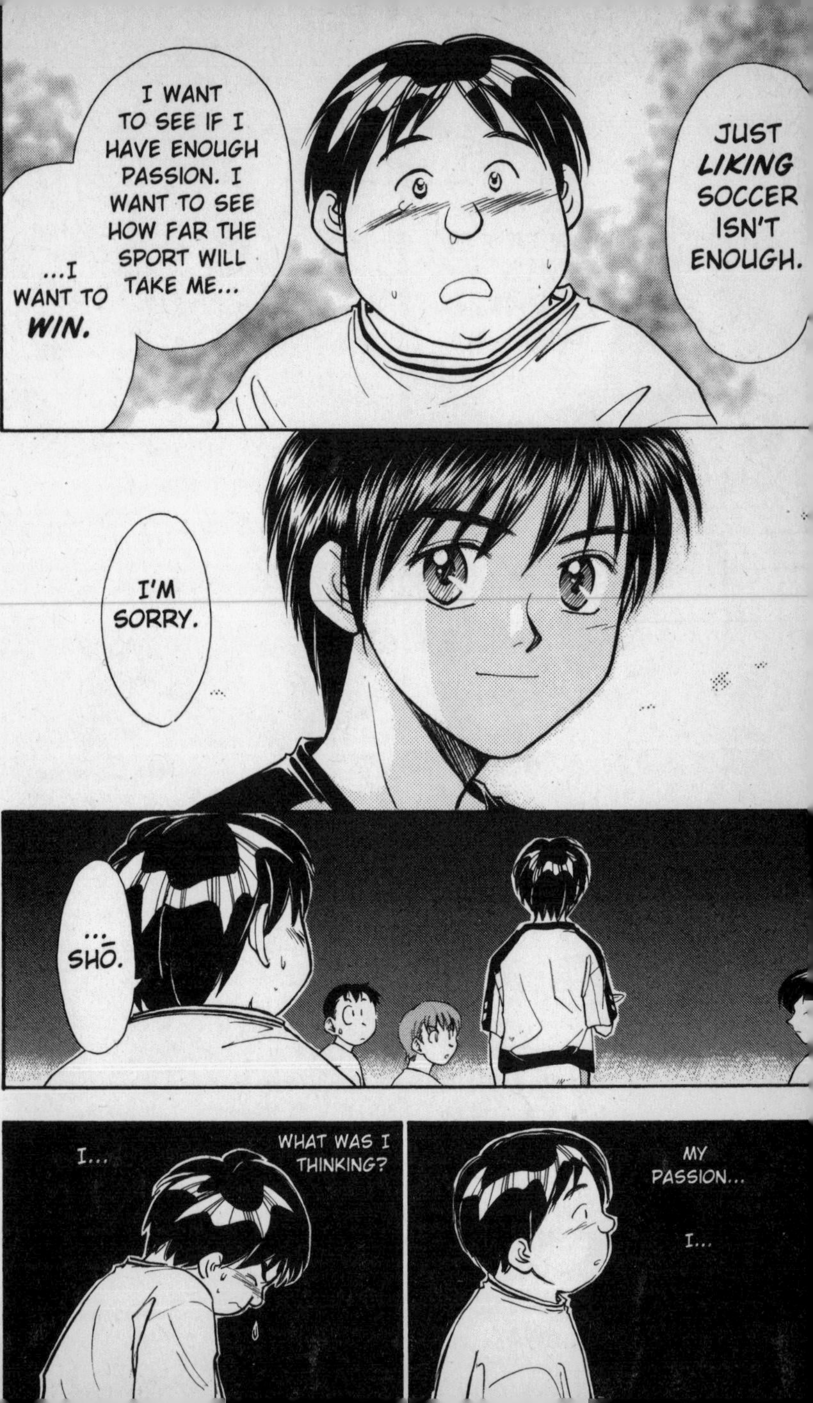
JUST *LIKING* SOCCER ISN'T ENOUGH.
I WANT TO SEE IF I HAVE ENOUGH PASSION. I WANT TO SEE HOW FAR THE SPORT WILL TAKE ME...
...I WANT TO *WIN.*
I'M SORRY.
...SHŌ.
MY PASSION...
I...
WHAT WAS I THINKING?
I...

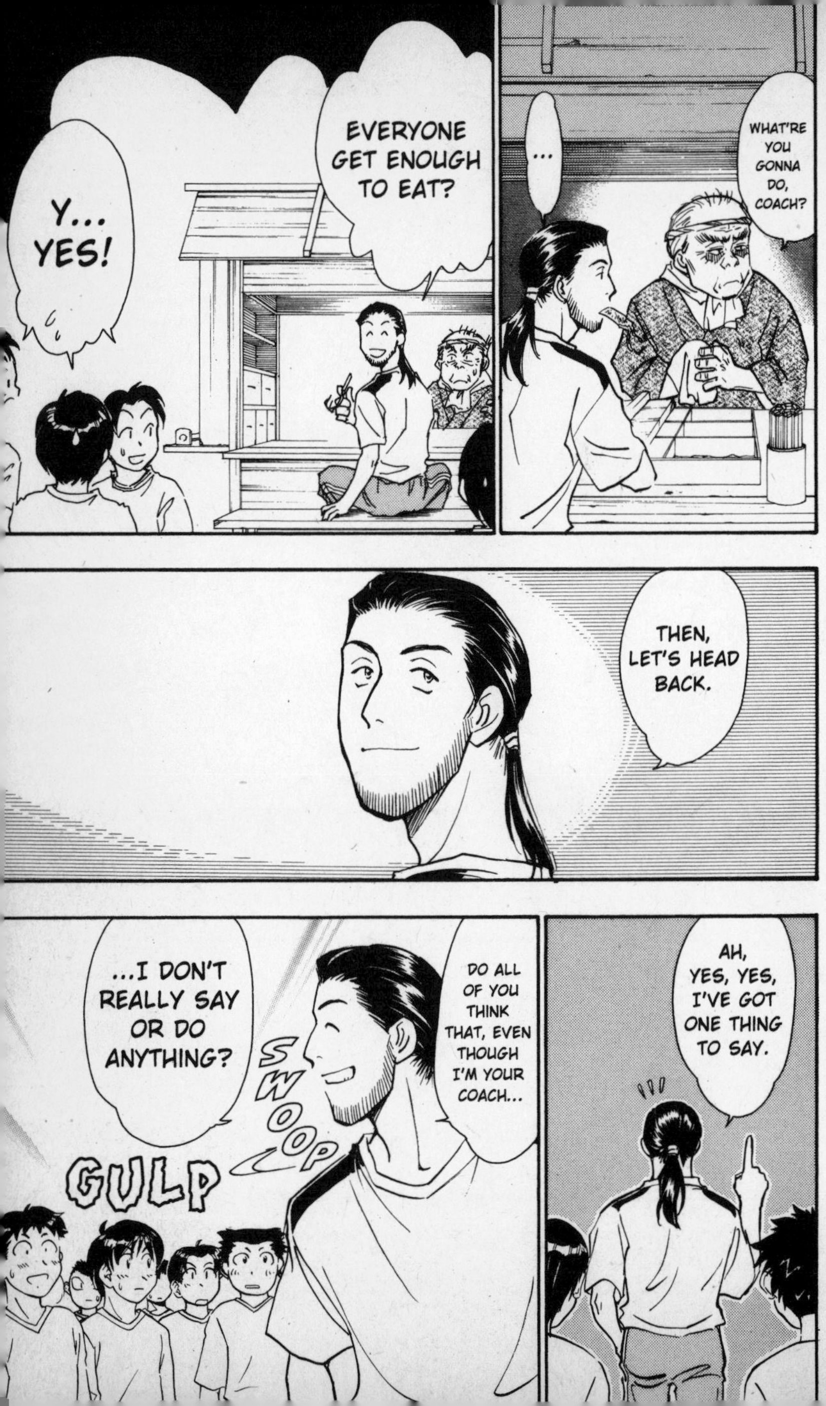
WHAT'RE YOU GONNA DO, COACH?
...
EVERYONE GET ENOUGH TO EAT?
Y... YES!
THEN, LET'S HEAD BACK.
AH, YES, YES, I'VE GOT ONE THING TO SAY.
DO ALL OF YOU THINK THAT, EVEN THOUGH I'M YOUR COACH...
...I DON'T REALLY SAY OR DO ANYTHING?
SWOOP
GULP

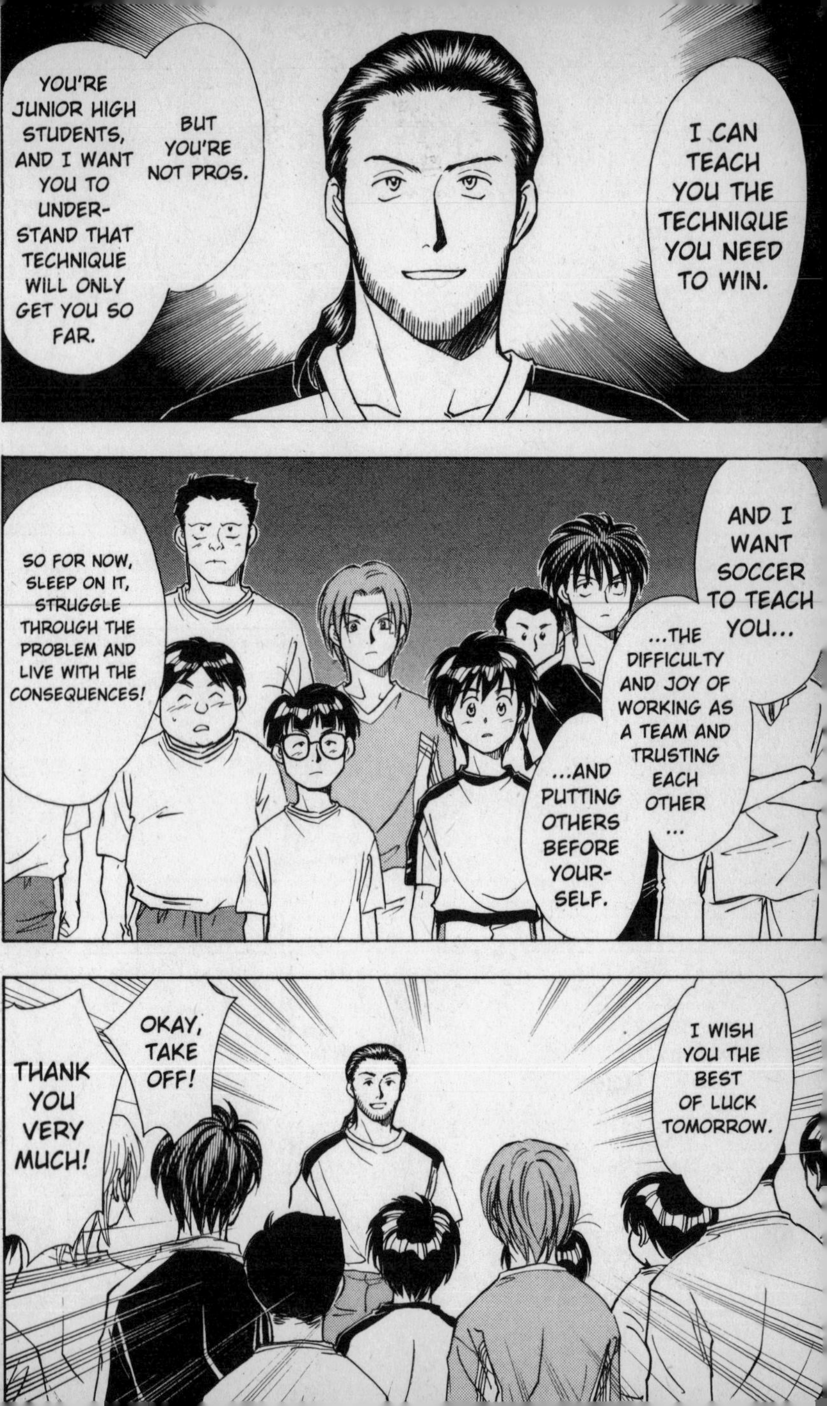
I CAN TEACH YOU THE TECHNIQUE YOU NEED TO WIN.
BUT YOU'RE NOT PROS.
YOU'RE JUNIOR HIGH STUDENTS, AND I WANT YOU TO UNDER-STAND THAT TECHNIQUE WILL ONLY GET YOU SO FAR.
AND I WANT SOCCER TO TEACH YOU...
...THE DIFFICULTY AND JOY OF WORKING AS A TEAM AND TRUSTING EACH OTHER...
...AND PUTTING OTHERS BEFORE YOUR-SELF.
SO FOR NOW, SLEEP ON IT, STRUGGLE THROUGH THE PROBLEM AND LIVE WITH THE CONSEQUENCES!
I WISH YOU THE BEST OF LUCK TOMORROW.
OKAY, TAKE OFF!
THANK YOU VERY MUCH!

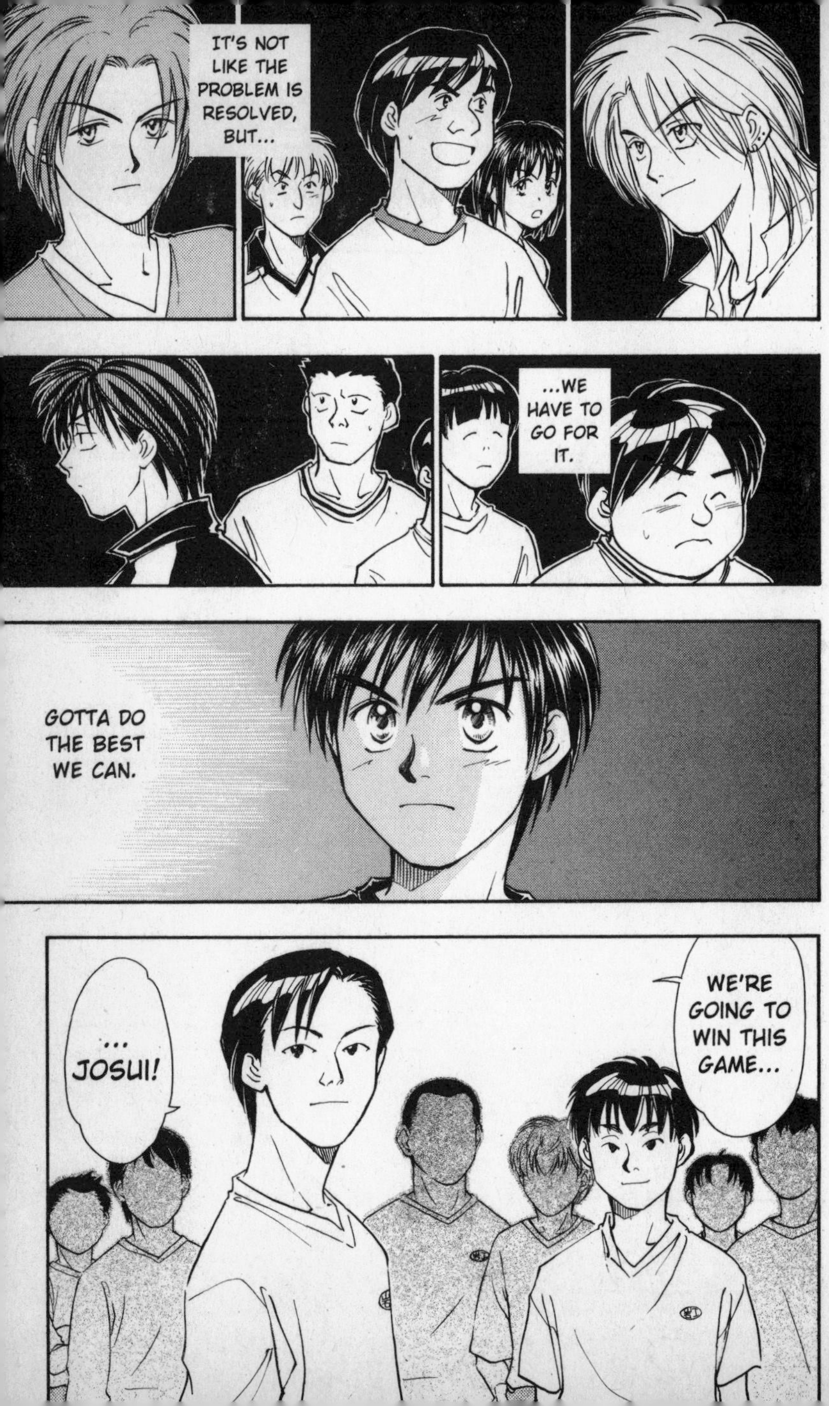
IT'S NOT LIKE THE PROBLEM IS RESOLVED, BUT...
...WE HAVE TO GO FOR IT.
GOTTA DO THE BEST WE CAN.
WE'RE GOING TO WIN THIS GAME...
...JOSUI!

WHISTLE! THEATRE

Well Past Curfew

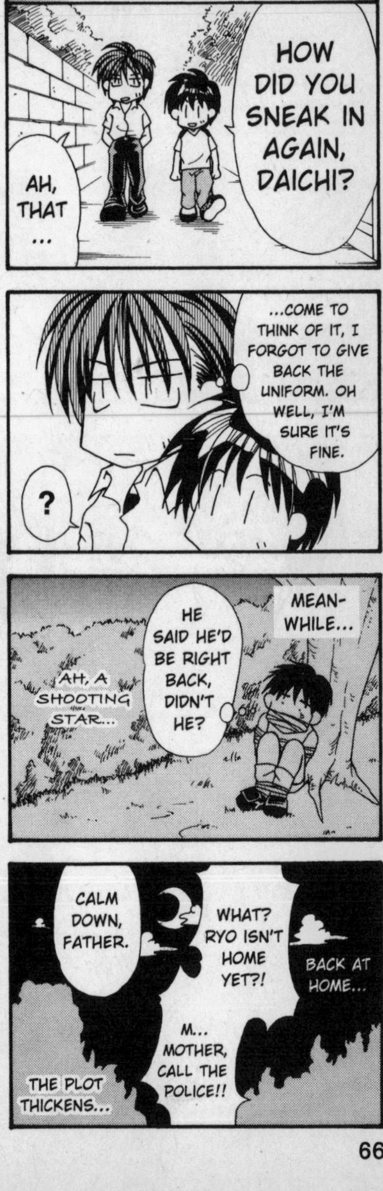
HOW DID YOU SNEAK IN AGAIN, DAICHI?
AH, THAT ...
...COME TO THINK OF IT, I FORGOT TO GIVE BACK THE UNIFORM. OH WELL, I'M SURE IT'S FINE.
?
MEAN-WHILE...
HE SAID HE'D BE RIGHT BACK, DIDN'T HE?
AH, A SHOOTING STAR...
BACK AT HOME...
WHAT? RYO ISN'T HOME YET?!
CALM DOWN, FATHER.
M... MOTHER, CALL THE POLICE!!
THE PLOT THICKENS...

Sorry

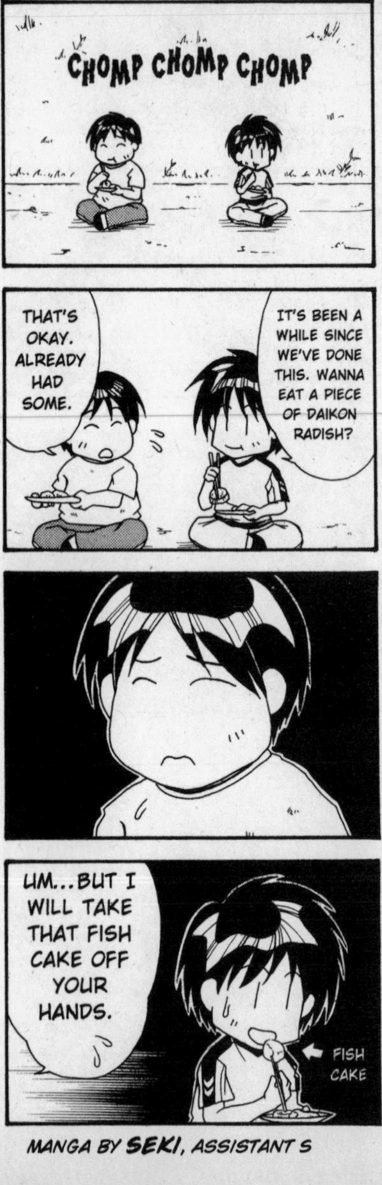
CHOMP CHOMP CHOMP
IT'S BEEN A WHILE SINCE WE'VE DONE THIS. WANNA EAT A PIECE OF DAIKON RADISH?
THAT'S OKAY. ALREADY HAD SOME.
UM...BUT I WILL TAKE THAT FISH CAKE OFF YOUR HANDS.
FISH CAKE

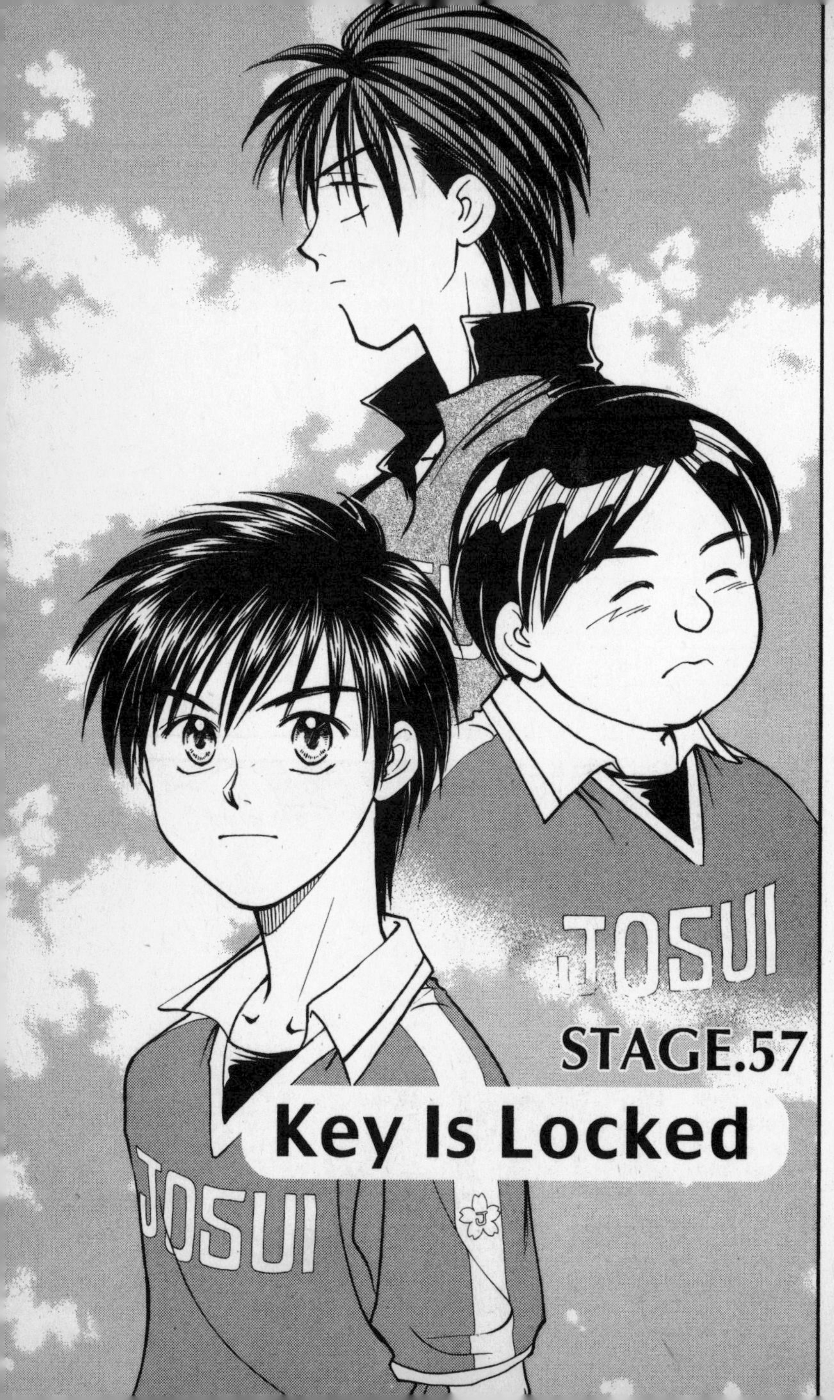
JOSUI
JOSUI

STAGE.57

Key Is Locked

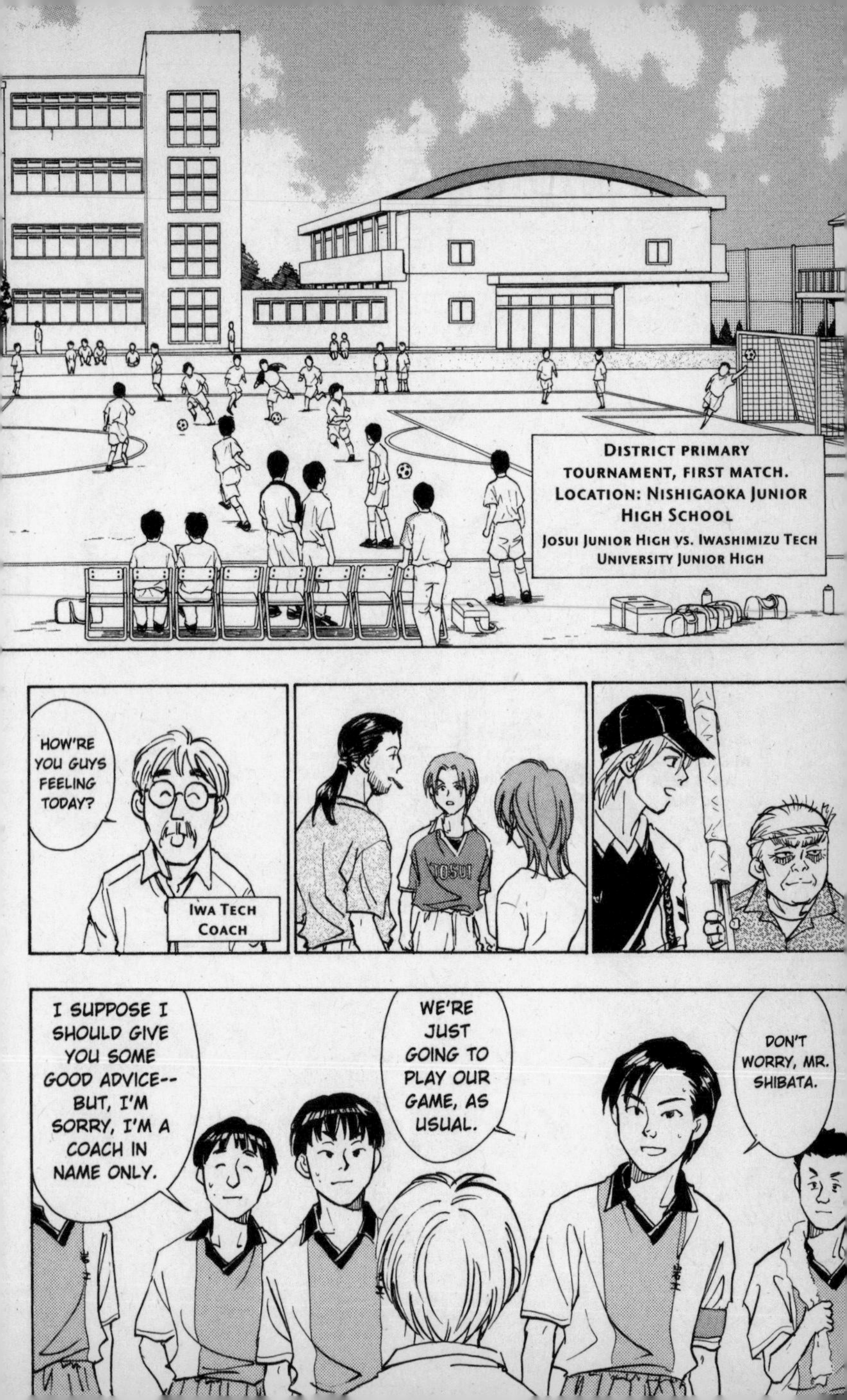
District primary tournament, first match. Location: Nishigaoka Junior High School
Josui Junior High vs. Iwashimizu Tech University Junior High
HOW'RE YOU GUYS FEELING TODAY?
Iwa Tech Coach
DON'T WORRY, MR. SHIBATA.
WE'RE JUST GOING TO PLAY OUR GAME, AS USUAL.
I SUPPOSE I SHOULD GIVE YOU SOME GOOD ADVICE-- BUT, I'M SORRY, I'M A COACH IN NAME ONLY.

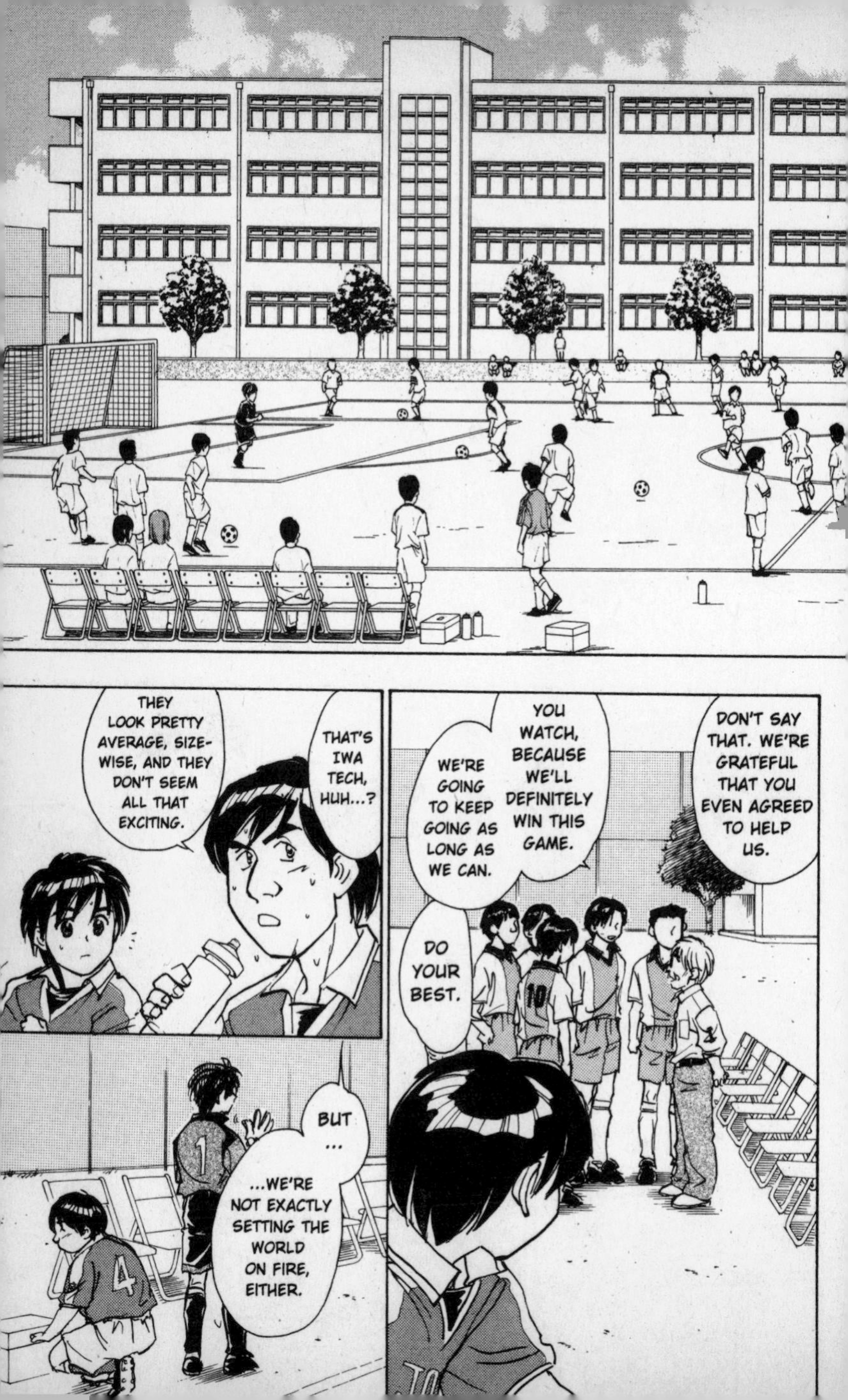
DON'T SAY THAT. WE'RE GRATEFUL THAT YOU EVEN AGREED TO HELP US.
YOU WATCH, BECAUSE WE'LL DEFINITELY WIN THIS GAME.
WE'RE GOING TO KEEP GOING AS LONG AS WE CAN.
DO YOUR BEST.
THAT'S IWA TECH, HUH...?
THEY LOOK PRETTY AVERAGE, SIZE-WISE, AND THEY DON'T SEEM ALL THAT EXCITING.
BUT...
...WE'RE NOT EXACTLY SETTING THE WORLD ON FIRE, EITHER.

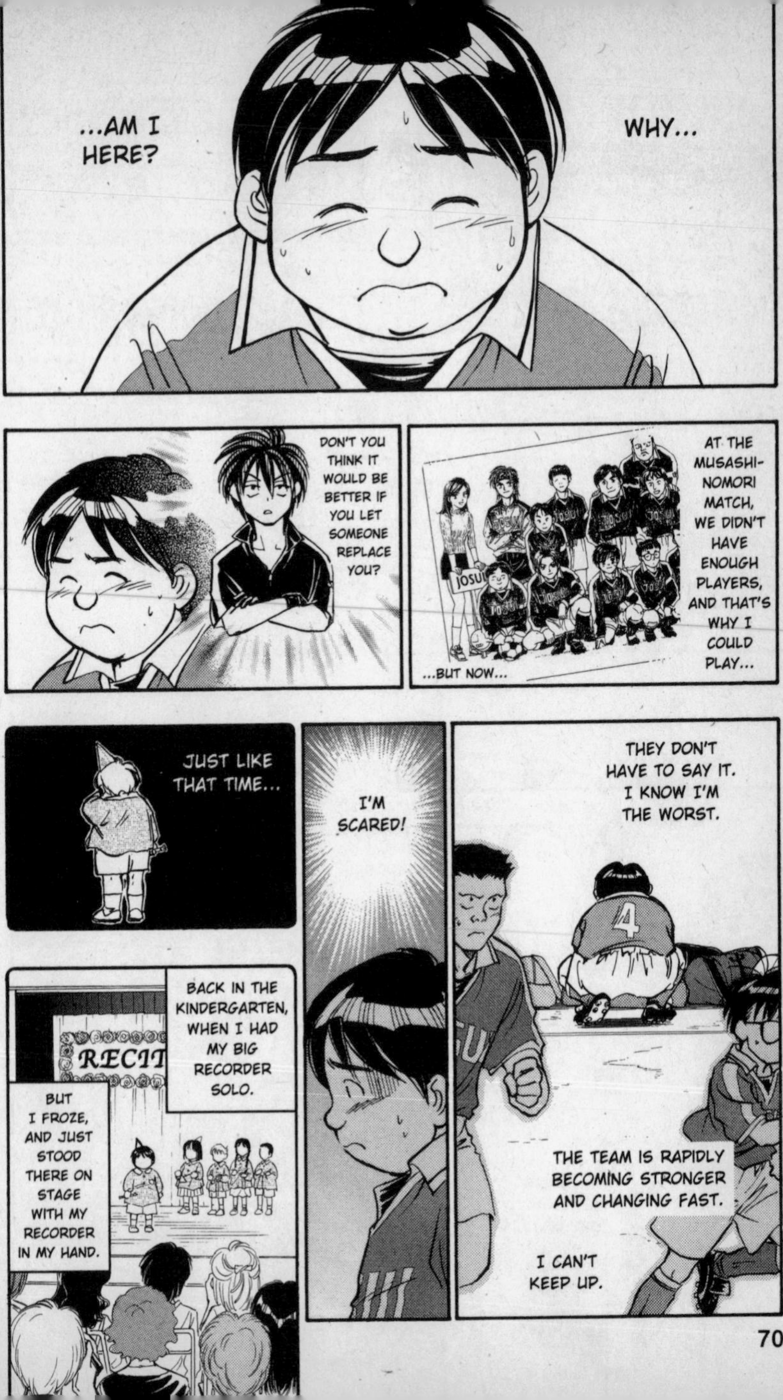

WHY...
...AM I HERE?
AT THE MUSASHI-NOMORI MATCH, WE DIDN'T HAVE ENOUGH PLAYERS, AND THAT'S WHY I COULD PLAY...
JOSUI
...BUT NOW...
DON'T YOU THINK IT WOULD BE BETTER IF YOU LET SOMEONE REPLACE YOU?
THEY DON'T HAVE TO SAY IT. I KNOW I'M THE WORST.
4
THE TEAM IS RAPIDLY BECOMING STRONGER AND CHANGING FAST.
I CAN'T KEEP UP.
I'M SCARED!
JUST LIKE THAT TIME...
BACK IN THE KINDERGARTEN, WHEN I HAD MY BIG RECORDER SOLO.
RECIT
BUT I FROZE, AND JUST STOOD THERE ON STAGE WITH MY RECORDER IN MY HAND.

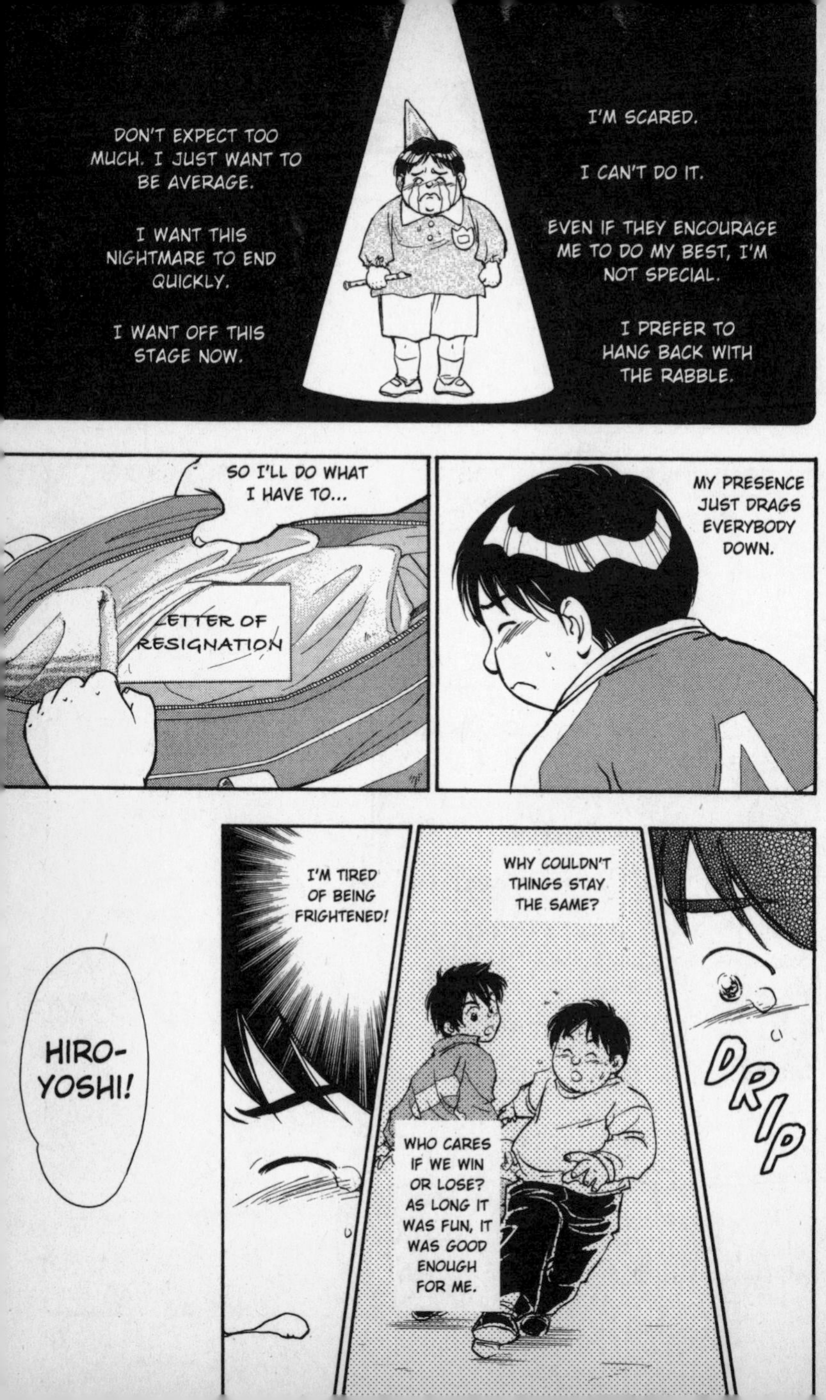
I'M SCARED.
I CAN'T DO IT.
EVEN IF THEY ENCOURAGE ME TO DO MY BEST, I'M NOT SPECIAL.
I PREFER TO HANG BACK WITH THE RABBLE.
DON'T EXPECT TOO MUCH. I JUST WANT TO BE AVERAGE.
I WANT THIS NIGHTMARE TO END QUICKLY.
I WANT OFF THIS STAGE NOW.
MY PRESENCE JUST DRAGS EVERYBODY DOWN.
SO I'LL DO WHAT I HAVE TO...
LETTER OF RESIGNATION
DRIP
WHY COULDN'T THINGS STAY THE SAME?
WHO CARES IF WE WIN OR LOSE? AS LONG IT WAS FUN, IT WAS GOOD ENOUGH FOR ME.
I'M TIRED OF BEING FRIGHTENED!
HIRO-YOSHI!

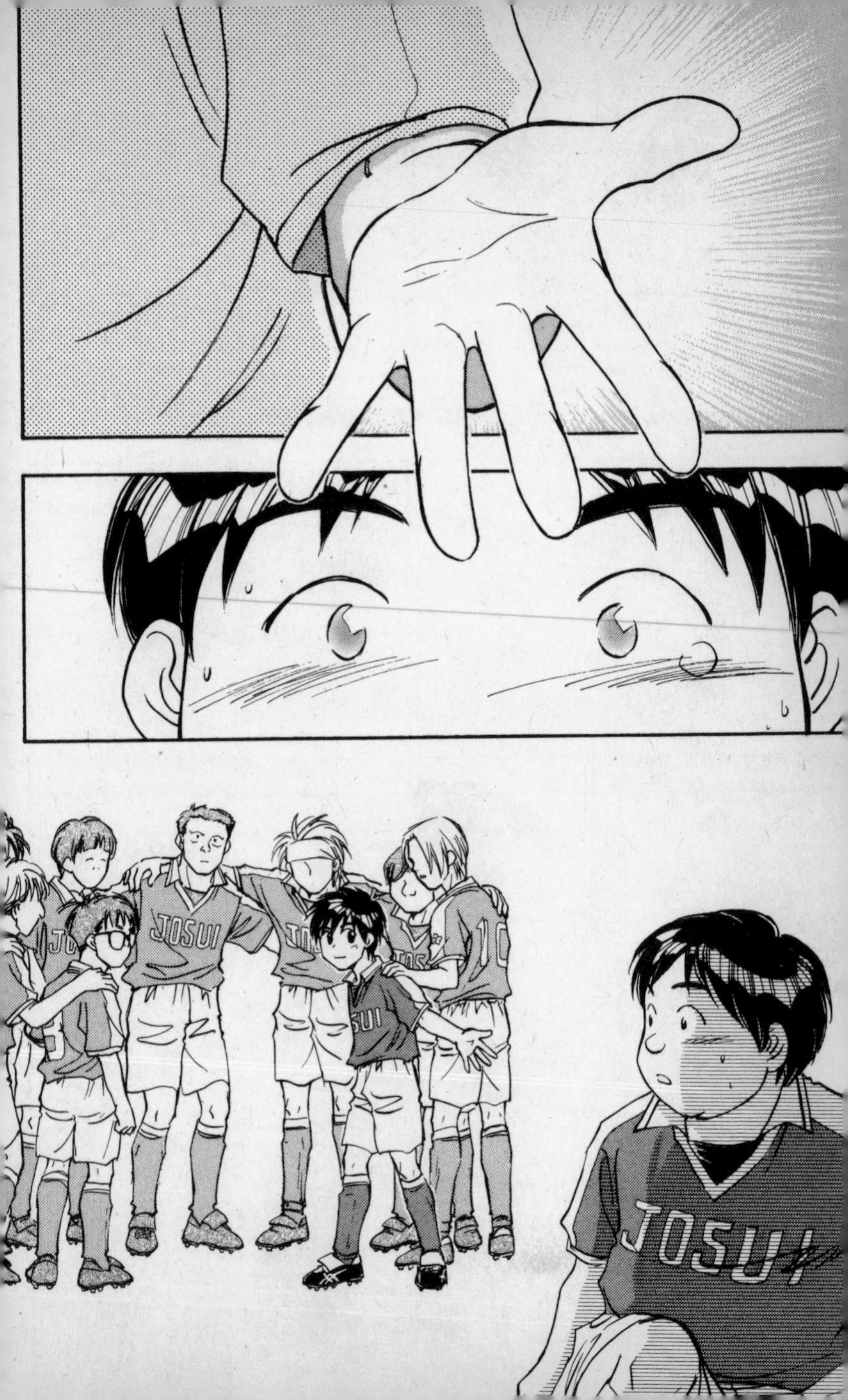
JOSUI
JOSUI

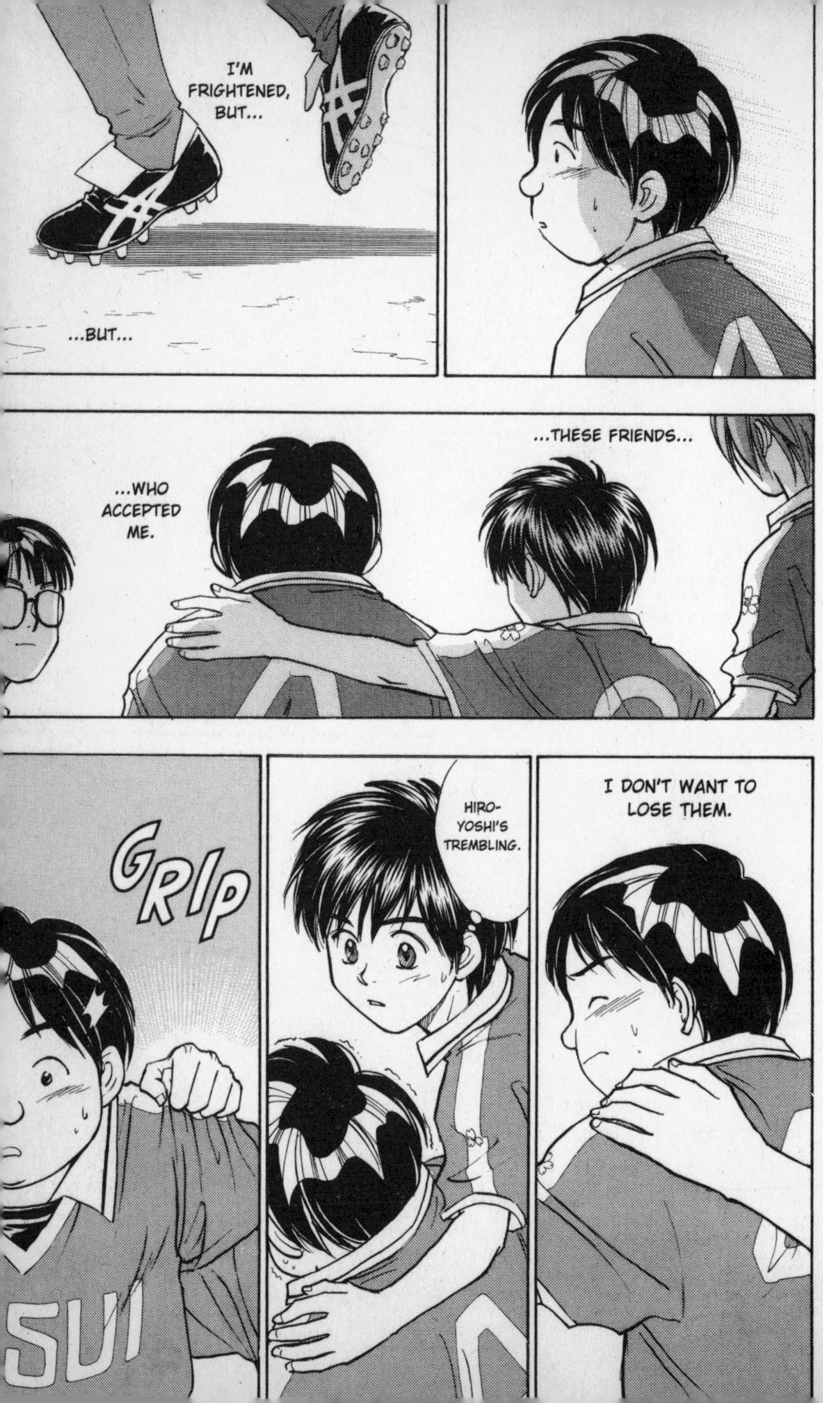
I'M FRIGHTENED, BUT...
...BUT...
...THESE FRIENDS...
...WHO ACCEPTED ME.
I DON'T WANT TO LOSE THEM.
HIRO-YOSHI'S TREMBLING.
GRIP
SUI

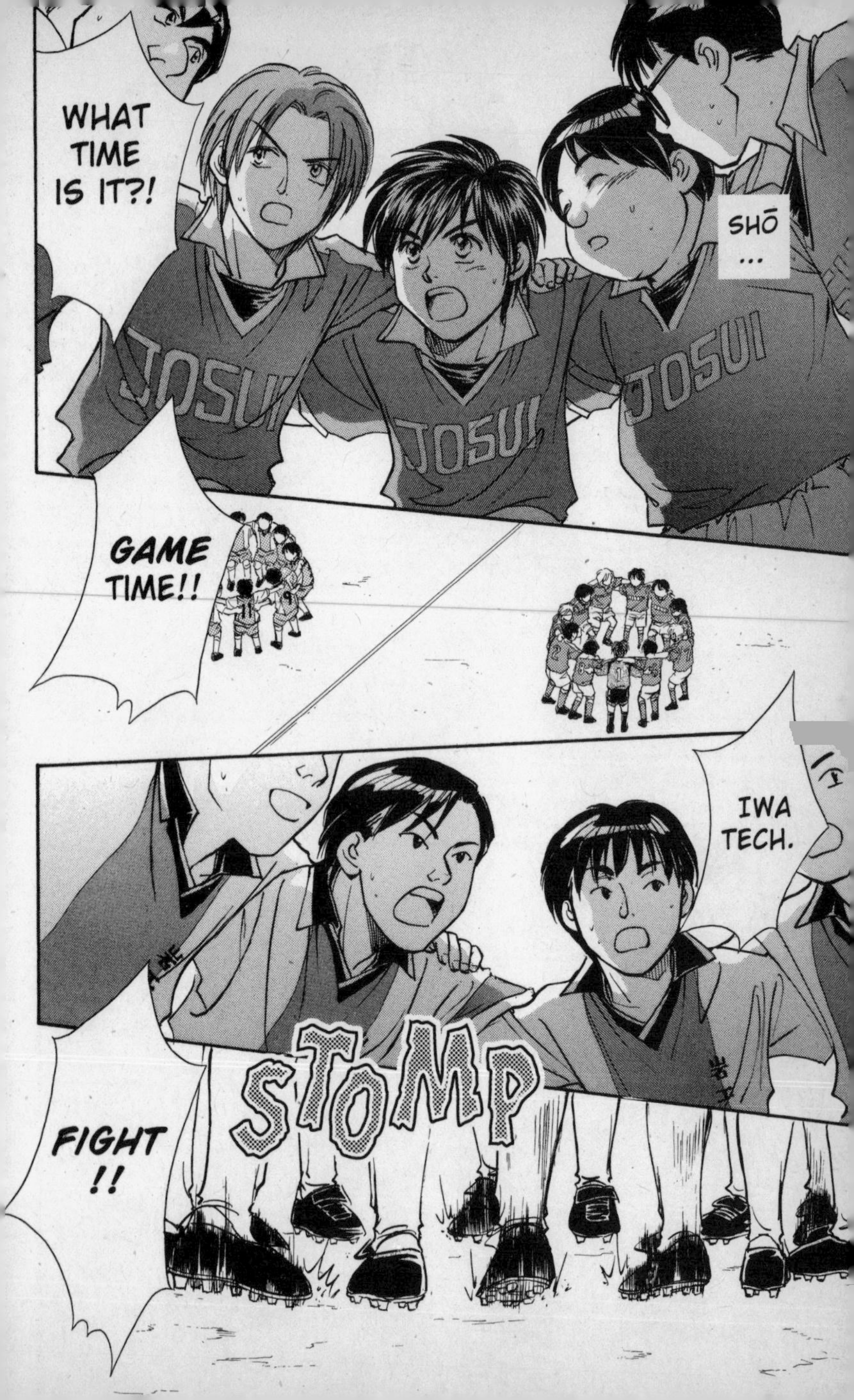
SHŌ ...
WHAT TIME IS IT?!
GAME TIME!!
IWA TECH.
STOMP
FIGHT !!

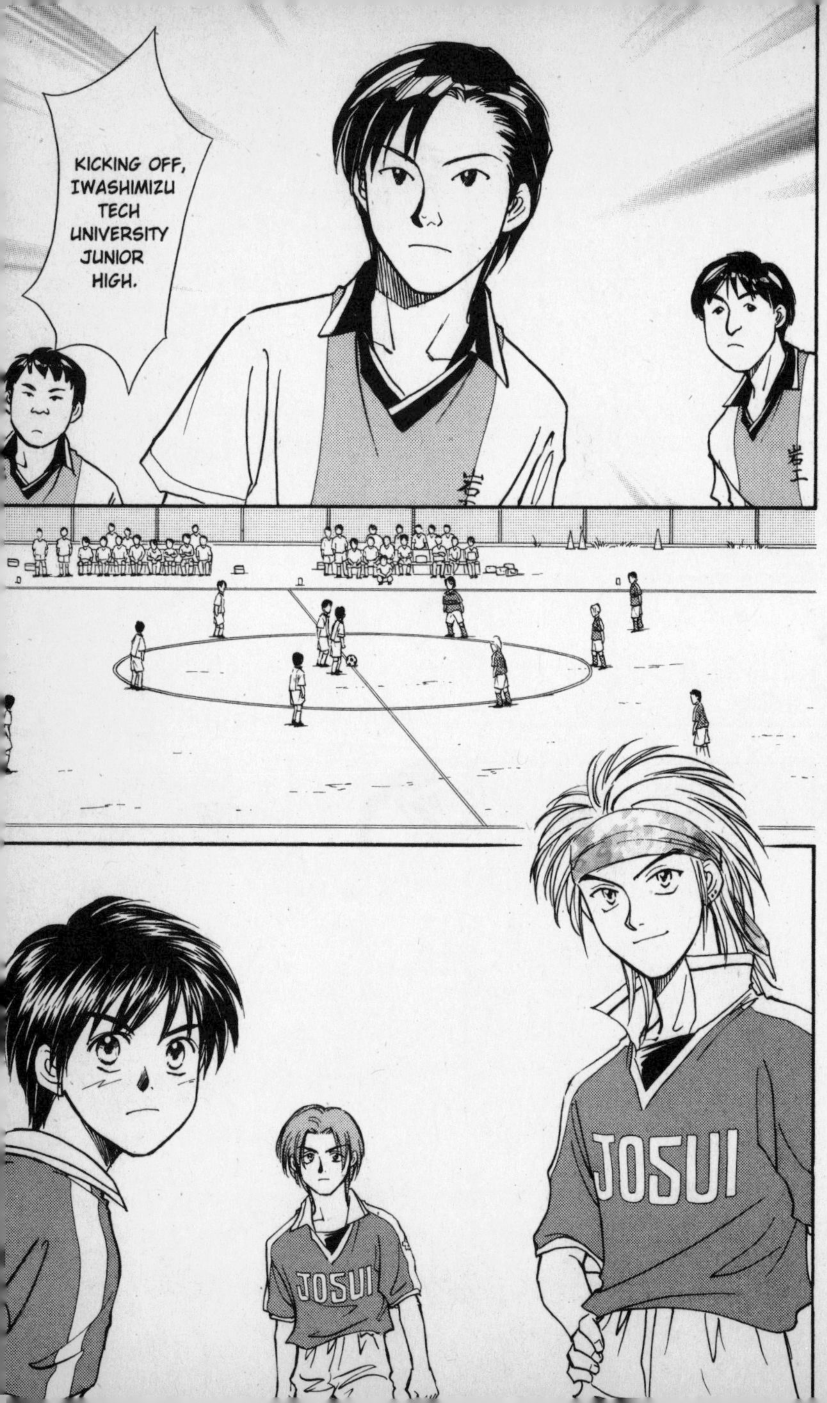
KICKING OFF, IWASHIMIZU TECH UNIVERSITY JUNIOR HIGH.
JOSUI
JOSUI

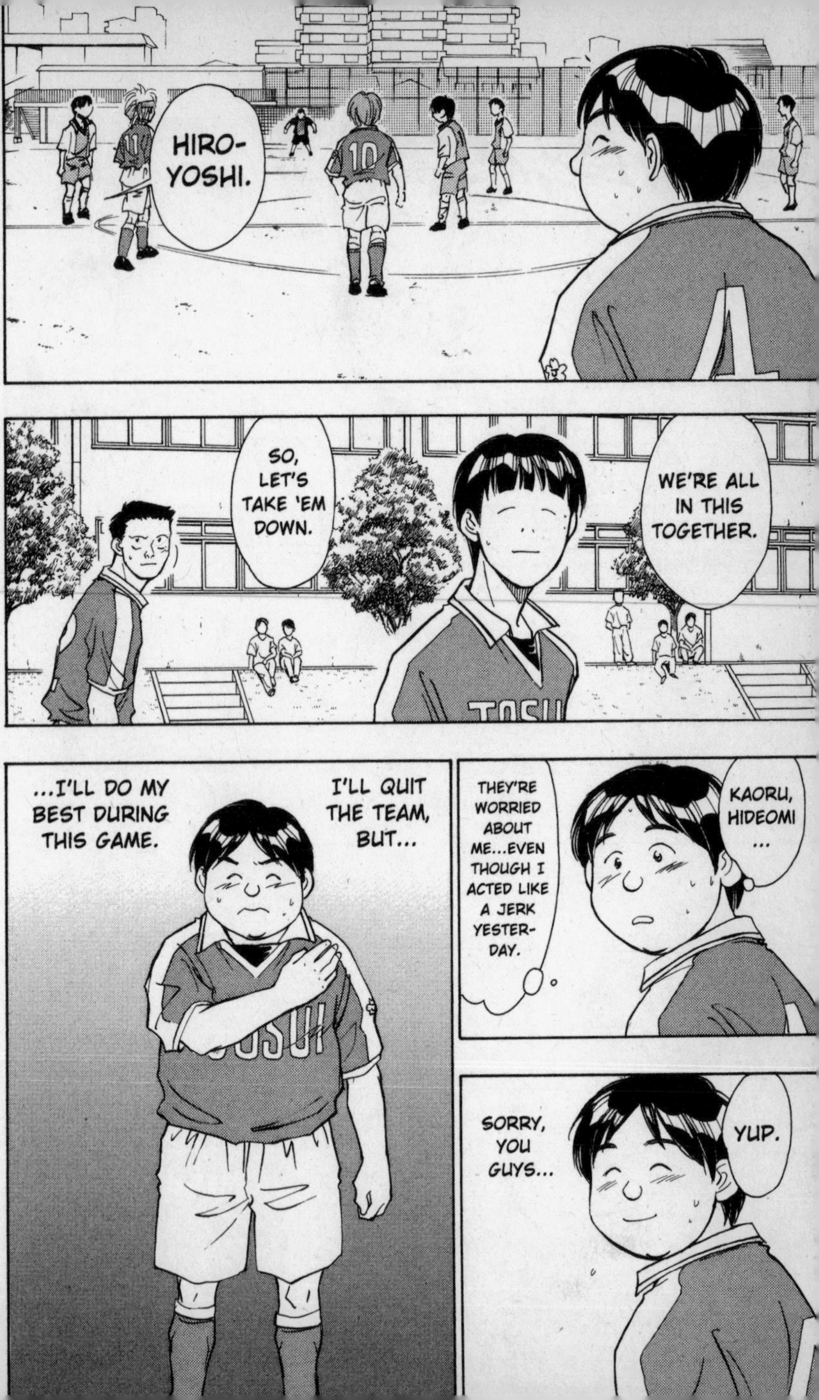
HIRO-YOSHI.
WE'RE ALL IN THIS TOGETHER.
SO, LET'S TAKE 'EM DOWN.
KAORU, HIDEOMI ...
THEY'RE WORRIED ABOUT ME...EVEN THOUGH I ACTED LIKE A JERK YESTER-DAY.
YUP.
SORRY, YOU GUYS...
I'LL QUIT THE TEAM, BUT...
...I'LL DO MY BEST DURING THIS GAME.

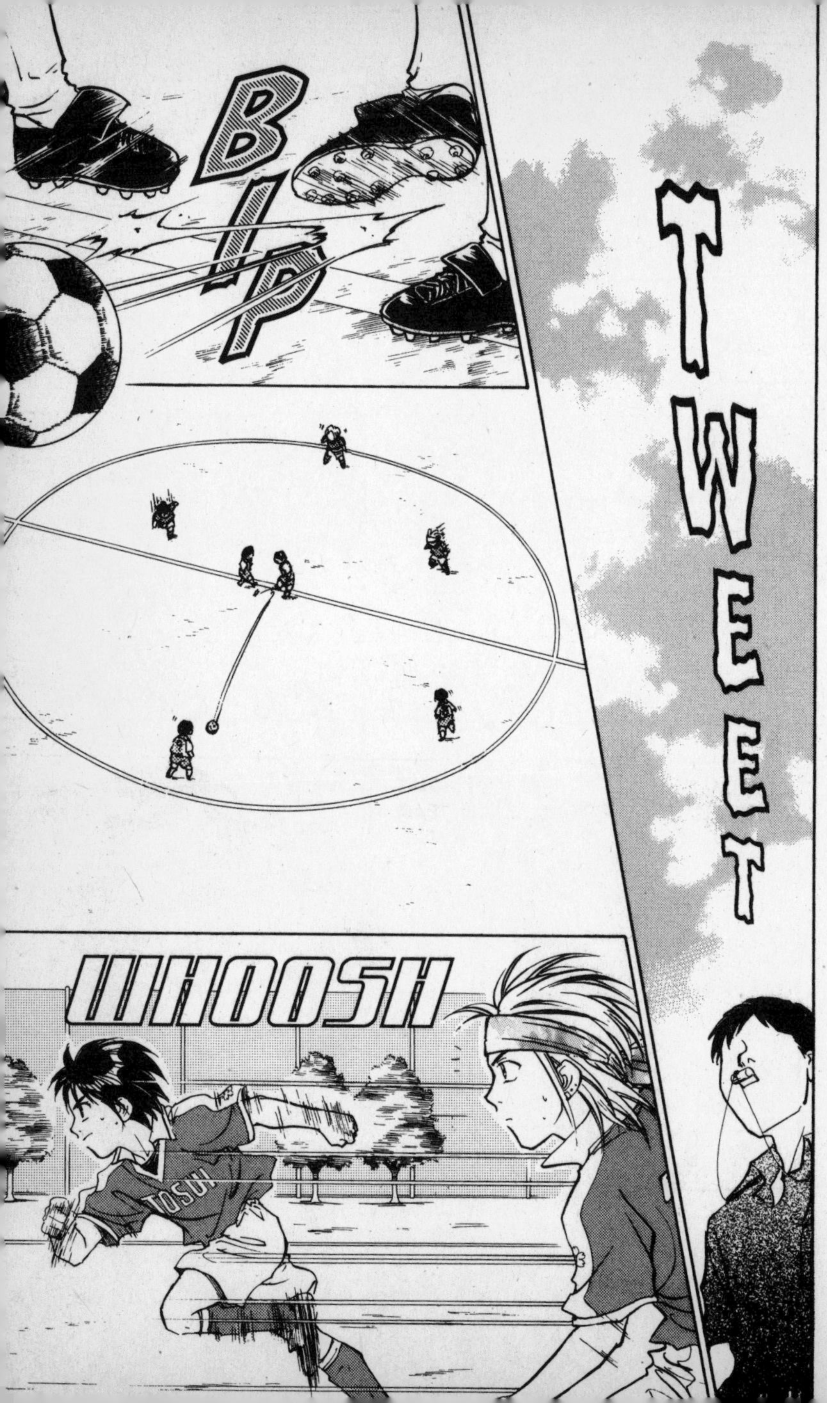
TWEET
BIP
WHOOSH

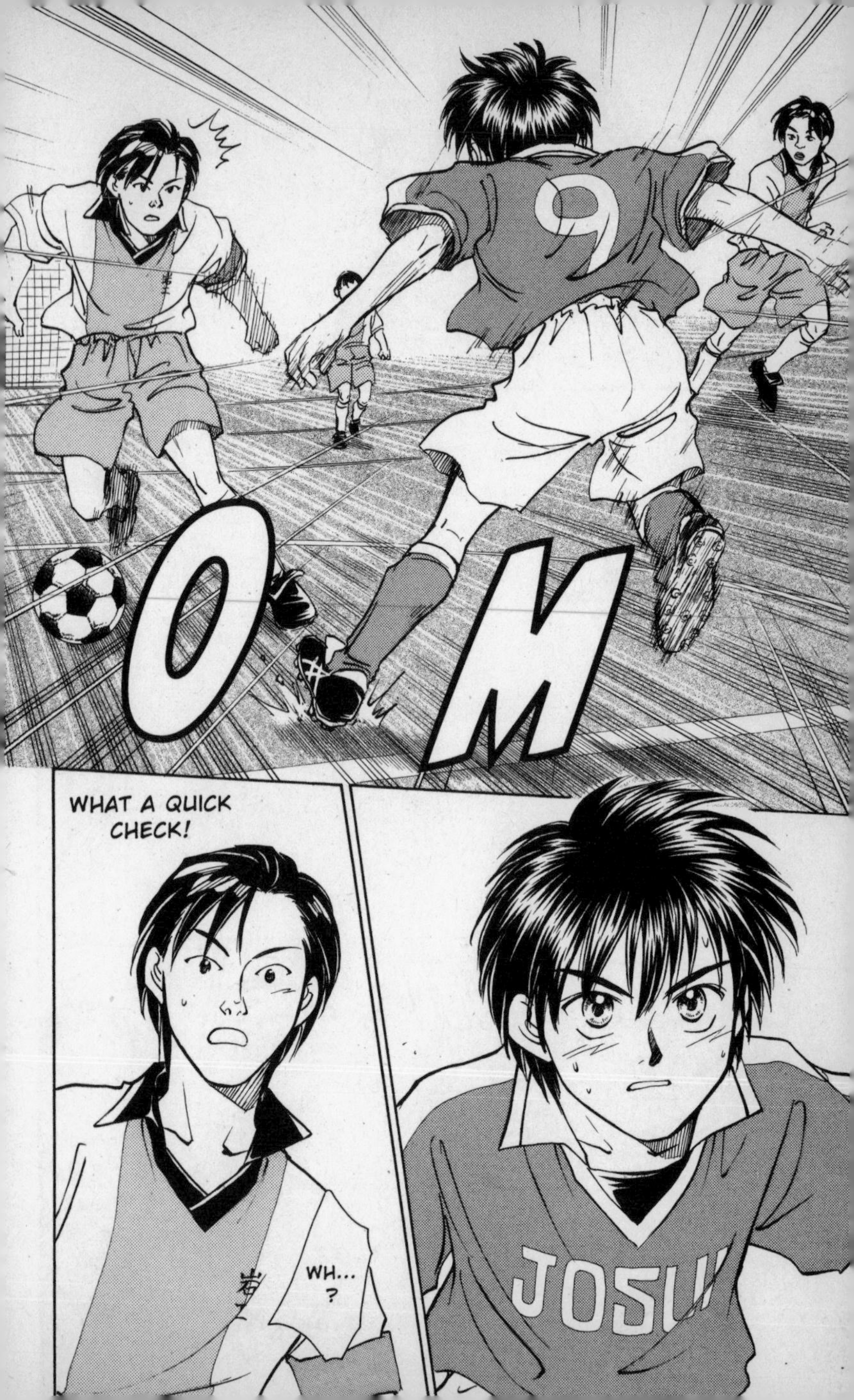
OM
JOSU
WHAT A QUICK CHECK!
WH... ?

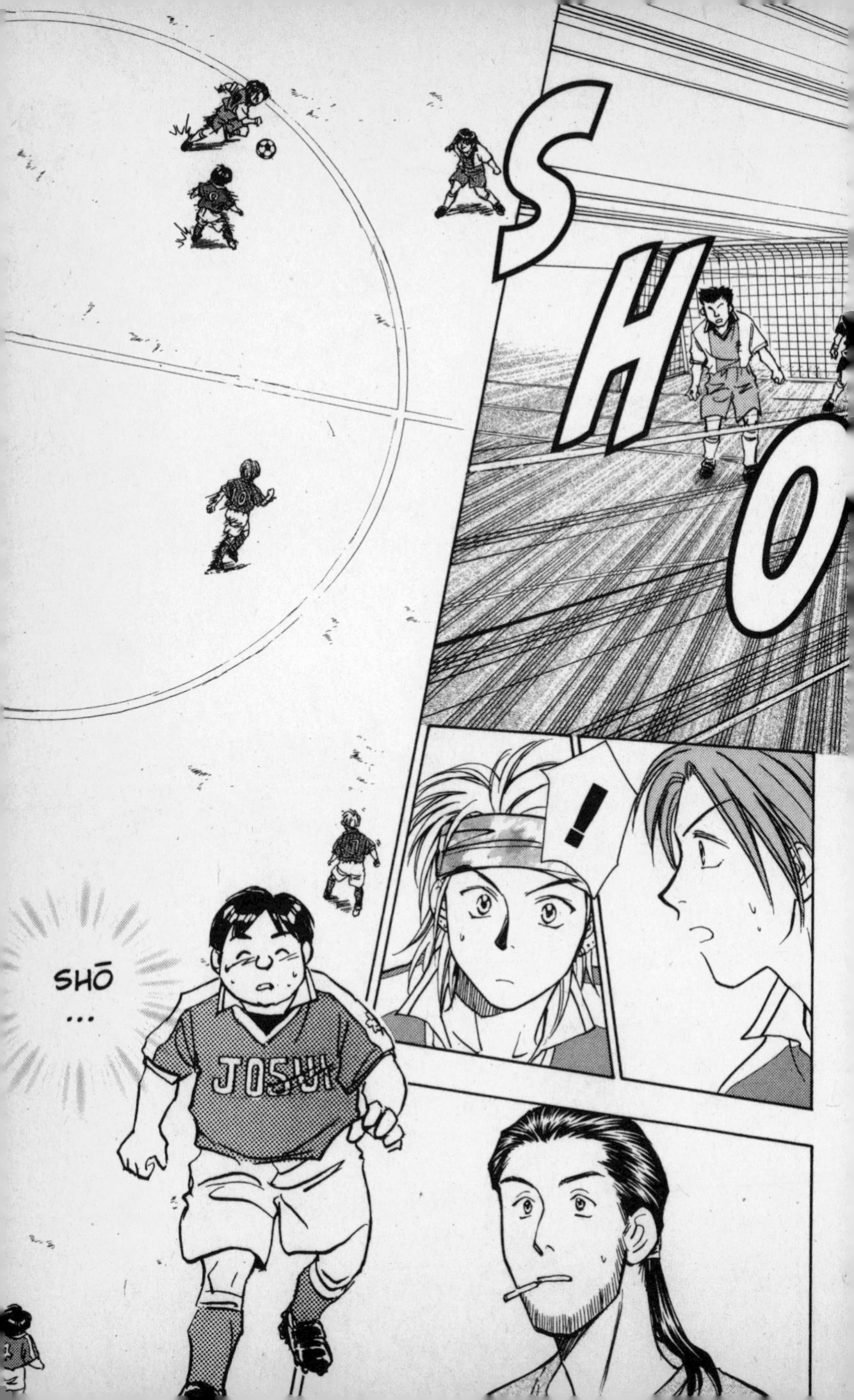
SHO
!
SHŌ
...
JOSUI

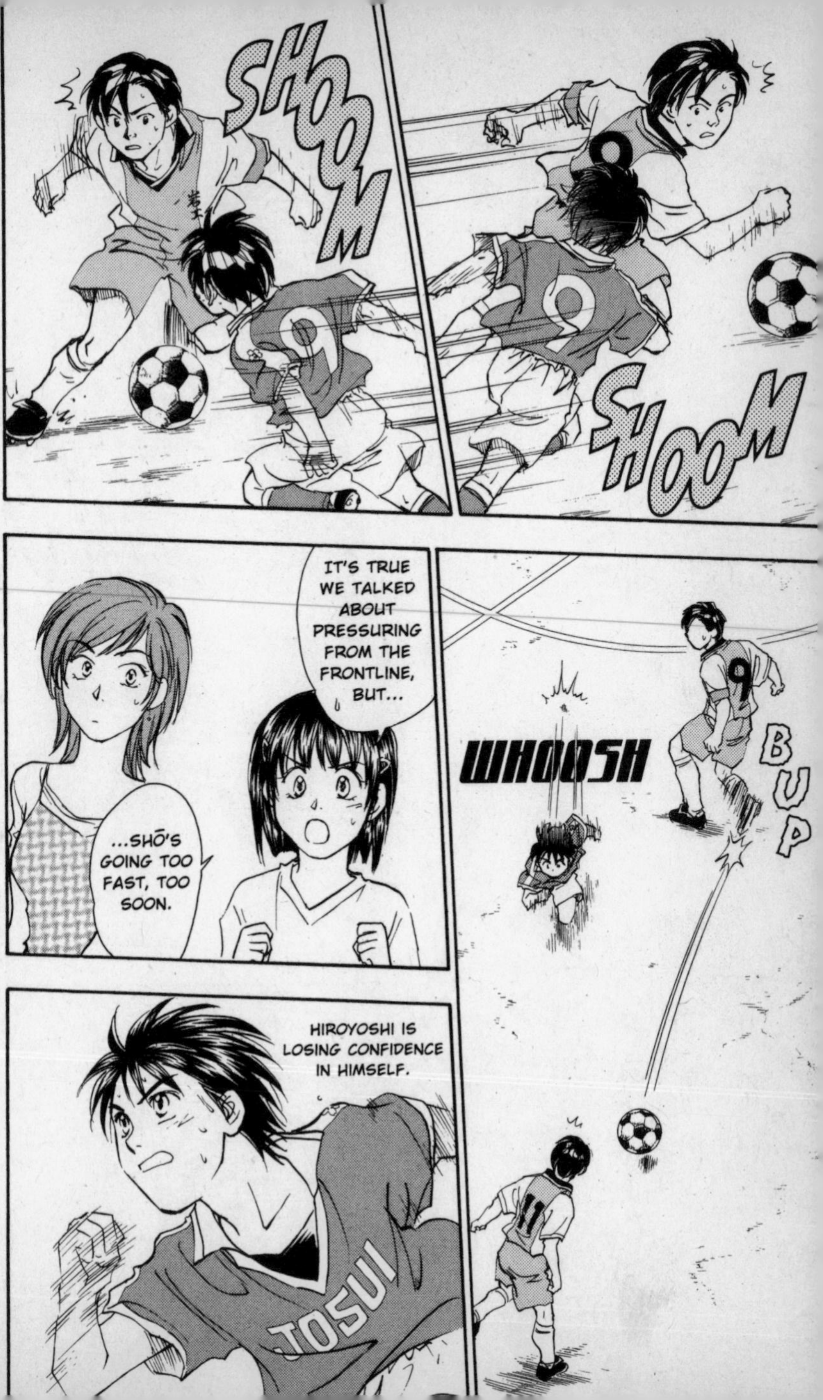
SHOOM
SHOOM
WHOOSH
BUP
IT'S TRUE WE TALKED ABOUT PRESSURING FROM THE FRONTLINE, BUT...
...SHŌ'S GOING TOO FAST, TOO SOON.
HIROYOSHI IS LOSING CONFIDENCE IN HIMSELF.
TOSUI

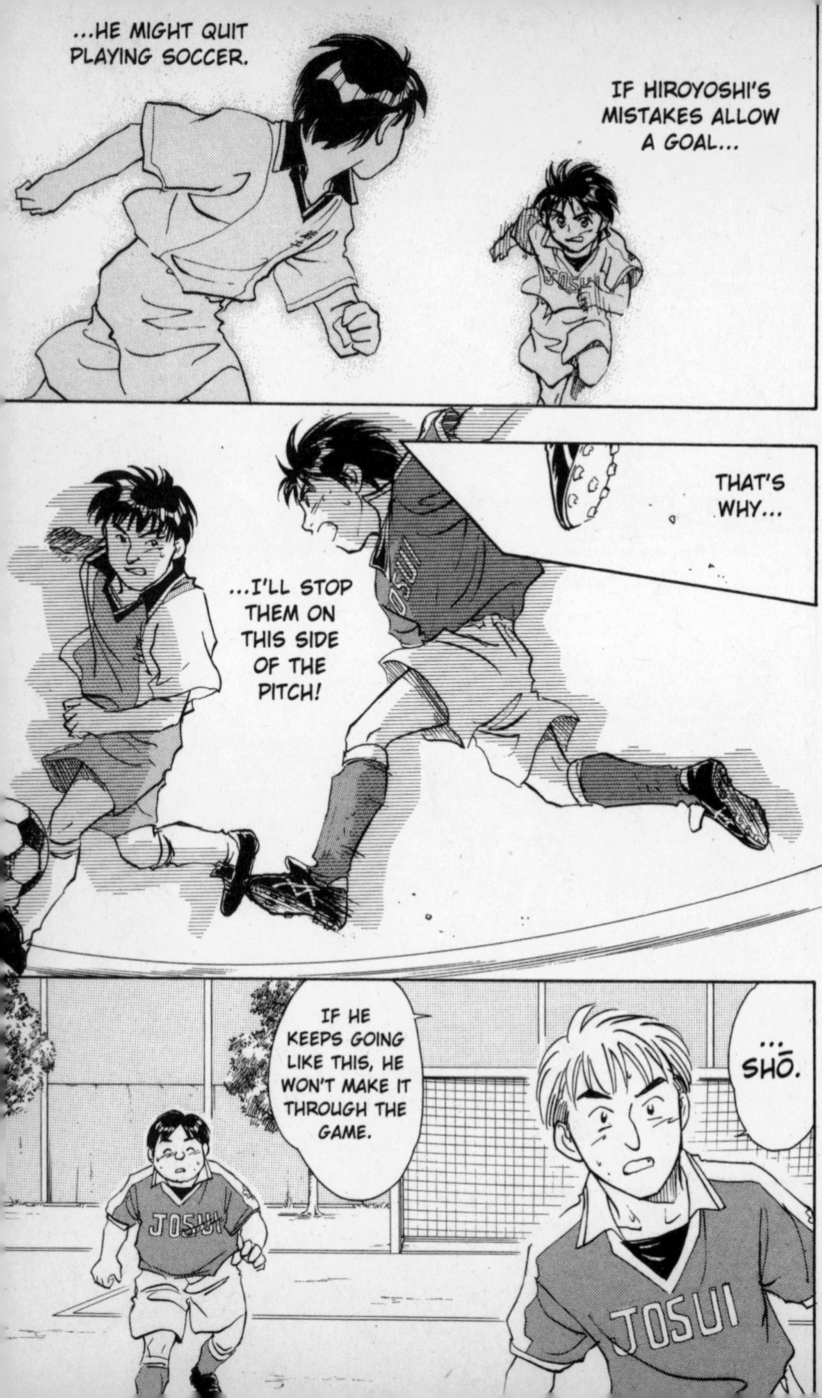
IF HIROYOSHI'S MISTAKES ALLOW A GOAL...
...HE MIGHT QUIT PLAYING SOCCER.
THAT'S WHY...
...I'LL STOP THEM ON THIS SIDE OF THE PITCH!
...SHŌ.
IF HE KEEPS GOING LIKE THIS, HE WON'T MAKE IT THROUGH THE GAME.

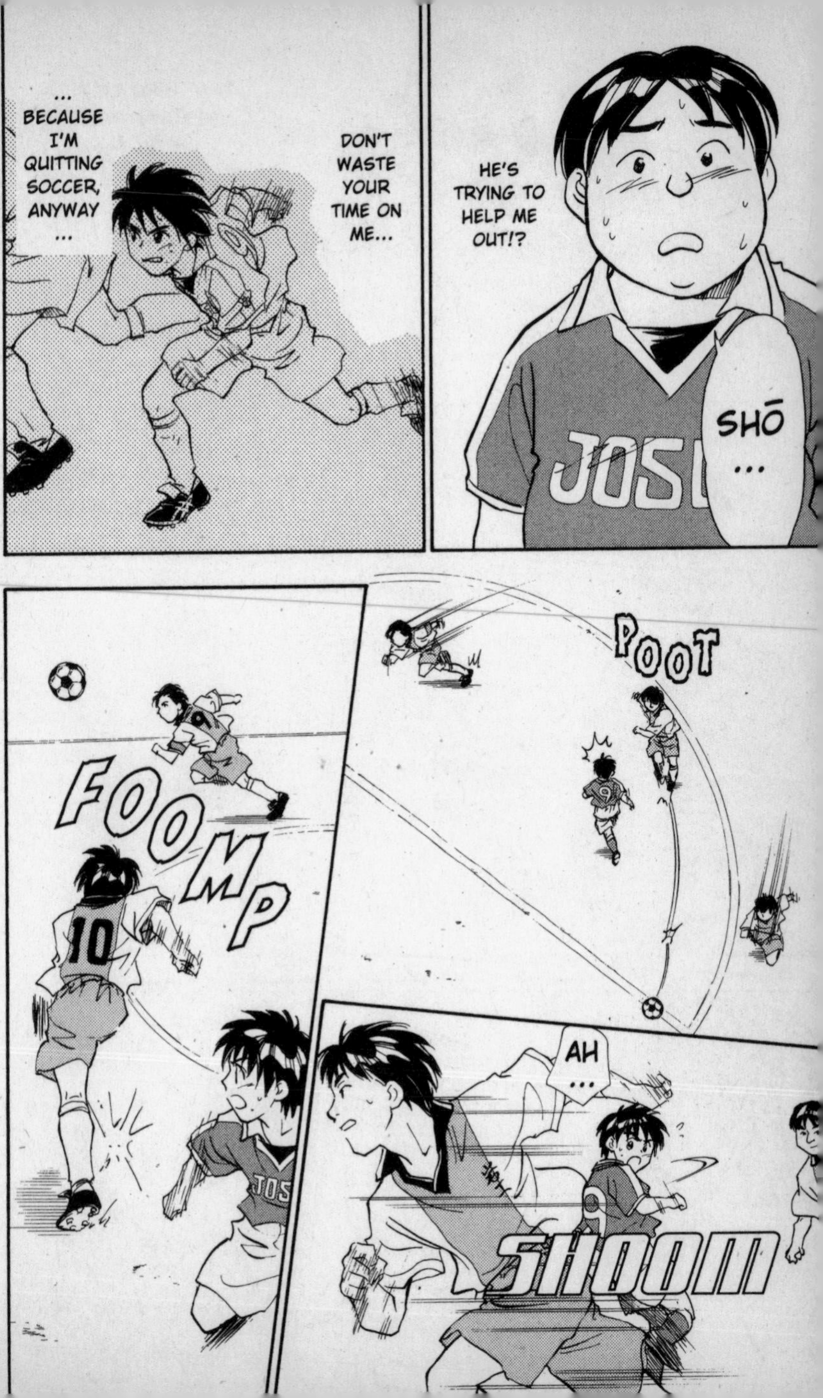
SHŌ ...
HE'S TRYING TO HELP ME OUT!?
DON'T WASTE YOUR TIME ON ME...
... BECAUSE I'M QUITTING SOCCER, ANYWAY ...
POOT
AH ...
SHOOM
FOOMP

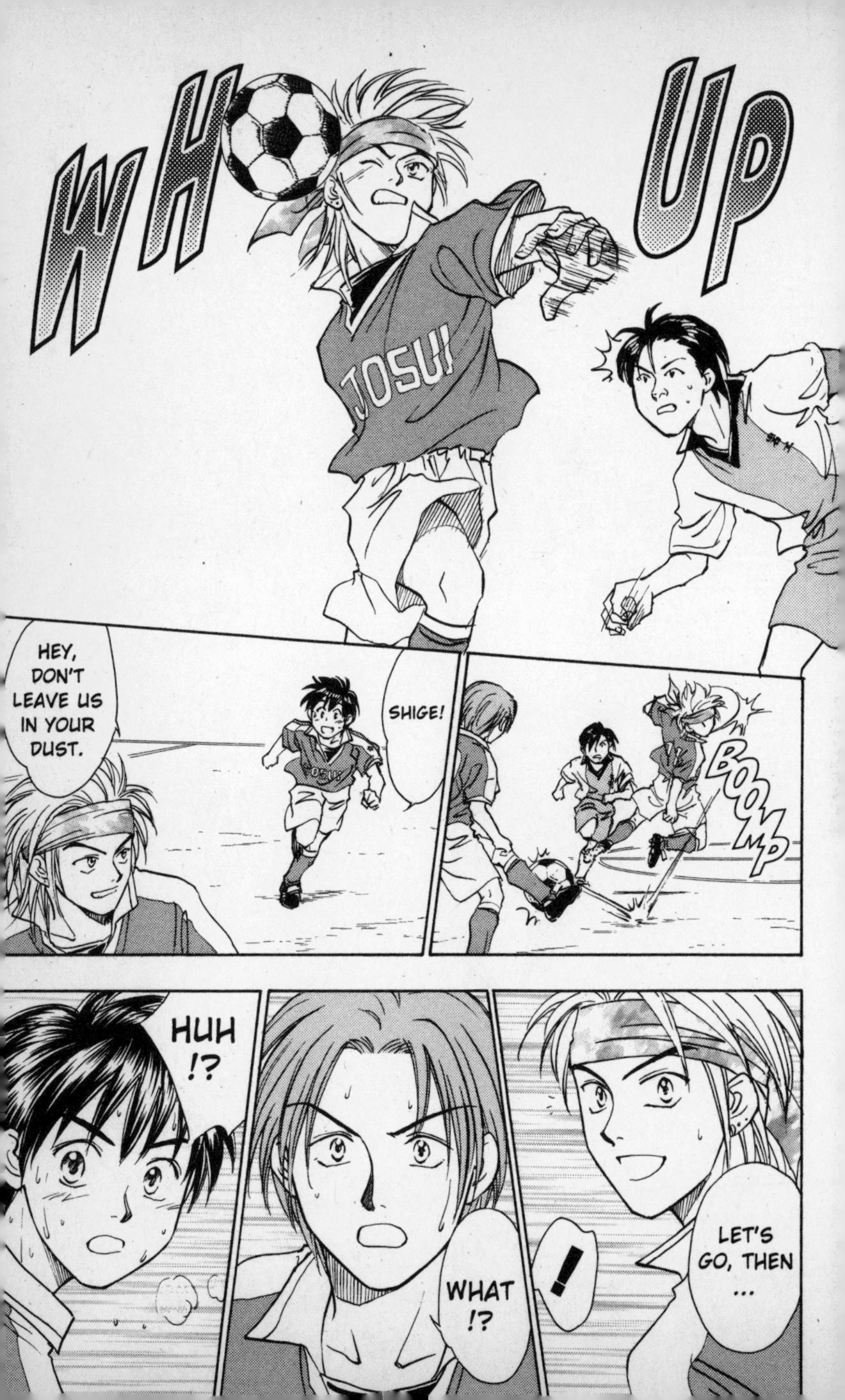
WH UP
BOOMP
SHIGE!
HEY, DON'T LEAVE US IN YOUR DUST.
LET'S GO, THEN ...
!
WHAT !?
HUH !?

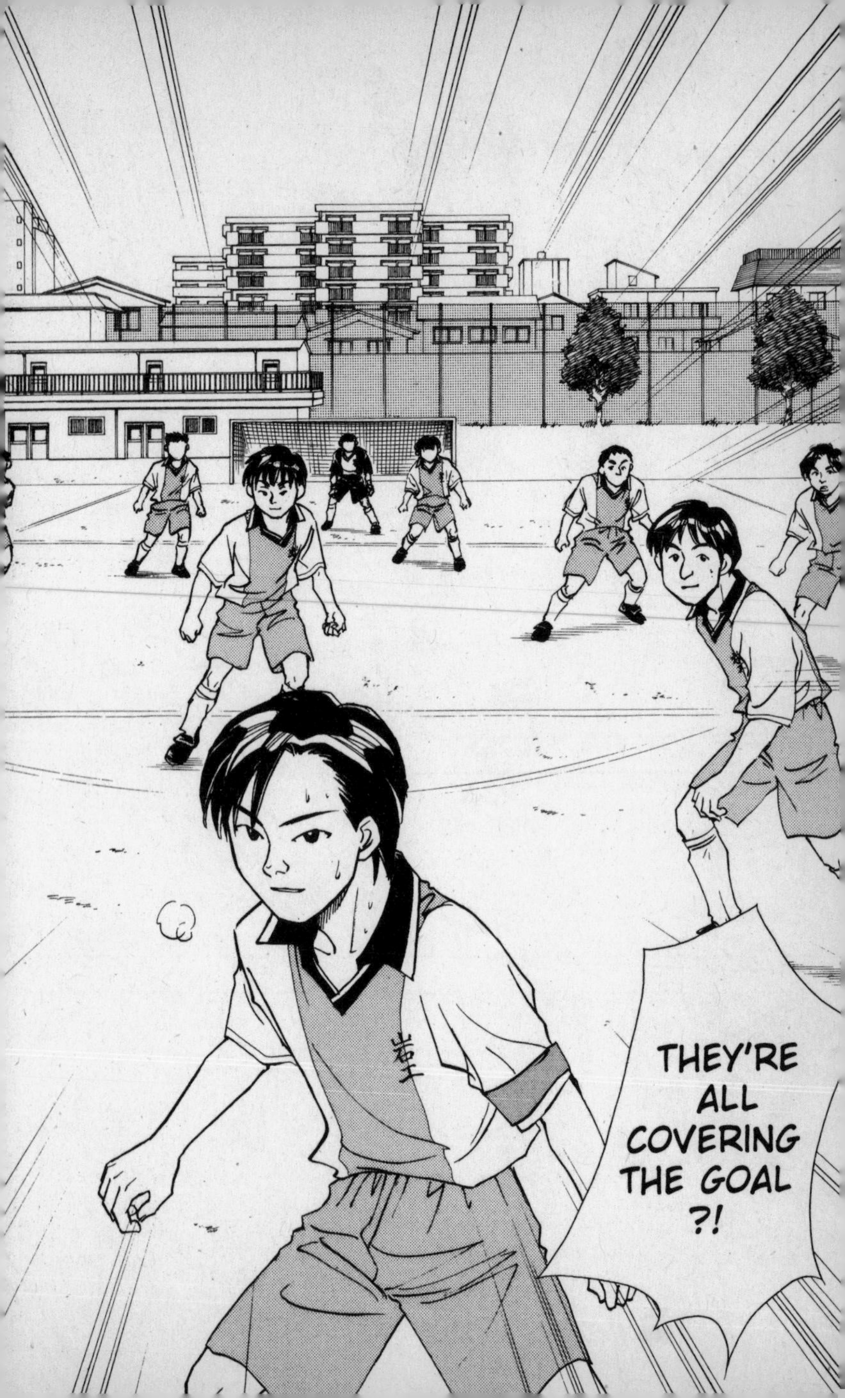
THEY'RE ALL COVERING THE GOAL ?!

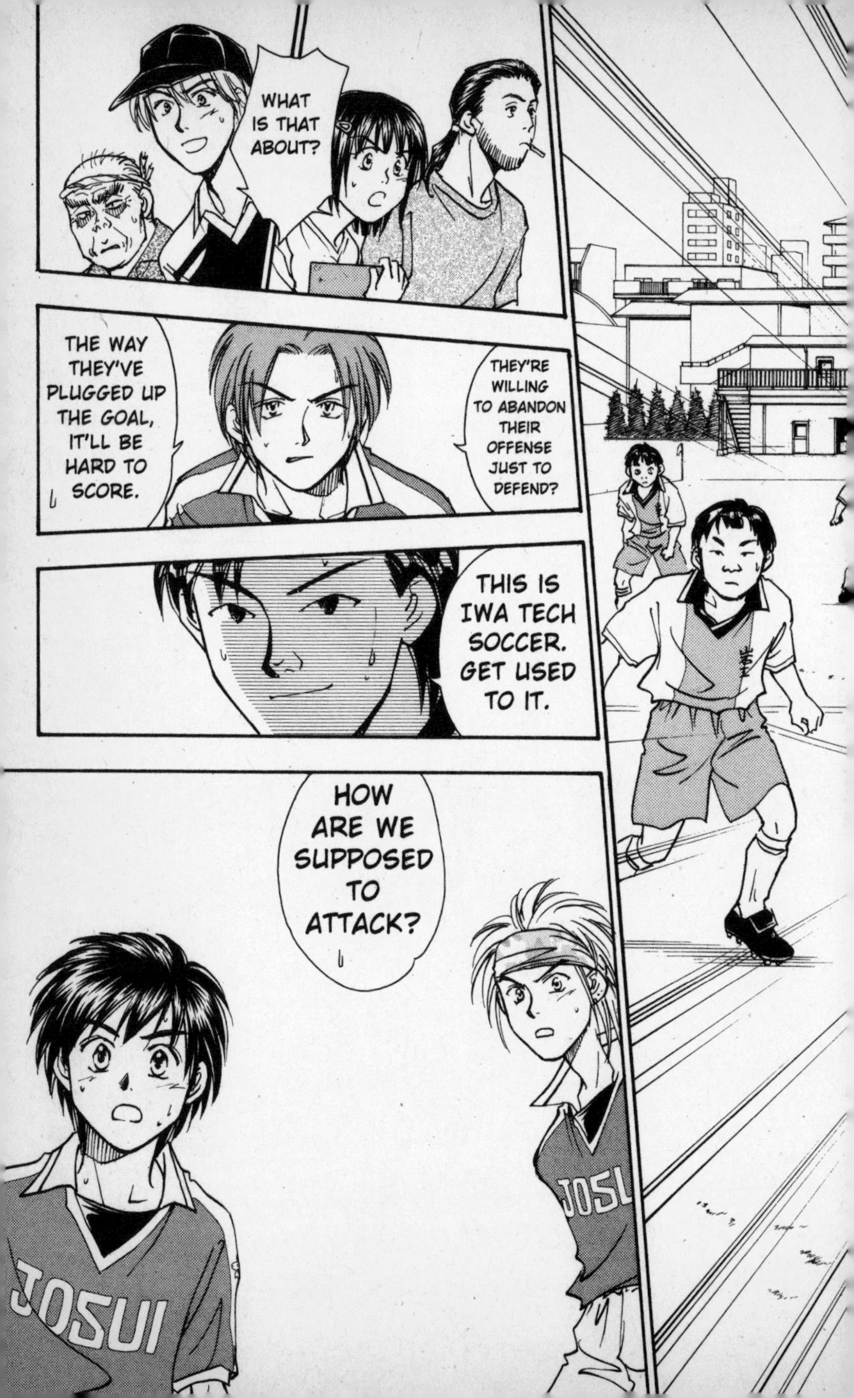
WHAT IS THAT ABOUT?
THEY'RE WILLING TO ABANDON THEIR OFFENSE JUST TO DEFEND?
THE WAY THEY'VE PLUGGED UP THE GOAL, IT'LL BE HARD TO SCORE.
THIS IS IWA TECH SOCCER. GET USED TO IT.
HOW ARE WE SUPPOSED TO ATTACK?
JOSUI
JOSUI

DAISUKE NOTE

Iwa Tech Side

SATORU OGATA

PERSONAL DATA

BIRTHDAY:	JAN 18, 1984
SIZE:	166 cm 53 kg
BLOOD TYPE:	O
FAVORITE FOOD:	FIGS
WHAT HE DISLIKES:	NOTHING IN PARTICULAR
HOBBY AND SPECIAL SKILLS:	BIRD WATCHING AND TINKERING WITH MACHINES

MASASHI HAYANO

PERSONAL DATA

BIRTHDAY:	AUG 30, 1984
SIZE:	162 cm 50 kg
BLOOD TYPE:	B
FAVORITE FOOD:	CHESTNUTS
WHAT HE DISLIKES:	TOFU
HOBBY AND SPECIAL SKILLS:	VIDEO EDITING AND PROGRAM SOFTWARE

STAGE.58
Nightmare of the Last Five Minutes

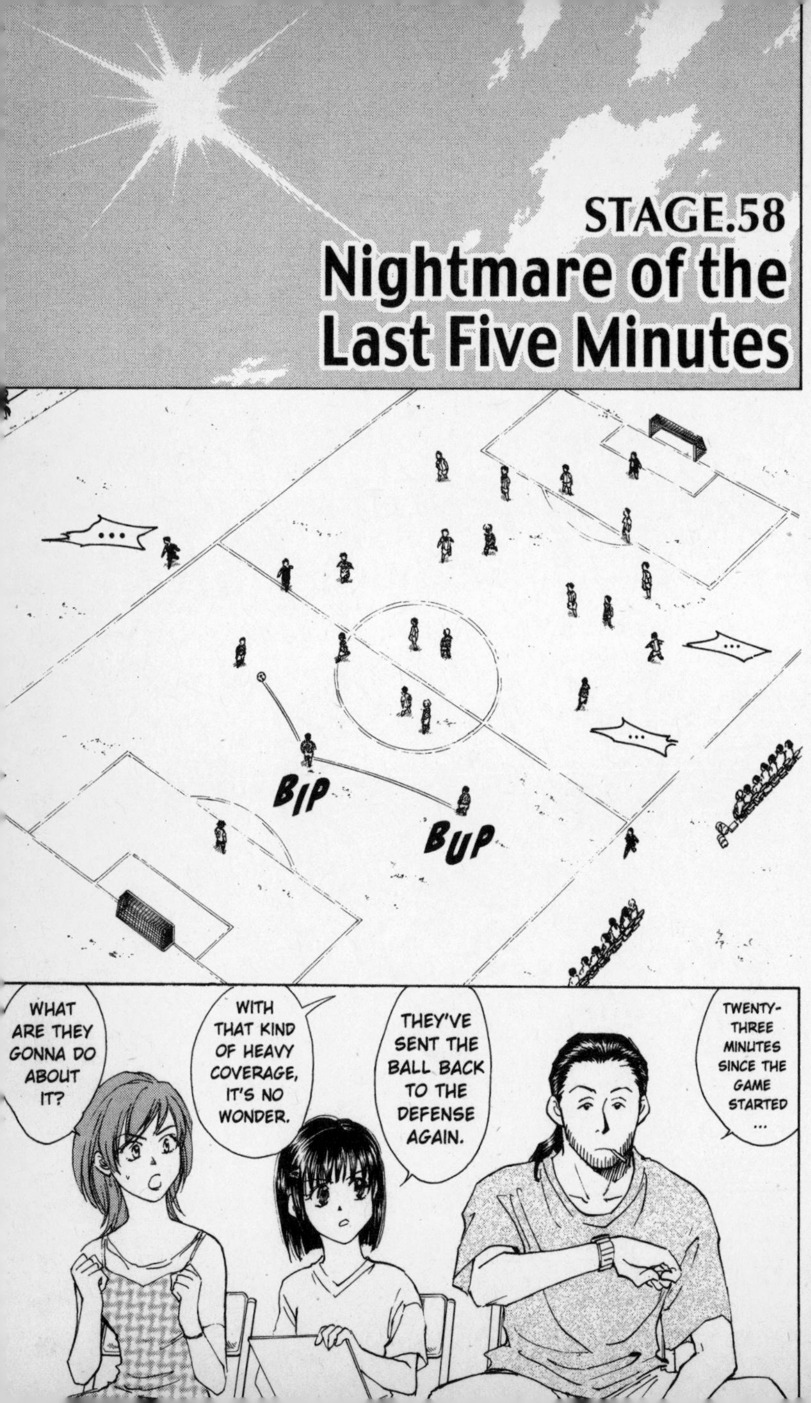
...
...
...
BIP
BUP
TWENTY-THREE MINUTES SINCE THE GAME STARTED ...
THEY'VE SENT THE BALL BACK TO THE DEFENSE AGAIN.
WITH THAT KIND OF HEAVY COVERAGE, IT'S NO WONDER.
WHAT ARE THEY GONNA DO ABOUT IT?

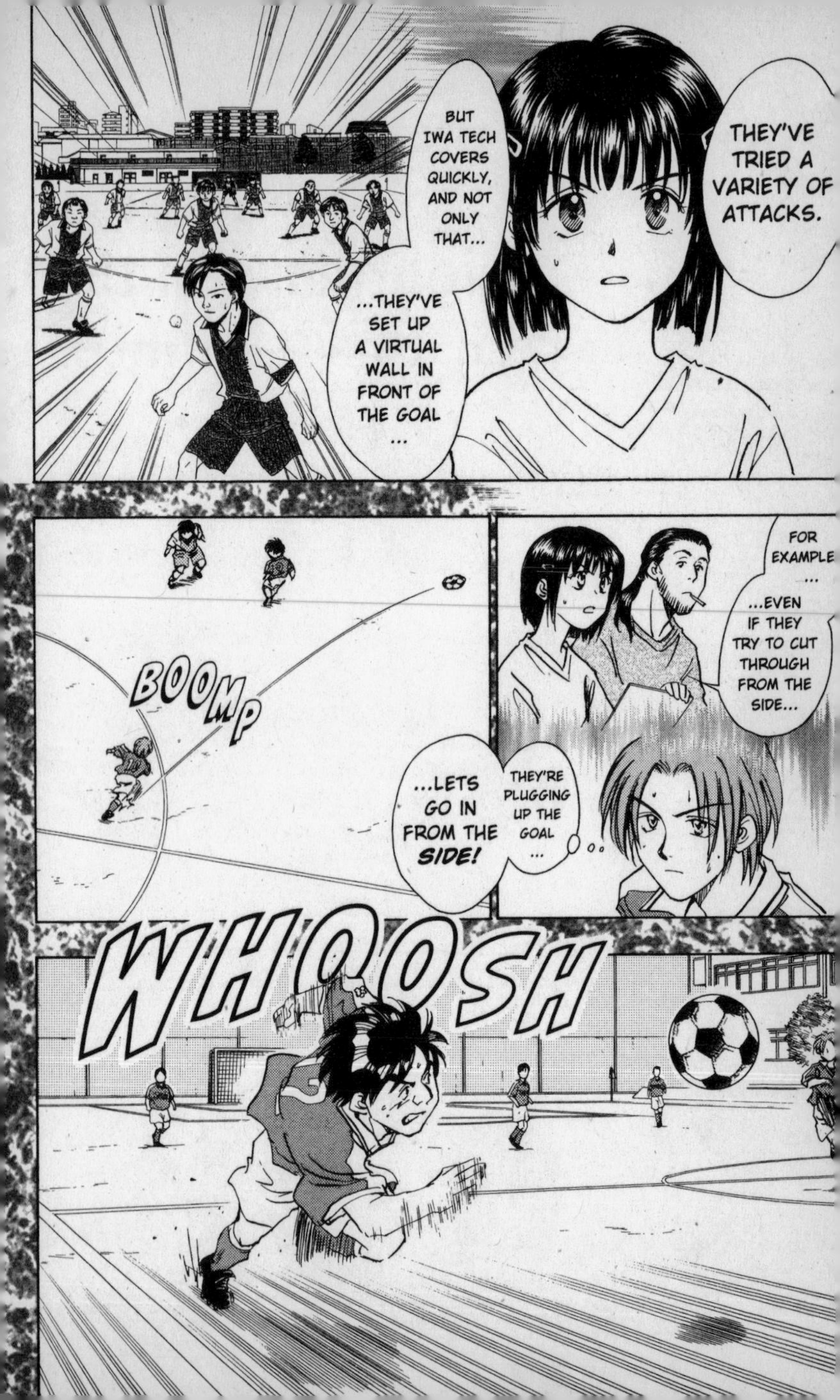
THEY'VE TRIED A VARIETY OF ATTACKS.
BUT IWA TECH COVERS QUICKLY, AND NOT ONLY THAT...
...THEY'VE SET UP A VIRTUAL WALL IN FRONT OF THE GOAL ...
FOR EXAMPLE ...
...EVEN IF THEY TRY TO CUT THROUGH FROM THE SIDE...
THEY'RE PLUGGING UP THE GOAL ...
...LETS GO IN FROM THE SIDE!
BOOMP
WHOOSH

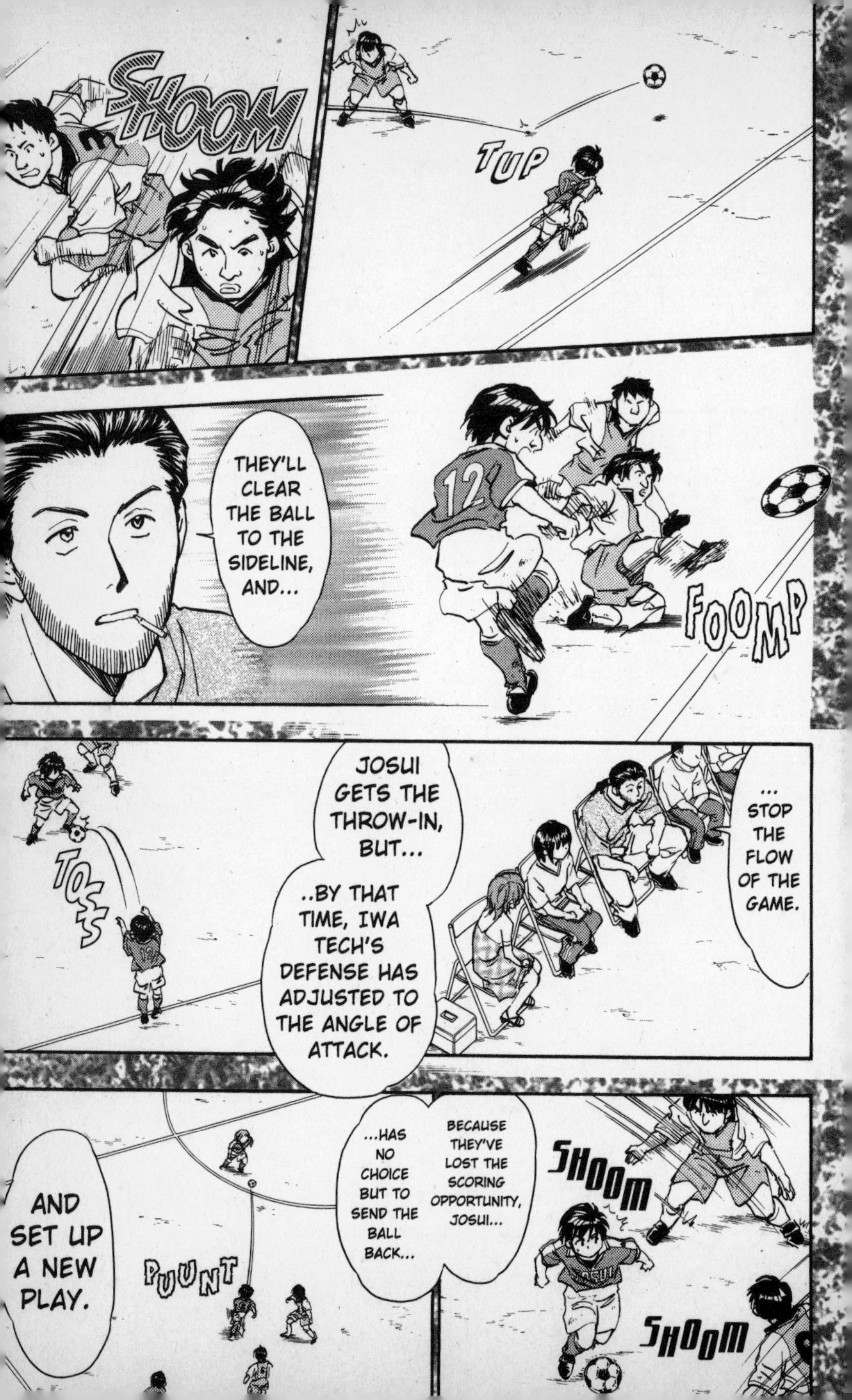
TUP
SHOOM
FOOMP
THEY'LL CLEAR THE BALL TO THE SIDELINE, AND...
... STOP THE FLOW OF THE GAME.
JOSUI GETS THE THROW-IN, BUT...
..BY THAT TIME, IWA TECH'S DEFENSE HAS ADJUSTED TO THE ANGLE OF ATTACK.
TOSS
SHOOM
SHOOM
BECAUSE THEY'VE LOST THE SCORING OPPORTUNITY, JOSUI...
...HAS NO CHOICE BUT TO SEND THE BALL BACK...
AND SET UP A NEW PLAY.
PUUNT

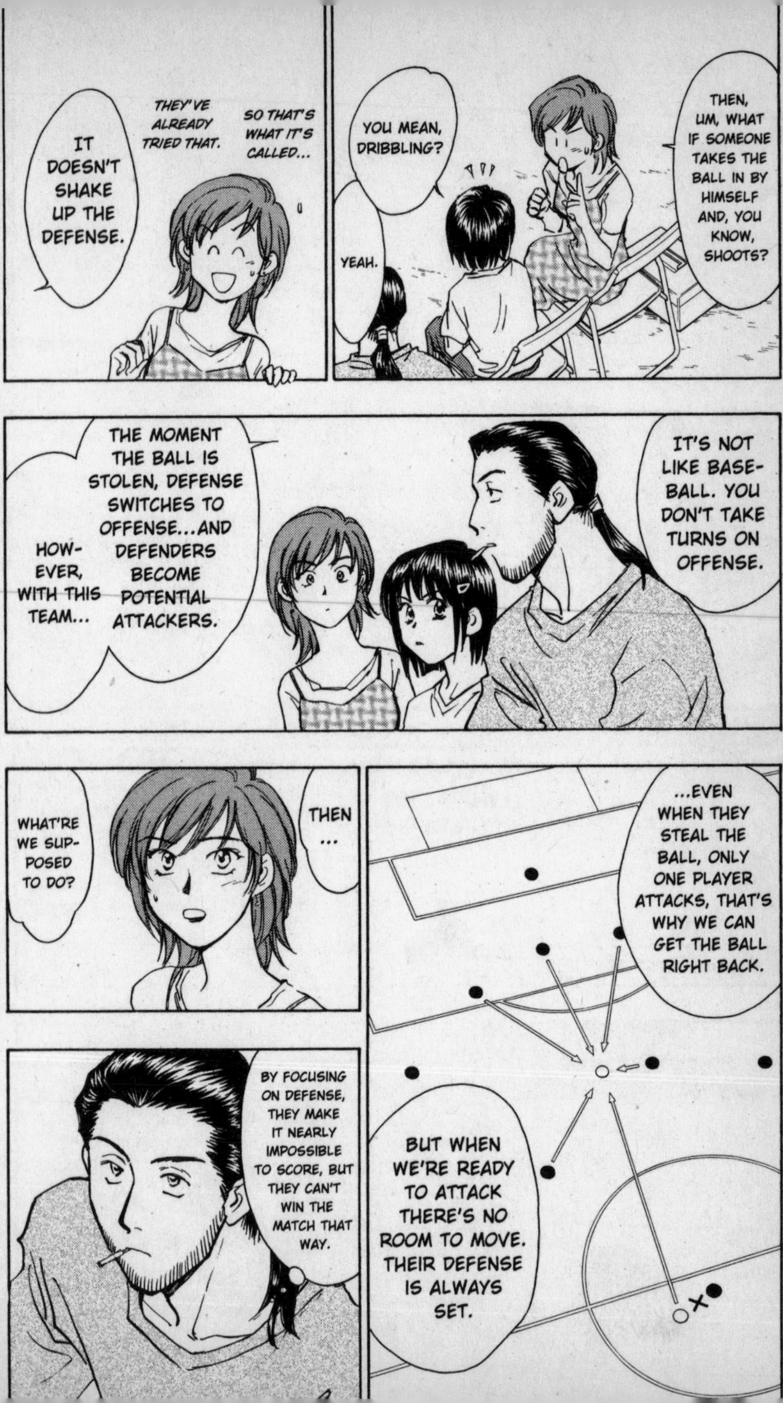

THEN, UM, WHAT IF SOMEONE TAKES THE BALL IN BY HIMSELF AND, YOU KNOW, SHOOTS?
YOU MEAN, DRIBBLING?
YEAH.
SO THAT'S WHAT IT'S CALLED...
THEY'VE ALREADY TRIED THAT.
IT DOESN'T SHAKE UP THE DEFENSE.
IT'S NOT LIKE BASE-BALL. YOU DON'T TAKE TURNS ON OFFENSE.
THE MOMENT THE BALL IS STOLEN, DEFENSE SWITCHES TO OFFENSE...AND DEFENDERS BECOME POTENTIAL ATTACKERS.
HOW-EVER, WITH THIS TEAM...
...EVEN WHEN THEY STEAL THE BALL, ONLY ONE PLAYER ATTACKS, THAT'S WHY WE CAN GET THE BALL RIGHT BACK.
BUT WHEN WE'RE READY TO ATTACK THERE'S NO ROOM TO MOVE. THEIR DEFENSE IS ALWAYS SET.
THEN...
WHAT'RE WE SUP-POSED TO DO?
BY FOCUSING ON DEFENSE, THEY MAKE IT NEARLY IMPOSSIBLE TO SCORE, BUT THEY CAN'T WIN THE MATCH THAT WAY.

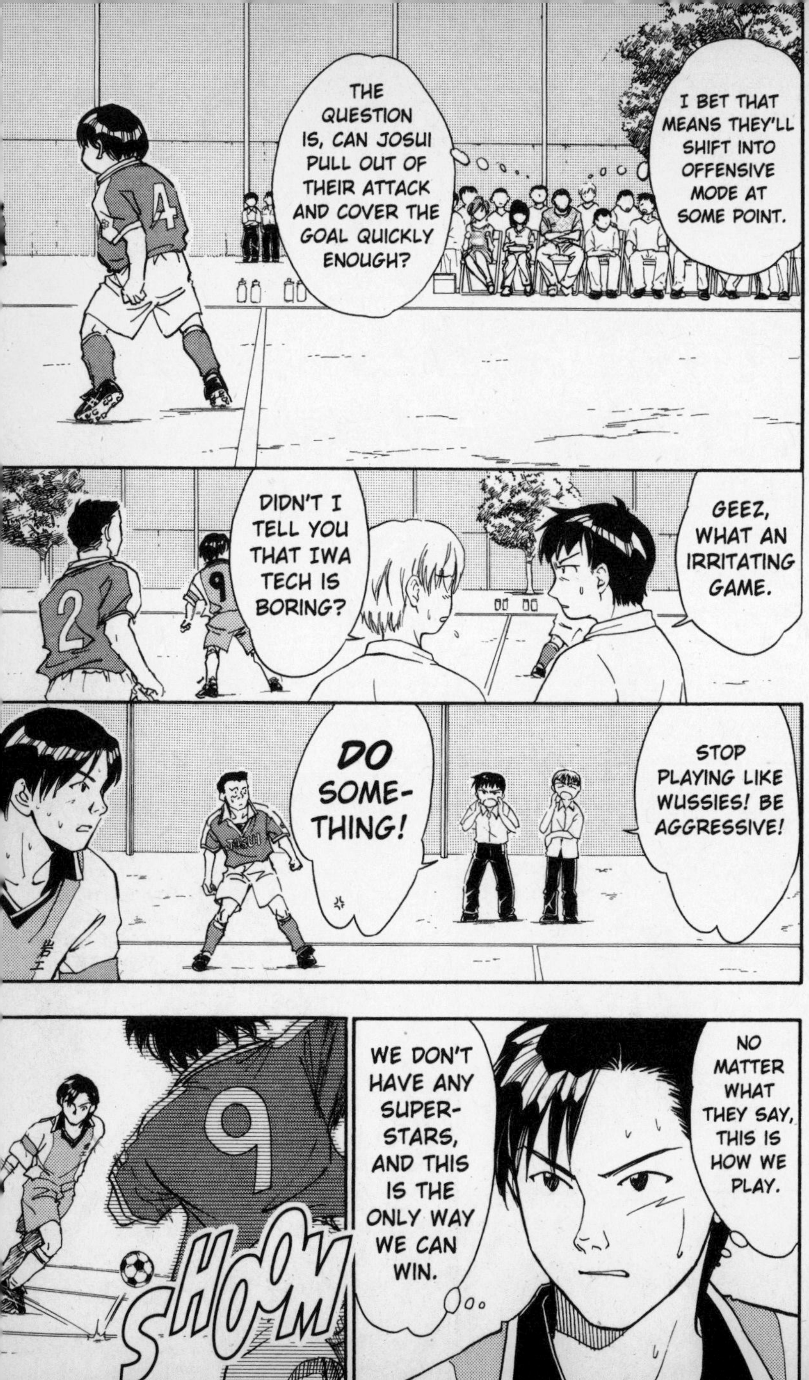
I BET THAT MEANS THEY'LL SHIFT INTO OFFENSIVE MODE AT SOME POINT.
THE QUESTION IS, CAN JOSUI PULL OUT OF THEIR ATTACK AND COVER THE GOAL QUICKLY ENOUGH?
GEEZ, WHAT AN IRRITATING GAME.
DIDN'T I TELL YOU THAT IWA TECH IS BORING?
STOP PLAYING LIKE WUSSIES! BE AGGRESSIVE!
DO SOME-THING!
JOSUI
NO MATTER WHAT THEY SAY, THIS IS HOW WE PLAY.
WE DON'T HAVE ANY SUPER-STARS, AND THIS IS THE ONLY WAY WE CAN WIN.
SHOOM

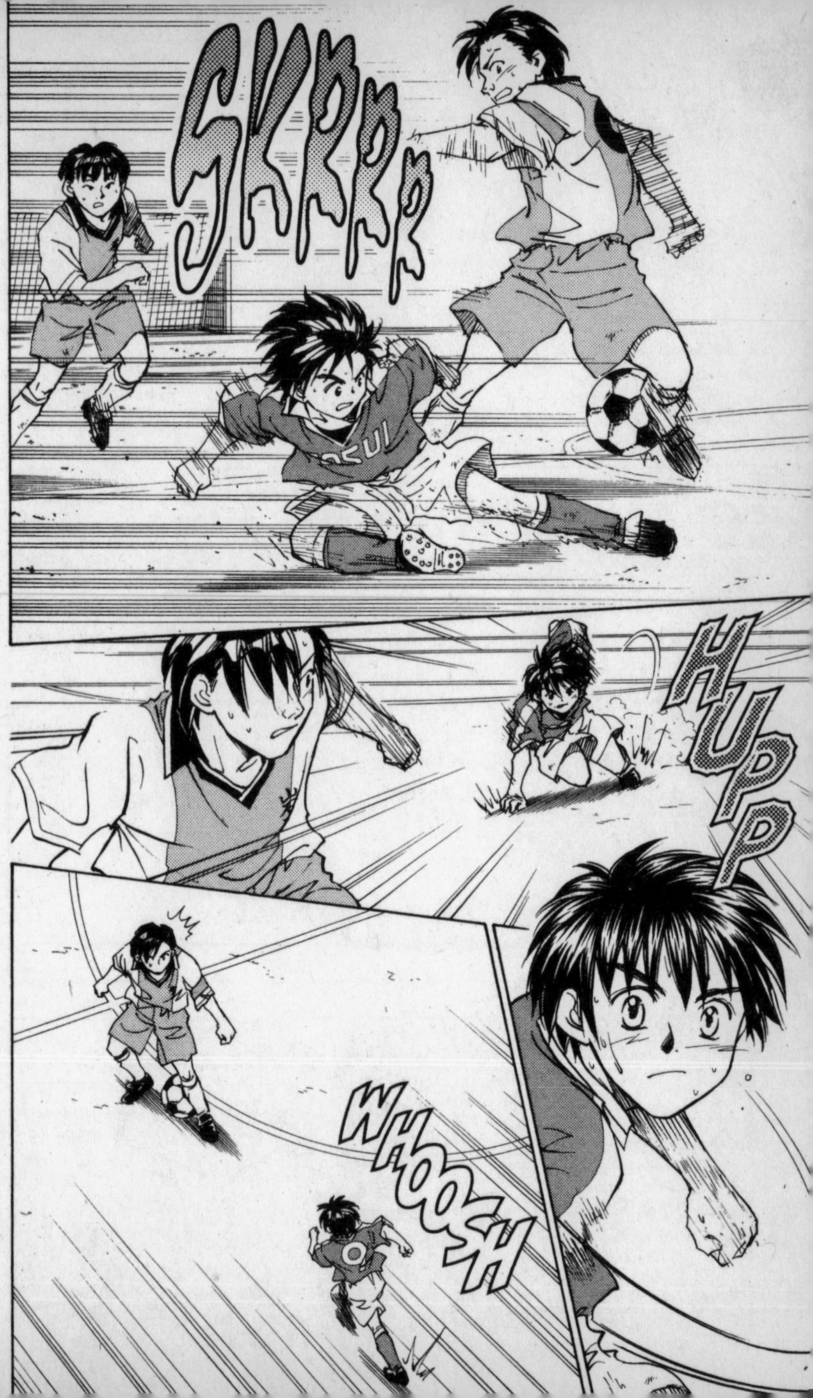
SKRRRR
HUPP!
WHOOSH

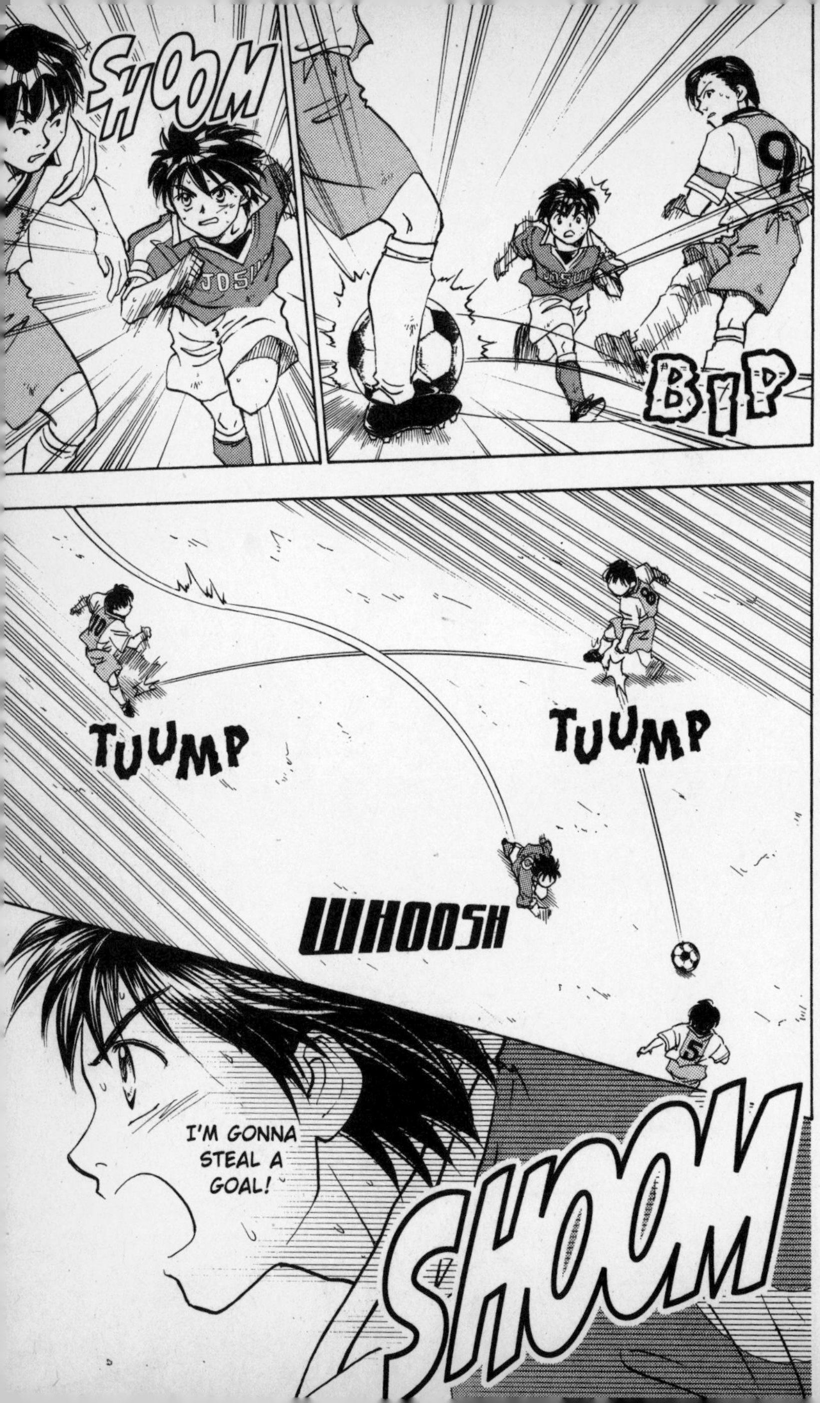
BIP
SHOOM
TUUMP
TUUMP
WHOOSH
I'M GONNA STEAL A GOAL!
SHOOM

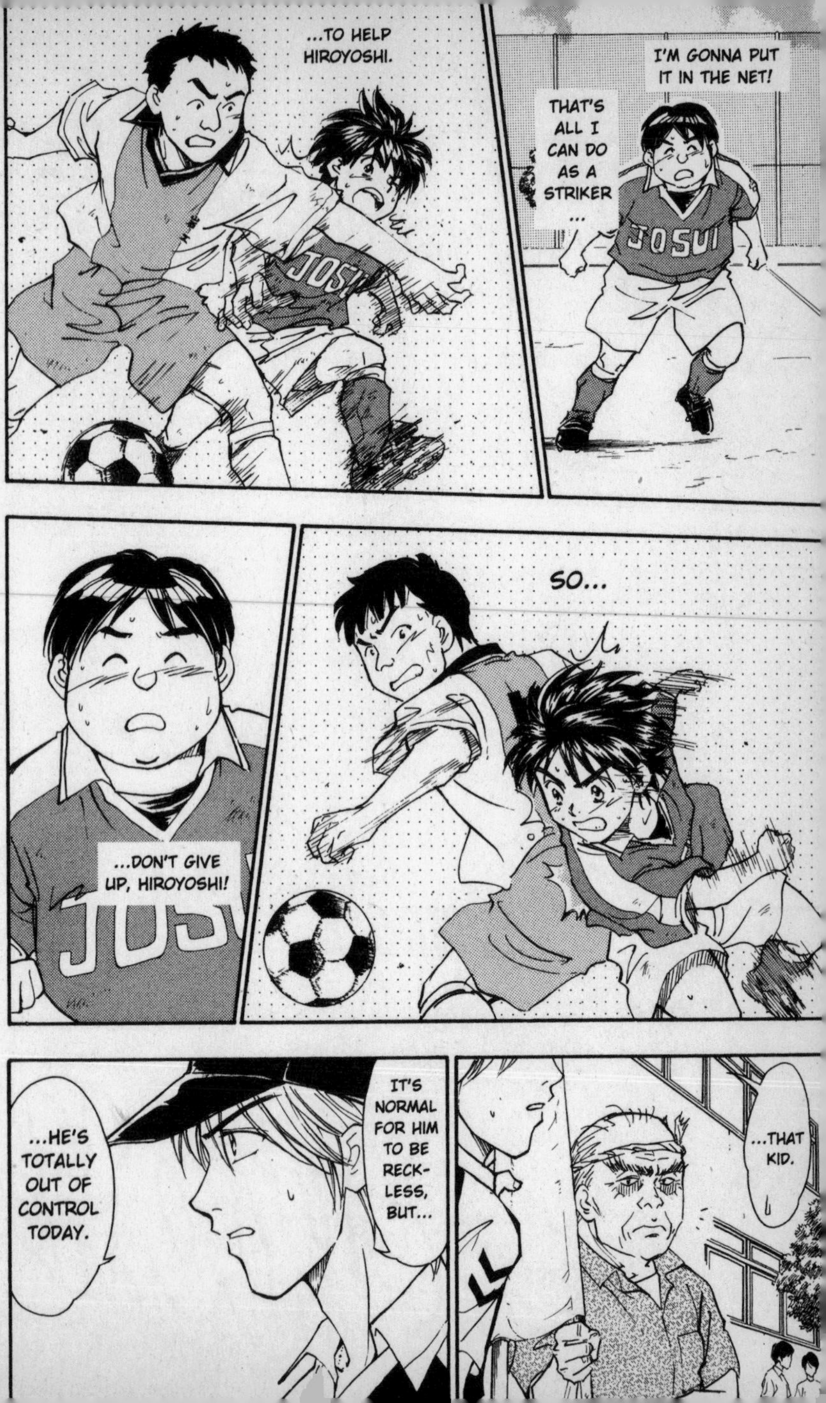
I'M GONNA PUT IT IN THE NET!
THAT'S ALL I CAN DO AS A STRIKER ...
...TO HELP HIROYOSHI.
SO...
...DON'T GIVE UP, HIROYOSHI!
...THAT KID.
IT'S NORMAL FOR HIM TO BE RECK-LESS, BUT...
...HE'S TOTALLY OUT OF CONTROL TODAY.

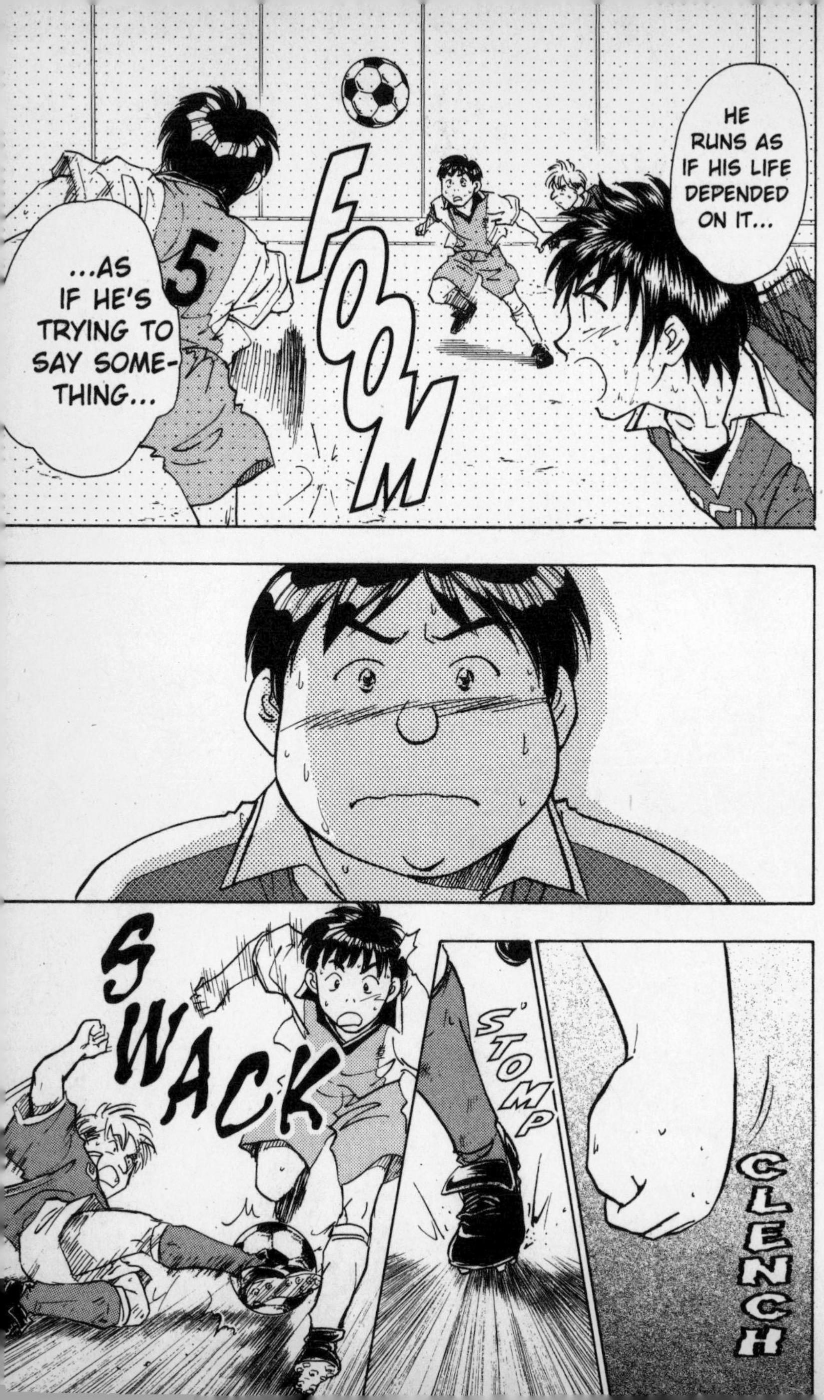
HE RUNS AS IF HIS LIFE DEPENDED ON IT...
...AS IF HE'S TRYING TO SAY SOME-THING...
FOOOM
CLENCH
STOMP
SWACK

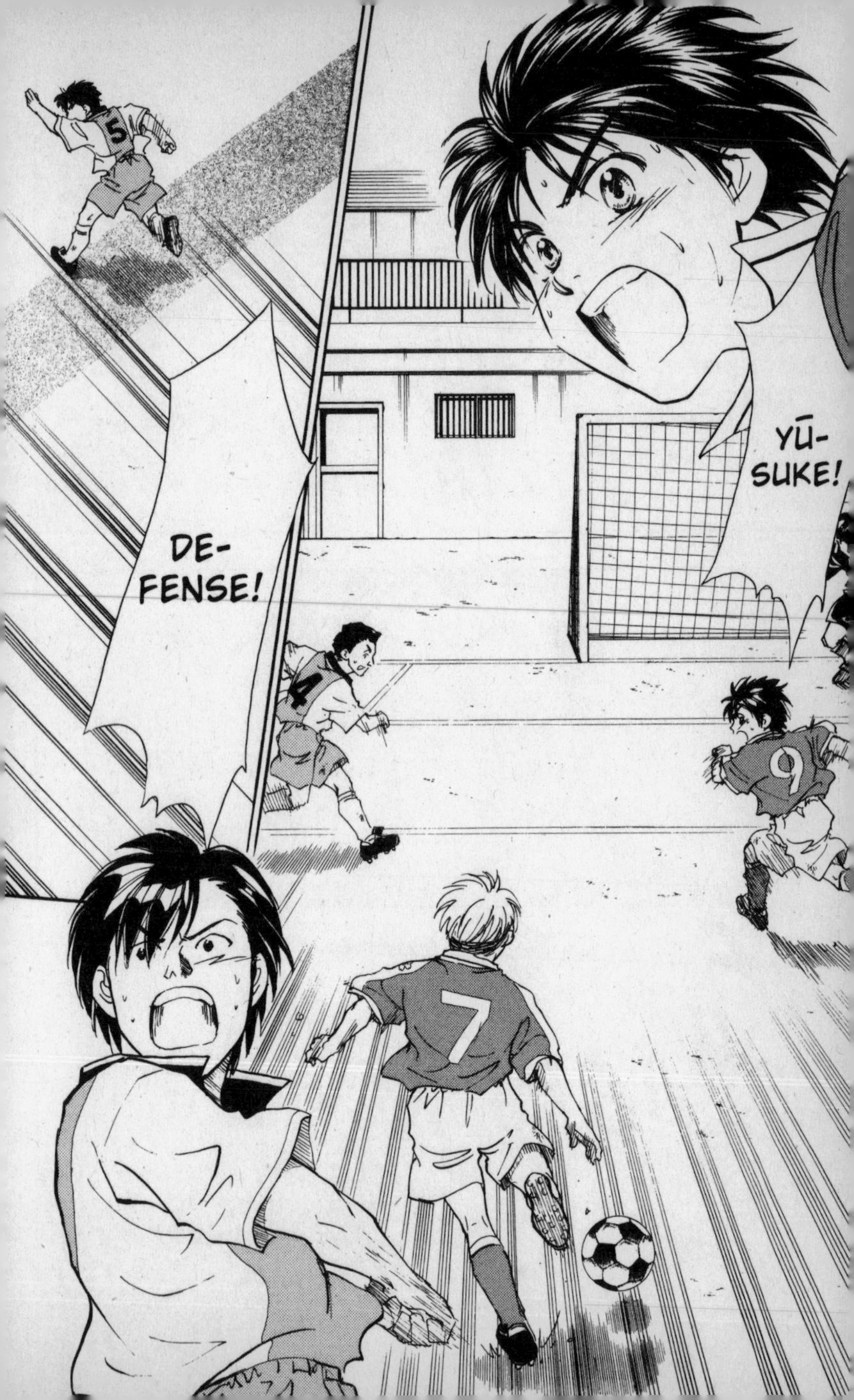
YŪ-
SUKE!
DE-
FENSE!

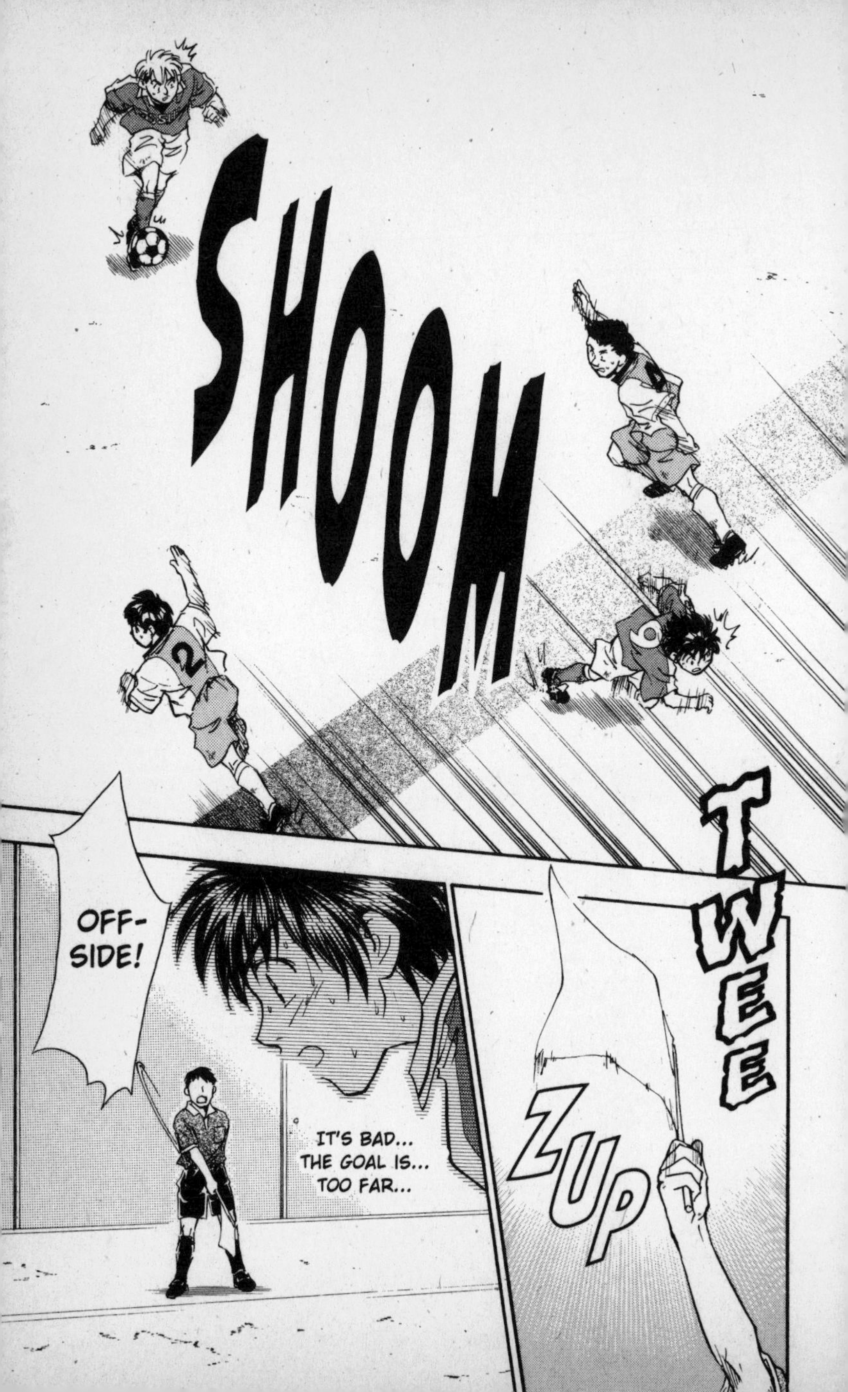
SHOOM
TWEE
ZUP
OFF-SIDE!
IT'S BAD... THE GOAL IS... TOO FAR...

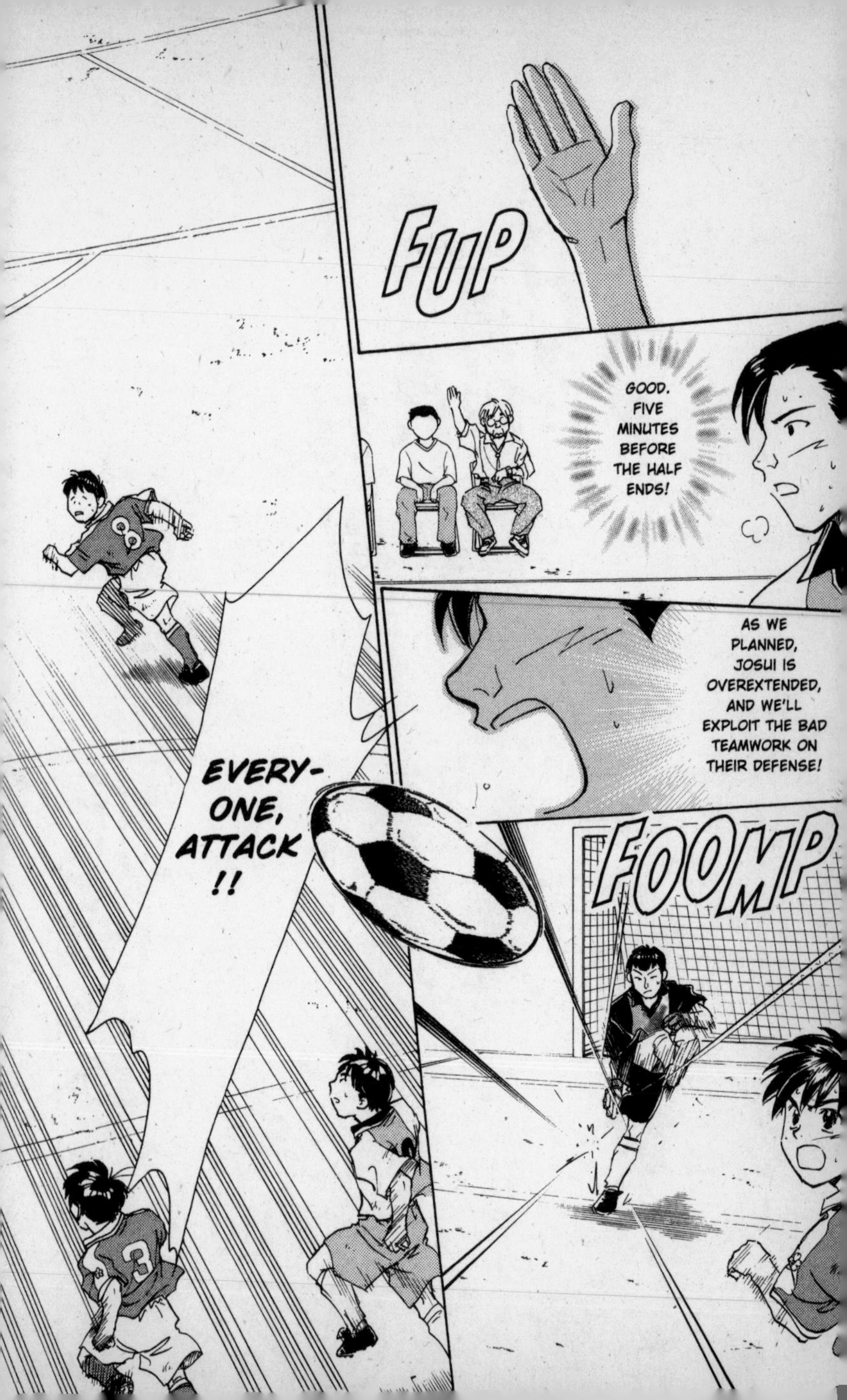
FUP
GOOD. FIVE MINUTES BEFORE THE HALF ENDS!
AS WE PLANNED, JOSUI IS OVEREXTENDED, AND WE'LL EXPLOIT THE BAD TEAMWORK ON THEIR DEFENSE!
FOOMP
EVERY-ONE, ATTACK !!

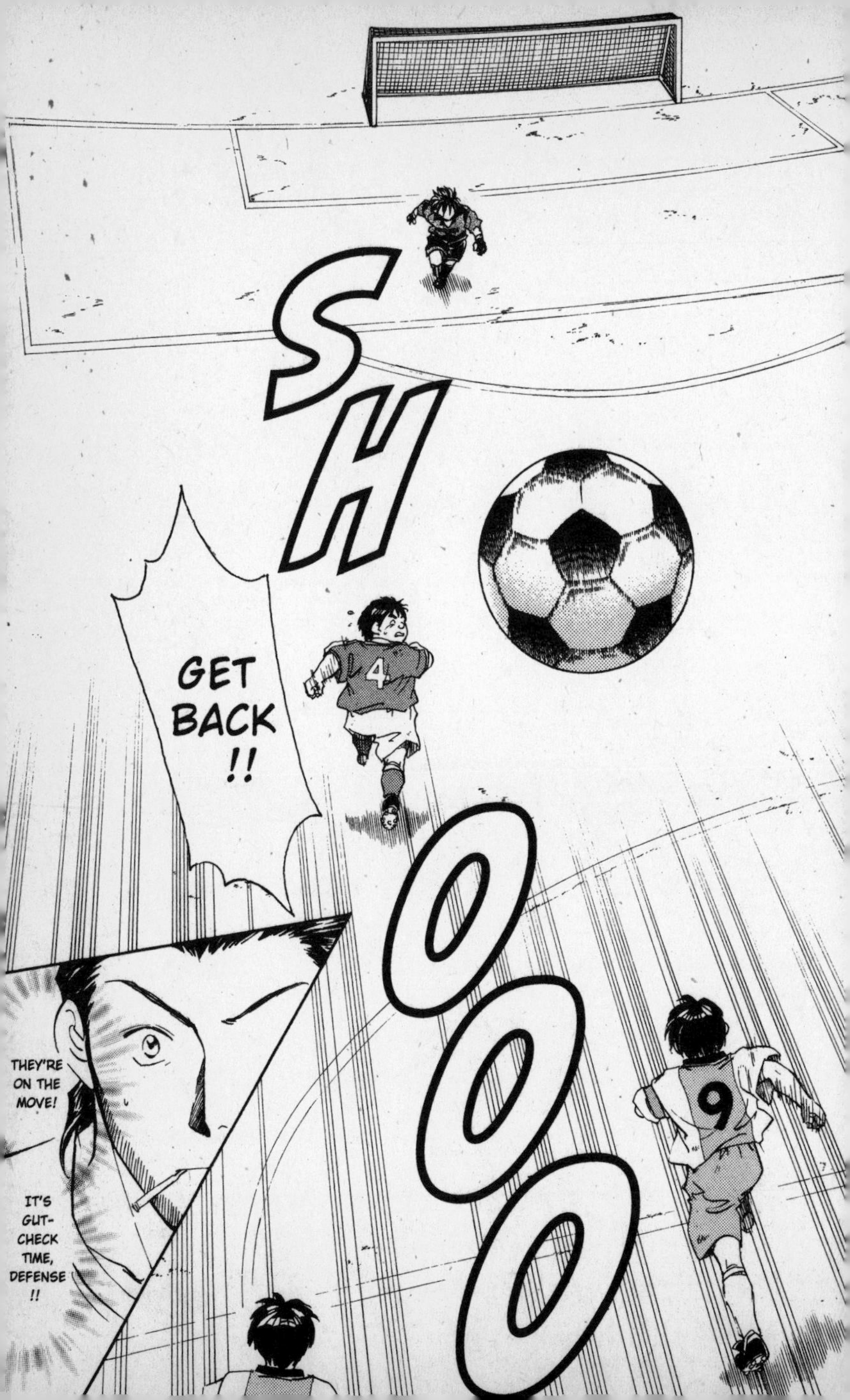
SHOOOOO
GET BACK !!
THEY'RE ON THE MOVE!
IT'S GUT-CHECK TIME, DEFENSE !!

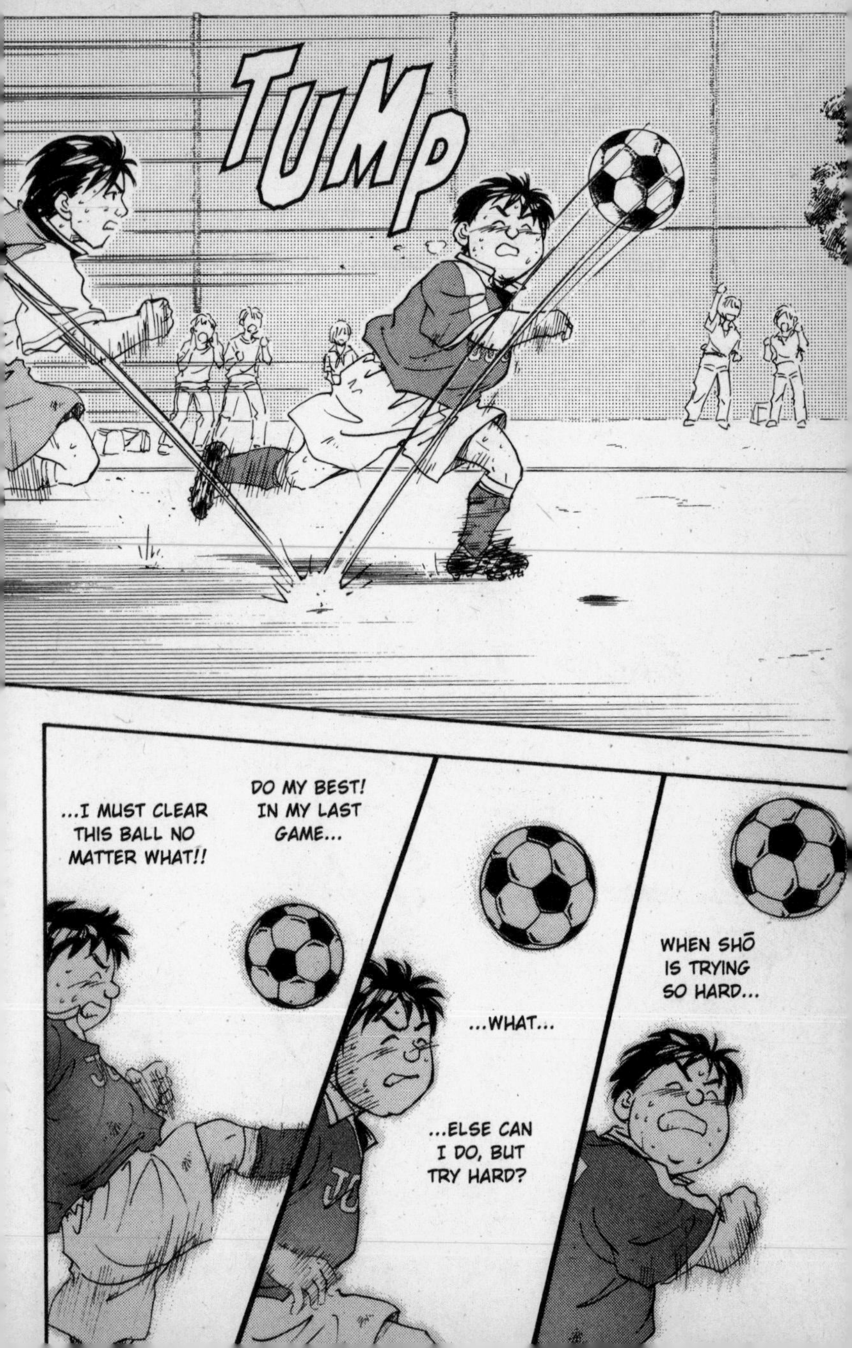
TUMP
WHEN SHŌ IS TRYING SO HARD...
...WHAT...
...ELSE CAN I DO, BUT TRY HARD?
DO MY BEST! IN MY LAST GAME...
...I MUST CLEAR THIS BALL NO MATTER WHAT!!

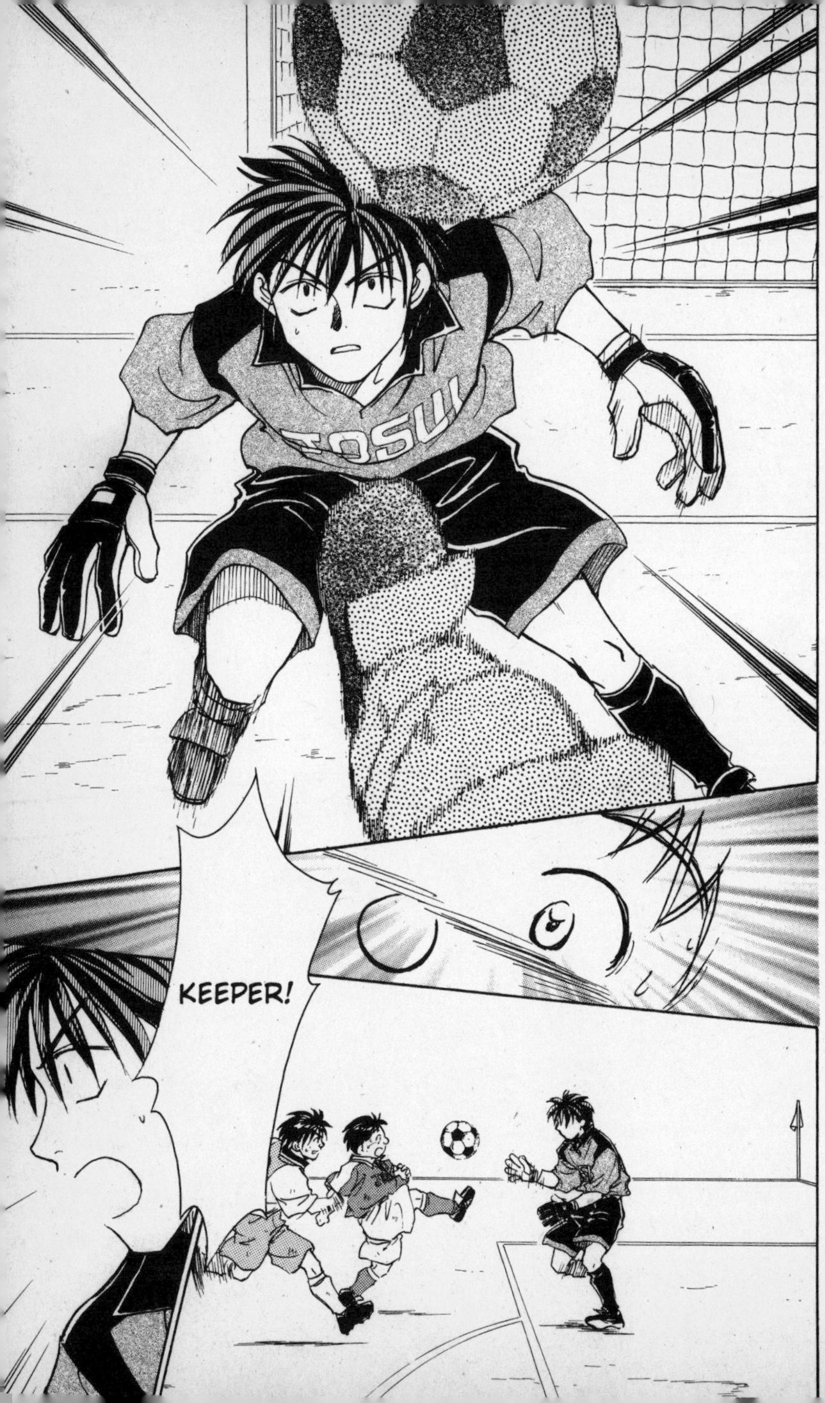
TOSU
KEEPER!

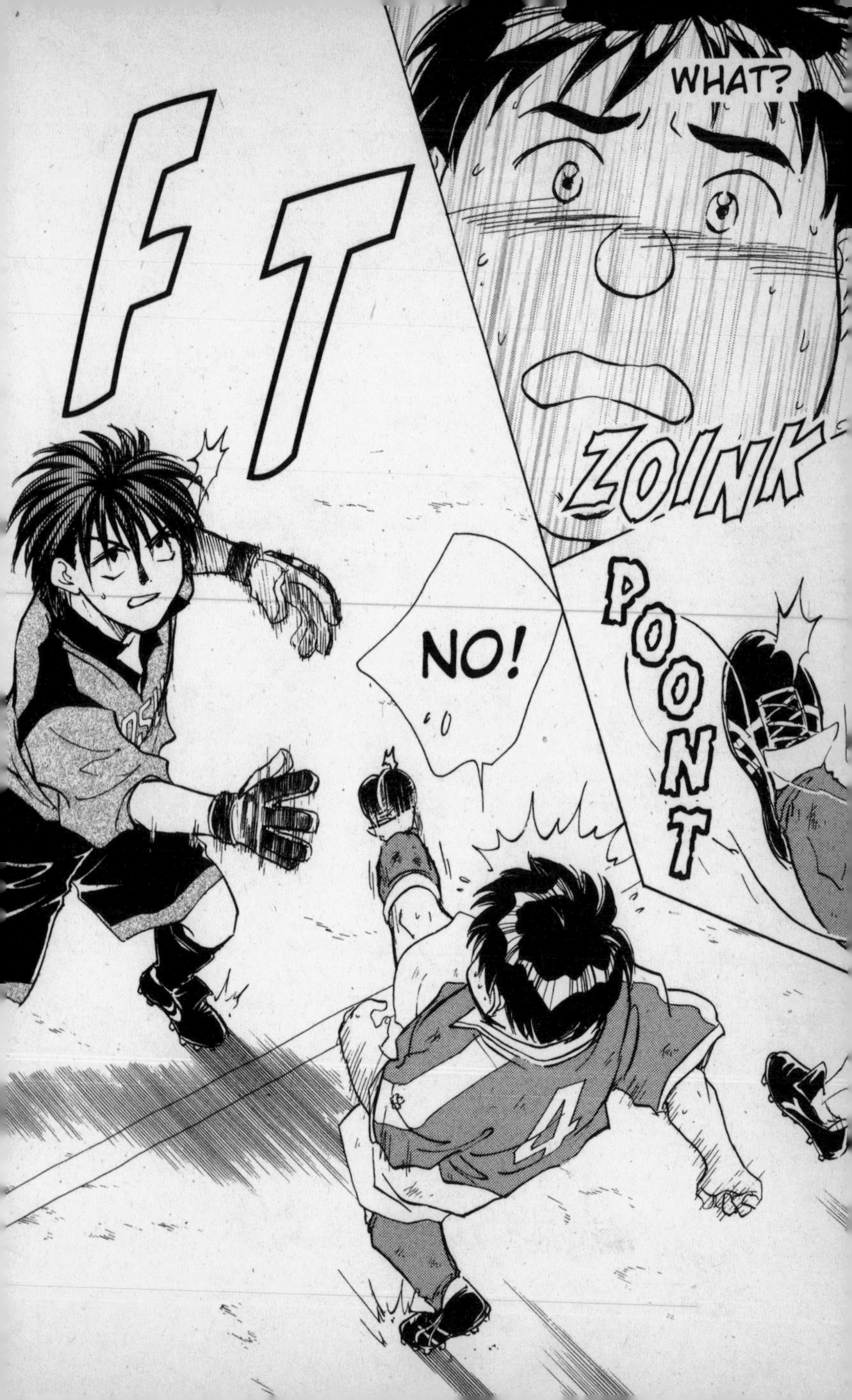
WHAT?
ZOINK
POONT
NO!
FT

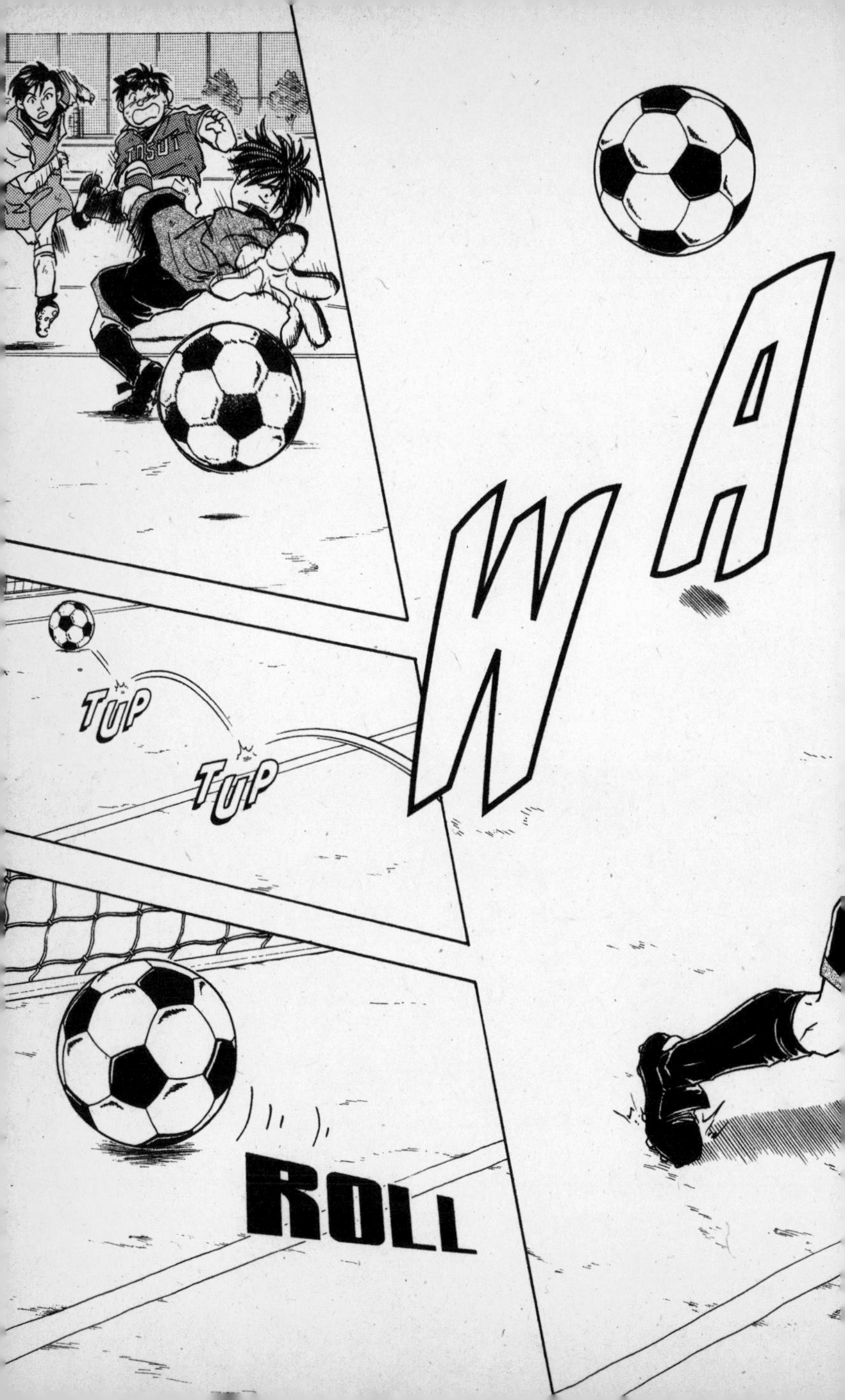
WA
TUP
TUP
ROLL

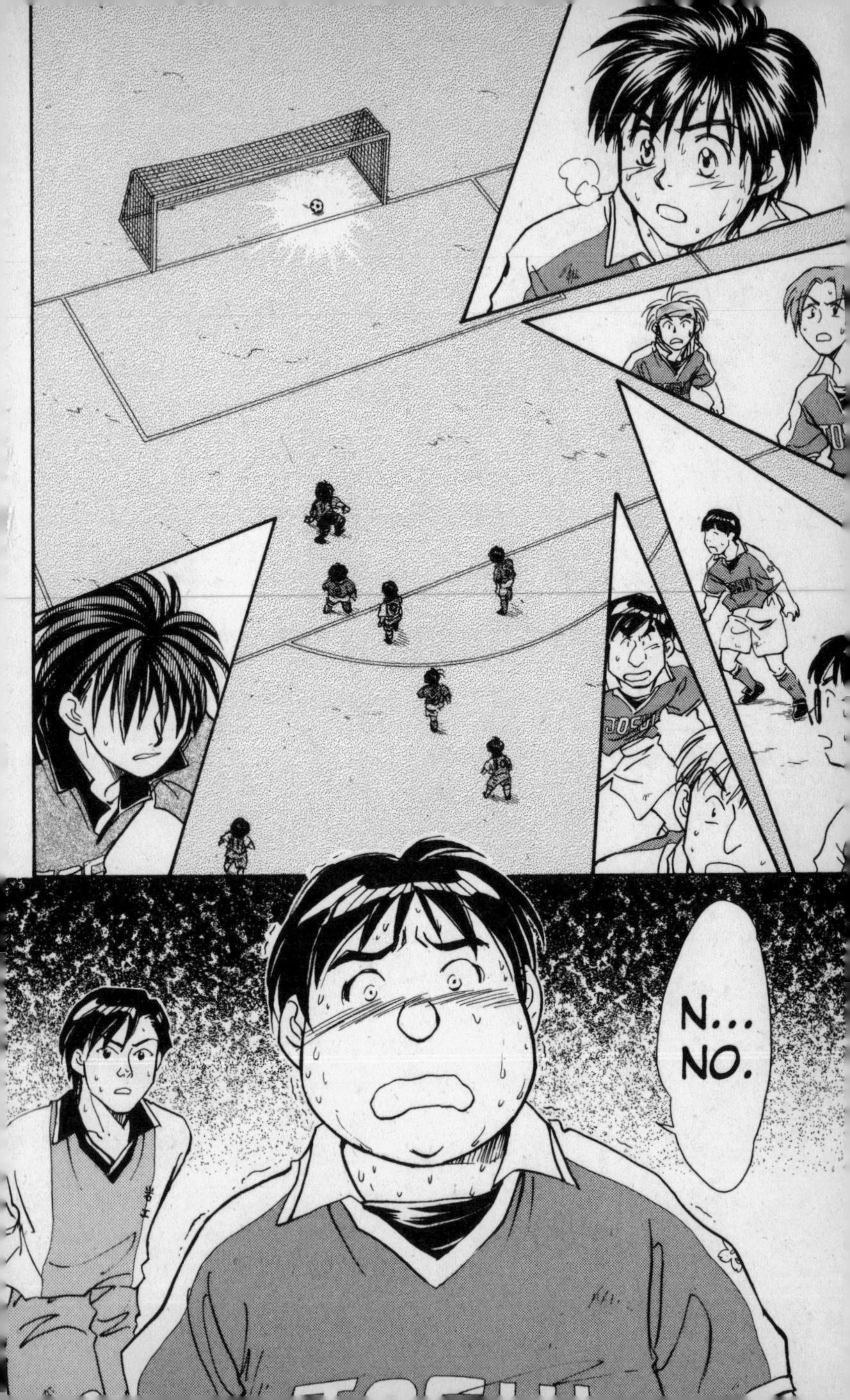
N... NO.

STAGE.59

What It Means to Be a Teammate

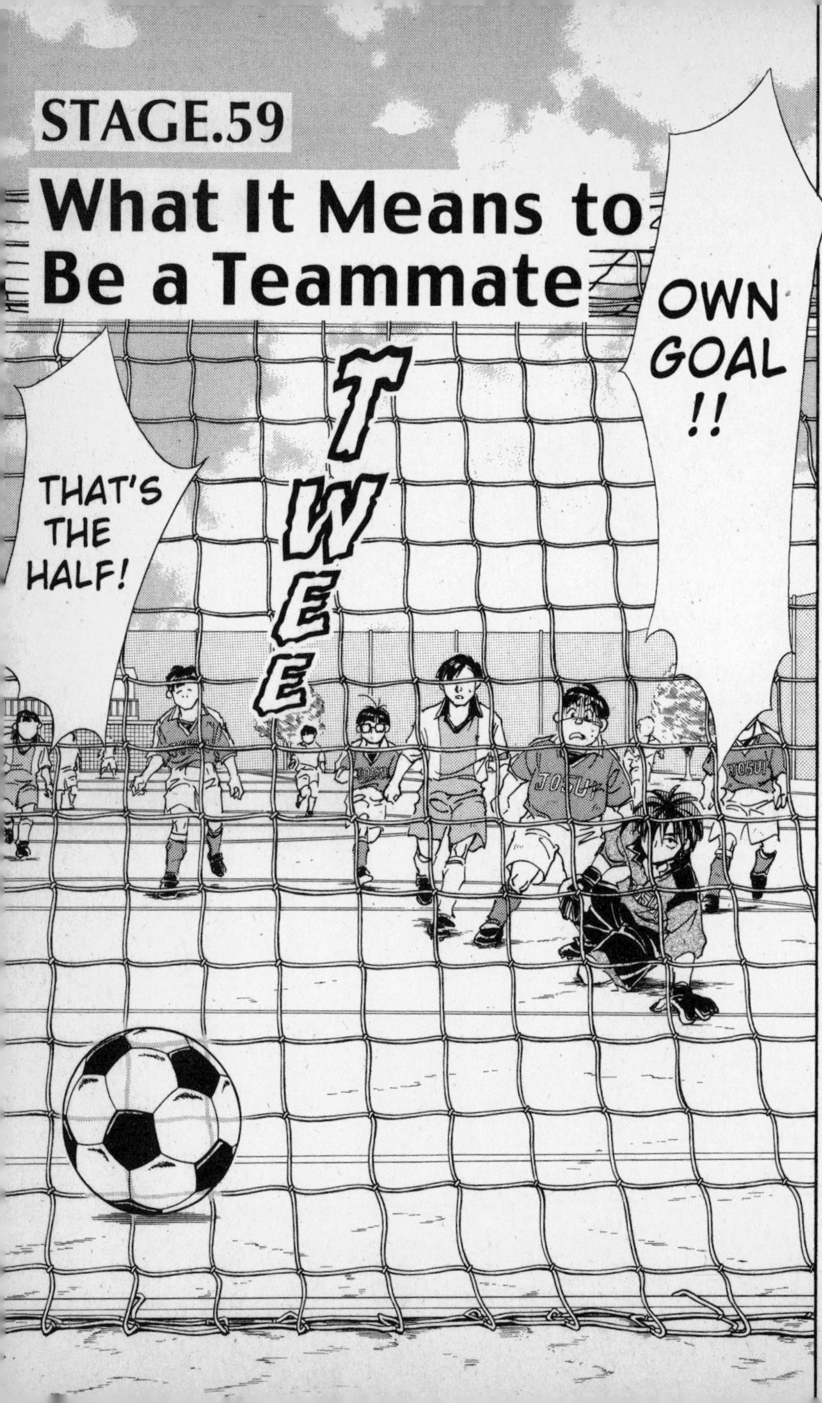
OWN GOAL !!
TWEEE
THAT'S THE HALF!

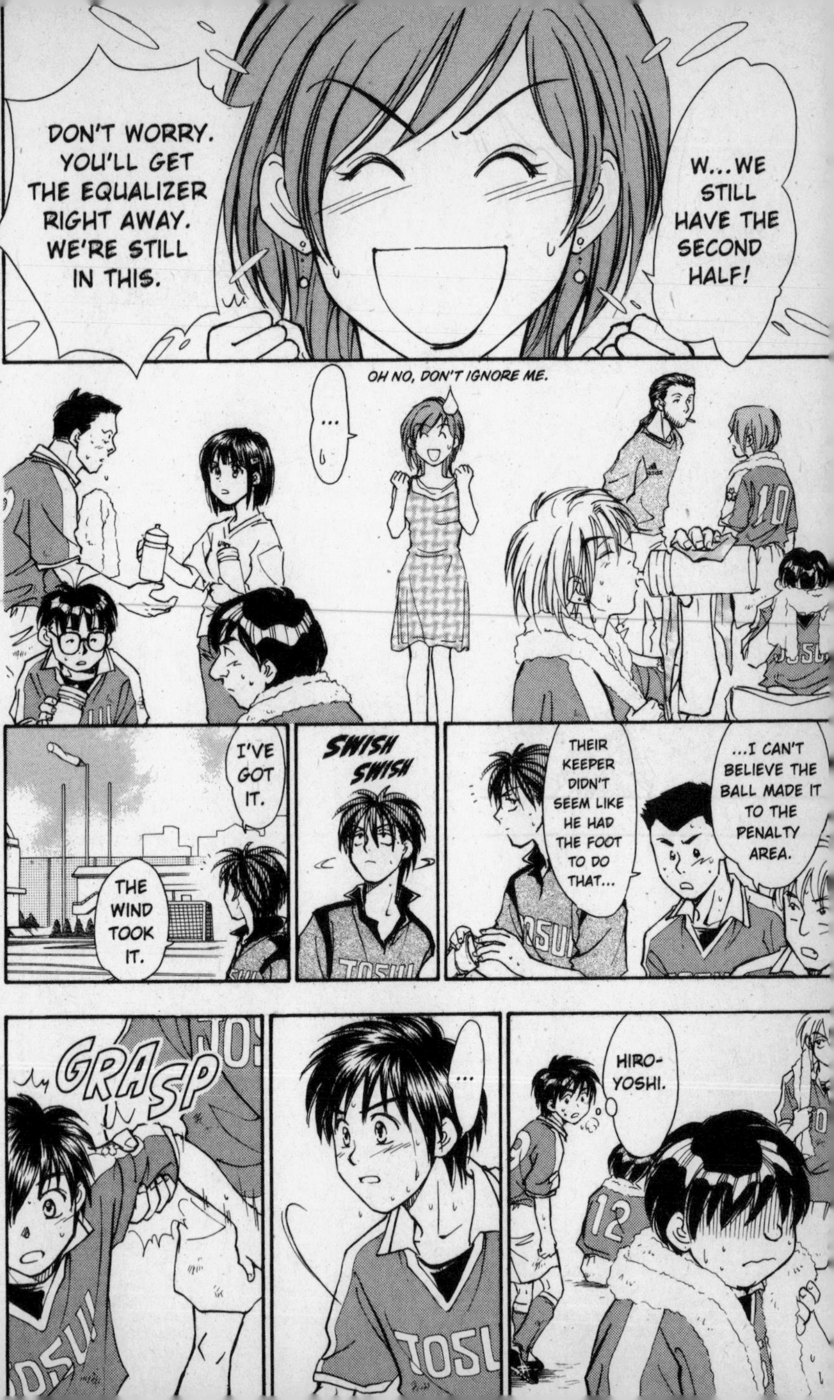
W...WE STILL HAVE THE SECOND HALF!
DON'T WORRY. YOU'LL GET THE EQUALIZER RIGHT AWAY. WE'RE STILL IN THIS.
...
OH NO, DON'T IGNORE ME.
...I CAN'T BELIEVE THE BALL MADE IT TO THE PENALTY AREA.
THEIR KEEPER DIDN'T SEEM LIKE HE HAD THE FOOT TO DO THAT...
SWISH SWISH
I'VE GOT IT.
THE WIND TOOK IT.
HIRO-YOSHI.
...
GRASP

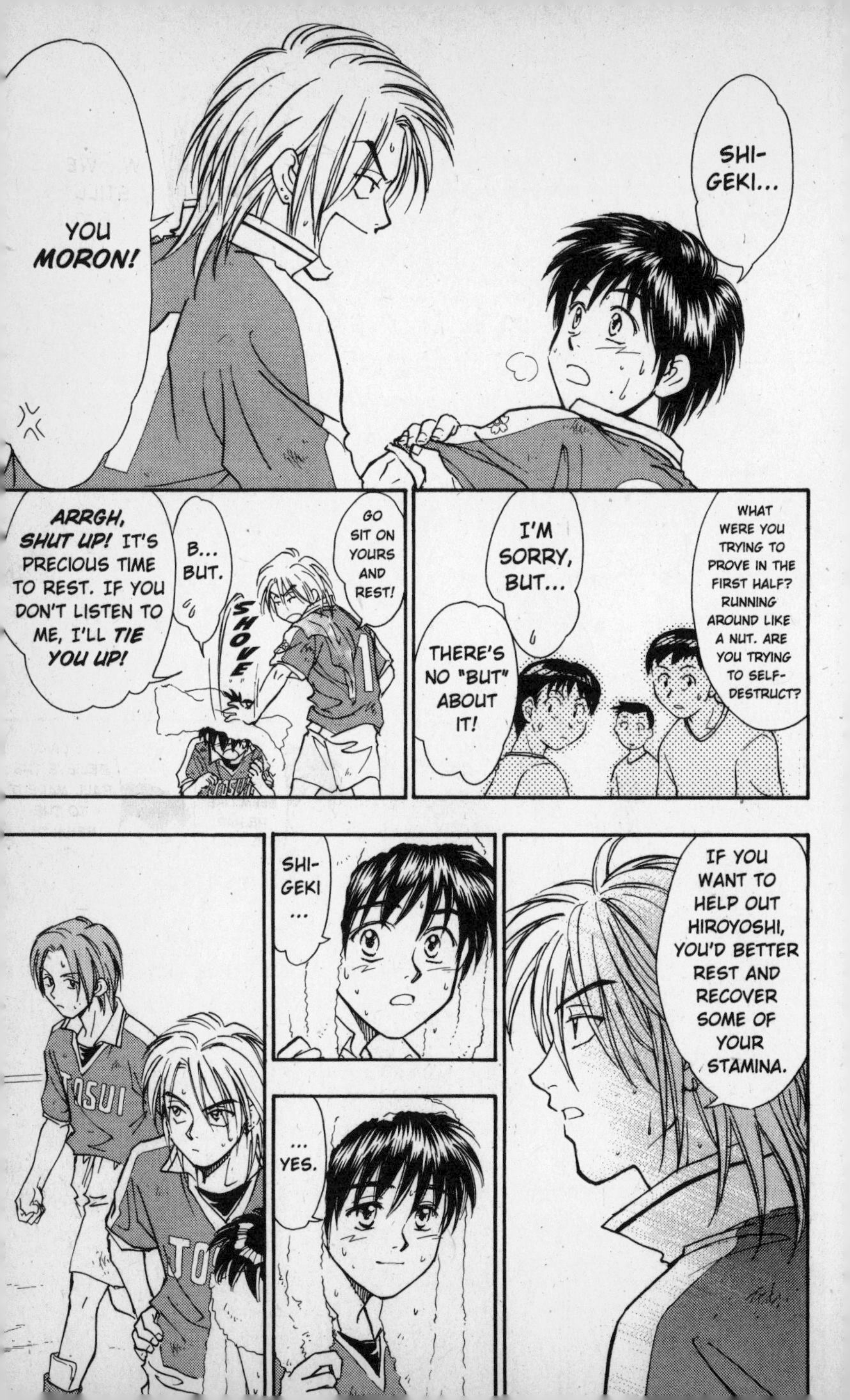
SHI-GEKI...
YOU MORON!
WHAT WERE YOU TRYING TO PROVE IN THE FIRST HALF? RUNNING AROUND LIKE A NUT. ARE YOU TRYING TO SELF-DESTRUCT?
I'M SORRY, BUT...
THERE'S NO "BUT" ABOUT IT!
GO SIT ON YOURS AND REST!
SHOVE
B... BUT.
ARRGH, SHUT UP! IT'S PRECIOUS TIME TO REST. IF YOU DON'T LISTEN TO ME, I'LL TIE YOU UP!
IF YOU WANT TO HELP OUT HIROYOSHI, YOU'D BETTER REST AND RECOVER SOME OF YOUR STAMINA.
SHI-GEKI ...
... YES.

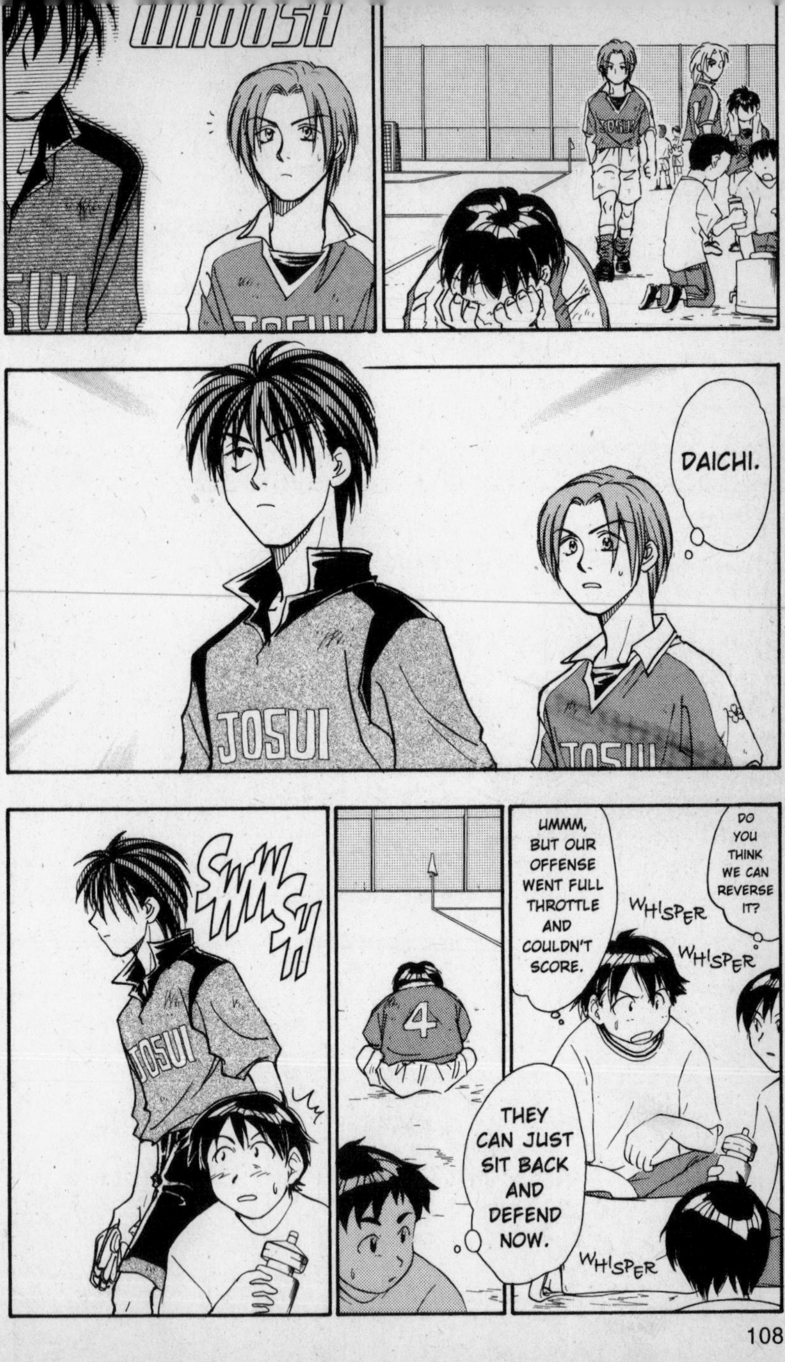
WHOOSH
DAICHI.
DO YOU THINK WE CAN REVERSE IT?
WHISPER
UMMM, BUT OUR OFFENSE WENT FULL THROTTLE AND COULDN'T SCORE.
WHISPER
THEY CAN JUST SIT BACK AND DEFEND NOW.
WHISPER
SWISH

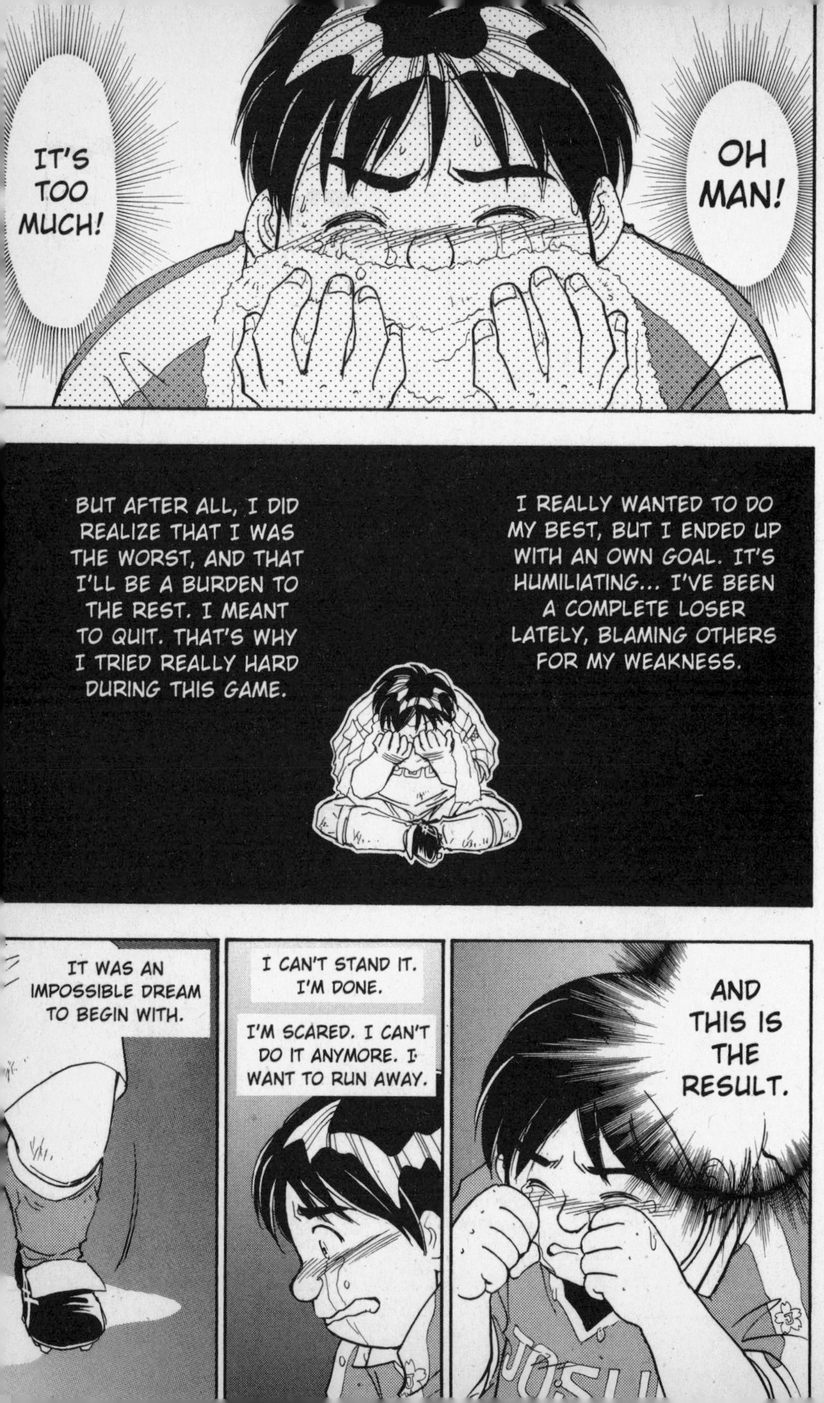

OH MAN!
IT'S TOO MUCH!
I REALLY WANTED TO DO MY BEST, BUT I ENDED UP WITH AN OWN GOAL. IT'S HUMILIATING... I'VE BEEN A COMPLETE LOSER LATELY, BLAMING OTHERS FOR MY WEAKNESS.
BUT AFTER ALL, I DID REALIZE THAT I WAS THE WORST, AND THAT I'LL BE A BURDEN TO THE REST. I MEANT TO QUIT. THAT'S WHY I TRIED REALLY HARD DURING THIS GAME.
AND THIS IS THE RESULT.
I CAN'T STAND IT. I'M DONE.
I'M SCARED. I CAN'T DO IT ANYMORE. I WANT TO RUN AWAY.
IT WAS AN IMPOSSIBLE DREAM TO BEGIN WITH.
JOSU

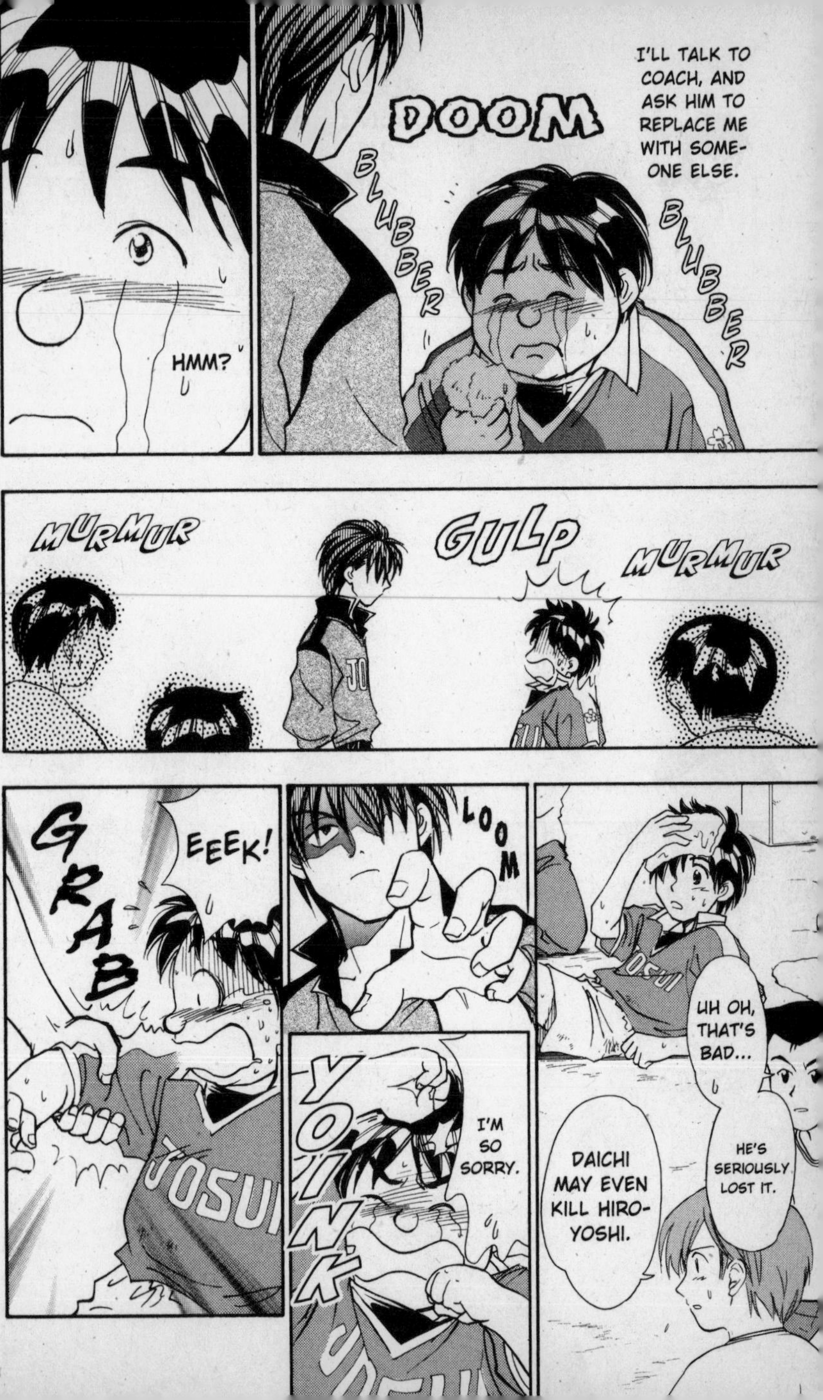

I'LL TALK TO COACH, AND ASK HIM TO REPLACE ME WITH SOME-ONE ELSE.
DOOM
BLUBBER
BLUBBER
HMM?
MURMUR
GULP
MURMUR
UH OH, THAT'S BAD...
HE'S SERIOUSLY LOST IT.
DAICHI MAY EVEN KILL HIRO-YOSHI.
LOOM
YOINK
I'M SO SORRY.
GRAB
EEEK!

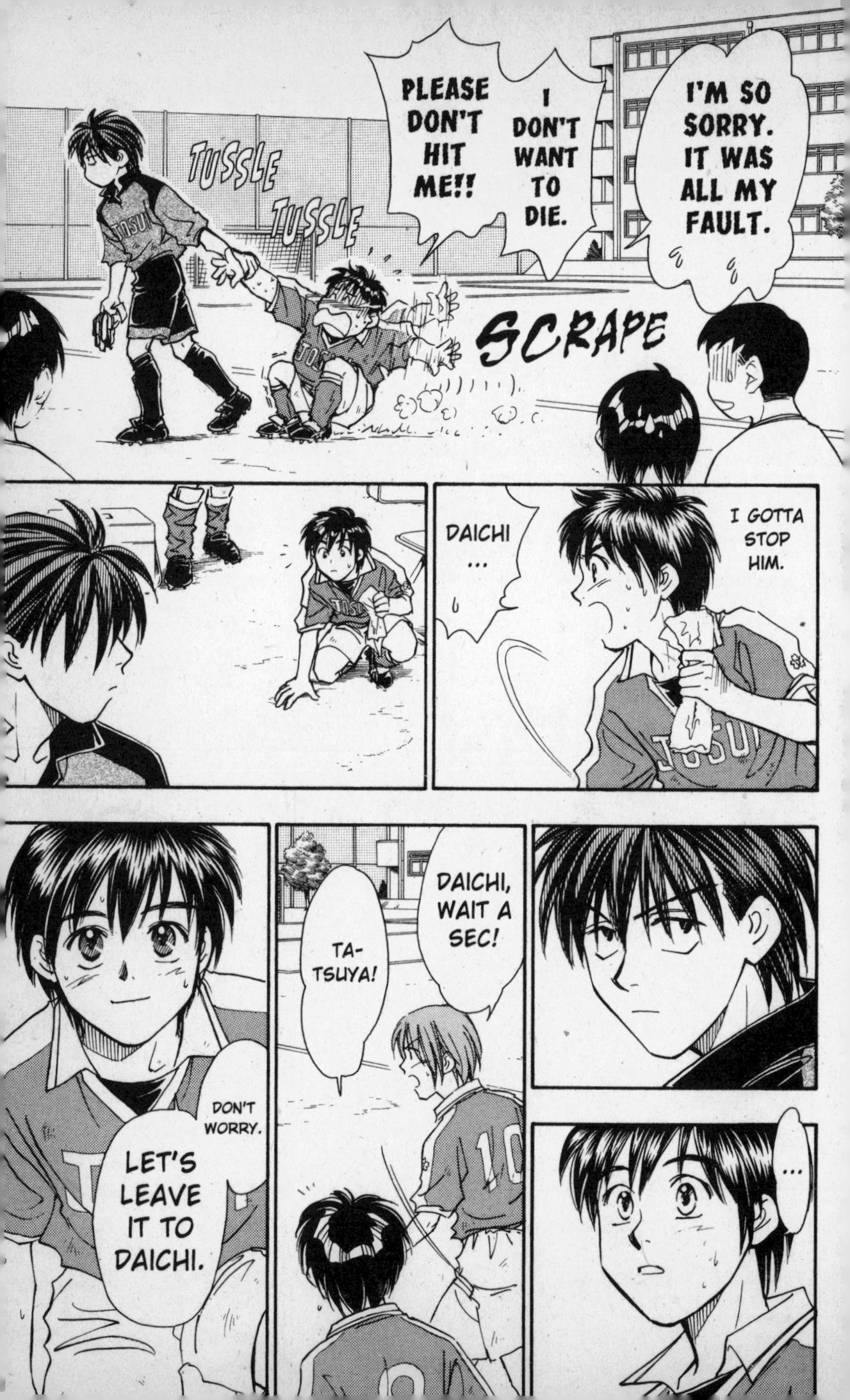
I'M SO SORRY. IT WAS ALL MY FAULT.
I DON'T WANT TO DIE.
PLEASE DON'T HIT ME!!
SCRAPE
TUSSLE
TUSSLE
I GOTTA STOP HIM.
DAICHI ...
...
DAICHI, WAIT A SEC!
TA-TSUYA!
DON'T WORRY.
LET'S LEAVE IT TO DAICHI.

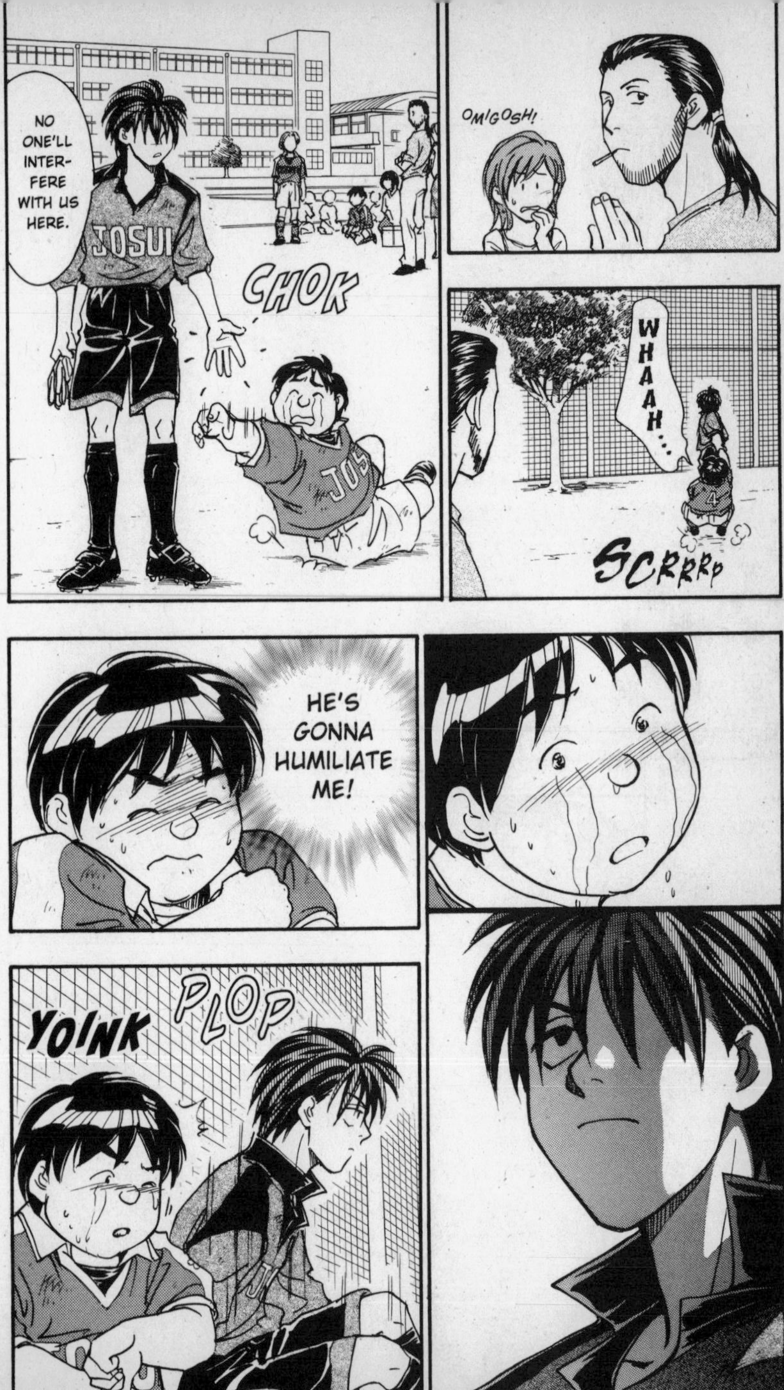
OMIGOSH!
WHAAAH...
SCRRRP
NO ONE'LL INTERFERE WITH US HERE.
CHOK
HE'S GONNA HUMILIATE ME!
PLOP
YOINK

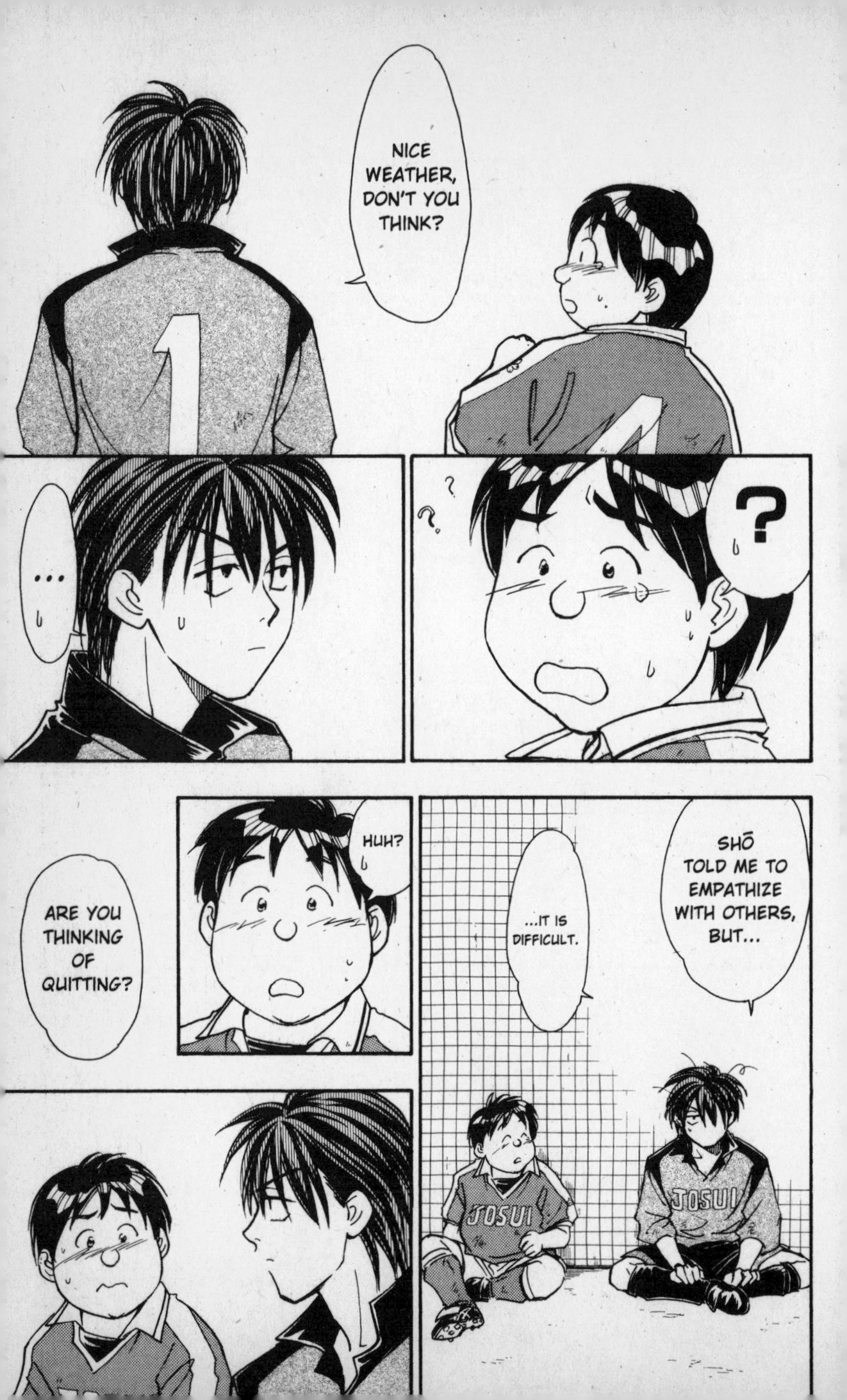
NICE WEATHER, DON'T YOU THINK?
?
...
SHŌ TOLD ME TO EMPATHIZE WITH OTHERS, BUT...
...IT IS DIFFICULT.
JOSUI
JOSUI
HUH?
ARE YOU THINKING OF QUITTING?

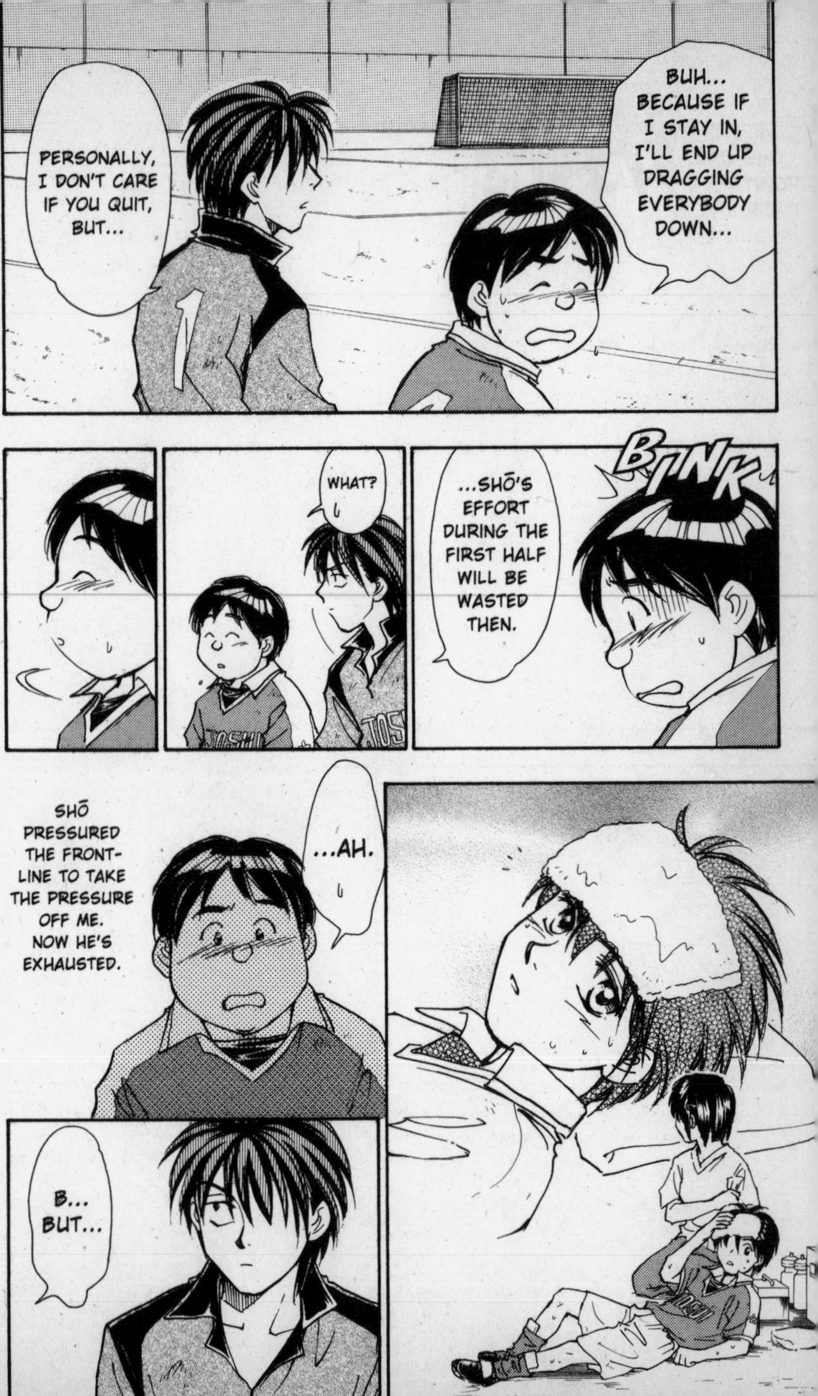
BUH... BECAUSE IF I STAY IN, I'LL END UP DRAGGING EVERYBODY DOWN...
PERSONALLY, I DON'T CARE IF YOU QUIT, BUT...
BLINK
...SHŌ'S EFFORT DURING THE FIRST HALF WILL BE WASTED THEN.
WHAT?
...AH.
SHŌ PRESSURED THE FRONT-LINE TO TAKE THE PRESSURE OFF ME. NOW HE'S EXHAUSTED.
B... BUT...

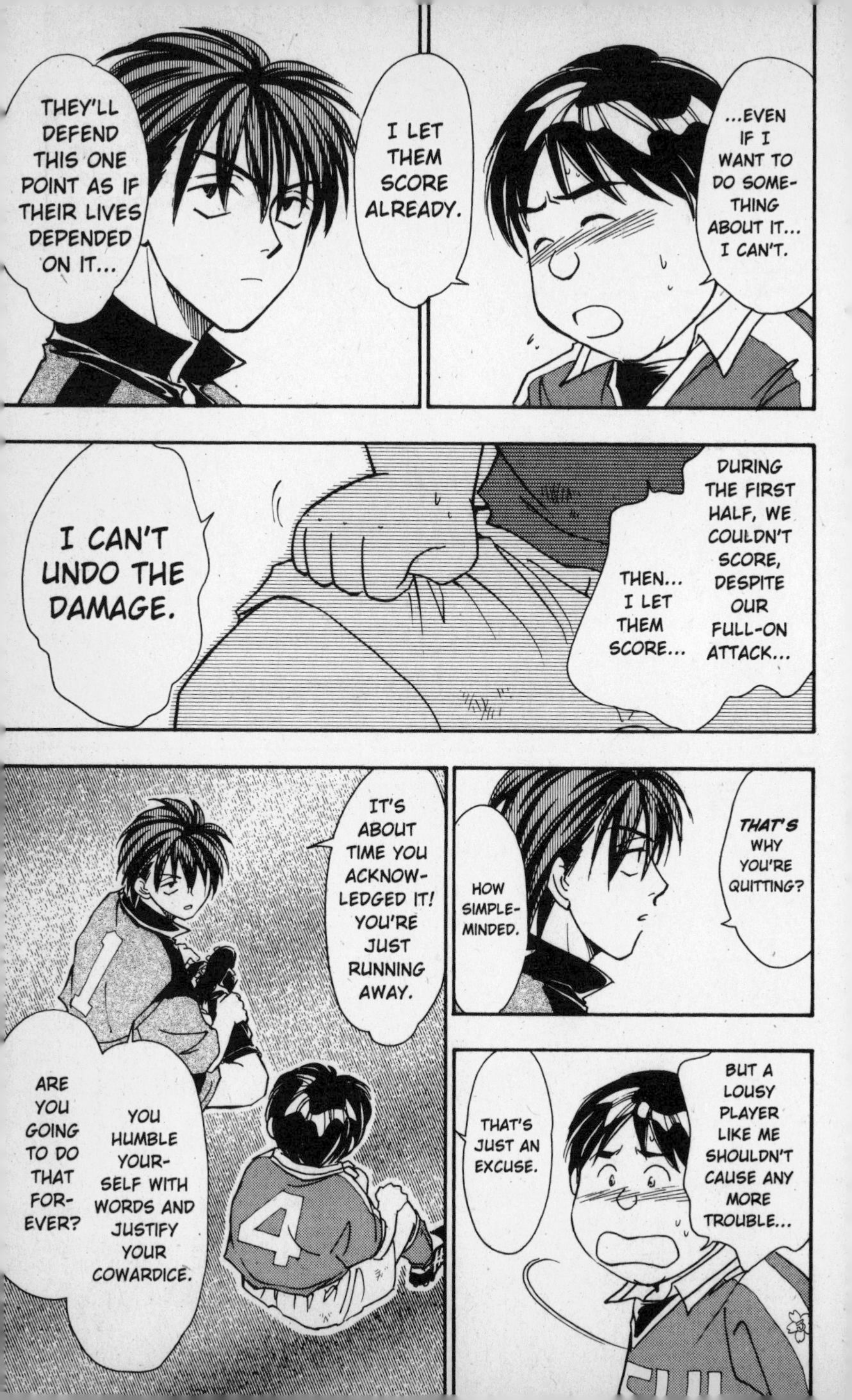
...EVEN IF I WANT TO DO SOMETHING ABOUT IT... I CAN'T.
I LET THEM SCORE ALREADY.
THEY'LL DEFEND THIS ONE POINT AS IF THEIR LIVES DEPENDED ON IT...
DURING THE FIRST HALF, WE COULDN'T SCORE, DESPITE OUR FULL-ON ATTACK...
THEN... I LET THEM SCORE...
I CAN'T UNDO THE DAMAGE.
THAT'S WHY YOU'RE QUITTING?
HOW SIMPLE-MINDED.
BUT A LOUSY PLAYER LIKE ME SHOULDN'T CAUSE ANY MORE TROUBLE...
THAT'S JUST AN EXCUSE.
IT'S ABOUT TIME YOU ACKNOWLEDGED IT! YOU'RE JUST RUNNING AWAY.
YOU HUMBLE YOURSELF WITH WORDS AND JUSTIFY YOUR COWARDICE.
ARE YOU GOING TO DO THAT FOREVER?

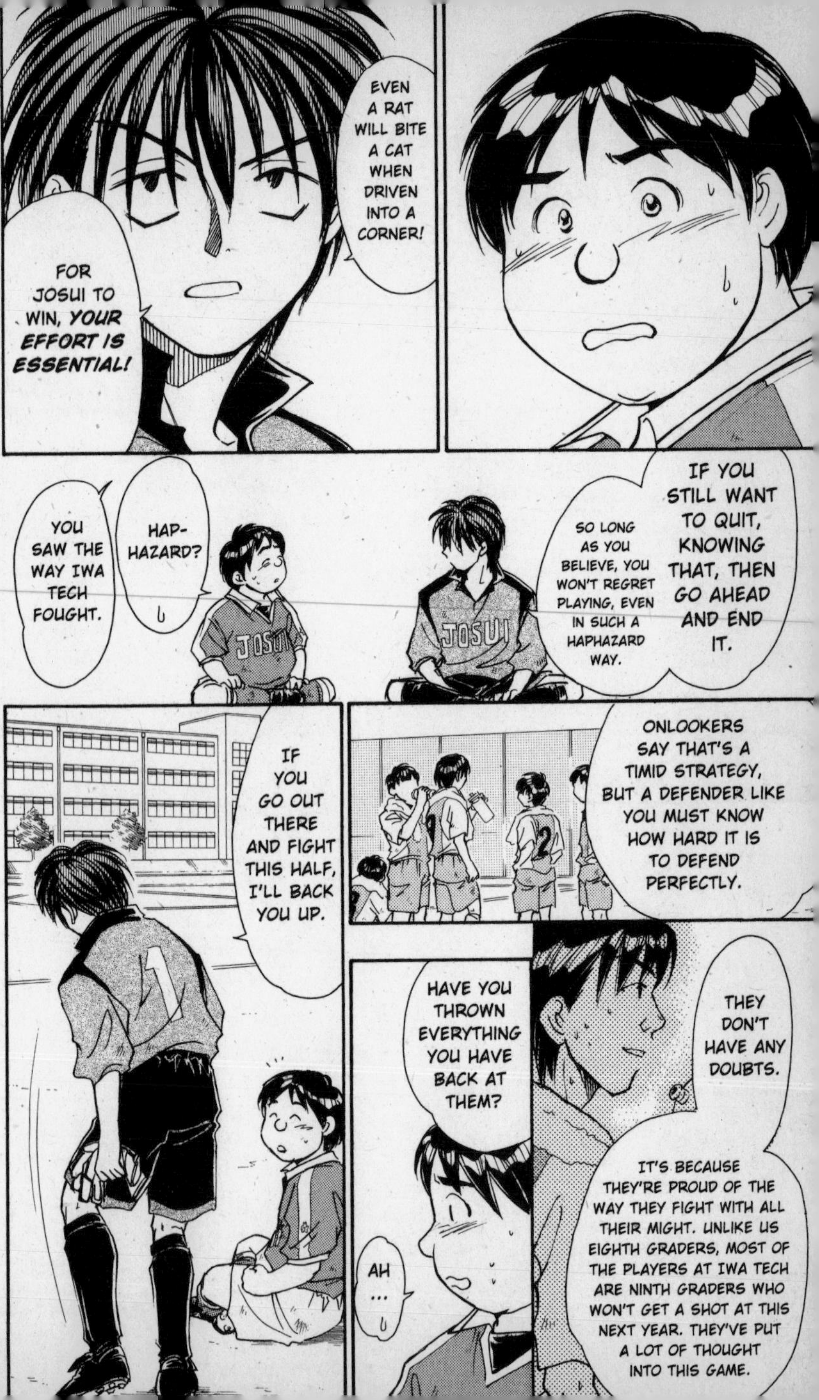
EVEN A RAT WILL BITE A CAT WHEN DRIVEN INTO A CORNER!
FOR JOSUI TO WIN, *YOUR EFFORT IS ESSENTIAL!*
IF YOU STILL WANT TO QUIT, KNOWING THAT, THEN GO AHEAD AND END IT.
SO LONG AS YOU BELIEVE, YOU WON'T REGRET PLAYING, EVEN IN SUCH A HAPHAZARD WAY.
JOSUI
JOSUI
HAP-HAZARD?
YOU SAW THE WAY IWA TECH FOUGHT.
ONLOOKERS SAY THAT'S A TIMID STRATEGY, BUT A DEFENDER LIKE YOU MUST KNOW HOW HARD IT IS TO DEFEND PERFECTLY.
THEY DON'T HAVE ANY DOUBTS.
IT'S BECAUSE THEY'RE PROUD OF THE WAY THEY FIGHT WITH ALL THEIR MIGHT. UNLIKE US EIGHTH GRADERS, MOST OF THE PLAYERS AT IWA TECH ARE NINTH GRADERS WHO WON'T GET A SHOT AT THIS NEXT YEAR. THEY'VE PUT A LOT OF THOUGHT INTO THIS GAME.
HAVE YOU THROWN EVERYTHING YOU HAVE BACK AT THEM?
AH ...
IF YOU GO OUT THERE AND FIGHT THIS HALF, I'LL BACK YOU UP.

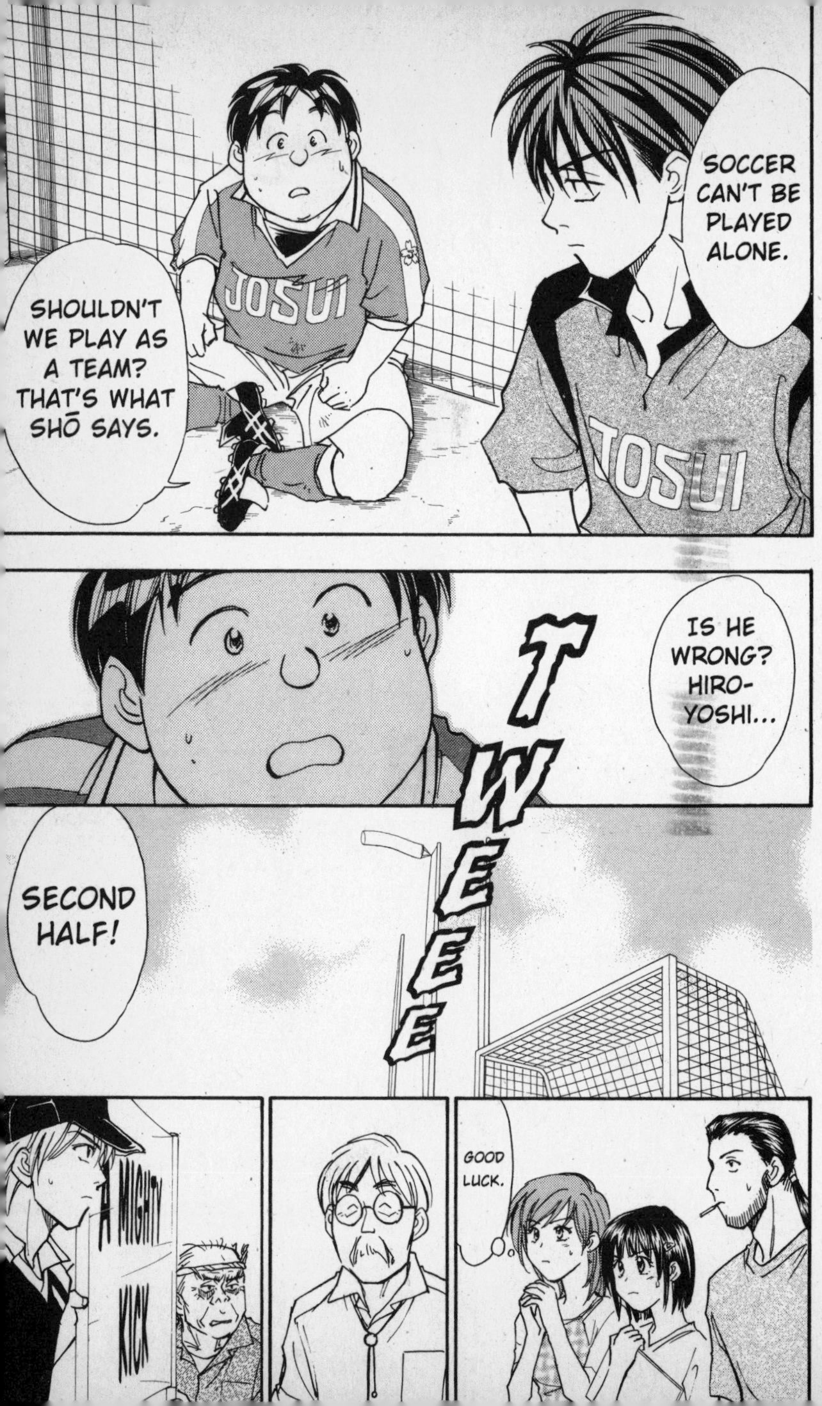

SOCCER CAN'T BE PLAYED ALONE.
SHOULDN'T WE PLAY AS A TEAM? THAT'S WHAT SHŌ SAYS.
IS HE WRONG? HIRO-YOSHI...
TWEEEE
SECOND HALF!
GOOD LUCK.
A MIGHTY KICK

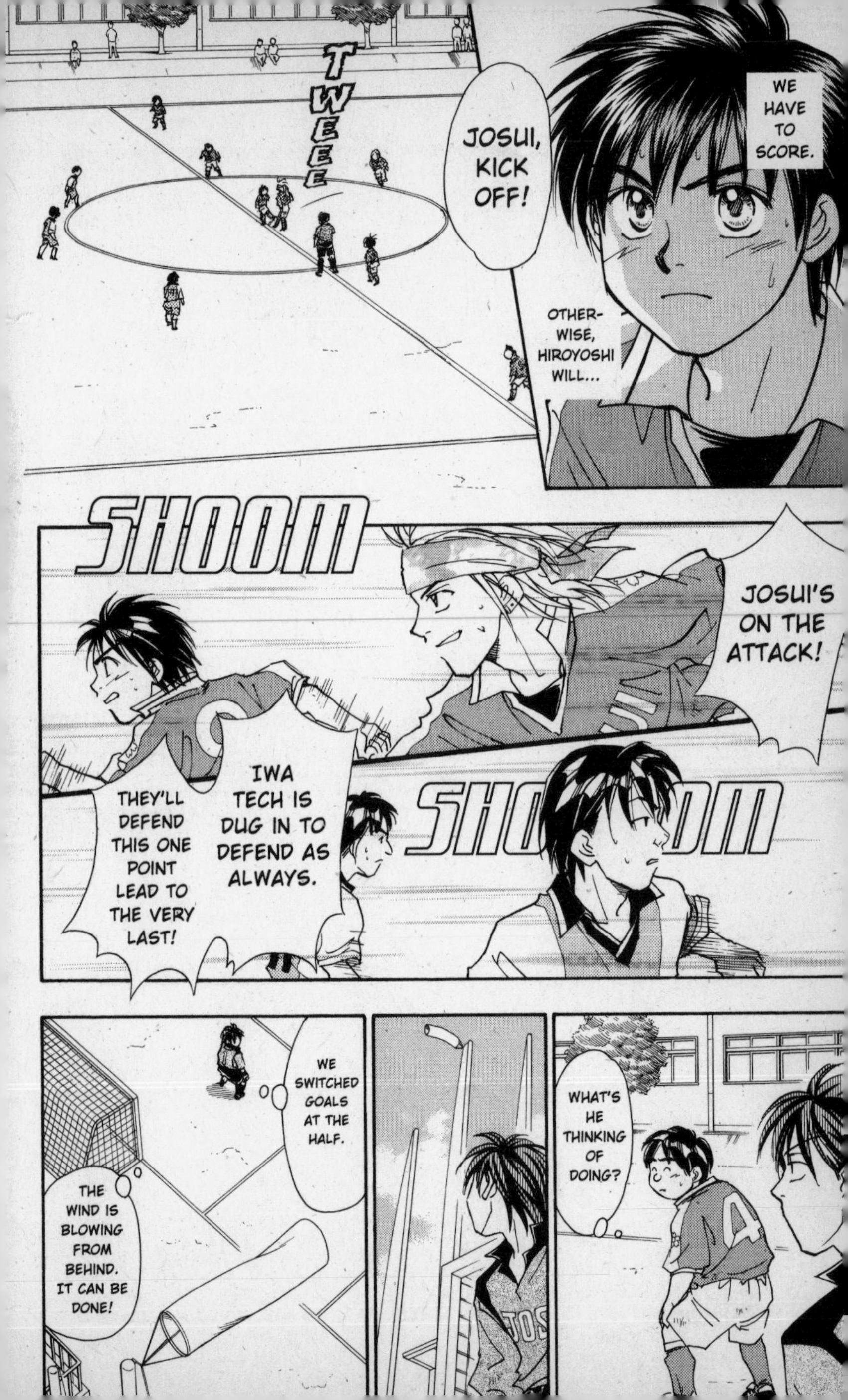
WE HAVE TO SCORE.
OTHER-WISE, HIROYOSHI WILL...
JOSUI, KICK OFF!
TWEEE
JOSUI'S ON THE ATTACK!
SHOOM
SHOOM
IWA TECH IS DUG IN TO DEFEND AS ALWAYS.
THEY'LL DEFEND THIS ONE POINT LEAD TO THE VERY LAST!
WHAT'S HE THINKING OF DOING?
WE SWITCHED GOALS AT THE HALF.
THE WIND IS BLOWING FROM BEHIND. IT CAN BE DONE!

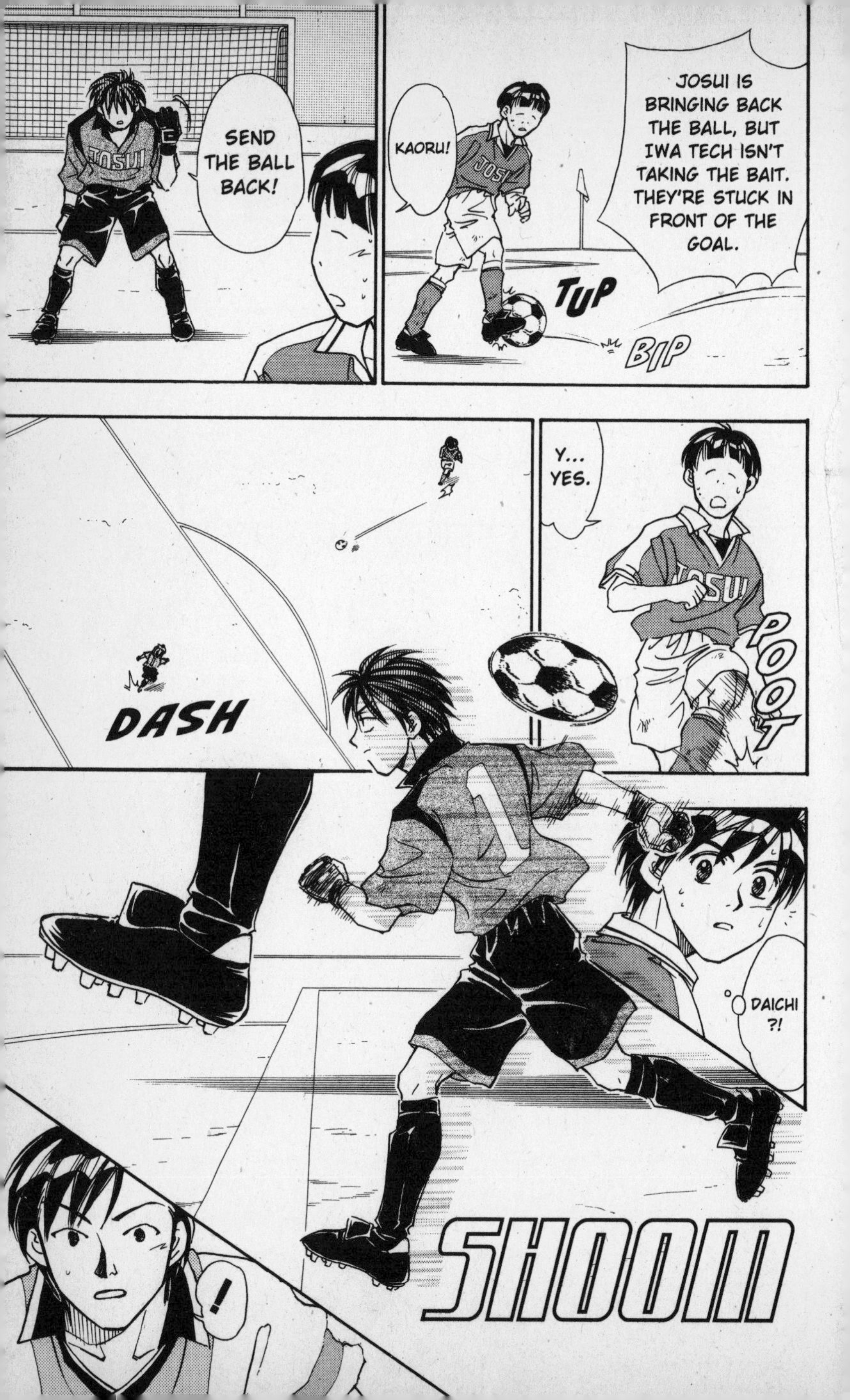
JOSUI IS BRINGING BACK THE BALL, BUT IWA TECH ISN'T TAKING THE BAIT. THEY'RE STUCK IN FRONT OF THE GOAL.
KAORU!
TUP
BIP
SEND THE BALL BACK!
Y... YES.
POOT
DASH
DAICHI ?!
SHOOM
!

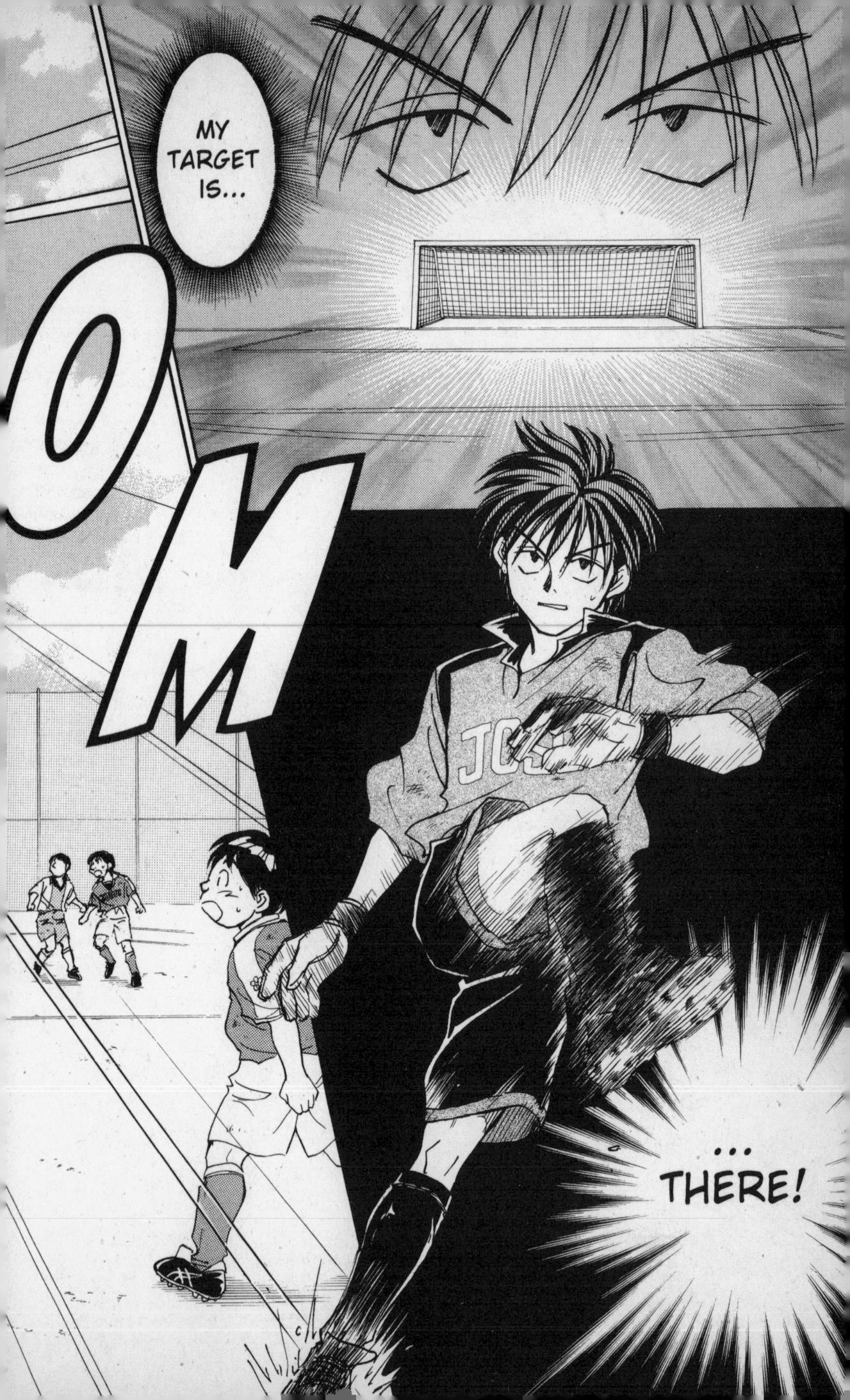
MY TARGET IS...
...THERE!
JOS

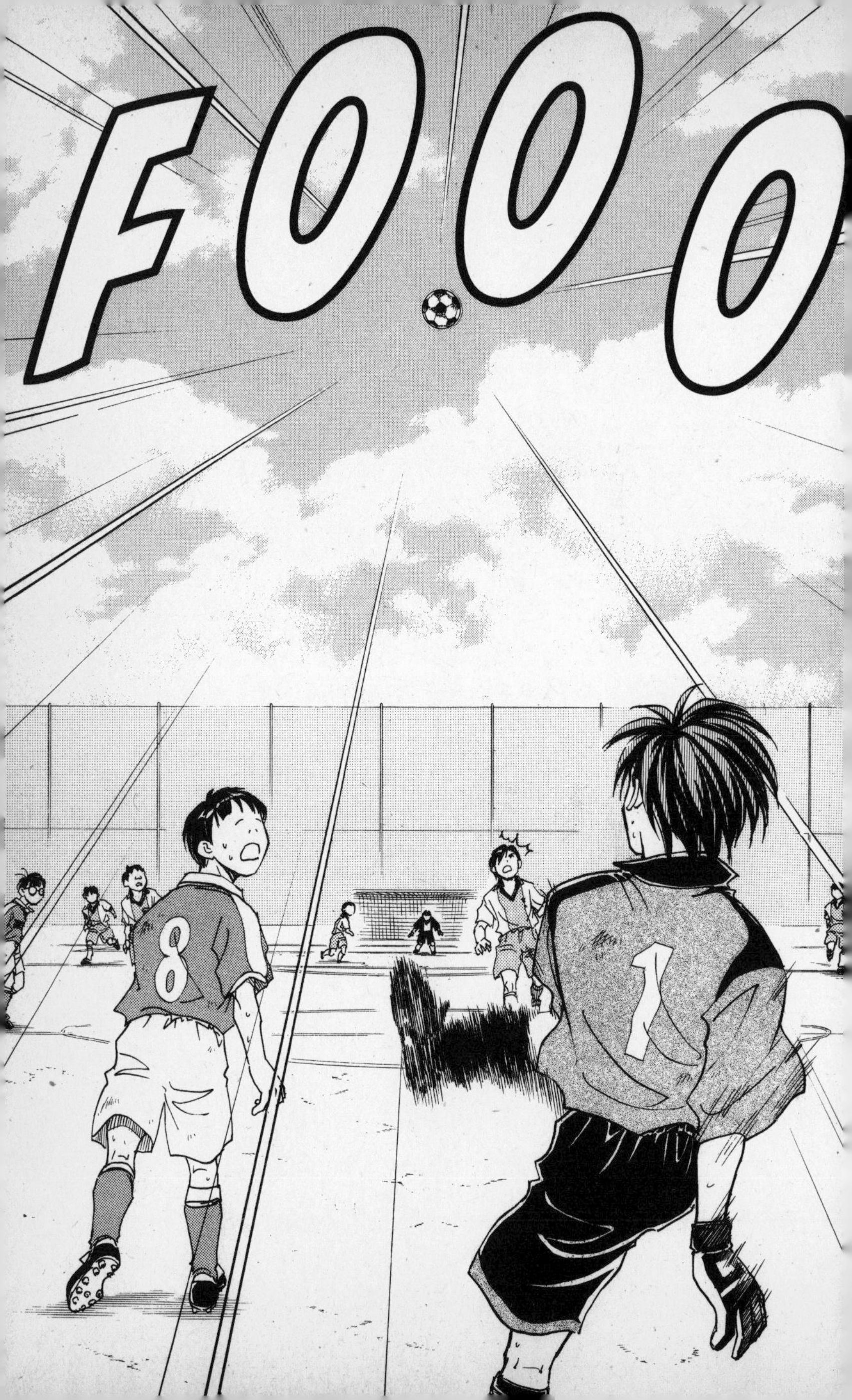
FOOO

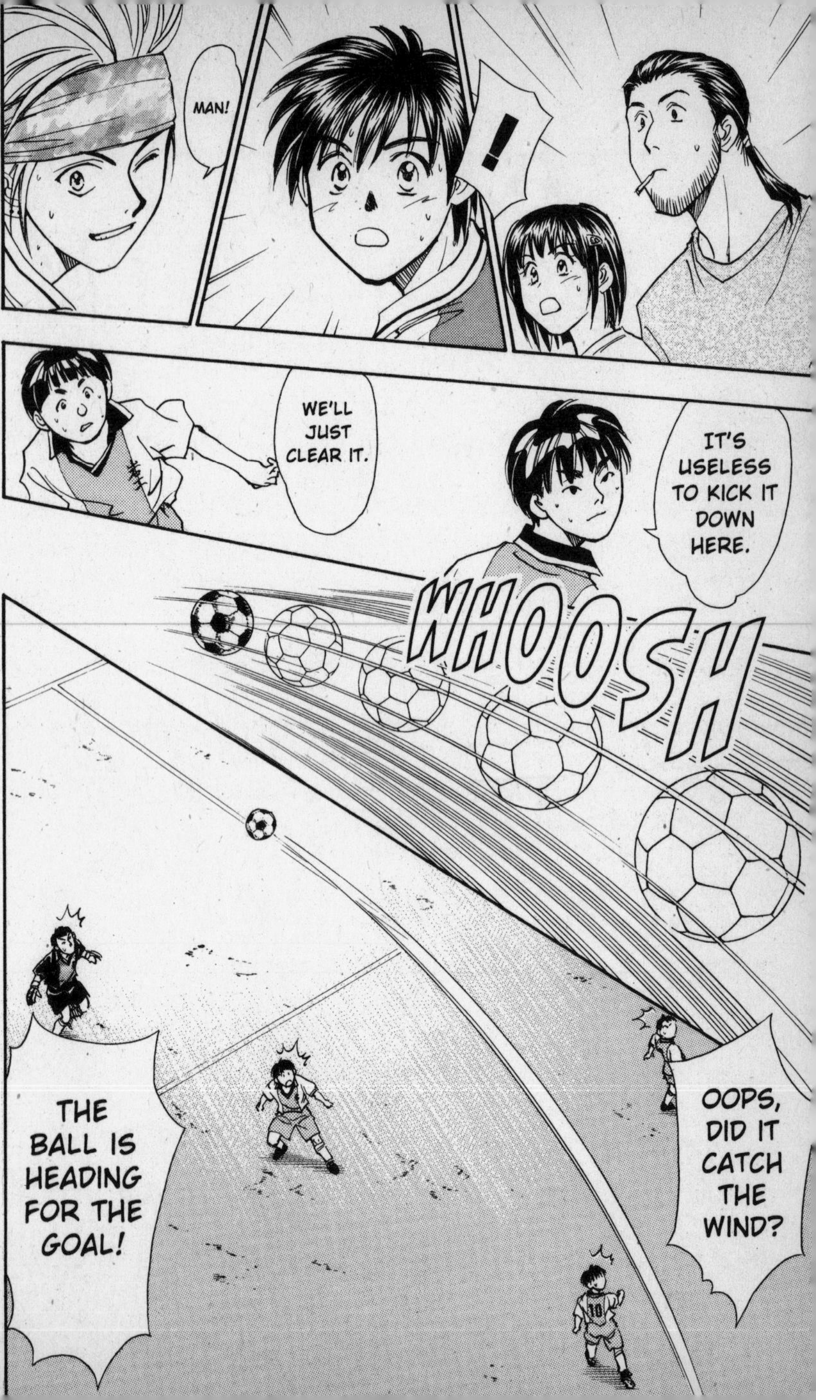
!
MAN!
IT'S USELESS TO KICK IT DOWN HERE.
WE'LL JUST CLEAR IT.
WHOOSH
OOPS, DID IT CATCH THE WIND?
THE BALL IS HEADING FOR THE GOAL!

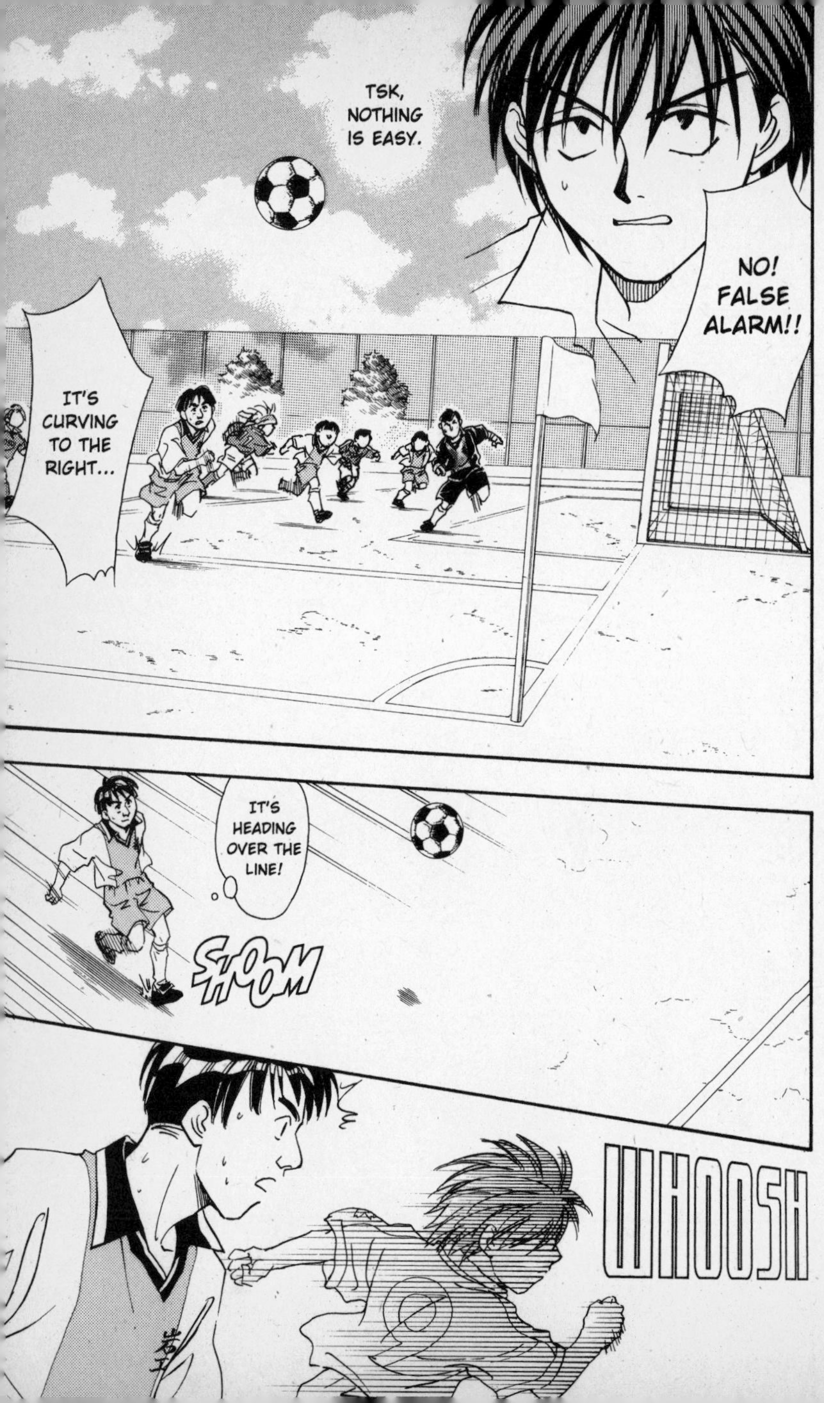
TSK, NOTHING IS EASY.
NO! FALSE ALARM!!
IT'S CURVING TO THE RIGHT...
IT'S HEADING OVER THE LINE!
SHOOM
WHOOSH

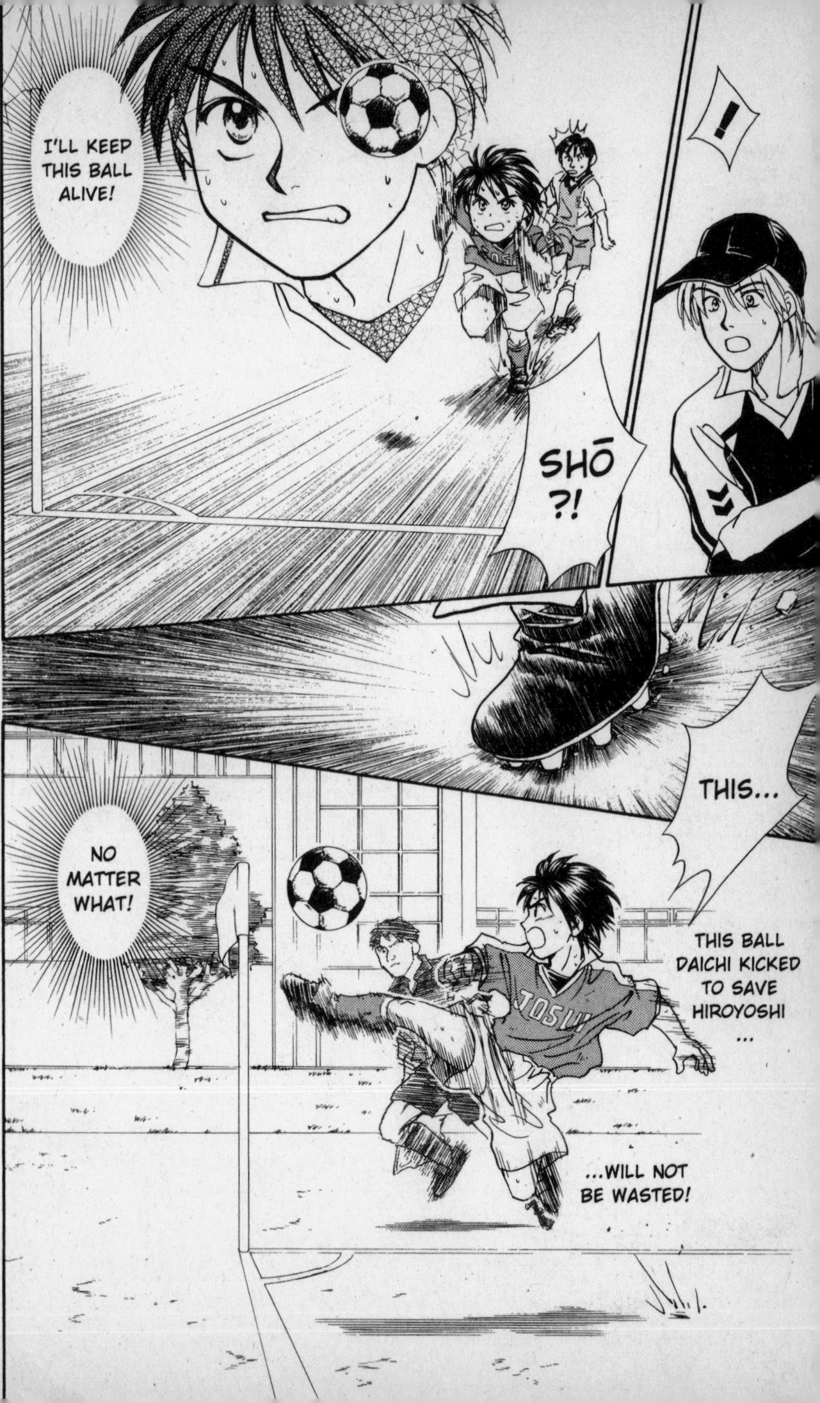
!
SHŌ ?!
I'LL KEEP THIS BALL ALIVE!
THIS...
THIS BALL DAICHI KICKED TO SAVE HIROYOSHI ...
...WILL NOT BE WASTED!
NO MATTER WHAT!

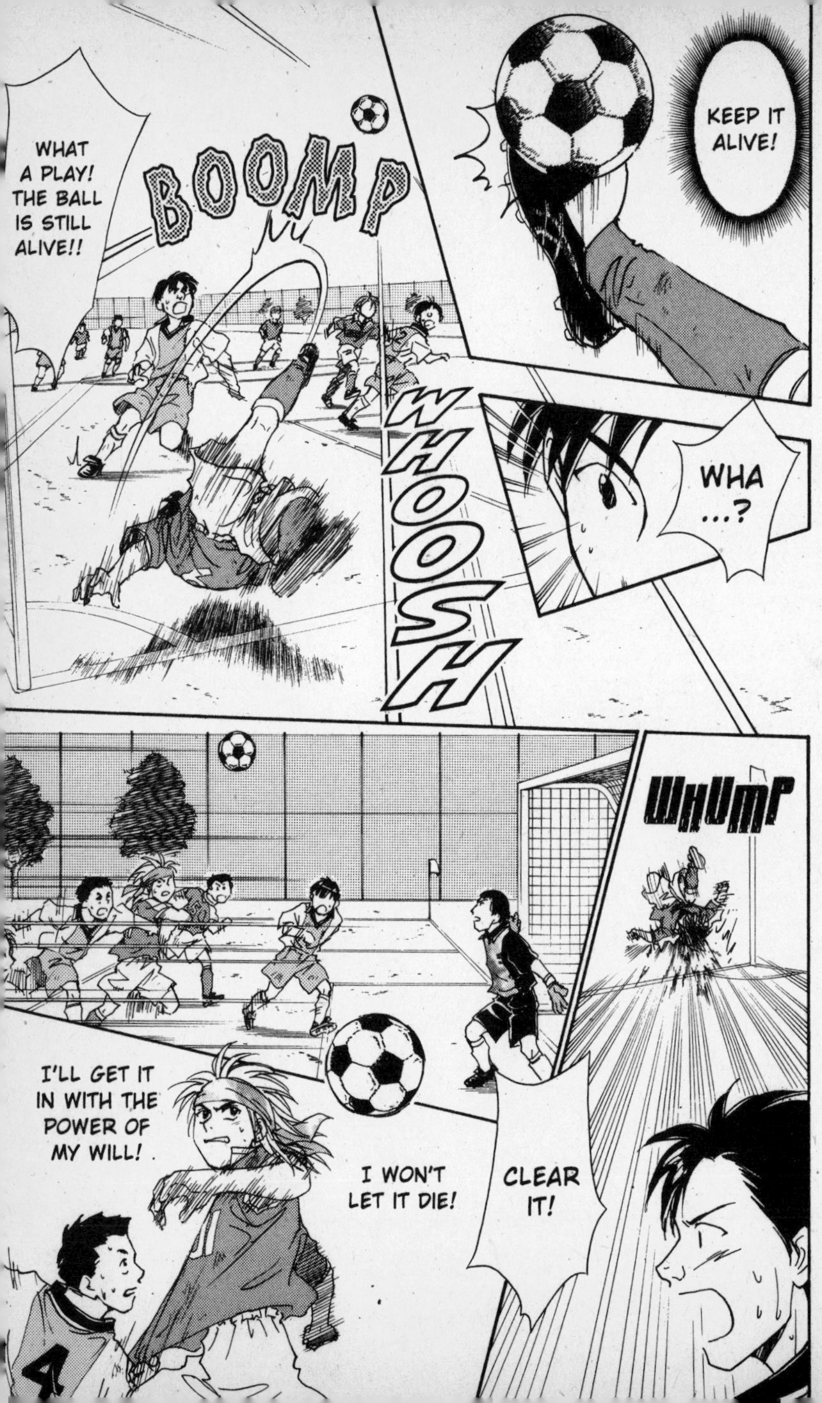
KEEP IT ALIVE!
WHA ...?
BOOMP
WHAT A PLAY! THE BALL IS STILL ALIVE!!
WHOOSH
WHUMP
CLEAR IT!
I WON'T LET IT DIE!
I'LL GET IT IN WITH THE POWER OF MY WILL!

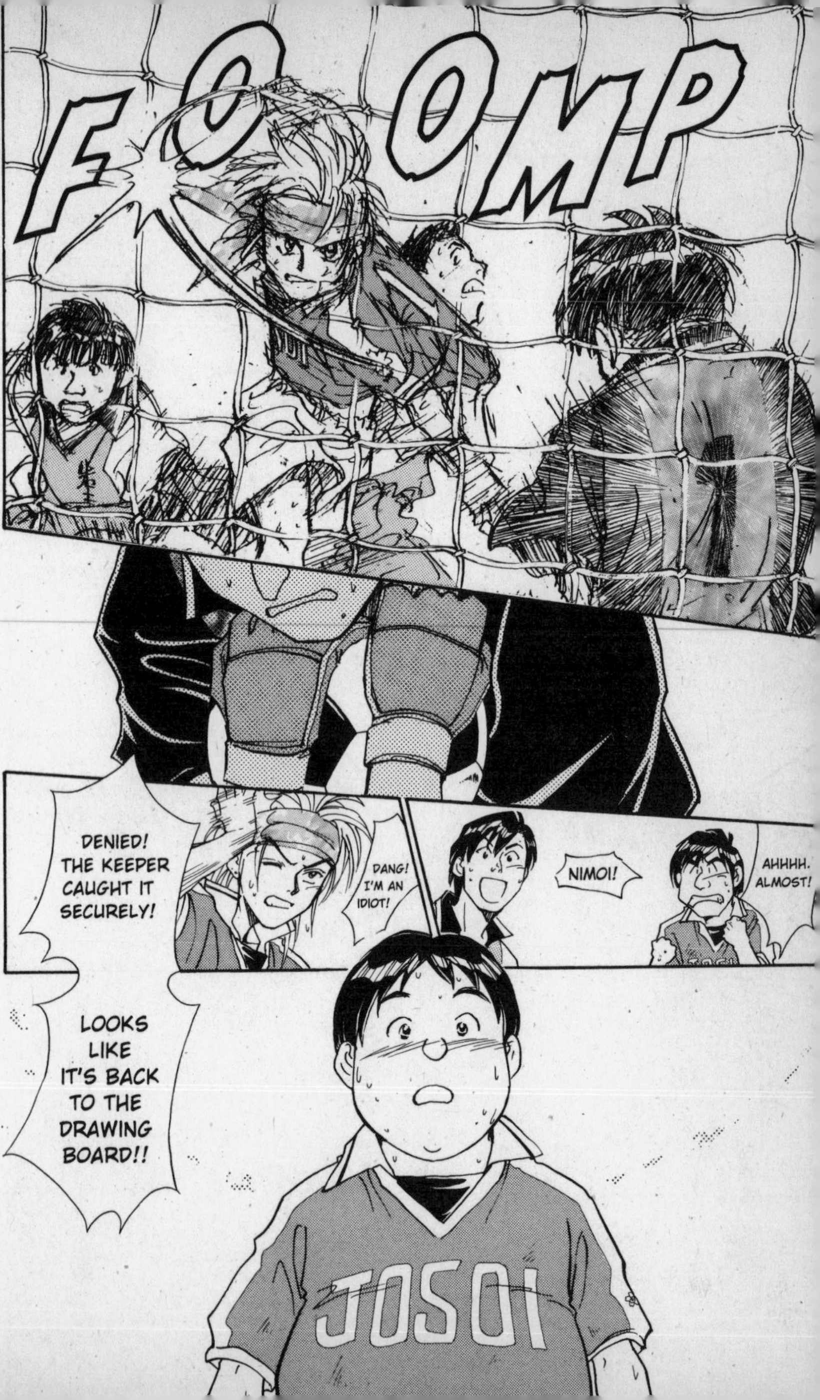
FOOMP
AHHHH. ALMOST!
NIMOI!
DANG! I'M AN IDIOT!
DENIED! THE KEEPER CAUGHT IT SECURELY!
LOOKS LIKE IT'S BACK TO THE DRAWING BOARD!!
JOSOI

STAGE.60 On Happiness

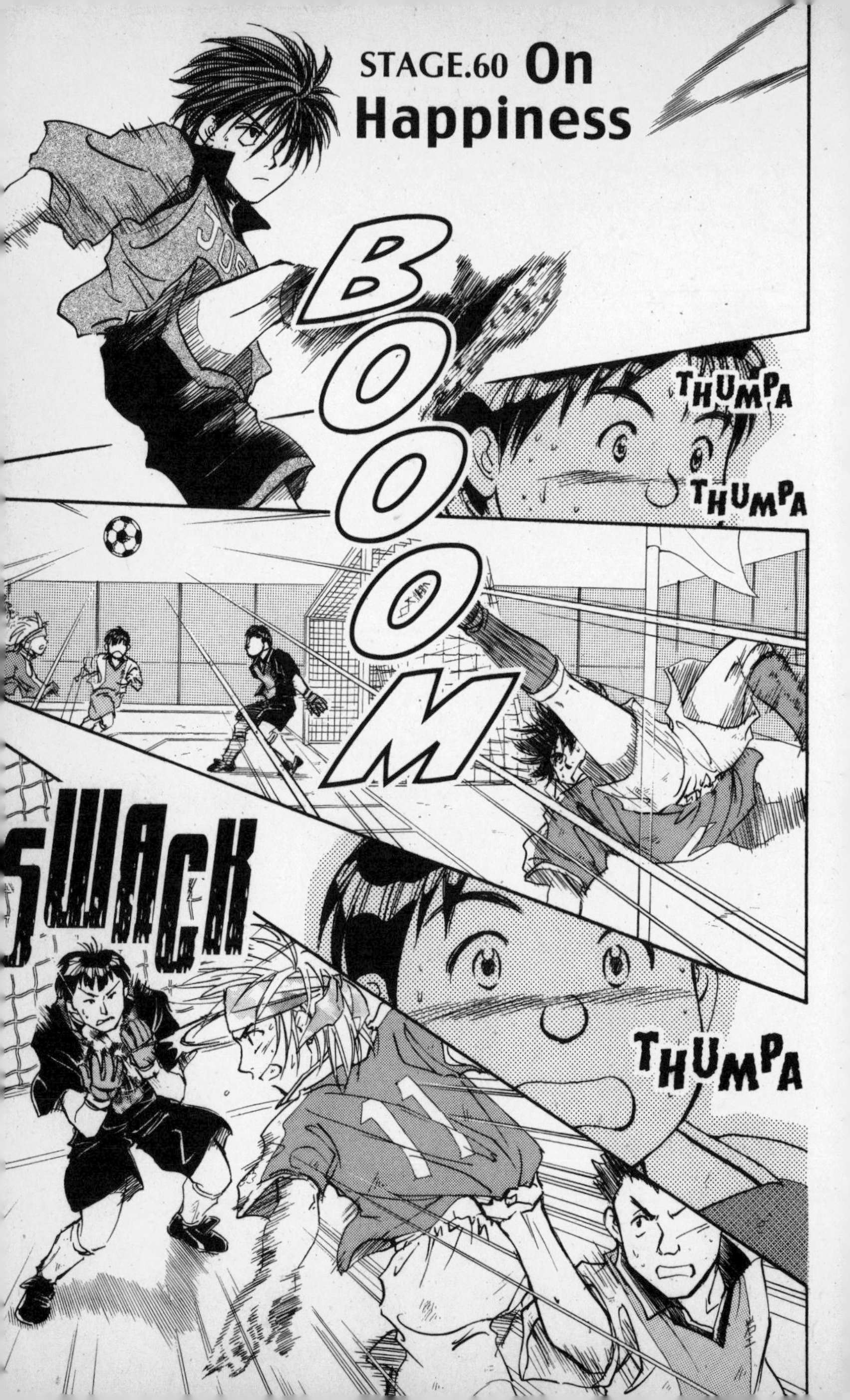
BOOOOM
THUMPA
THUMPA
THUMPA
SWACK

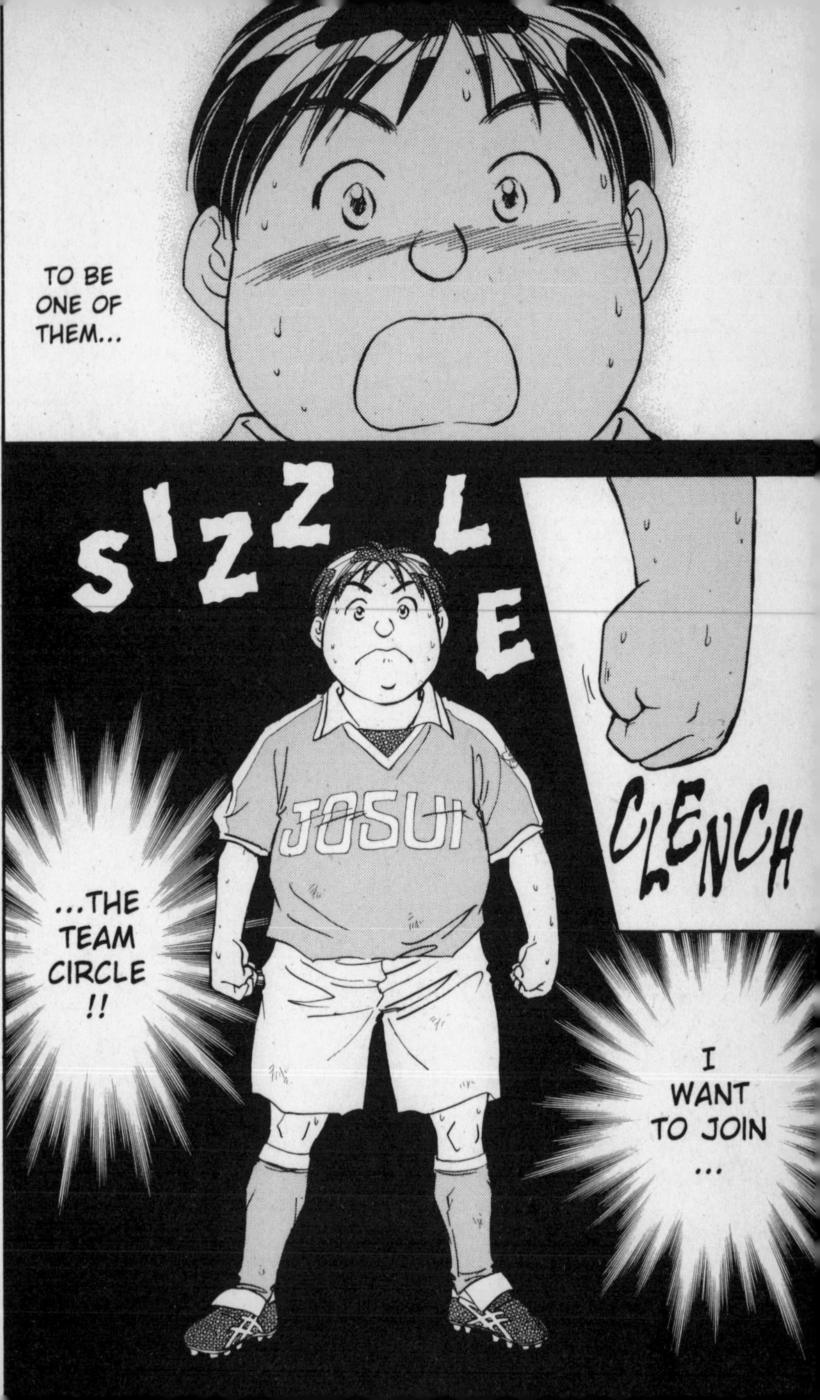
TO BE ONE OF THEM...
CLENCH
SIZZLE
I WANT TO JOIN ...
...THE TEAM CIRCLE !!
JOSUI

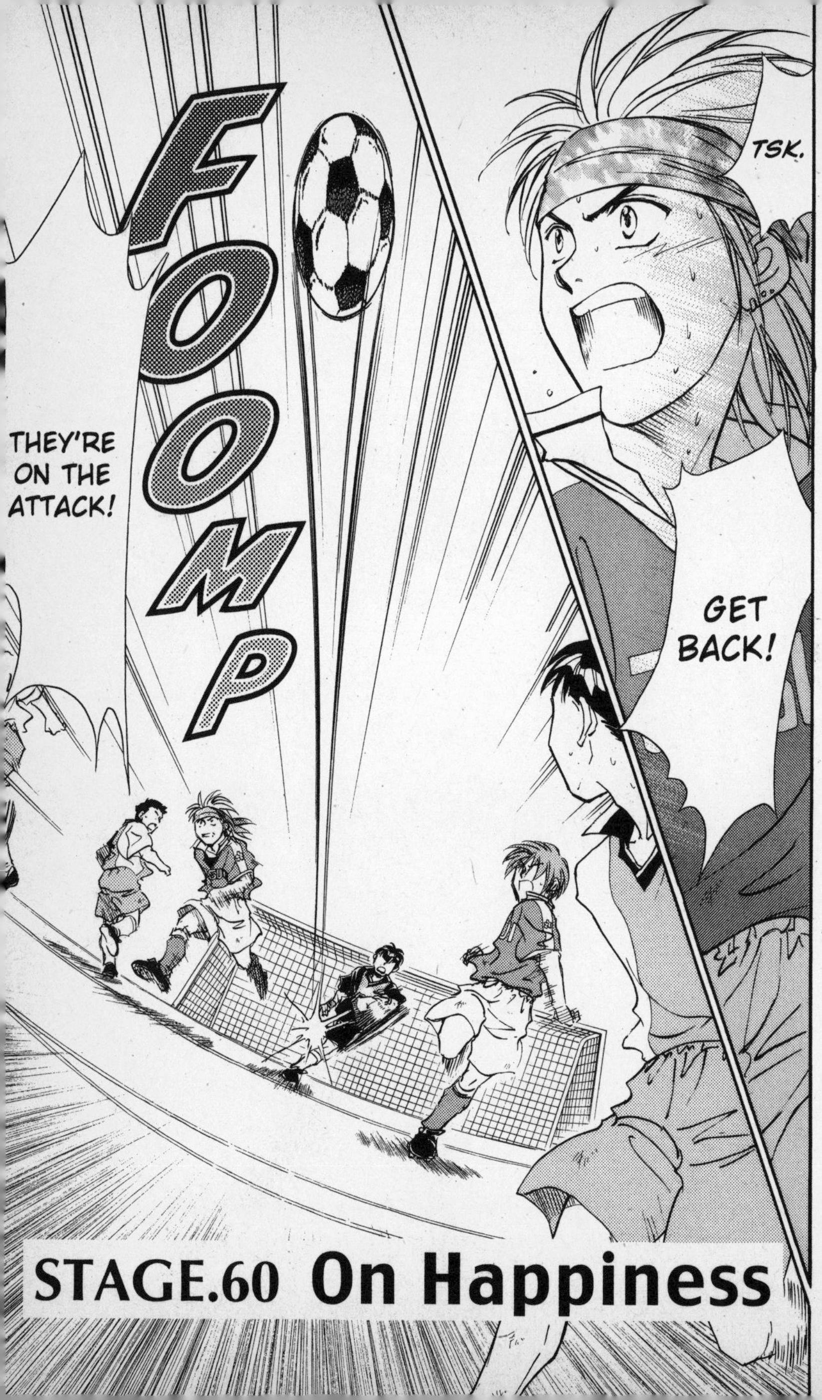
TSK.
GET BACK!
THEY'RE ON THE ATTACK!
FOOMP

STAGE.60 On Happiness

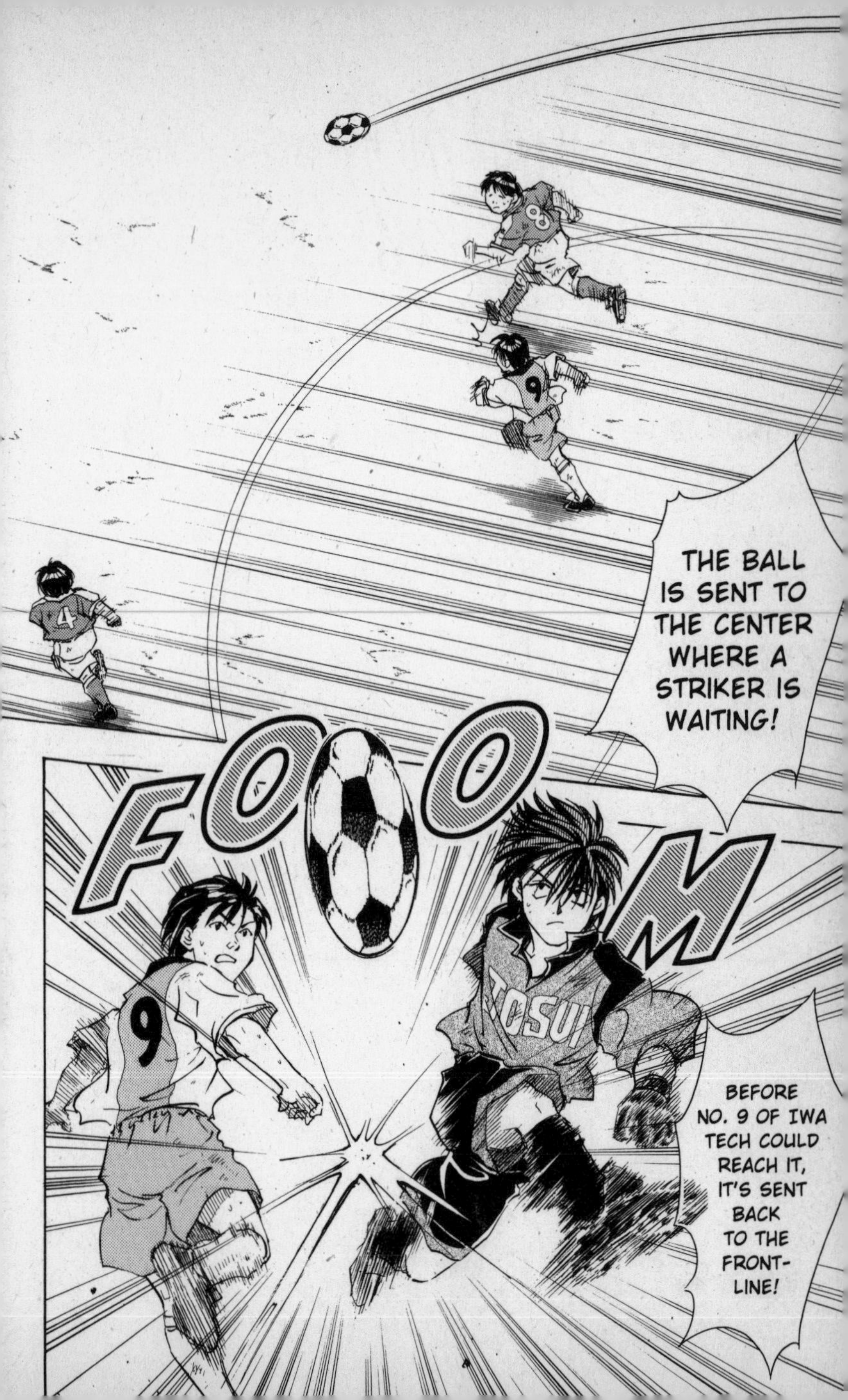
THE BALL IS SENT TO THE CENTER WHERE A STRIKER IS WAITING!
FOOOM
BEFORE NO. 9 OF IWA TECH COULD REACH IT, IT'S SENT BACK TO THE FRONT-LINE!
TOSUI

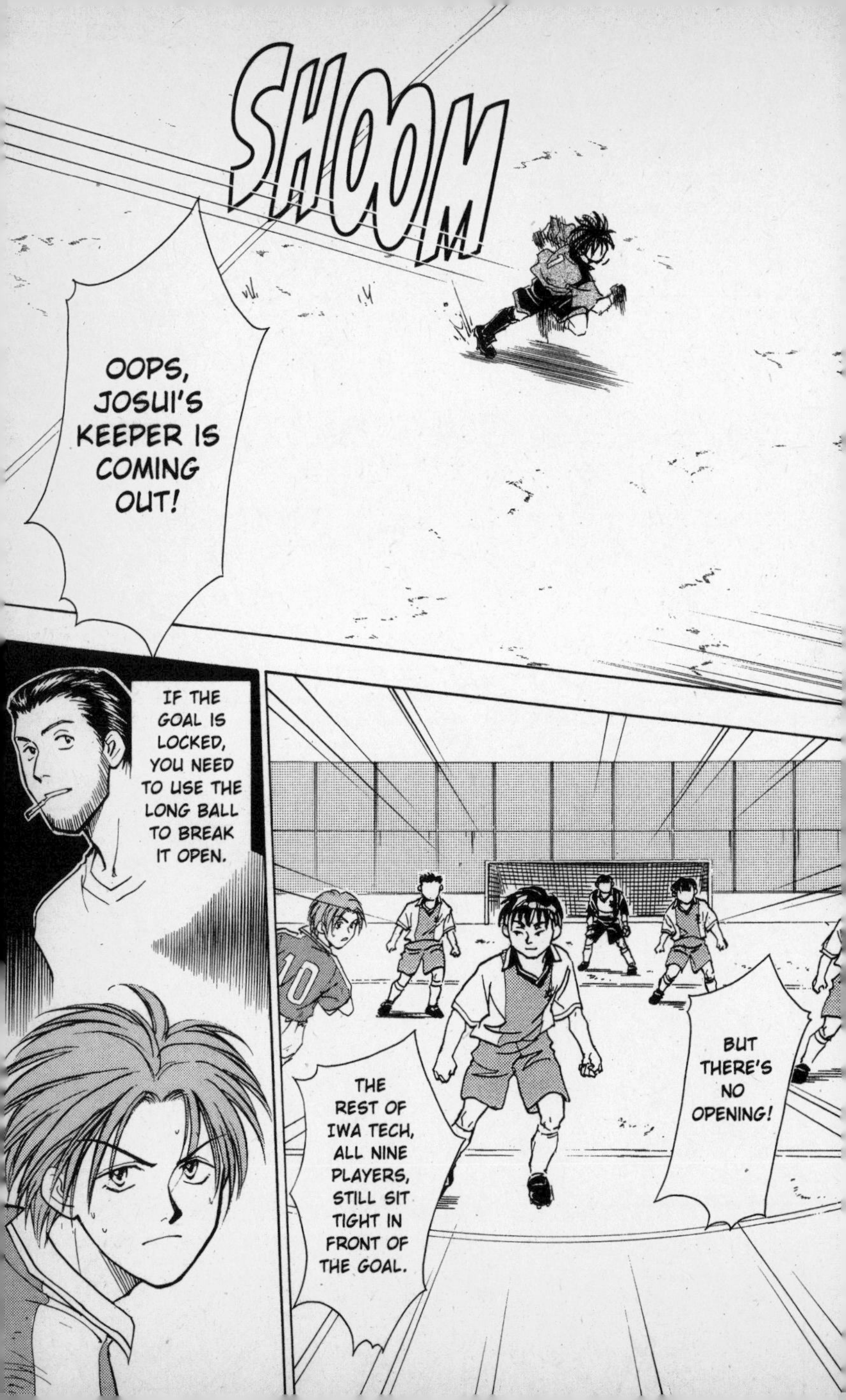
SHOOM
OOPS, JOSUI'S KEEPER IS COMING OUT!
BUT THERE'S NO OPENING!
THE REST OF IWA TECH, ALL NINE PLAYERS, STILL SIT TIGHT IN FRONT OF THE GOAL.
IF THE GOAL IS LOCKED, YOU NEED TO USE THE LONG BALL TO BREAK IT OPEN.

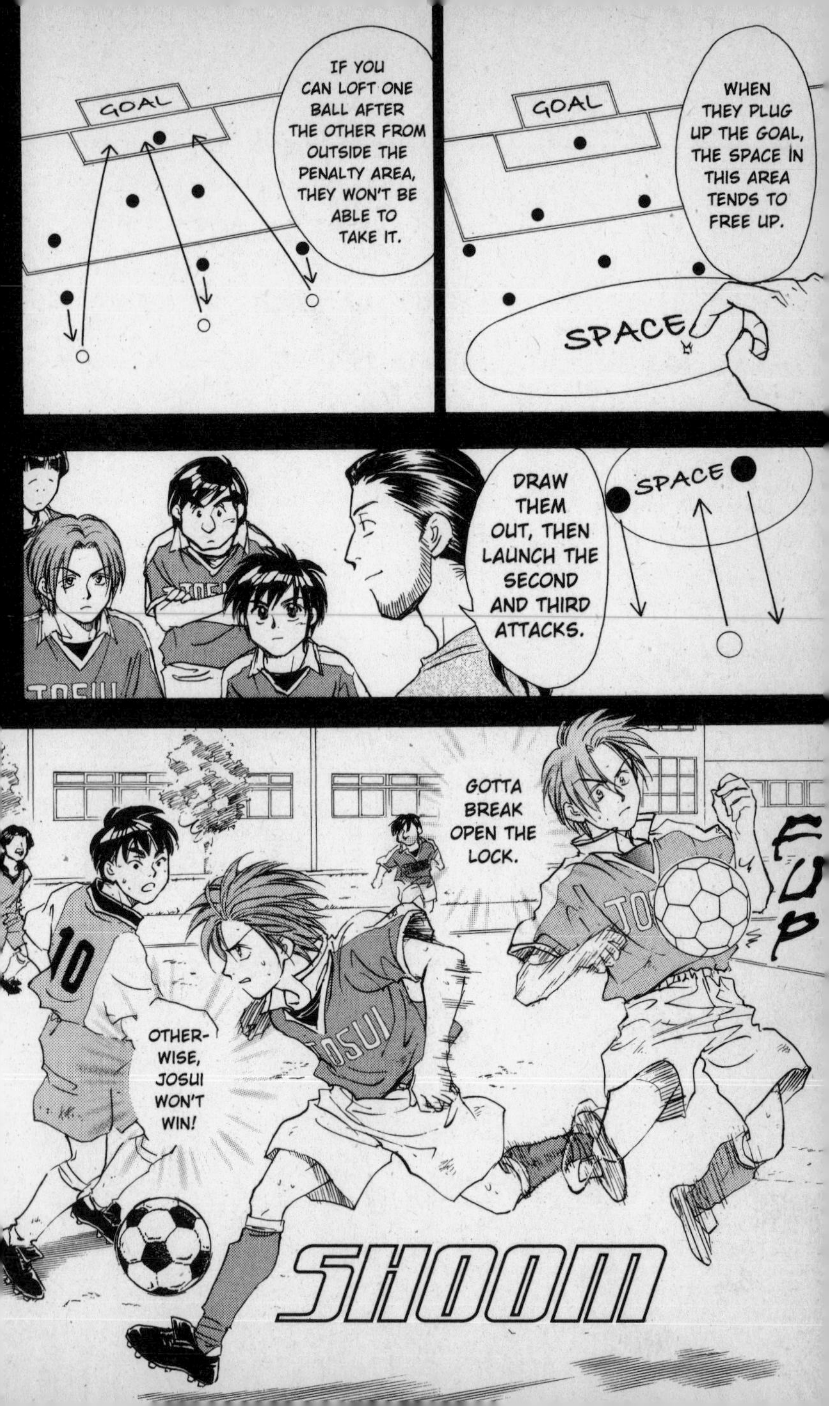
GOAL
WHEN THEY PLUG UP THE GOAL, THE SPACE IN THIS AREA TENDS TO FREE UP.
SPACE
GOAL
IF YOU CAN LOFT ONE BALL AFTER THE OTHER FROM OUTSIDE THE PENALTY AREA, THEY WON'T BE ABLE TO TAKE IT.
SPACE
DRAW THEM OUT, THEN LAUNCH THE SECOND AND THIRD ATTACKS.
FUP
GOTTA BREAK OPEN THE LOCK.
OTHER-WISE, JOSUI WON'T WIN!
SHOOM

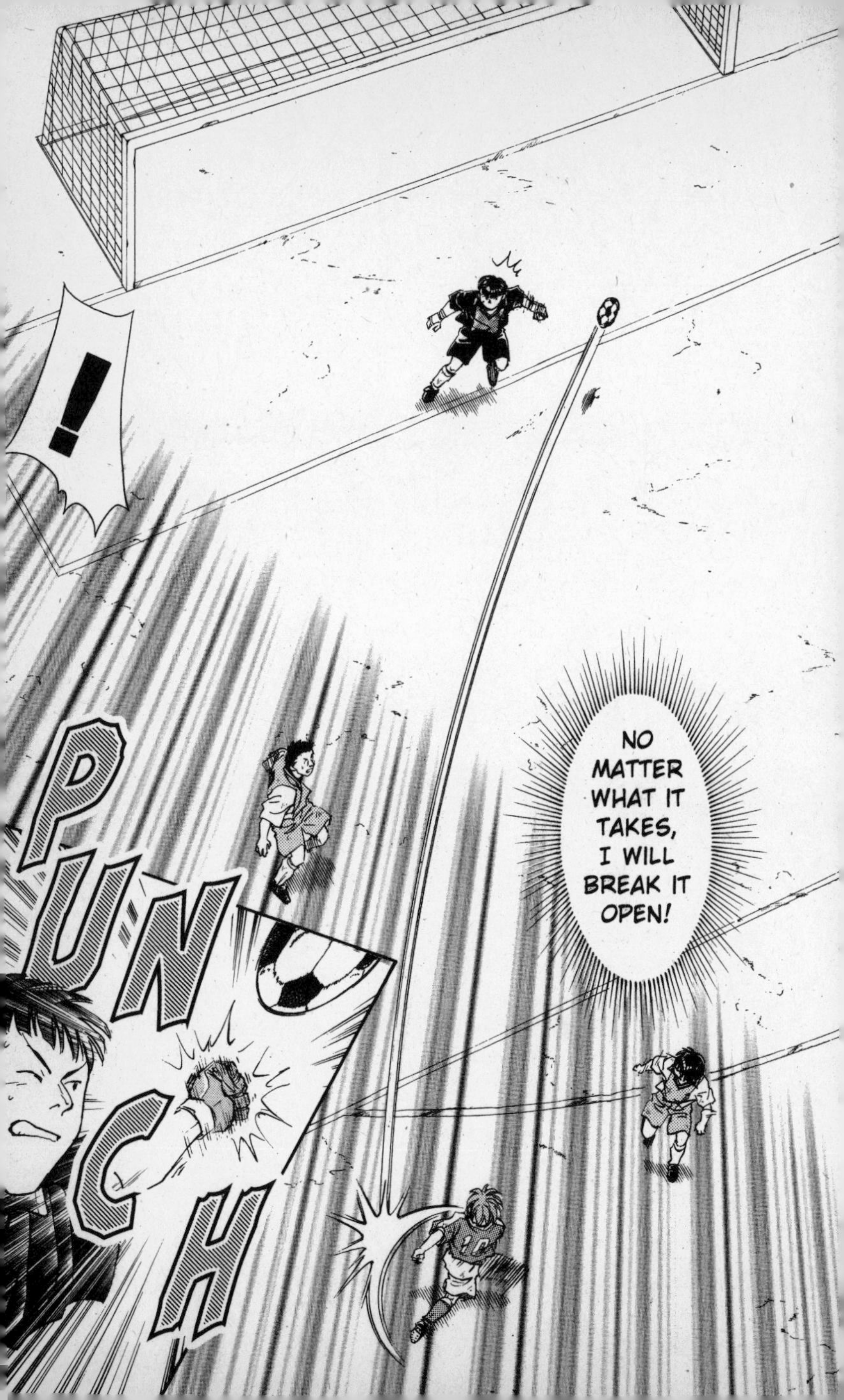
!
NO MATTER WHAT IT TAKES, I WILL BREAK IT OPEN!
PUNCH

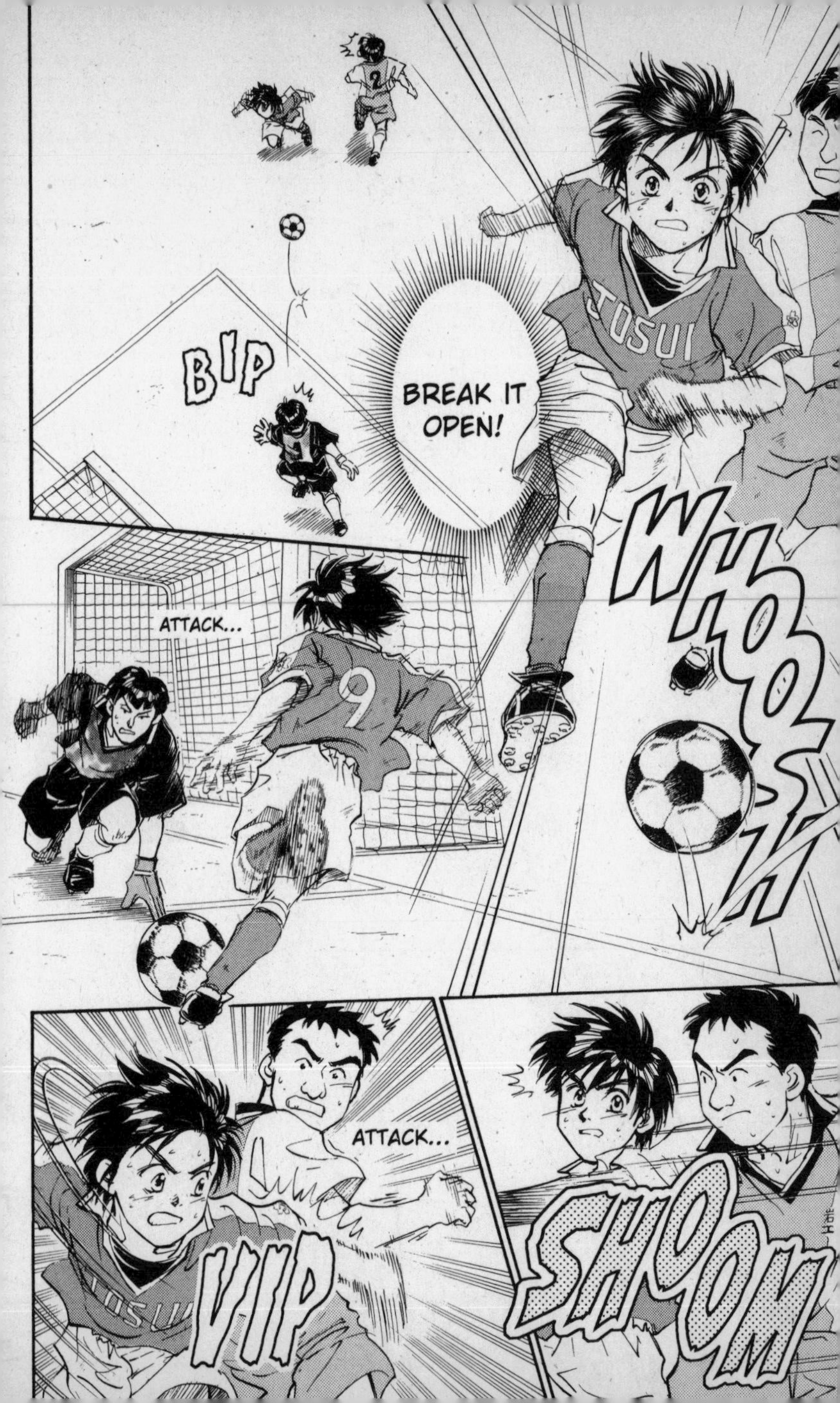
BREAK IT OPEN!
WHOOSH
BIP
ATTACK...
SHOOM
ATTACK...
VIP

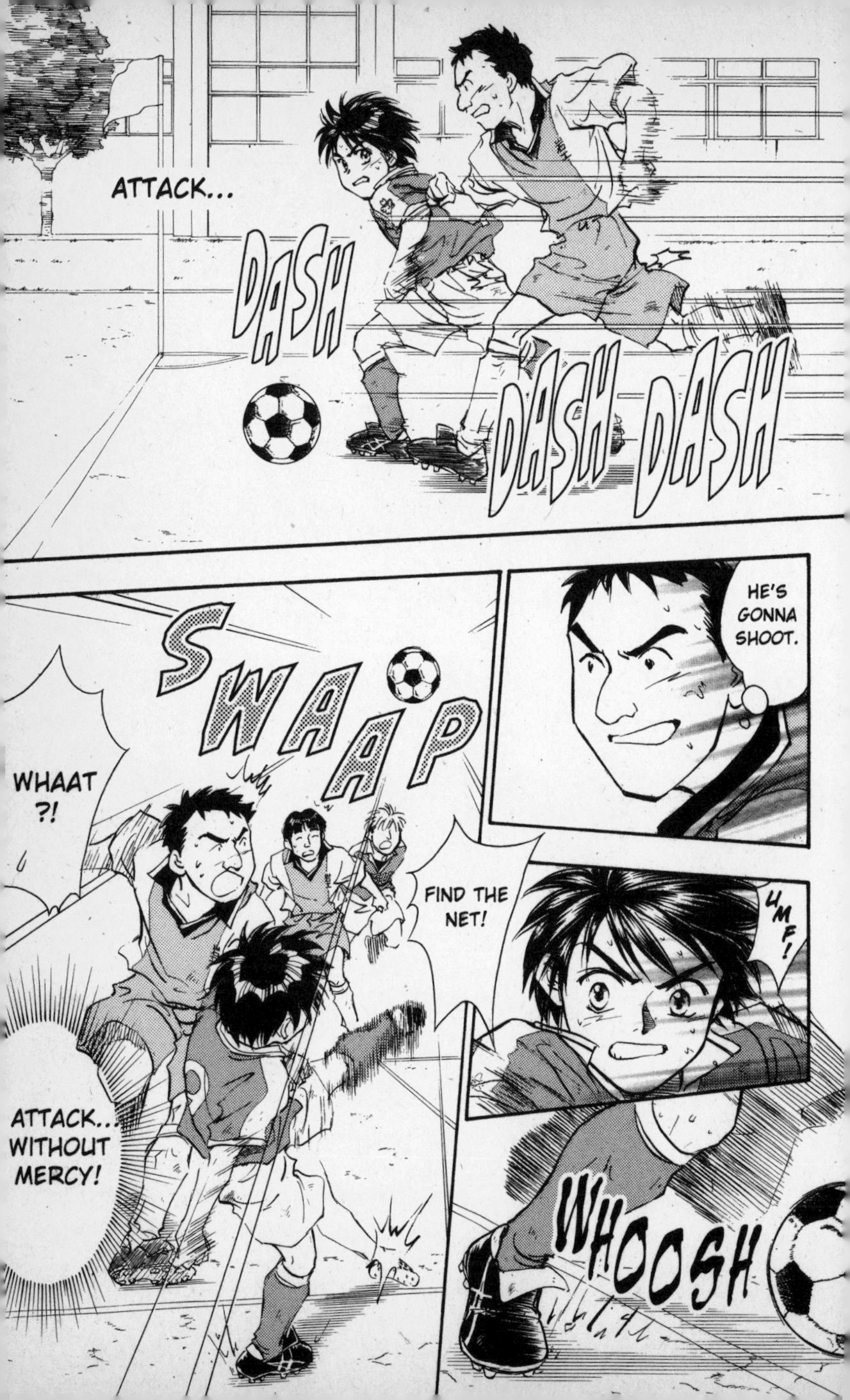
ATTACK...
DASH
DASH DASH
HE'S GONNA SHOOT.
UMF!
WHOOSH
SWAAP
WHAAT ?!
FIND THE NET!
ATTACK... WITHOUT MERCY!

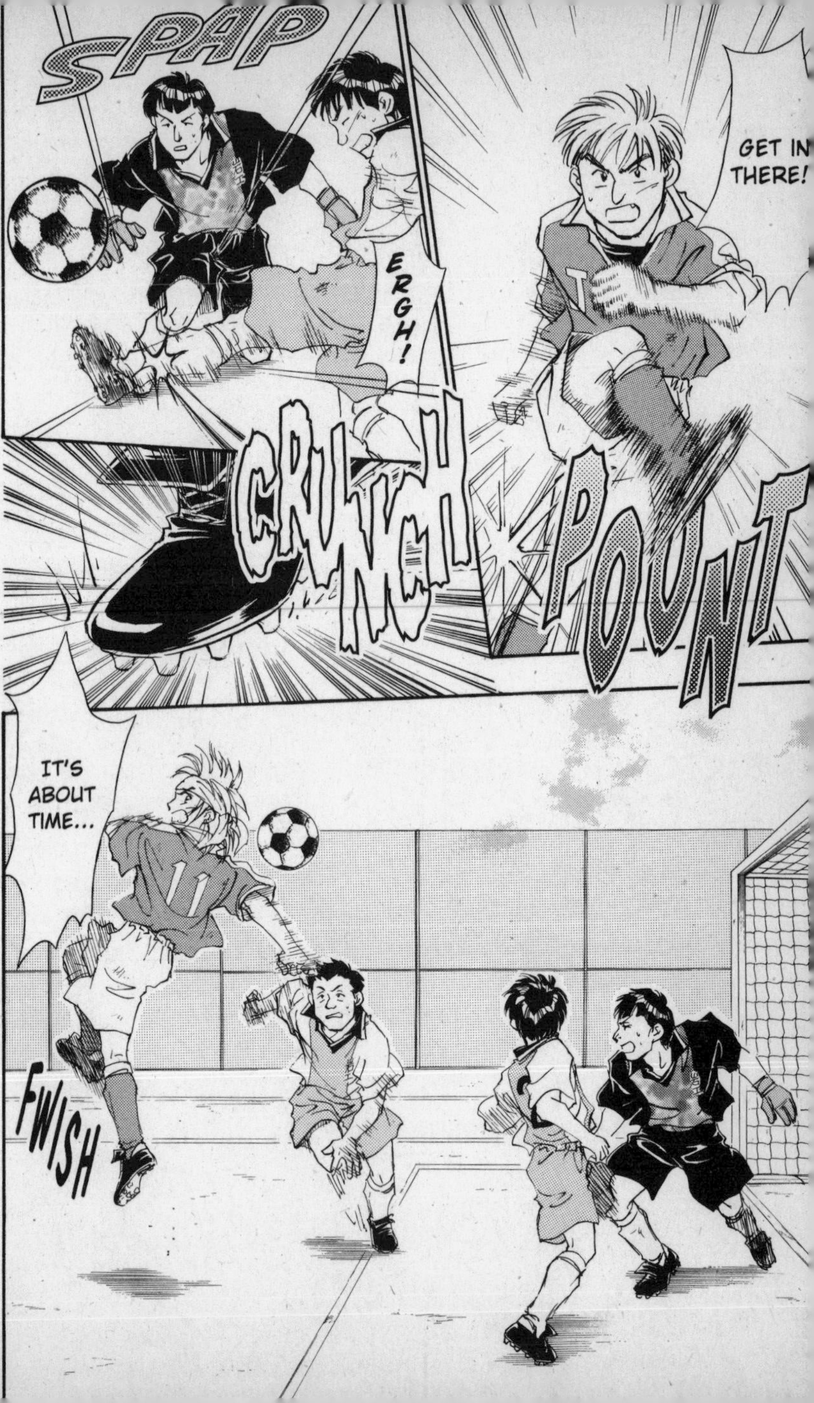
GET IN THERE!
SPAP
ERGH!
POUNT
CRUNCH
IT'S ABOUT TIME...
FWISH

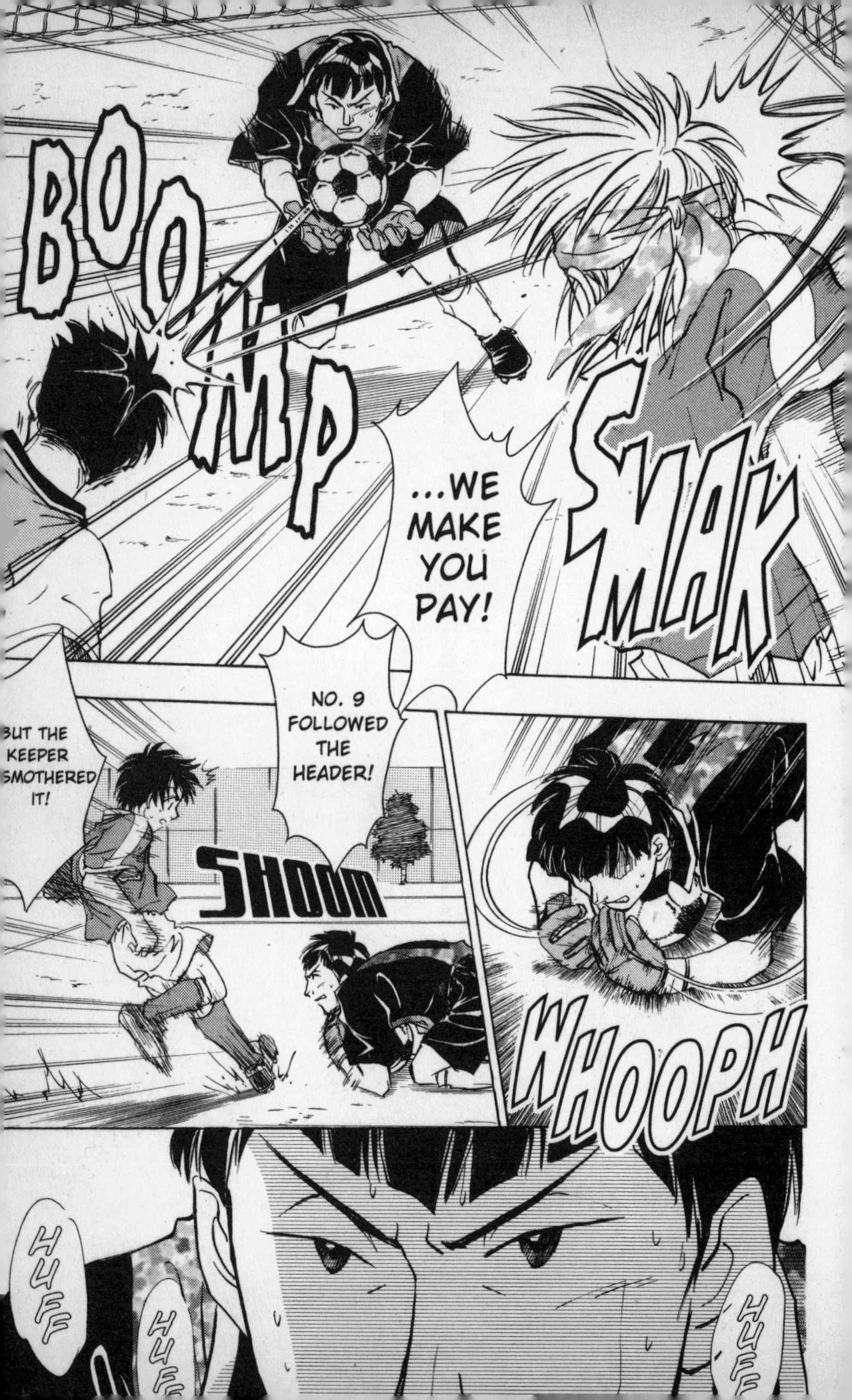
SMAK
...WE MAKE YOU PAY!
BOOMP
WHOOPH
NO. 9 FOLLOWED THE HEADER!
BUT THE KEEPER SMOTHERED IT!
SHOOM
HUFF HUFF
HUFF HUFF

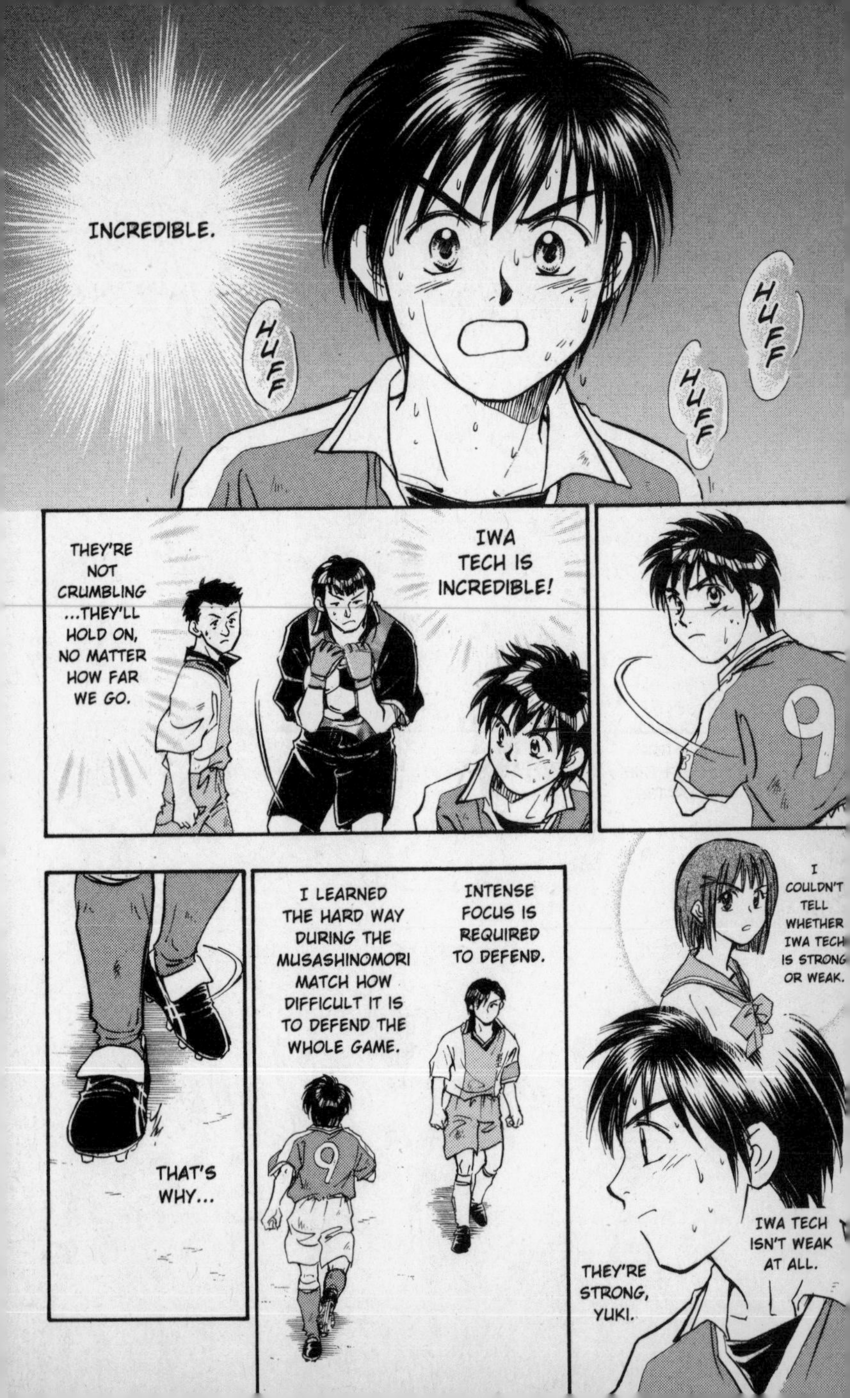

HUFF
HUFF
INCREDIBLE.
HUFF
IWA TECH IS INCREDIBLE!
THEY'RE NOT CRUMBLING ...THEY'LL HOLD ON, NO MATTER HOW FAR WE GO.
I COULDN'T TELL WHETHER IWA TECH IS STRONG OR WEAK.
IWA TECH ISN'T WEAK AT ALL.
THEY'RE STRONG, YUKI.
INTENSE FOCUS IS REQUIRED TO DEFEND.
I LEARNED THE HARD WAY DURING THE MUSASHINOMORI MATCH HOW DIFFICULT IT IS TO DEFEND THE WHOLE GAME.
THAT'S WHY...

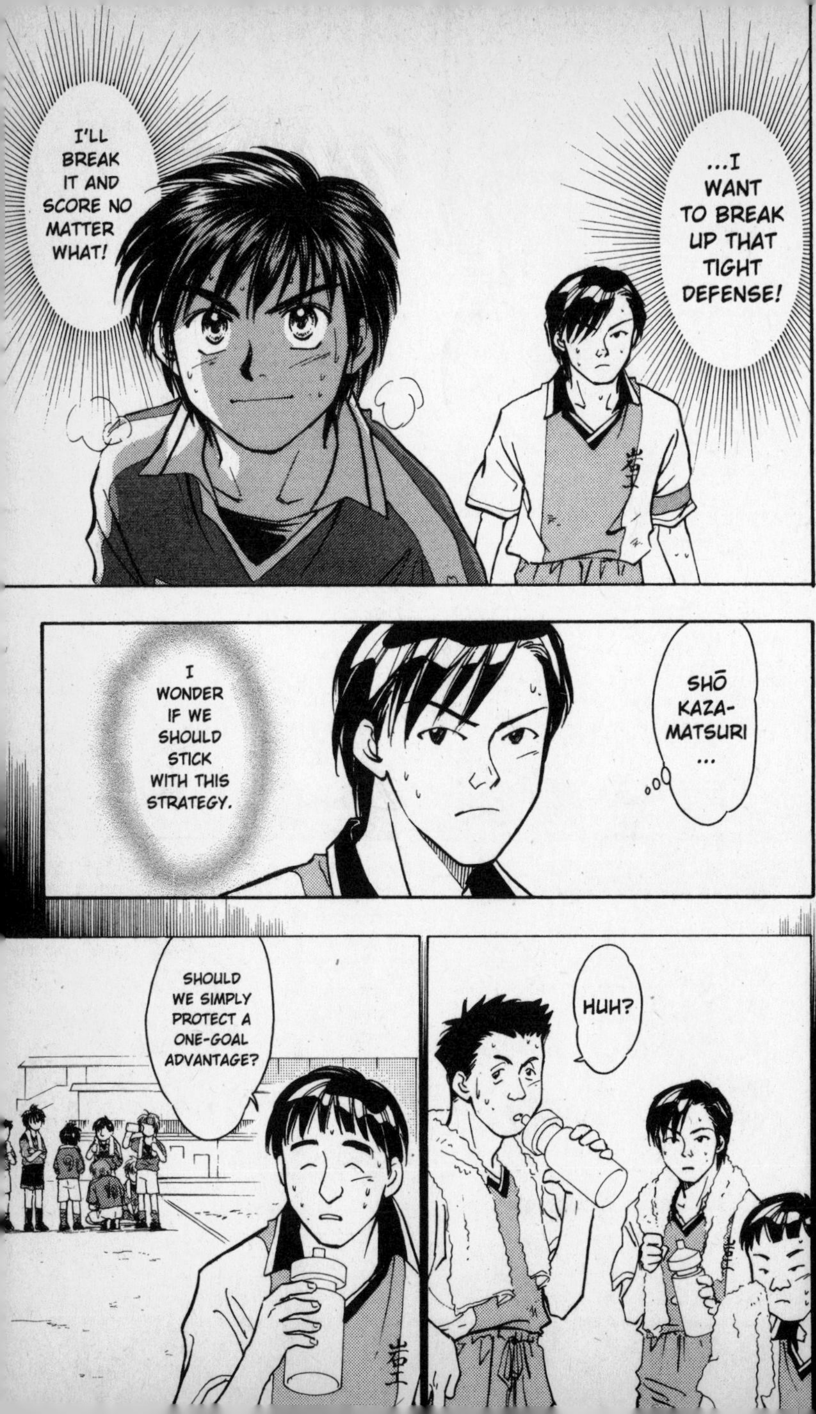
...I WANT TO BREAK UP THAT TIGHT DEFENSE!
I'LL BREAK IT AND SCORE NO MATTER WHAT!
SHŌ KAZA-MATSURI...
I WONDER IF WE SHOULD STICK WITH THIS STRATEGY.
HUH?
SHOULD WE SIMPLY PROTECT A ONE-GOAL ADVANTAGE?

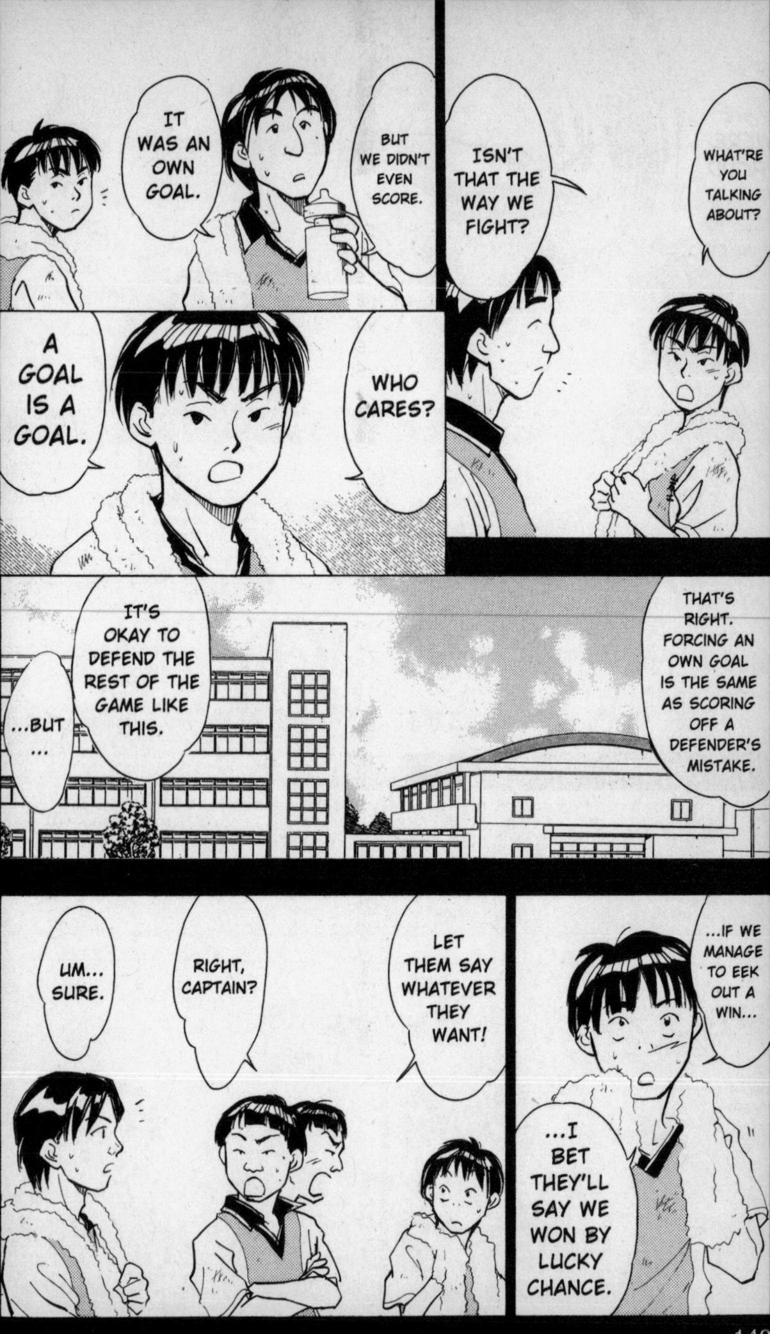
WHAT'RE YOU TALKING ABOUT?
ISN'T THAT THE WAY WE FIGHT?
BUT WE DIDN'T EVEN SCORE.
IT WAS AN OWN GOAL.
WHO CARES?
A GOAL IS A GOAL.
THAT'S RIGHT. FORCING AN OWN GOAL IS THE SAME AS SCORING OFF A DEFENDER'S MISTAKE.
IT'S OKAY TO DEFEND THE REST OF THE GAME LIKE THIS.
...BUT ...
...IF WE MANAGE TO EEK OUT A WIN...
...I BET THEY'LL SAY WE WON BY LUCKY CHANCE.
LET THEM SAY WHATEVER THEY WANT!
RIGHT, CAPTAIN?
UM... SURE.

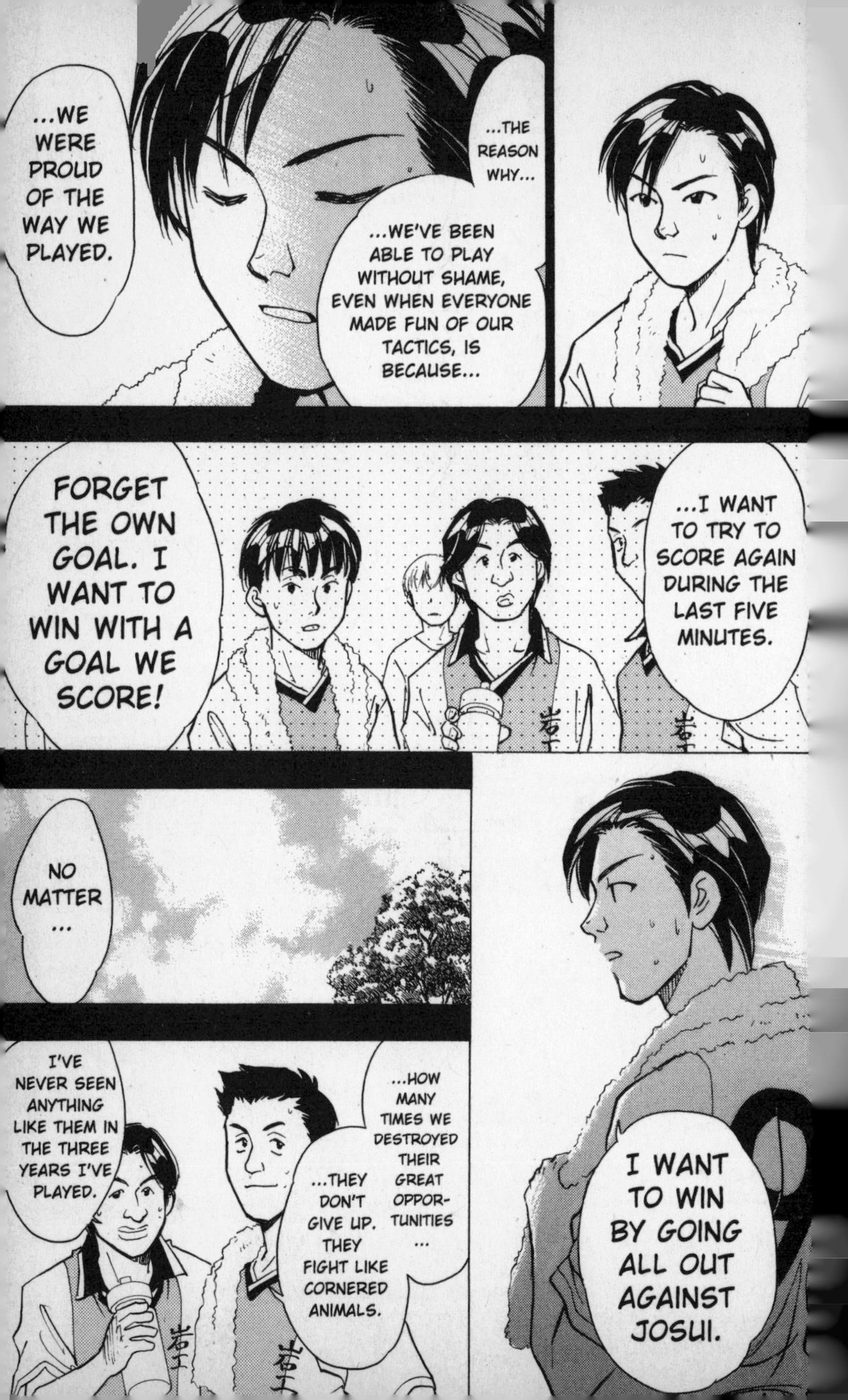
...THE REASON WHY...
...WE'VE BEEN ABLE TO PLAY WITHOUT SHAME, EVEN WHEN EVERYONE MADE FUN OF OUR TACTICS, IS BECAUSE...
...WE WERE PROUD OF THE WAY WE PLAYED.
...I WANT TO TRY TO SCORE AGAIN DURING THE LAST FIVE MINUTES.
FORGET THE OWN GOAL. I WANT TO WIN WITH A GOAL WE SCORE!
I WANT TO WIN BY GOING ALL OUT AGAINST JOSUI.
NO MATTER...
...HOW MANY TIMES WE DESTROYED THEIR GREAT OPPOR-TUNITIES...
...THEY DON'T GIVE UP. THEY FIGHT LIKE CORNERED ANIMALS.
I'VE NEVER SEEN ANYTHING LIKE THEM IN THE THREE YEARS I'VE PLAYED.

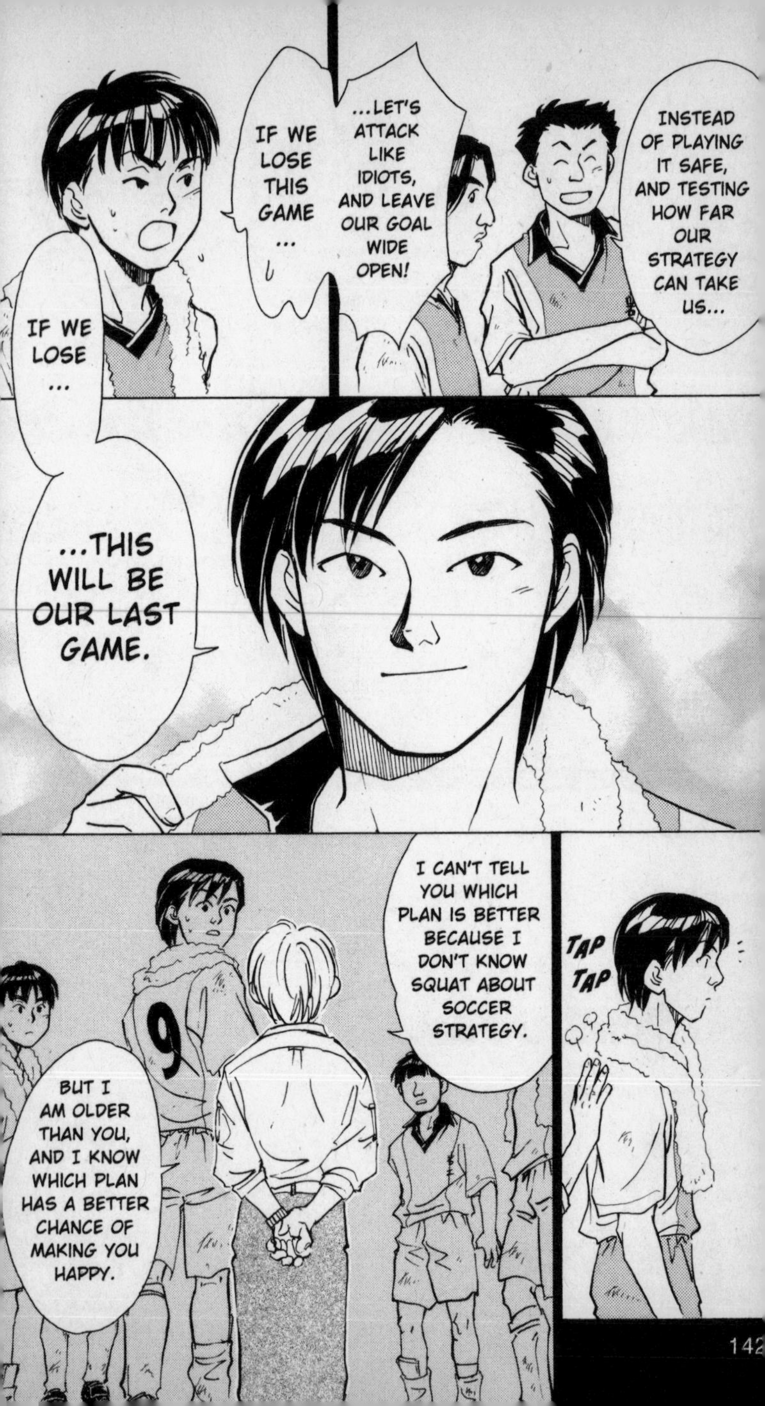
INSTEAD OF PLAYING IT SAFE, AND TESTING HOW FAR OUR STRATEGY CAN TAKE US...
...LET'S ATTACK LIKE IDIOTS, AND LEAVE OUR GOAL WIDE OPEN!
IF WE LOSE THIS GAME ...
IF WE LOSE ...
...THIS WILL BE OUR LAST GAME.
TAP TAP
I CAN'T TELL YOU WHICH PLAN IS BETTER BECAUSE I DON'T KNOW SQUAT ABOUT SOCCER STRATEGY.
BUT I AM OLDER THAN YOU, AND I KNOW WHICH PLAN HAS A BETTER CHANCE OF MAKING YOU HAPPY.

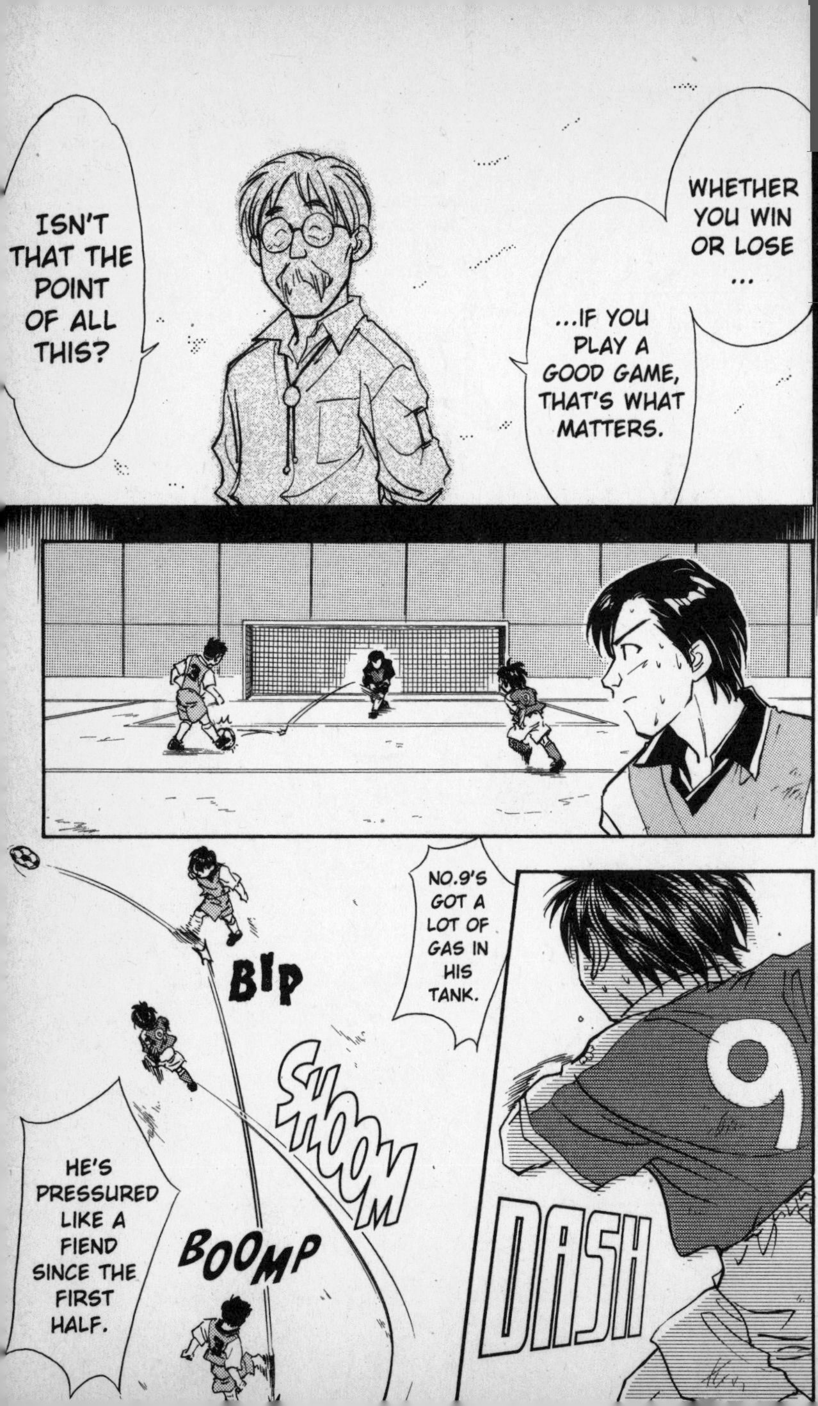
WHETHER YOU WIN OR LOSE ...
...IF YOU PLAY A GOOD GAME, THAT'S WHAT MATTERS.
ISN'T THAT THE POINT OF ALL THIS?
NO.9'S GOT A LOT OF GAS IN HIS TANK.
DASH
BIP
SHOOM
BOOMP
HE'S PRESSURED LIKE A FIEND SINCE THE FIRST HALF.

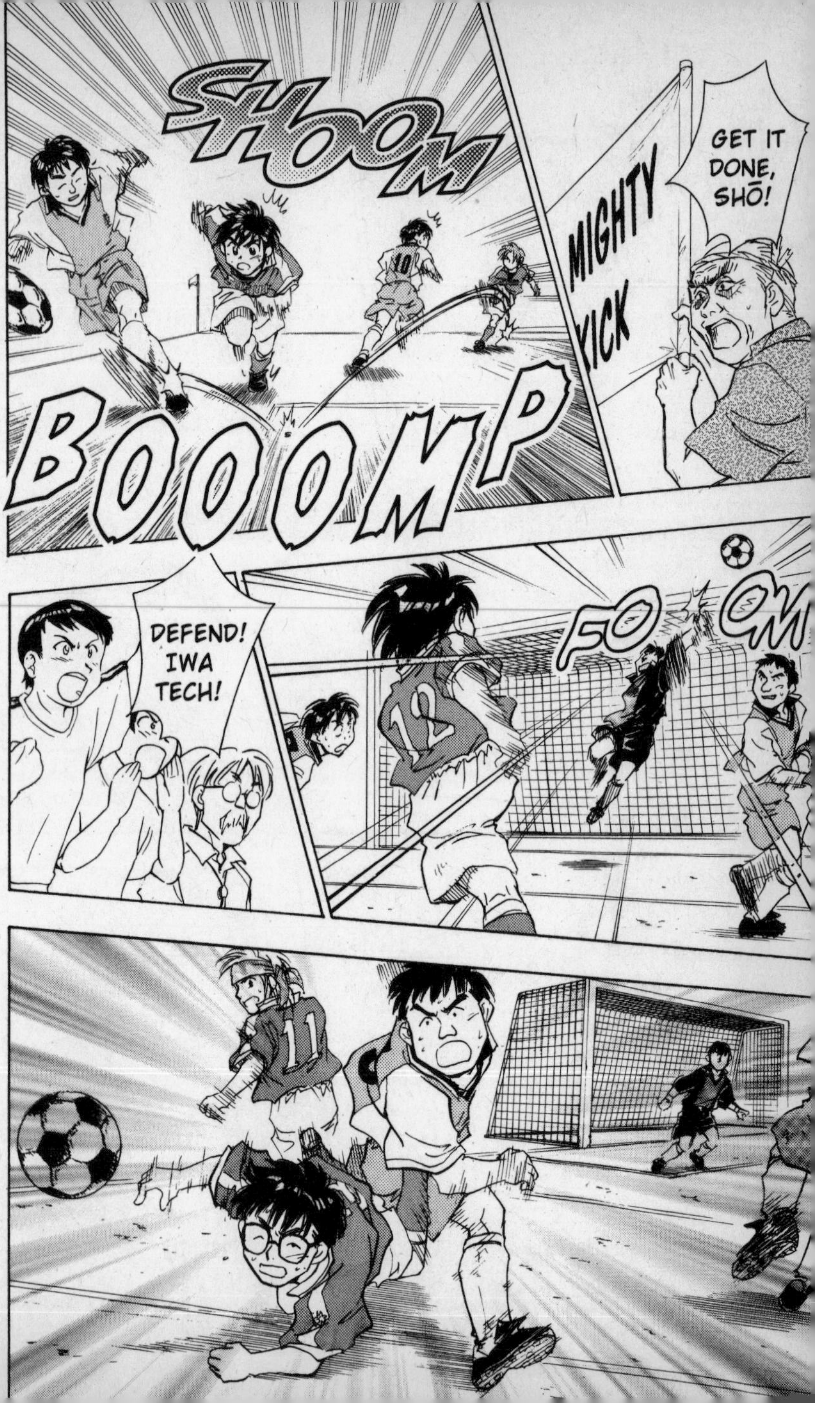
GET IT DONE, SHŌ!
MIGHTY KICK
SHOOM
BOOOMP
FO OM
DEFEND! IWA TECH!

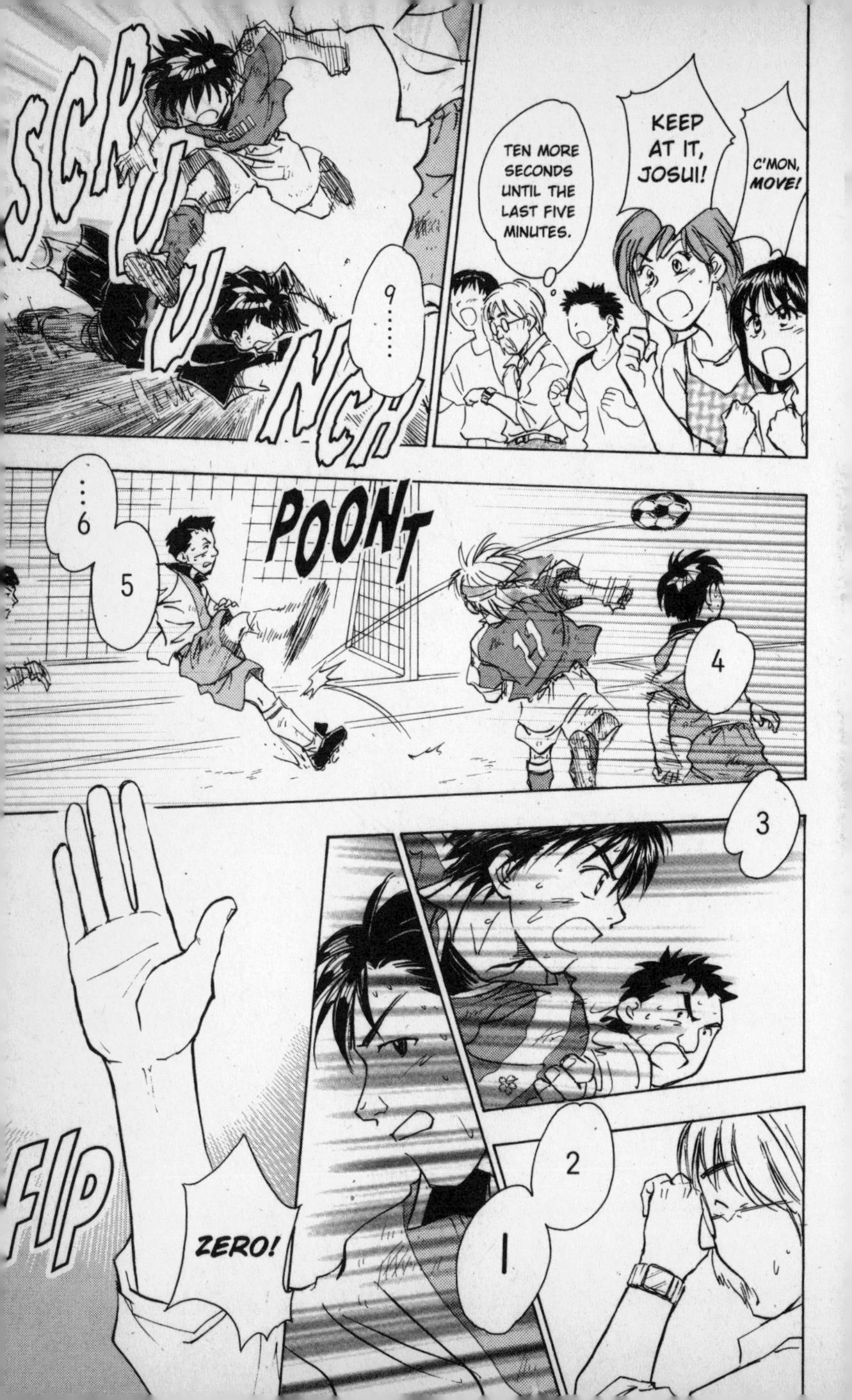
C'MON, MOVE!
KEEP AT IT, JOSUI!
TEN MORE SECONDS UNTIL THE LAST FIVE MINUTES.
9......
SCRUUNCH
......6
5
POONT
4
3
2
1
ZERO!
FLIP

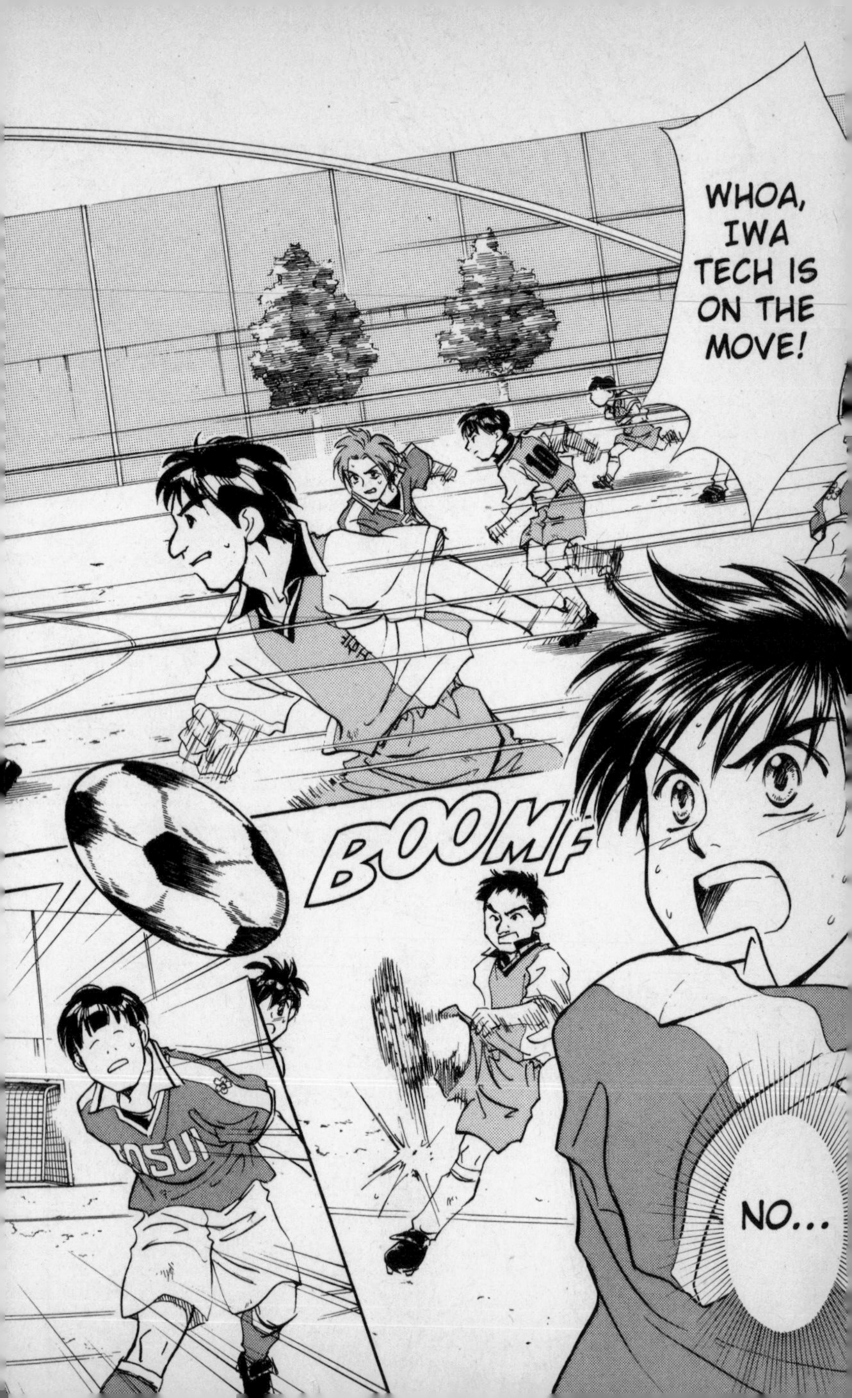
WHOA, IWA TECH IS ON THE MOVE!
BOOMF
NO...

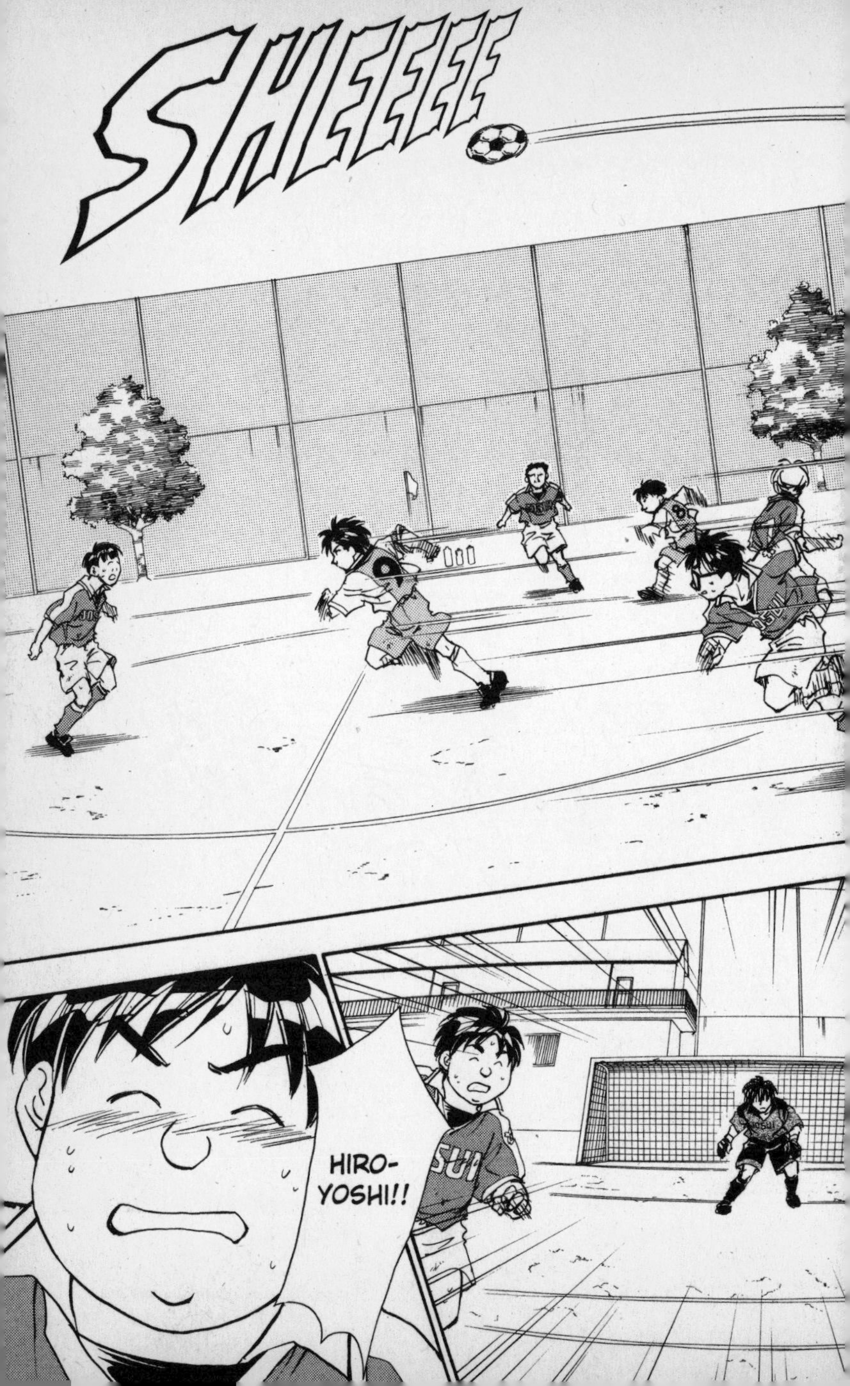
SHEEEEE
HIRO-
YOSHI!!

Daichi Computes

EEEEK
BINK
NO ONE WILL INTER-FERE WITH US HERE.
NOW, HOW SHOULD I BEGIN...
YOU SUCK!! THAT WON' DO. IF YO TO QUIT, WH YOU? NOT GO EITHER...UMM, ISN'T THERE A B WAY TO SAY IT? AH, THIS IS IT!! NO, NO, NO...SOMETHING. ANYTHING!!...AH, A BUTTERFLY...NO, NO THE TIME FOR THAT!!
WHIRR
CLICK
CLICK
BING
BING
GOT IT. THIS IS IT!!
ZOINK
FUMP
NICE WEATHER, DON'T YOU THINK?

WHISTLE! THEATRE !!

MANGA BY **SEKI**, ASSISTANT S

DID YOU KNOW 72% OF THE SOCCER PLAYERS AT IWA TECH ARE MADE OF SPECIAL ALLOY? ACCORDING TO THE EX-CAPTAIN, HONMA.
CLANK CLANK
VREEE BRIIING CLANK
IWA TECH COACH NO. 3
HONMA JOURNAL
MESO
← AIKO

STAGE.61 Time to Go

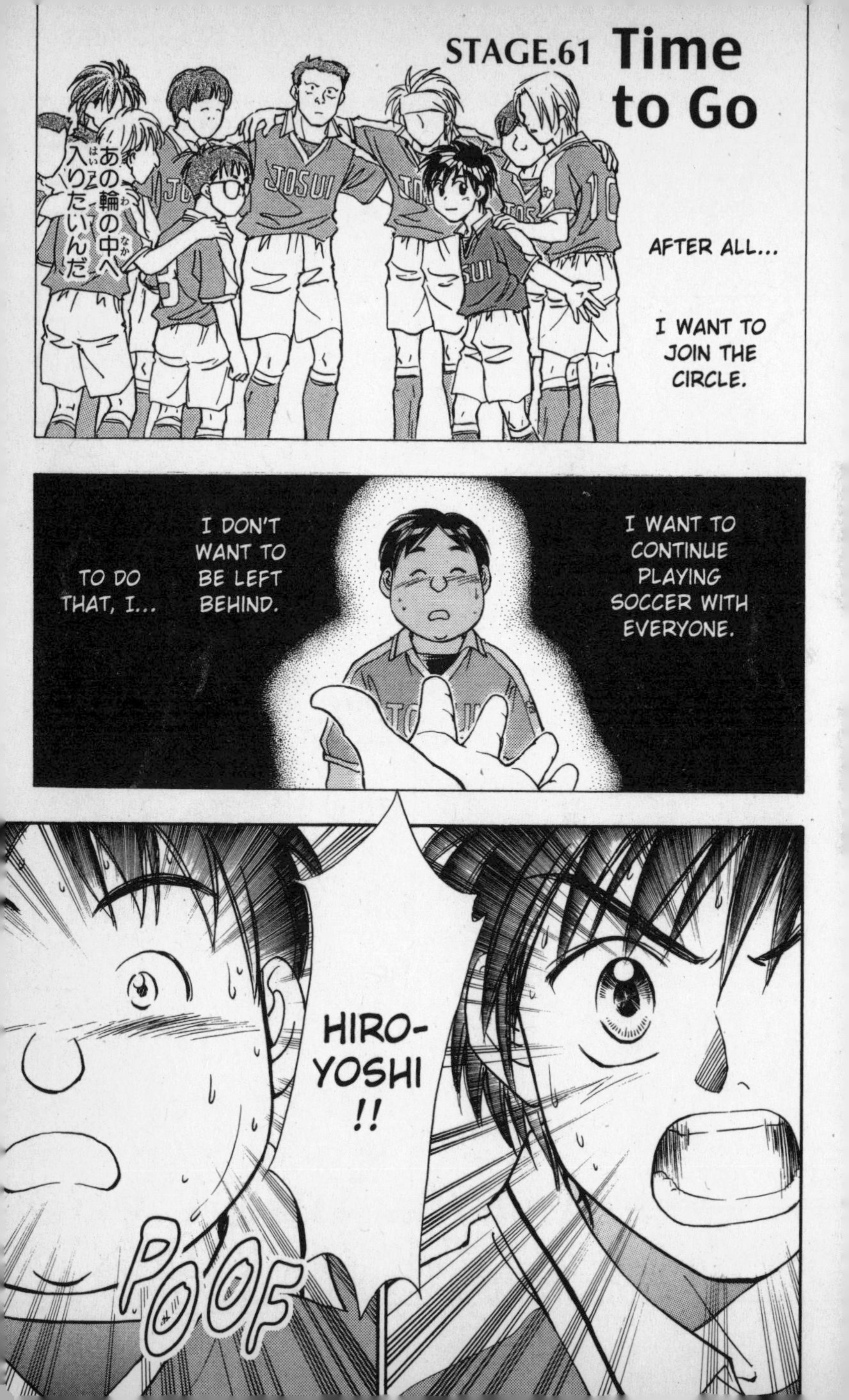
AFTER ALL...
I WANT TO JOIN THE CIRCLE.
あの輪の中へ入りたいんだ
I WANT TO CONTINUE PLAYING SOCCER WITH EVERYONE.
I DON'T WANT TO BE LEFT BEHIND.
TO DO THAT, I...
HIRO-YOSHI !!
POOF

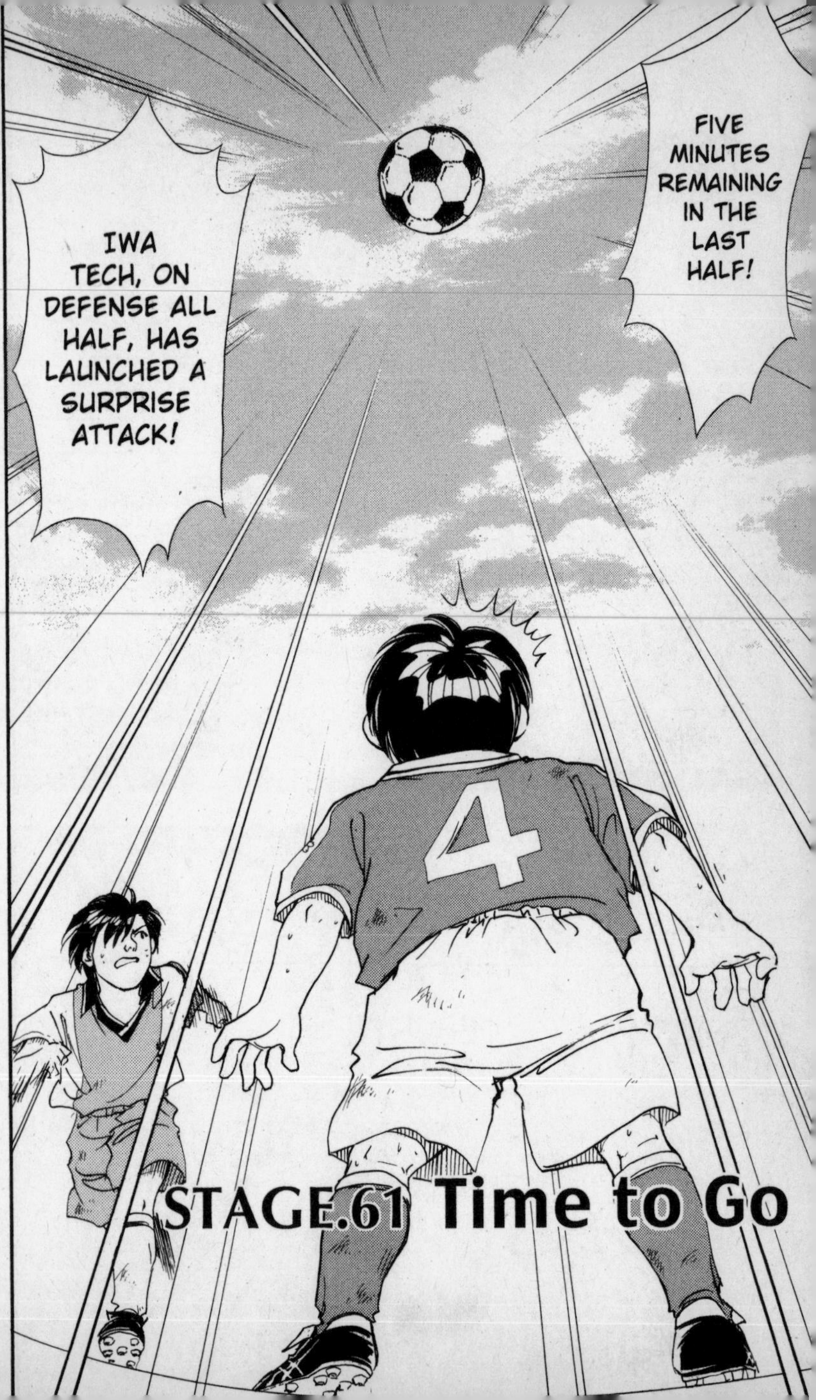
FIVE MINUTES REMAINING IN THE LAST HALF!
IWA TECH, ON DEFENSE ALL HALF, HAS LAUNCHED A SURPRISE ATTACK!
STAGE.61 Time to Go

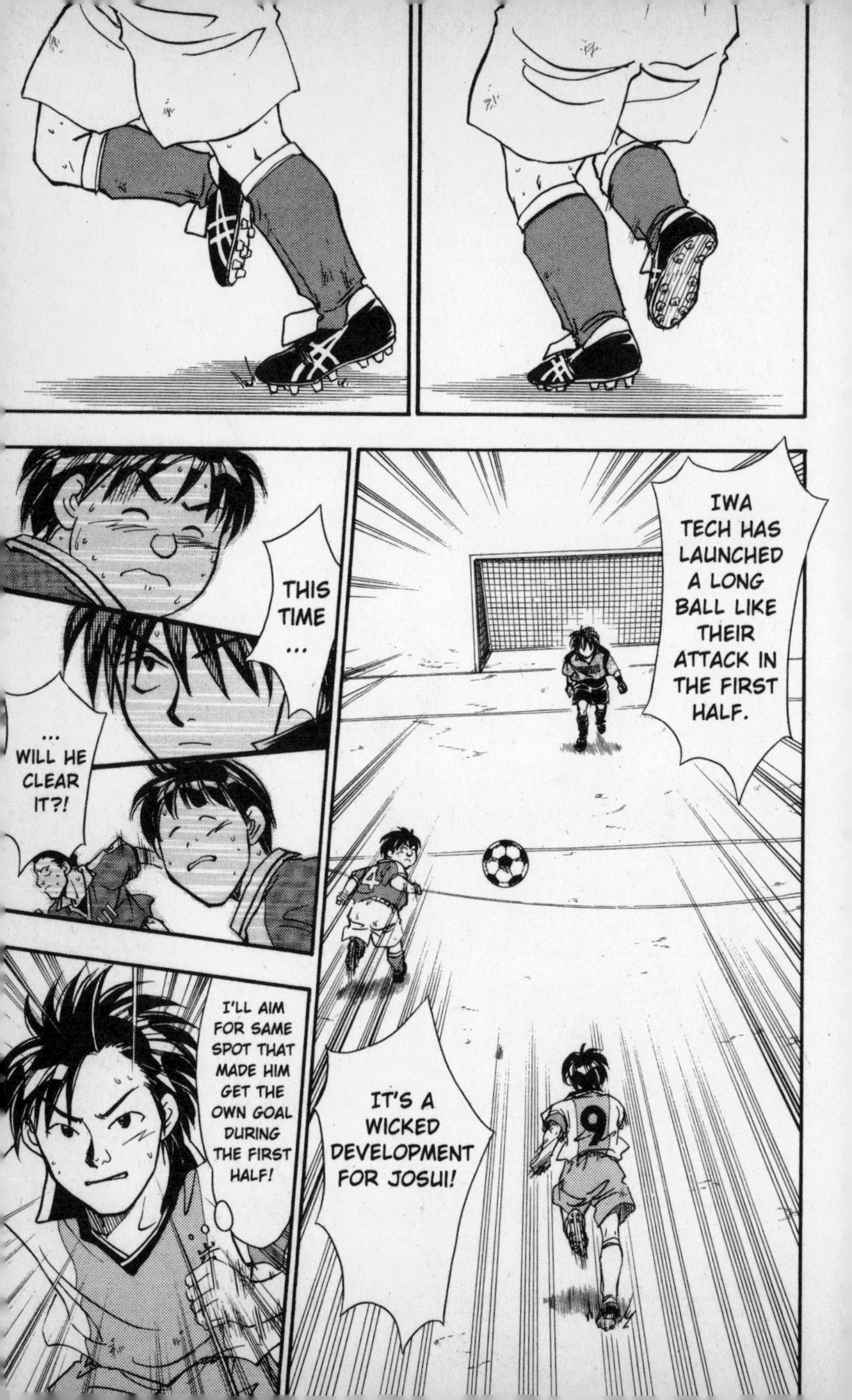
IWA TECH HAS LAUNCHED A LONG BALL LIKE THEIR ATTACK IN THE FIRST HALF.
IT'S A WICKED DEVELOPMENT FOR JOSUI!
THIS TIME ...
... WILL HE CLEAR IT?!
I'LL AIM FOR SAME SPOT THAT MADE HIM GET THE OWN GOAL DURING THE FIRST HALF!

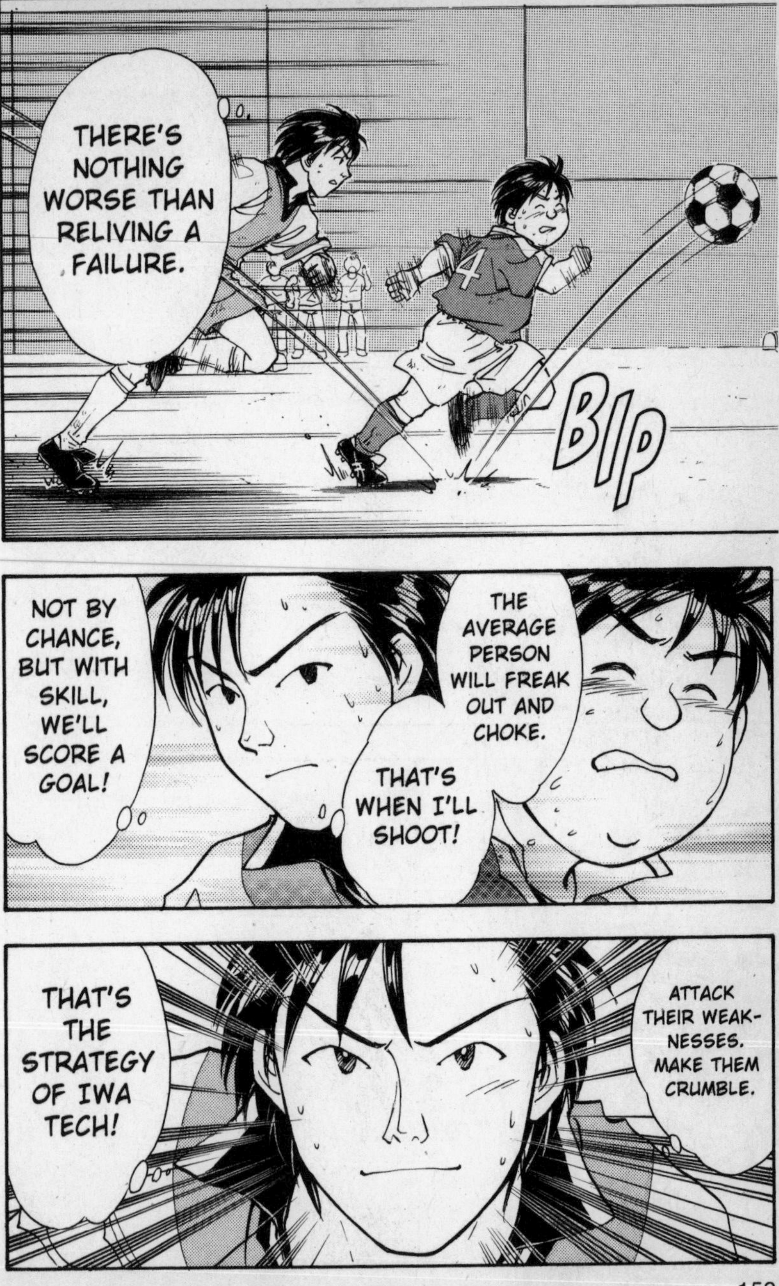

THERE'S NOTHING WORSE THAN RELIVING A FAILURE.
BIP
THE AVERAGE PERSON WILL FREAK OUT AND CHOKE.
THAT'S WHEN I'LL SHOOT!
NOT BY CHANCE, BUT WITH SKILL, WE'LL SCORE A GOAL!
ATTACK THEIR WEAK-NESSES. MAKE THEM CRUMBLE.
THAT'S THE STRATEGY OF IWA TECH!

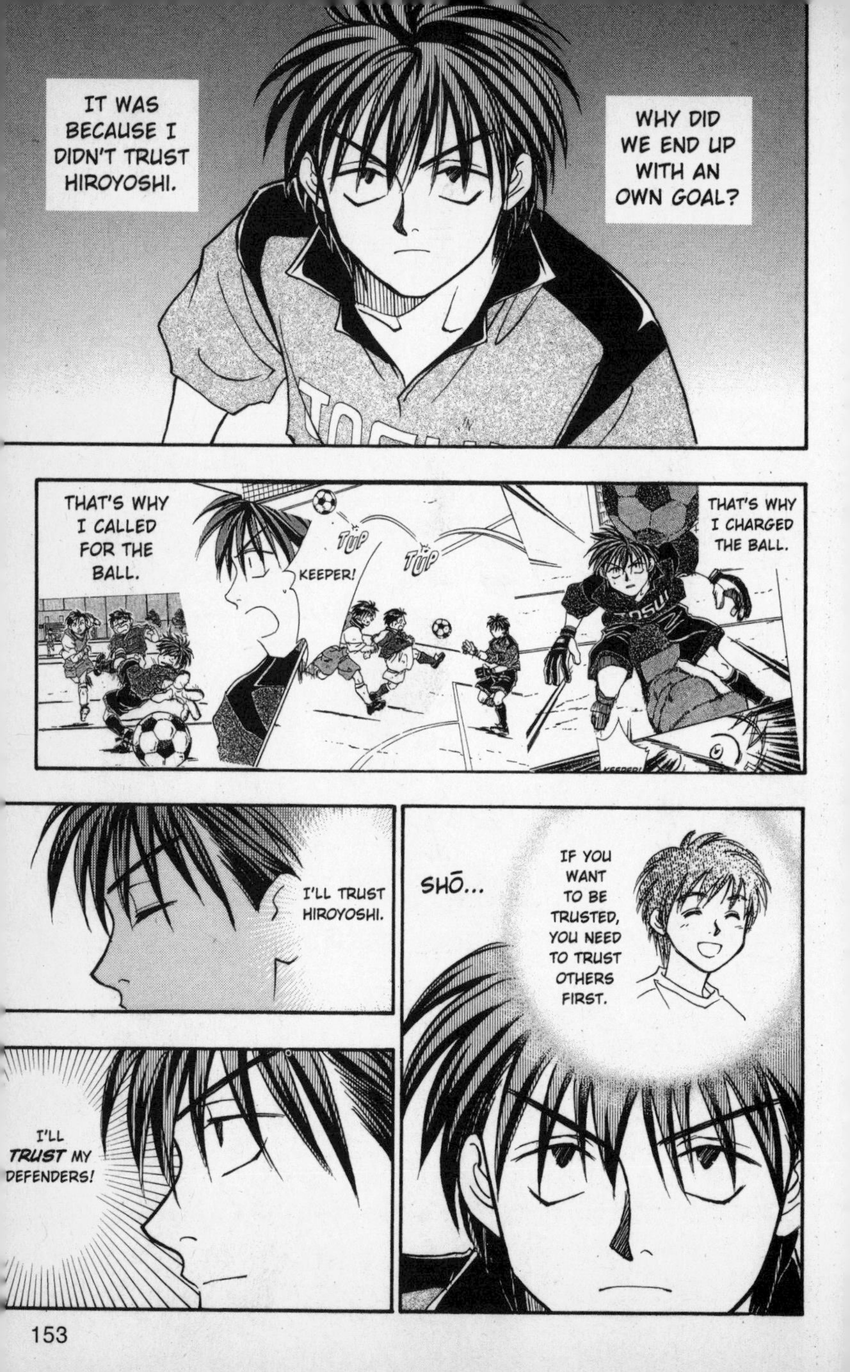
WHY DID WE END UP WITH AN OWN GOAL?
IT WAS BECAUSE I DIDN'T TRUST HIROYOSHI.
THAT'S WHY I CHARGED THE BALL.
TUP
TUP
KEEPER!
THAT'S WHY I CALLED FOR THE BALL.
IF YOU WANT TO BE TRUSTED, YOU NEED TO TRUST OTHERS FIRST.
SHŌ...
I'LL TRUST HIROYOSHI.
I'LL TRUST MY DEFENDERS!

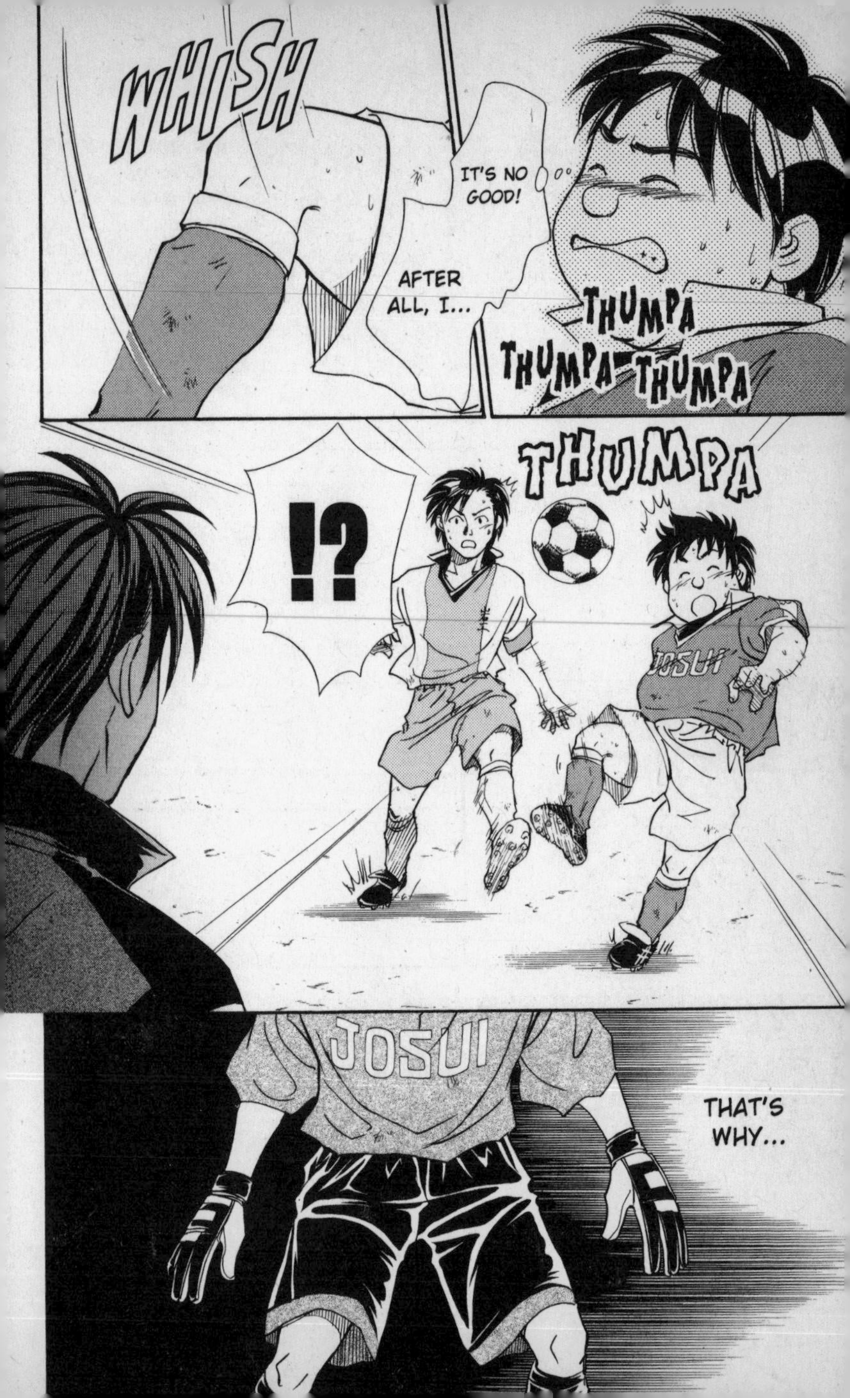
IT'S NO GOOD!
AFTER ALL, I...
THUMPA
THUMPA THUMPA
WHISH
THUMPA
!?
THAT'S WHY...

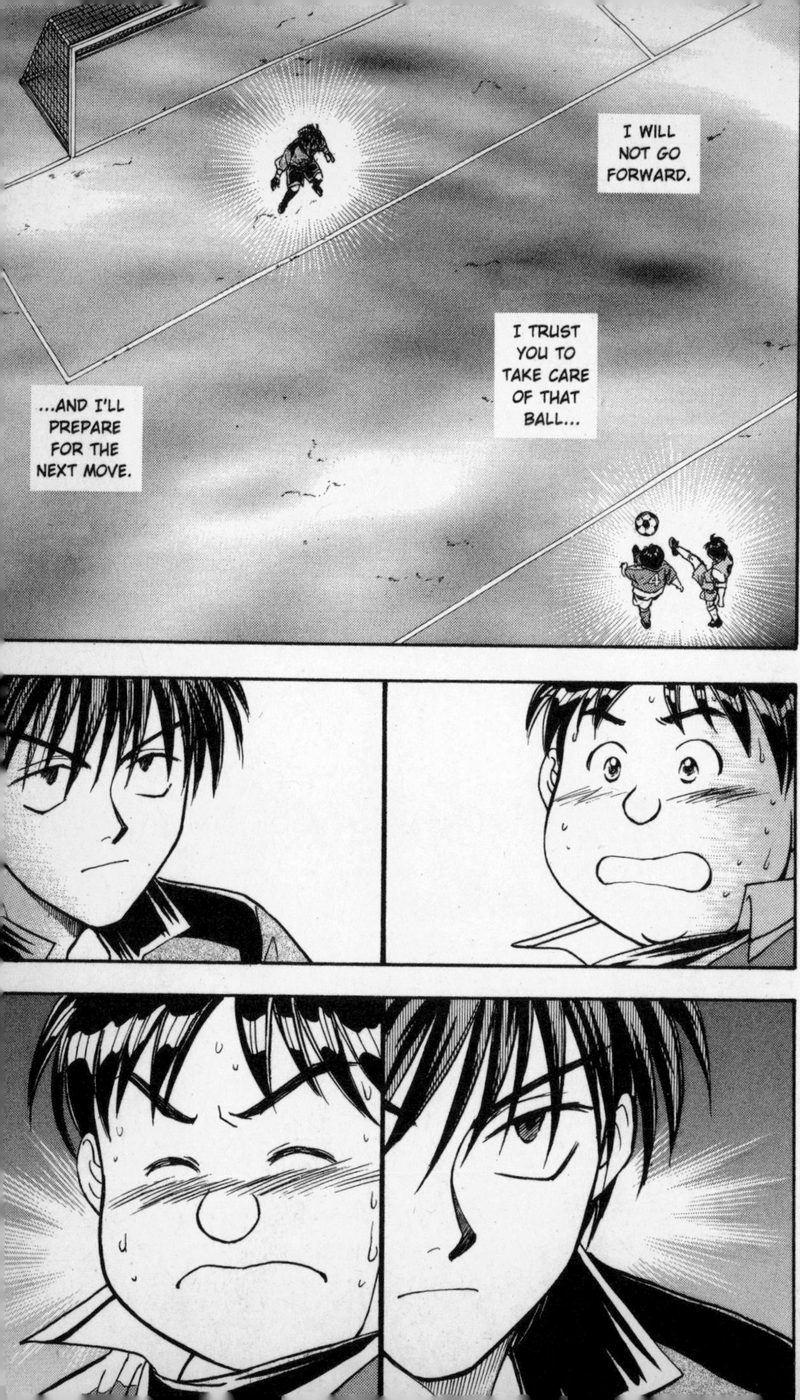
I WILL NOT GO FORWARD.
I TRUST YOU TO TAKE CARE OF THAT BALL...
...AND I'LL PREPARE FOR THE NEXT MOVE.

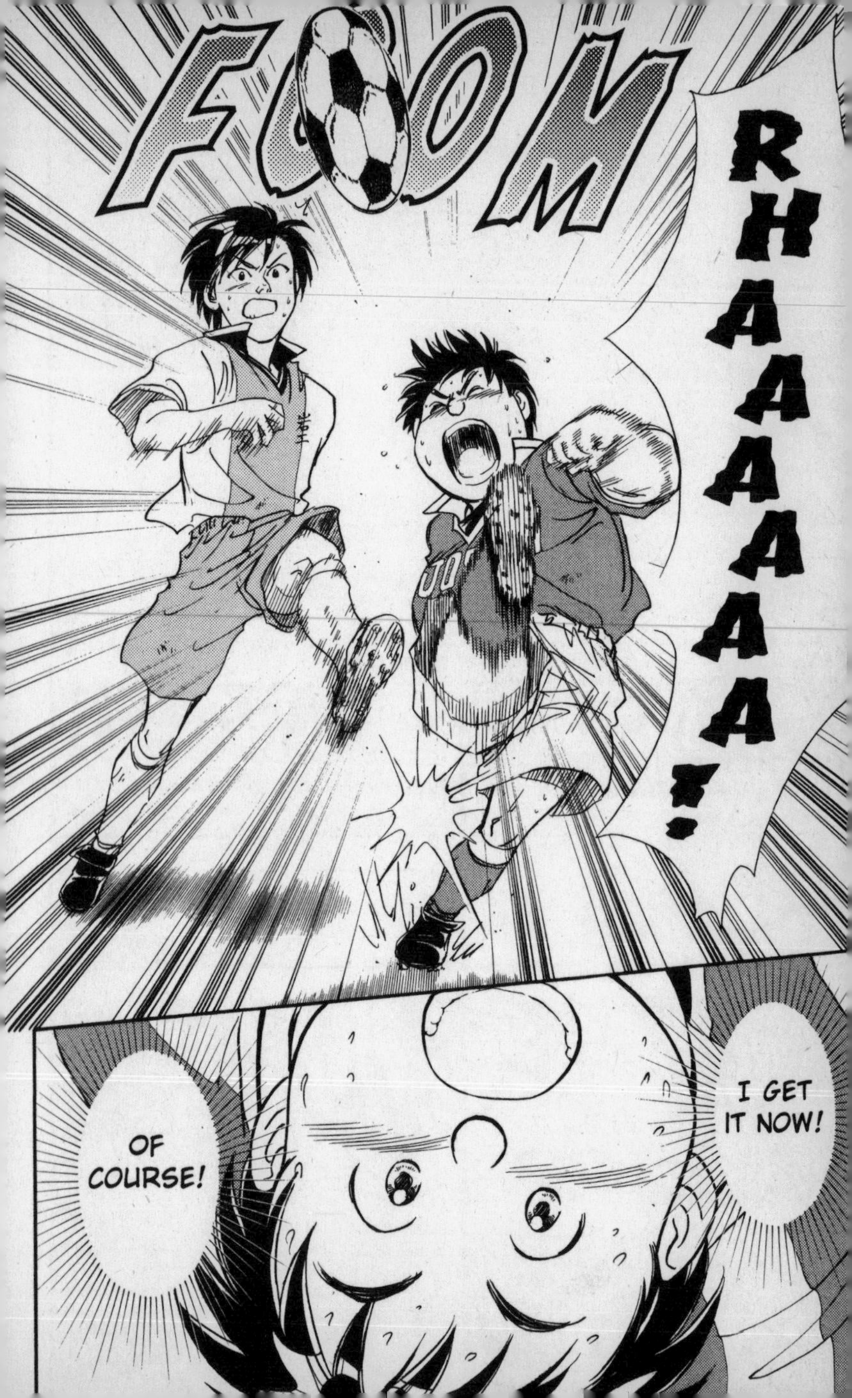
FOOM
RHAAAAAA!!
I GET IT NOW!
OF COURSE!

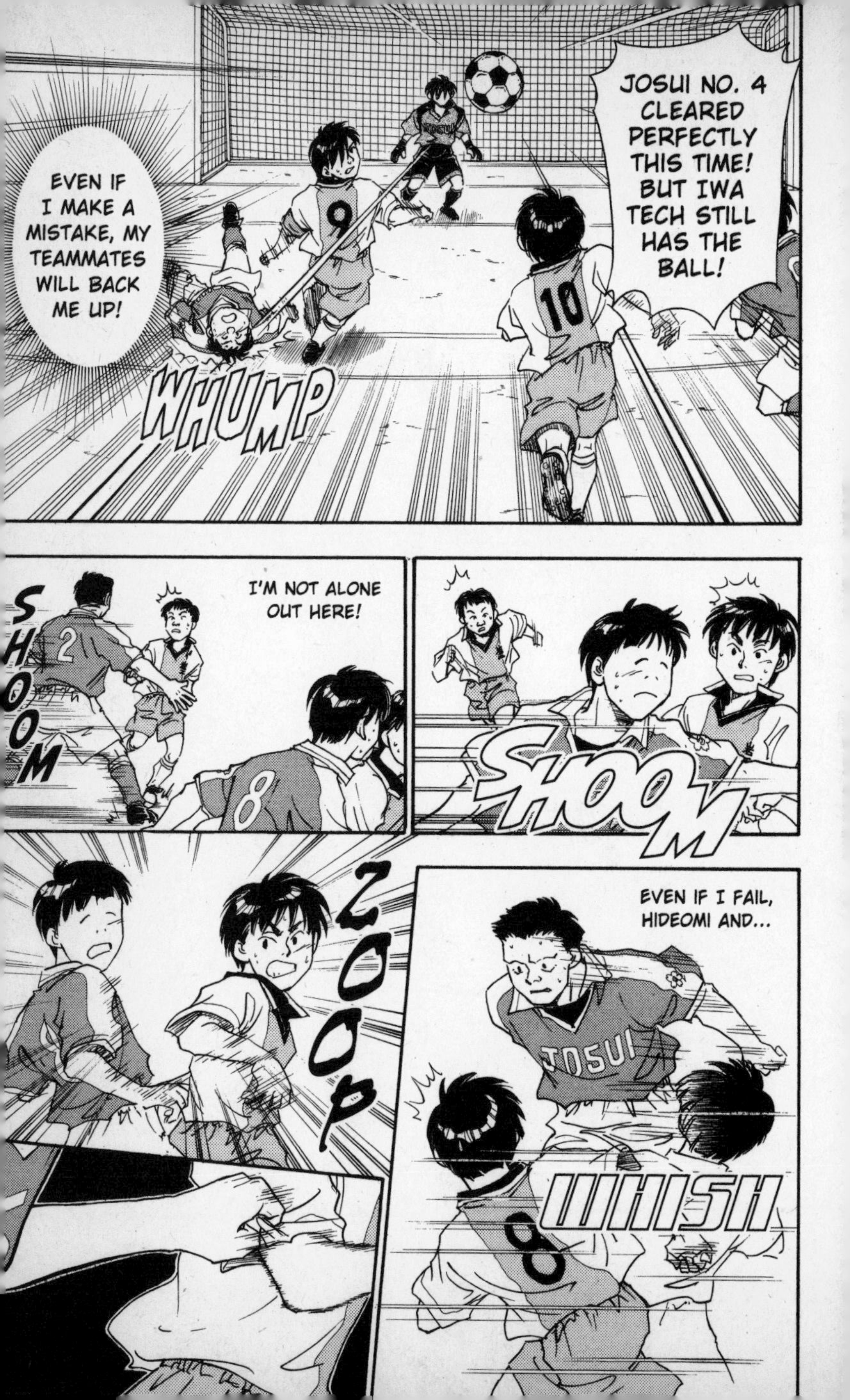
JOSUI NO. 4 CLEARED PERFECTLY THIS TIME! BUT IWA TECH STILL HAS THE BALL!
EVEN IF I MAKE A MISTAKE, MY TEAMMATES WILL BACK ME UP!
WHUMP
SHOOM
I'M NOT ALONE OUT HERE!
SHOOM
EVEN IF I FAIL, HIDEOMI AND...
WHISH
ZOOP

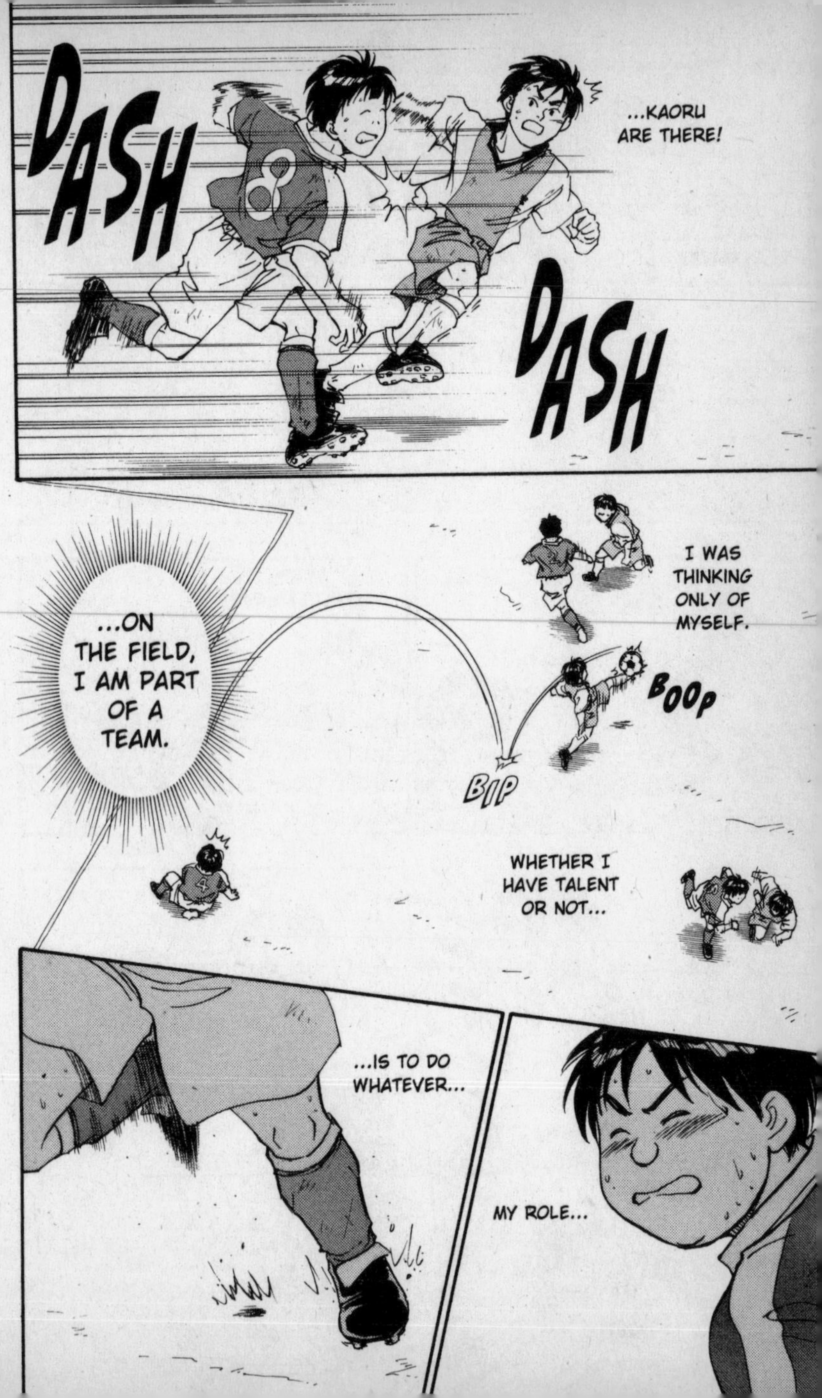
...KAORU ARE THERE!
DASH
DASH
I WAS THINKING ONLY OF MYSELF.
BOOP
BIP
WHETHER I HAVE TALENT OR NOT...
...ON THE FIELD, I AM PART OF A TEAM.
MY ROLE...
...IS TO DO WHATEVER...

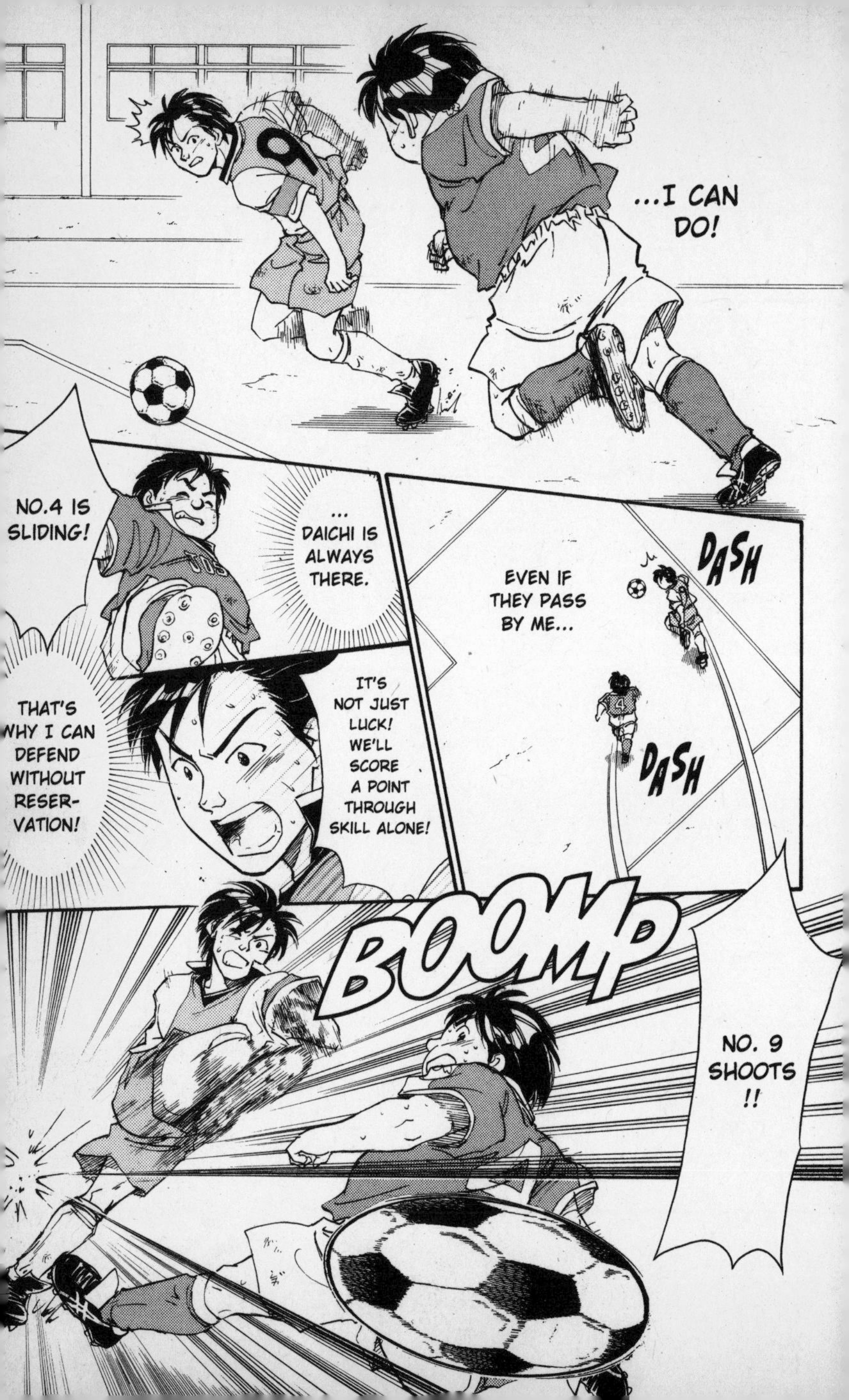
...I CAN DO!
EVEN IF THEY PASS BY ME...
DASH
DASH
... DAICHI IS ALWAYS THERE.
NO.4 IS SLIDING!
IT'S NOT JUST LUCK! WE'LL SCORE A POINT THROUGH SKILL ALONE!
THAT'S WHY I CAN DEFEND WITHOUT RESER-VATION!
NO. 9 SHOOTS !!
BOOMP

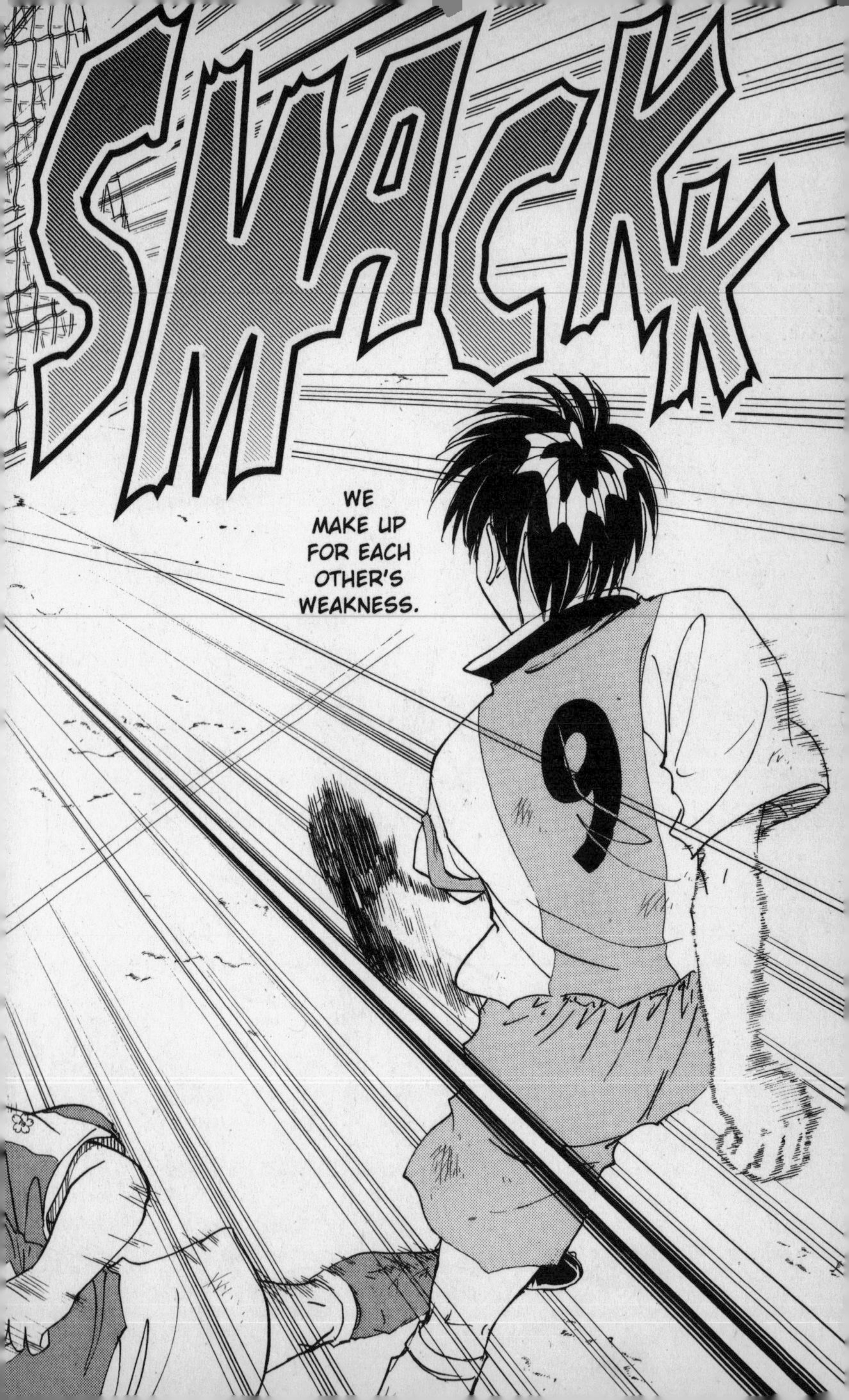
SMACK
WE MAKE UP FOR EACH OTHER'S WEAKNESS.

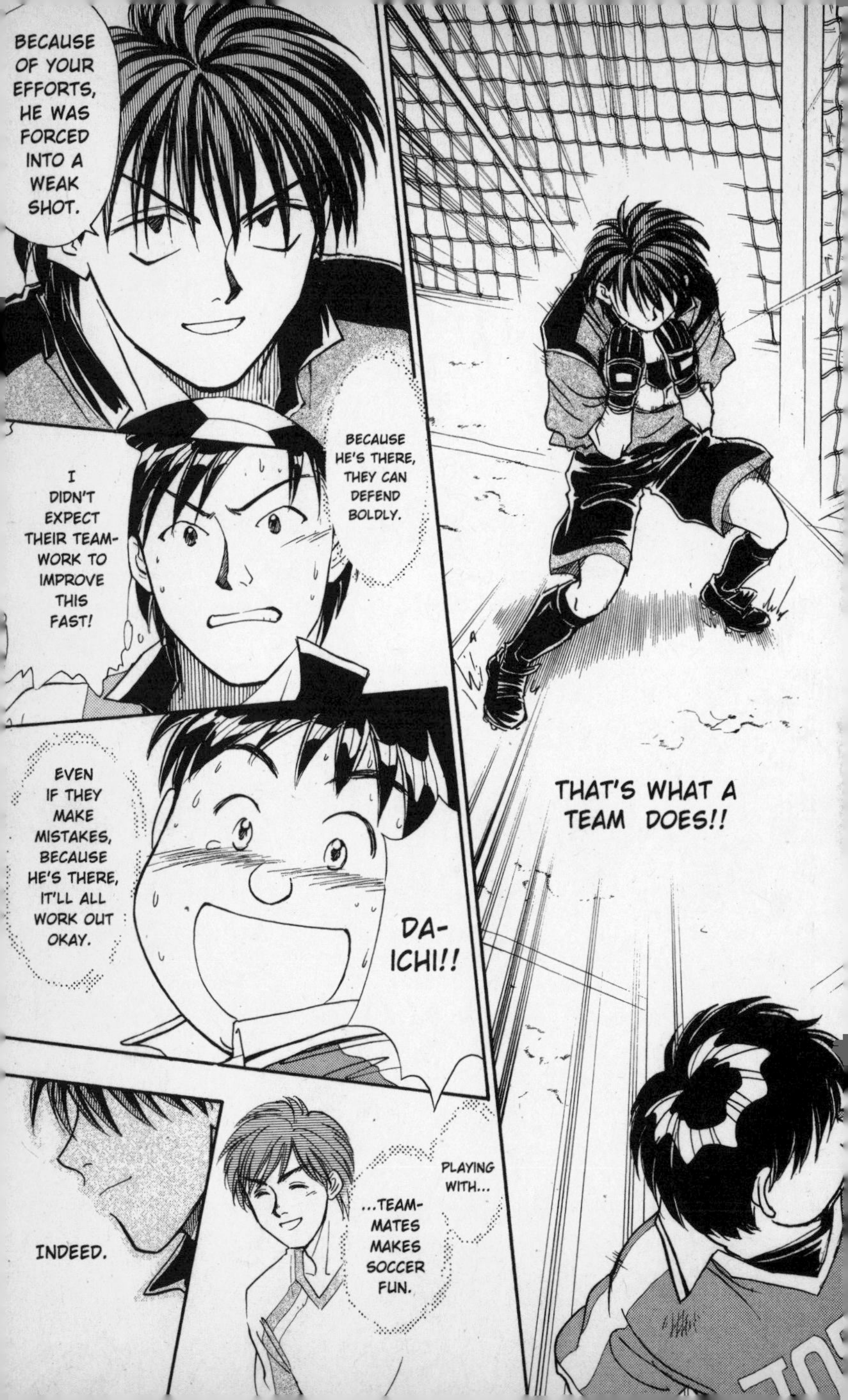
THAT'S WHAT A TEAM DOES!!
BECAUSE OF YOUR EFFORTS, HE WAS FORCED INTO A WEAK SHOT.
BECAUSE HE'S THERE, THEY CAN DEFEND BOLDLY.
I DIDN'T EXPECT THEIR TEAM-WORK TO IMPROVE THIS FAST!
EVEN IF THEY MAKE MISTAKES, BECAUSE HE'S THERE, IT'LL ALL WORK OUT OKAY.
DA-ICHI!!
PLAYING WITH...
...TEAM-MATES MAKES SOCCER FUN.
INDEED.

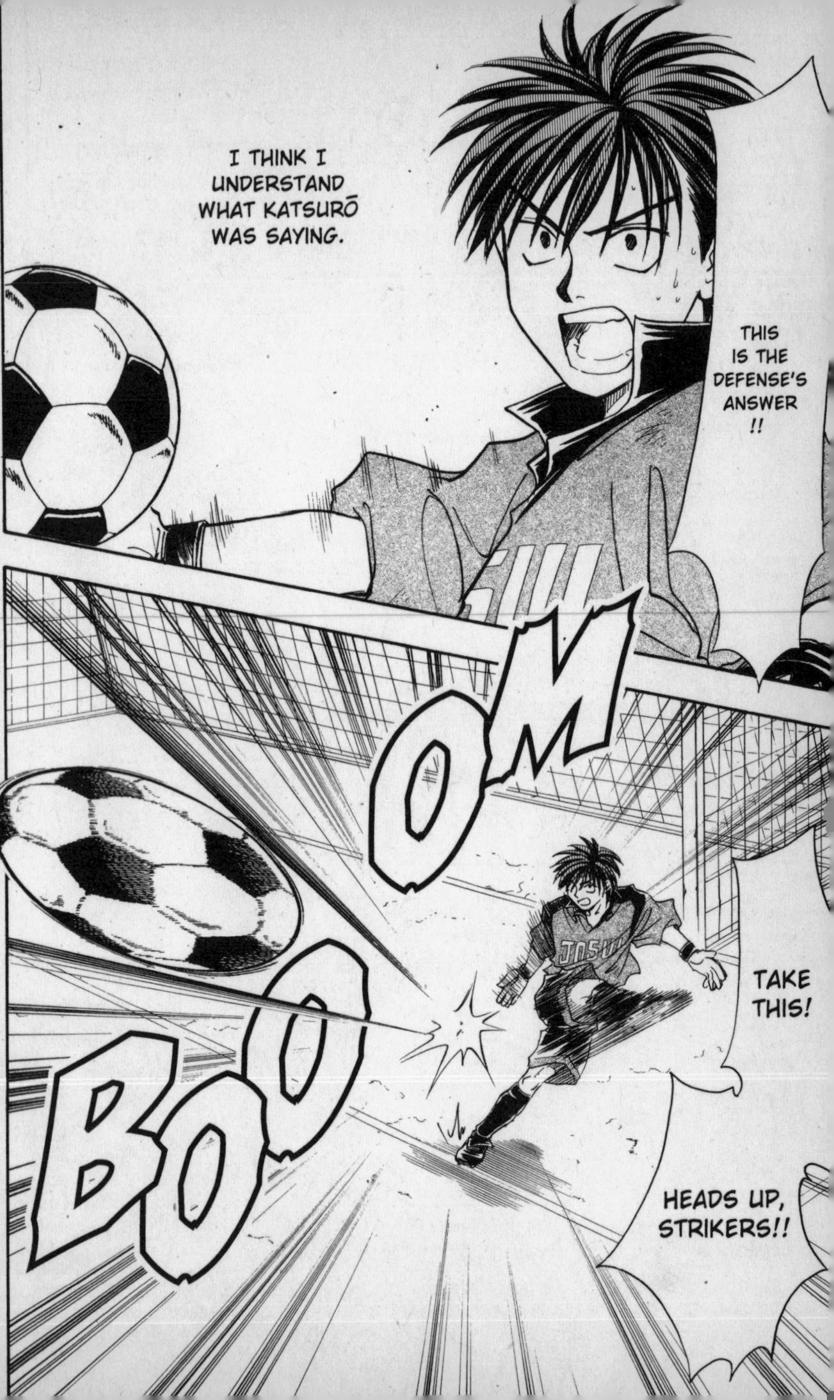
THIS IS THE DEFENSE'S ANSWER !!
I THINK I UNDERSTAND WHAT KATSURŌ WAS SAYING.
TAKE THIS!
HEADS UP, STRIKERS!!
BOOOM

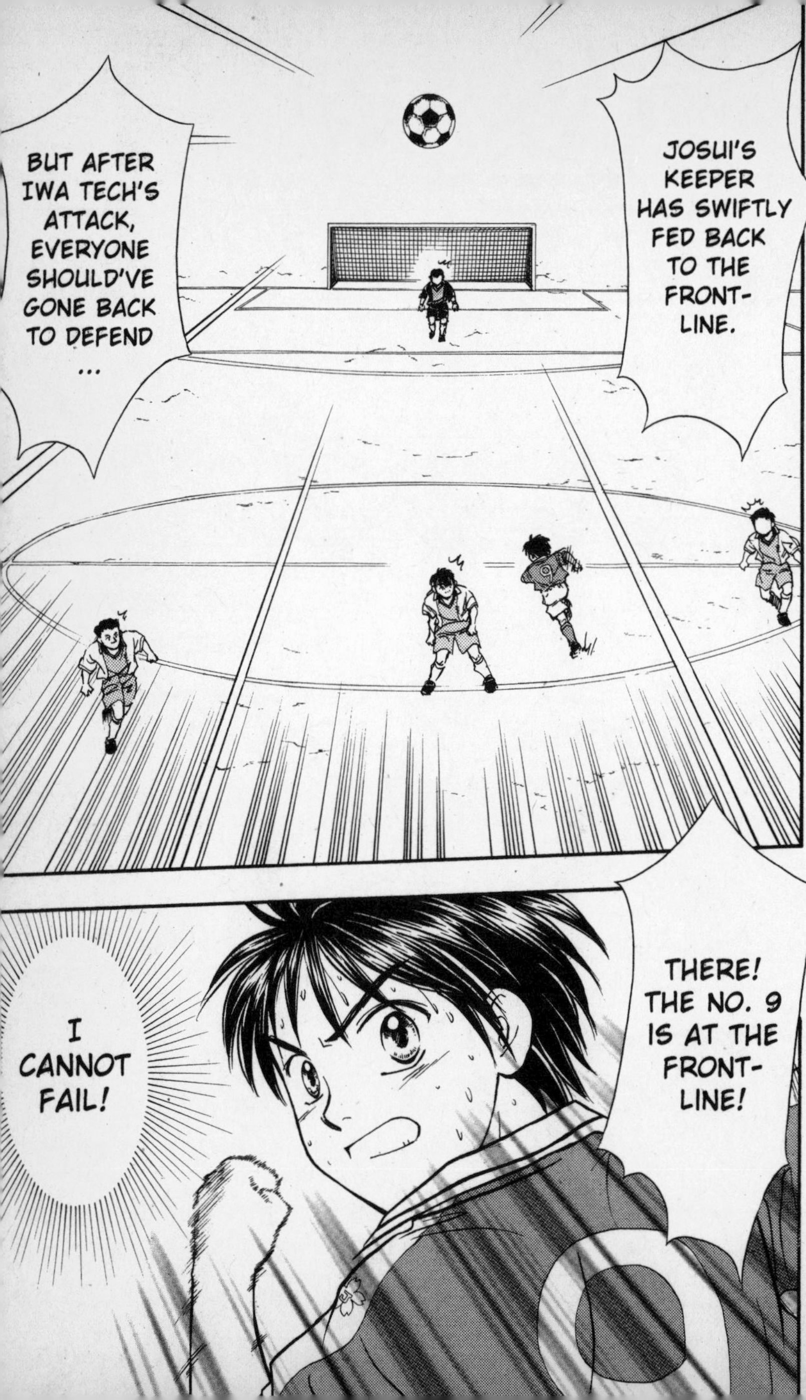
JOSUI'S KEEPER HAS SWIFTLY FED BACK TO THE FRONT-LINE.
BUT AFTER IWA TECH'S ATTACK, EVERYONE SHOULD'VE GONE BACK TO DEFEND ...
THERE! THE NO. 9 IS AT THE FRONT-LINE!
I CANNOT FAIL!

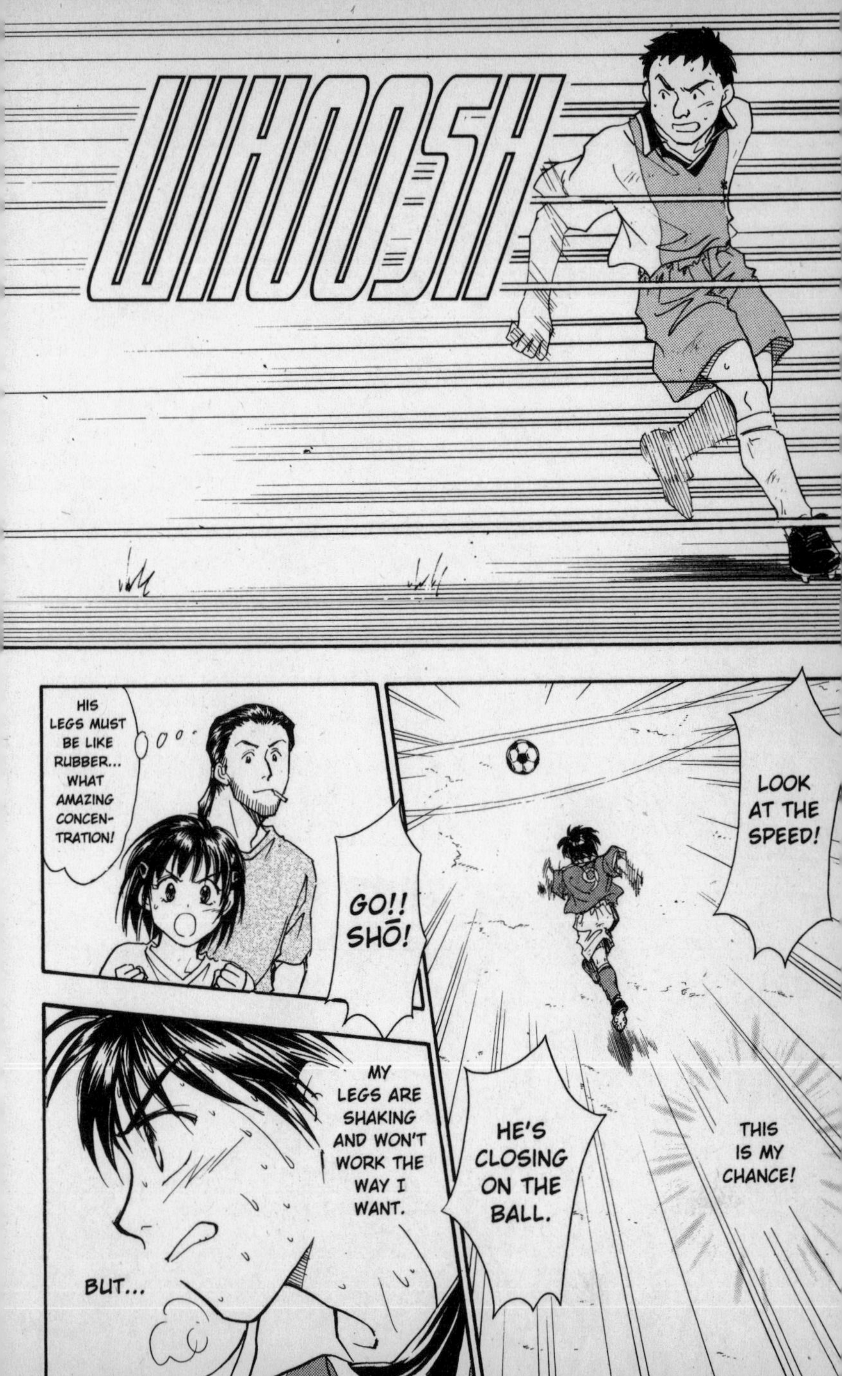
WHOOSH
LOOK AT THE SPEED!
THIS IS MY CHANCE!
HE'S CLOSING ON THE BALL.
GO!! SHŌ!
HIS LEGS MUST BE LIKE RUBBER... WHAT AMAZING CONCEN-TRATION!
MY LEGS ARE SHAKING AND WON'T WORK THE WAY I WANT.
BUT...

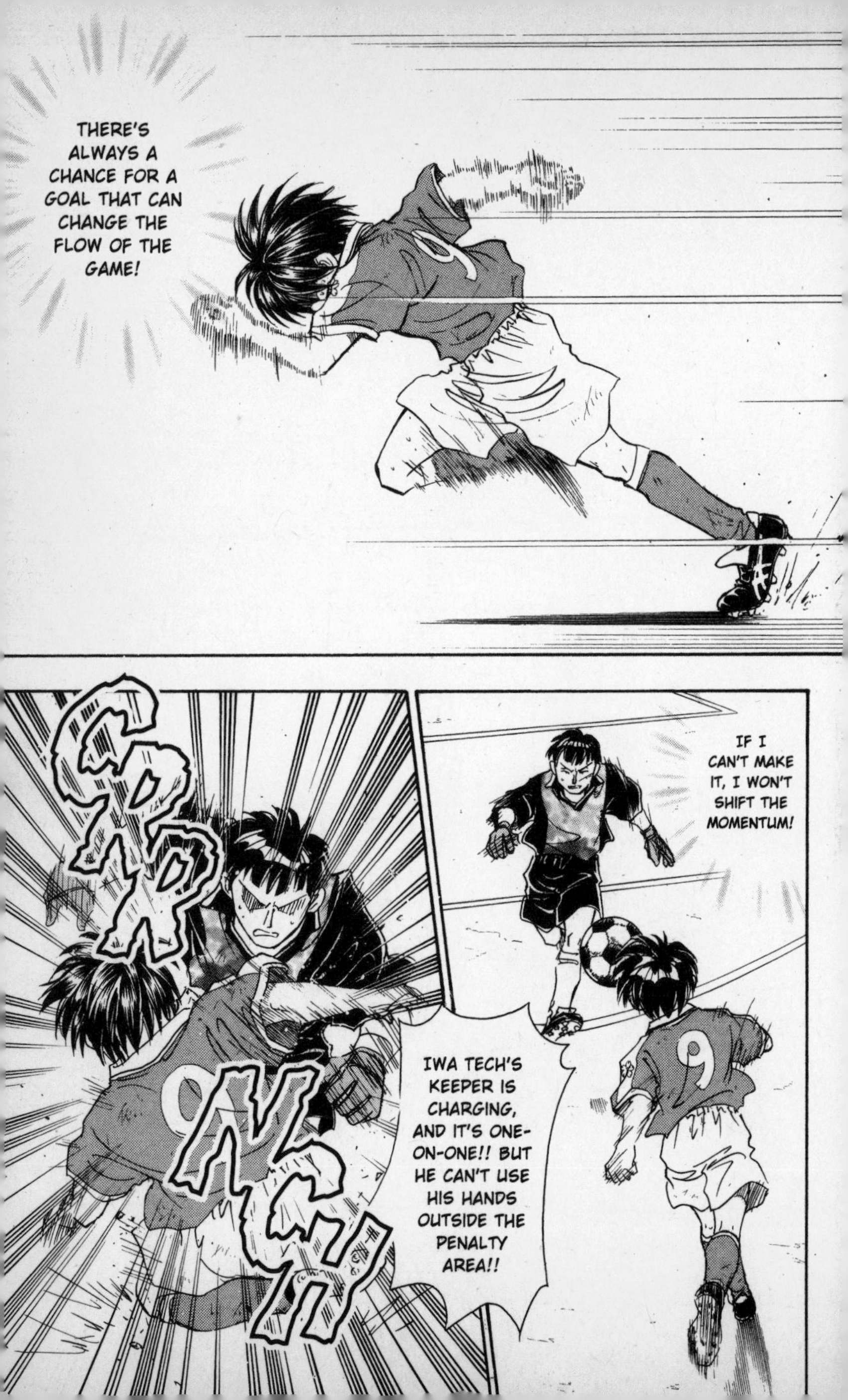
THERE'S ALWAYS A CHANCE FOR A GOAL THAT CAN CHANGE THE FLOW OF THE GAME!
IF I CAN'T MAKE IT, I WON'T SHIFT THE MOMENTUM!
IWA TECH'S KEEPER IS CHARGING, AND IT'S ONE-ON-ONE!! BUT HE CAN'T USE HIS HANDS OUTSIDE THE PENALTY AREA!!

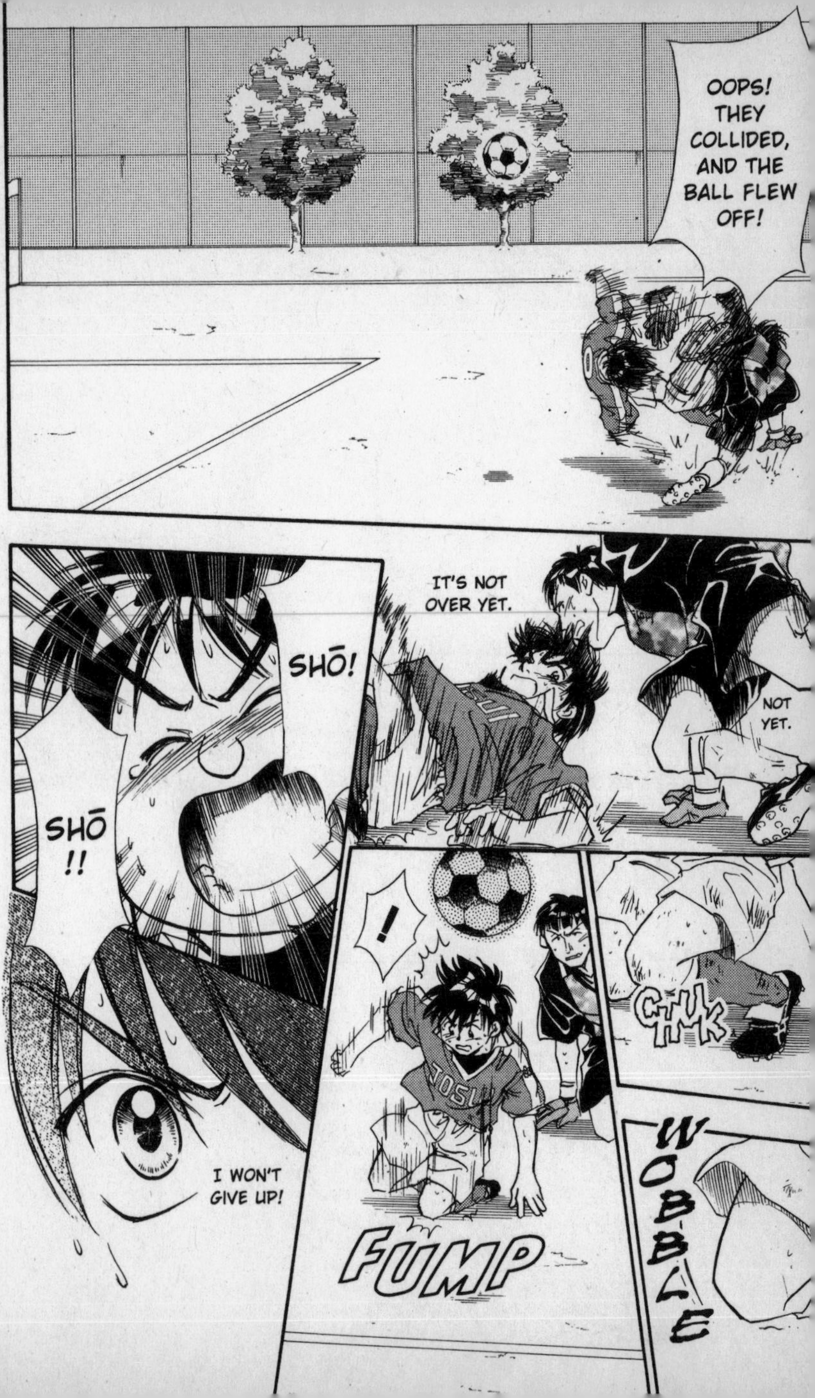
OOPS! THEY COLLIDED, AND THE BALL FLEW OFF!
IT'S NOT OVER YET.
NOT YET.
CHUK
WOBBLE
!
FUMP
SHŌ!
SHŌ !!
I WON'T GIVE UP!

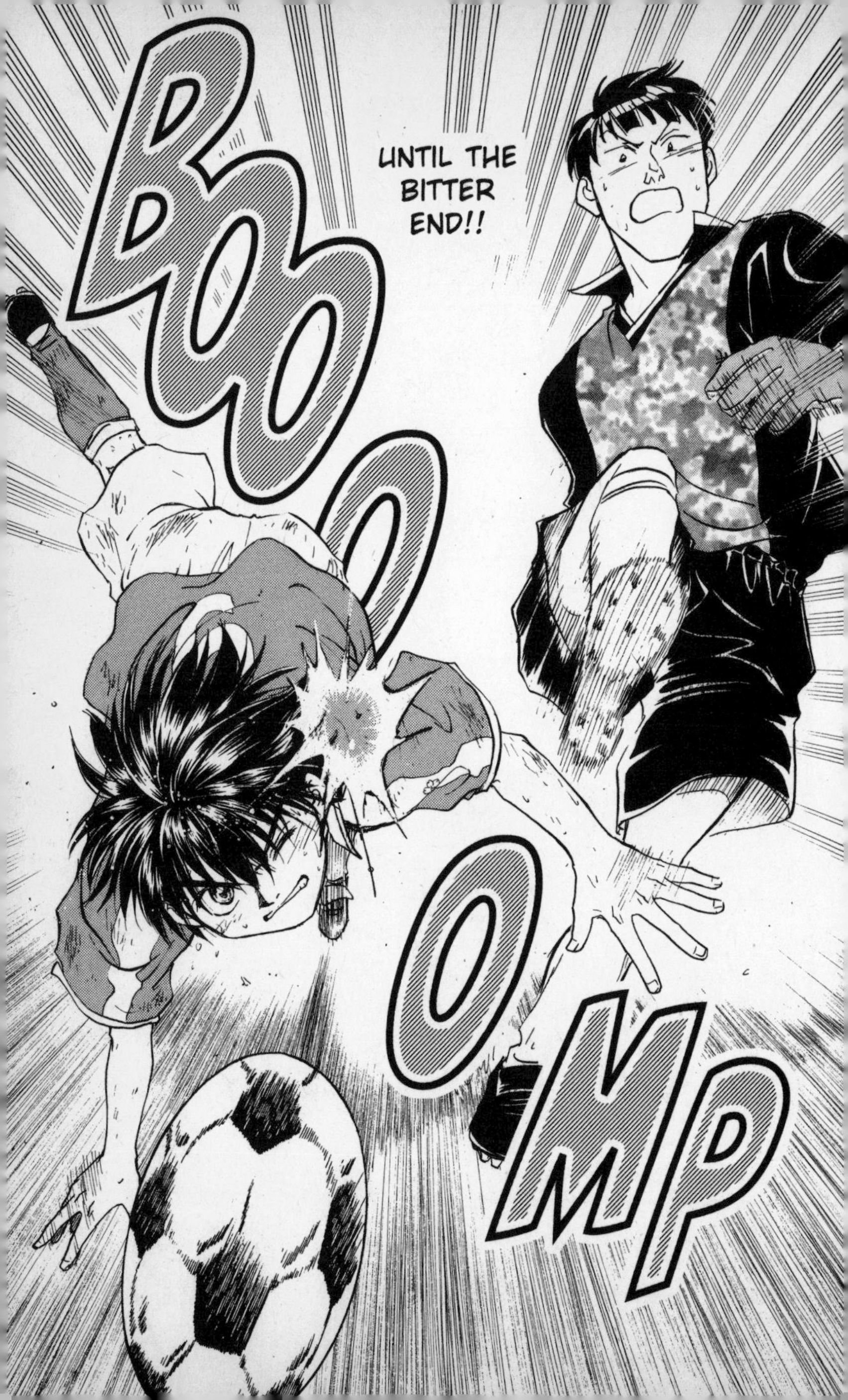
UNTIL THE BITTER END!!
BOOOOOMP

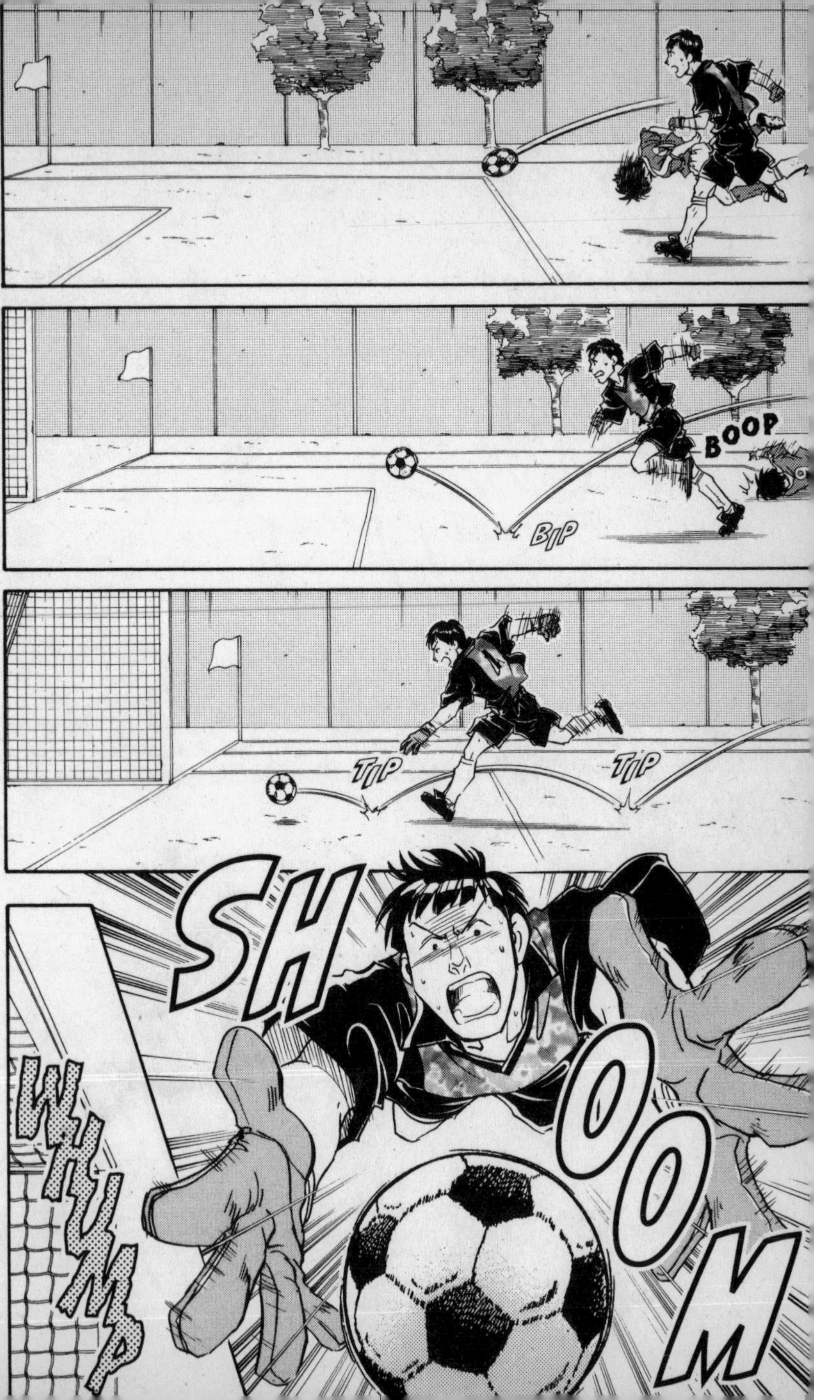
BOOP
BIP
TIP
TIP
SHOOOM
WHUMP

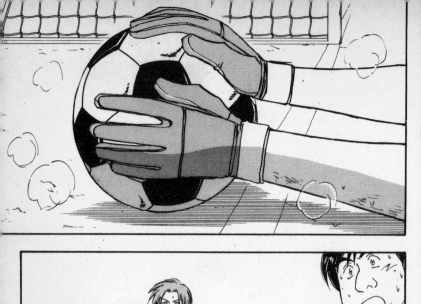

RO OAA RR

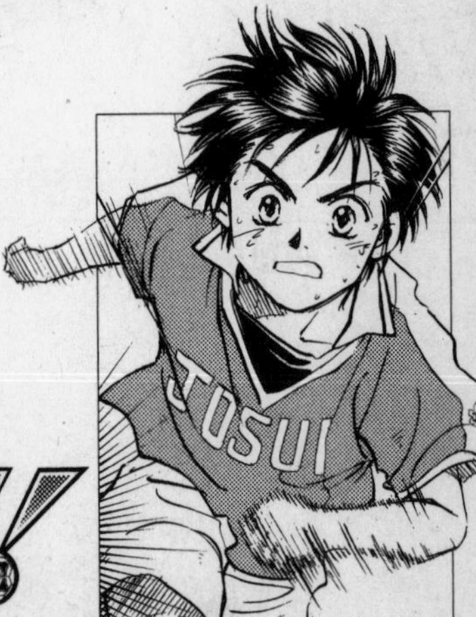
JOSUI

WHISTLE!

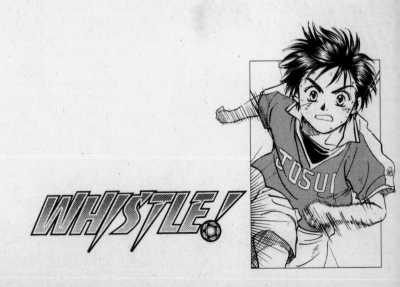

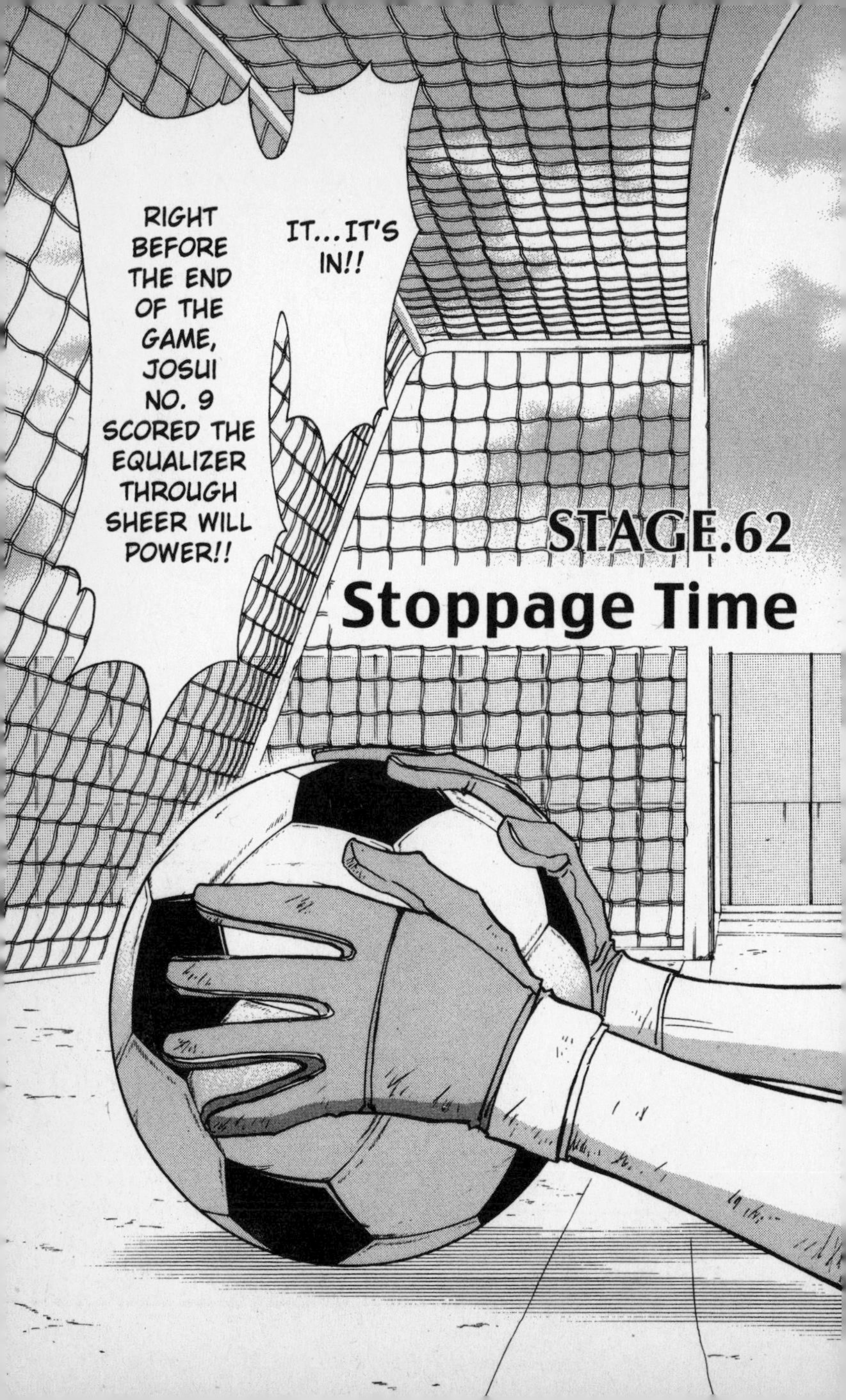
IT... IT'S IN!!
RIGHT BEFORE THE END OF THE GAME, JOSUI NO. 9 SCORED THE EQUALIZER THROUGH SHEER WILL POWER!!
STAGE.62
Stoppage Time

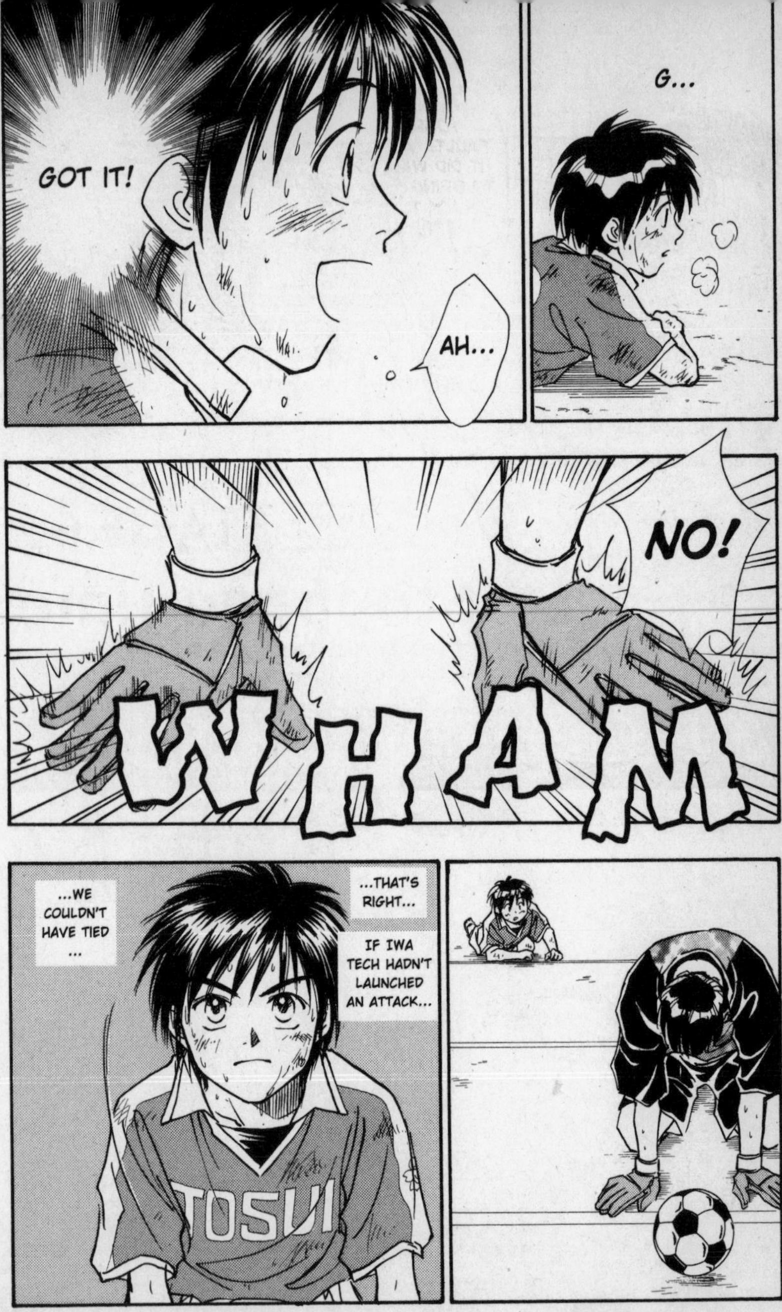
G...
GOT IT!
AH...
NO!
WHAM
...THAT'S RIGHT...
IF IWA TECH HADN'T LAUNCHED AN ATTACK...
...WE COULDN'T HAVE TIED ...

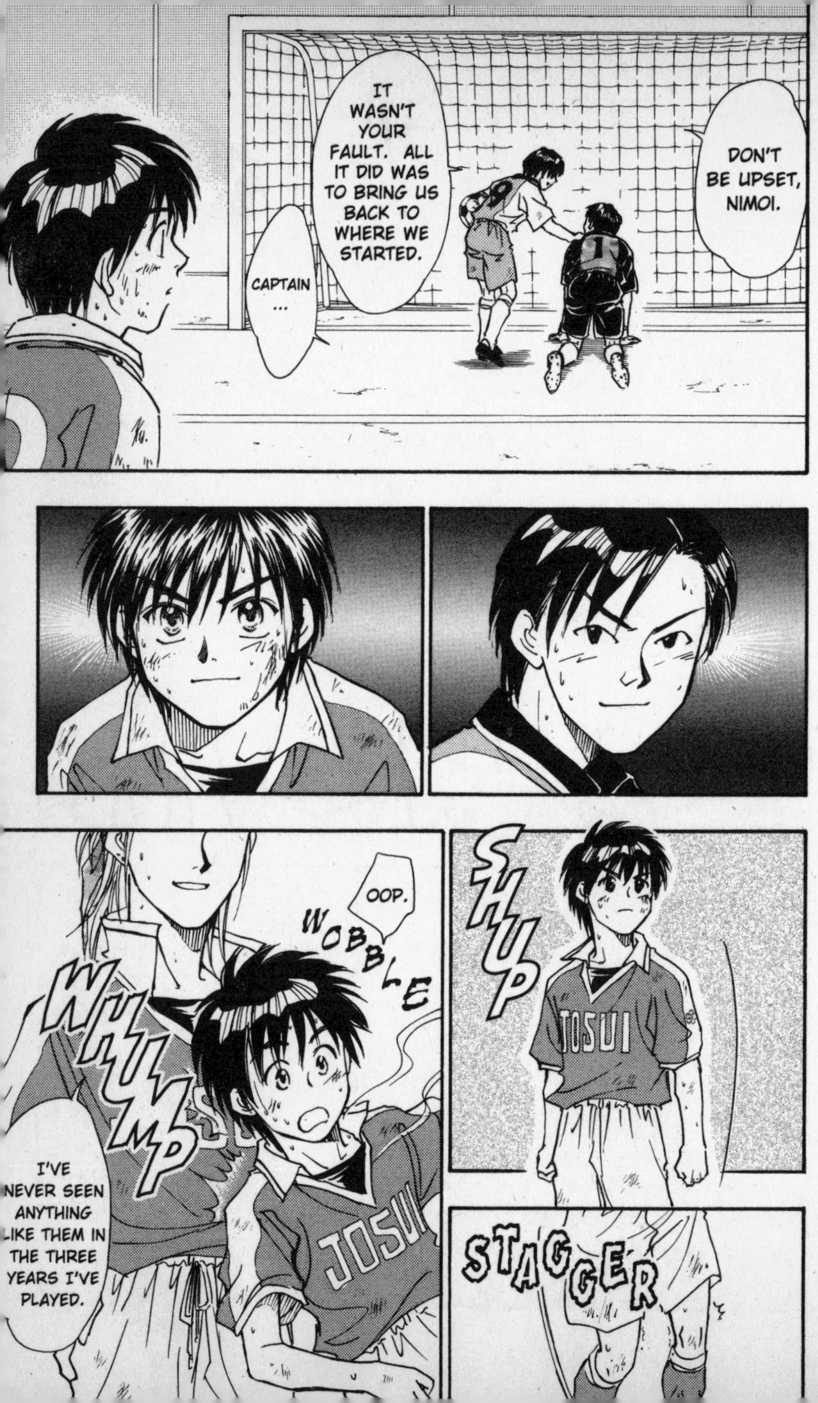
DON'T BE UPSET, NIMOI.
IT WASN'T YOUR FAULT. ALL IT DID WAS TO BRING US BACK TO WHERE WE STARTED.
CAPTAIN ...
SHUP
STAGGER
OOP.
WOBBLE
WHUMP
I'VE NEVER SEEN ANYTHING LIKE THEM IN THE THREE YEARS I'VE PLAYED.

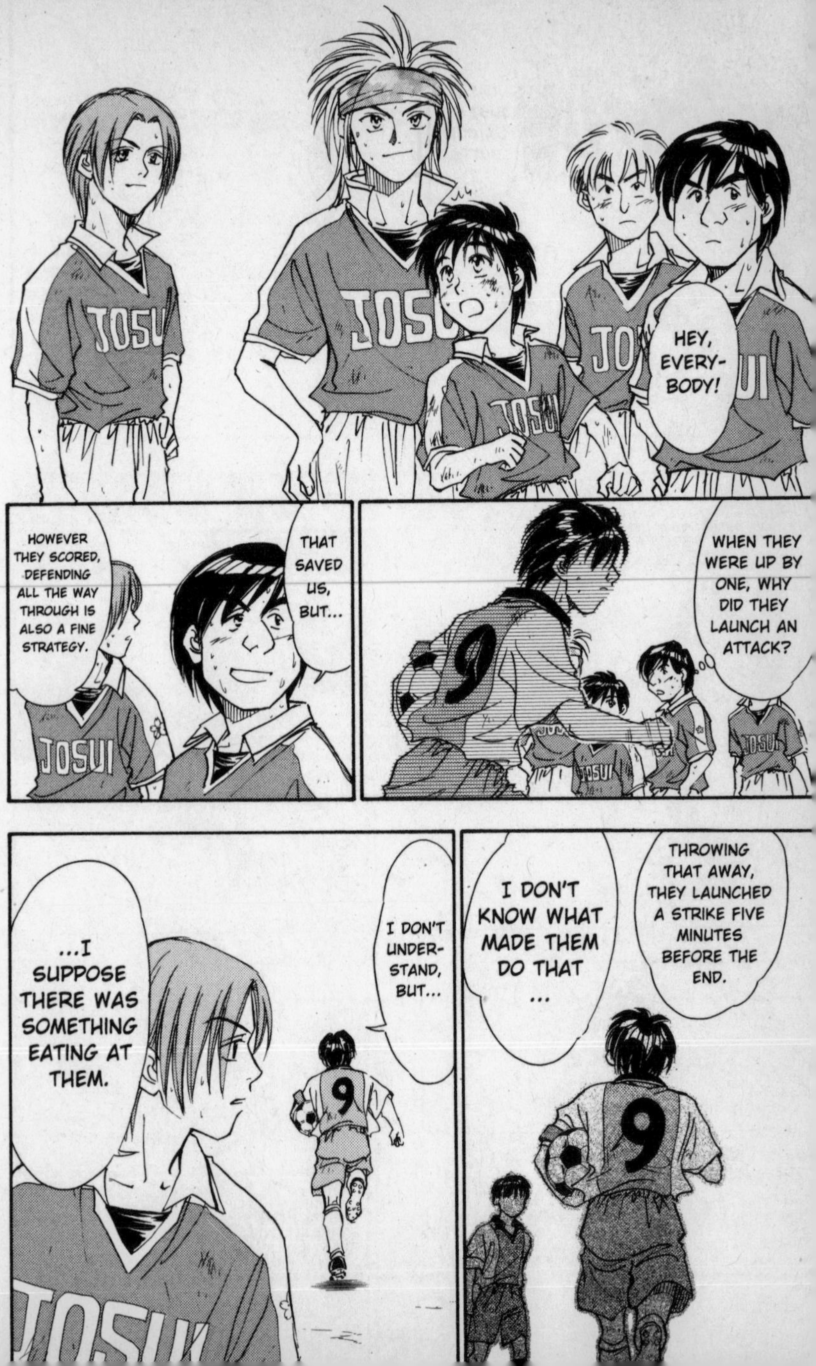
HEY, EVERY-BODY!
WHEN THEY WERE UP BY ONE, WHY DID THEY LAUNCH AN ATTACK?
THAT SAVED US, BUT...
HOWEVER THEY SCORED, DEFENDING ALL THE WAY THROUGH IS ALSO A FINE STRATEGY.
THROWING THAT AWAY, THEY LAUNCHED A STRIKE FIVE MINUTES BEFORE THE END.
I DON'T KNOW WHAT MADE THEM DO THAT ...
I DON'T UNDER-STAND, BUT...
...I SUPPOSE THERE WAS SOMETHING EATING AT THEM.

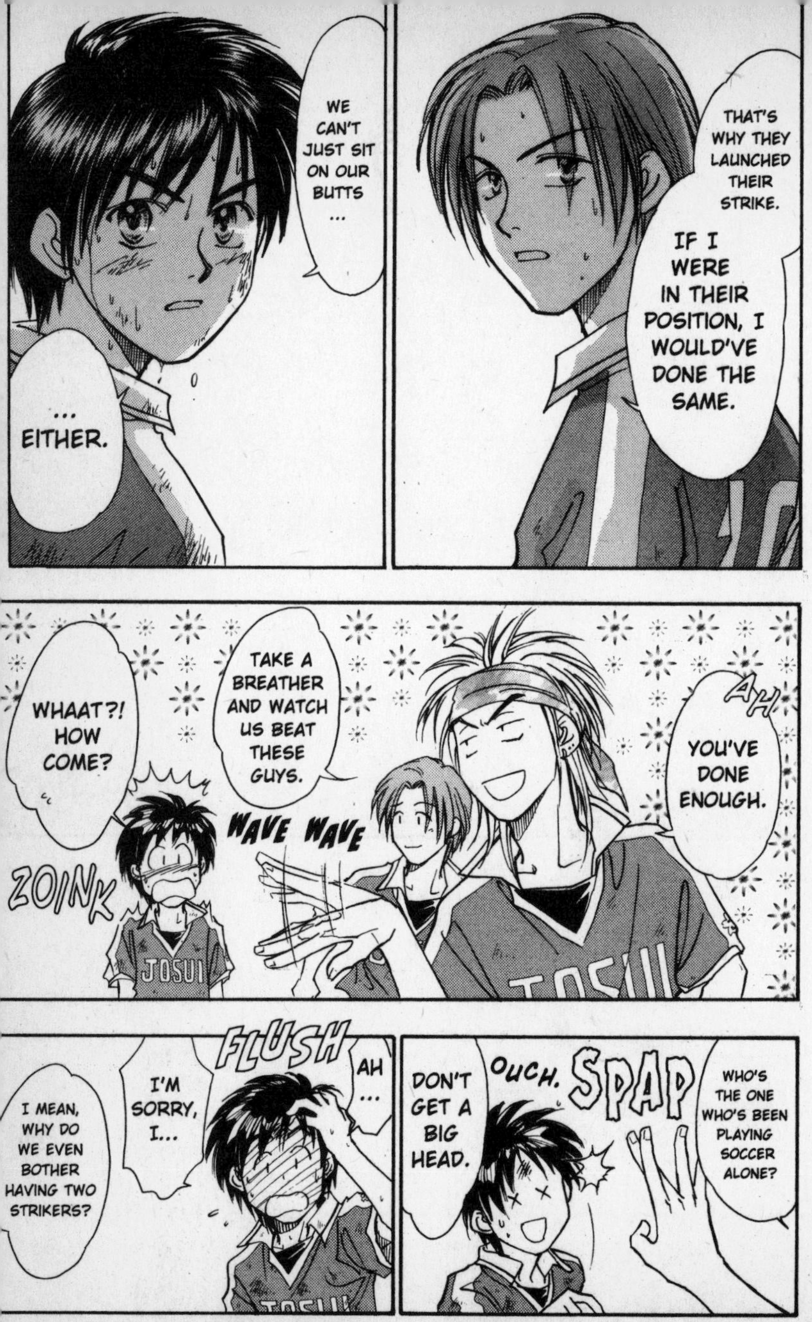
THAT'S WHY THEY LAUNCHED THEIR STRIKE.
IF I WERE IN THEIR POSITION, I WOULD'VE DONE THE SAME.
WE CAN'T JUST SIT ON OUR BUTTS ...
... EITHER.
AH
YOU'VE DONE ENOUGH.
WAVE WAVE
TAKE A BREATHER AND WATCH US BEAT THESE GUYS.
WHAAT?! HOW COME?
ZOINK
JOSUI
WHO'S THE ONE WHO'S BEEN PLAYING SOCCER ALONE?
SPAP
OUCH.
DON'T GET A BIG HEAD.
AH ...
FLUSH
I'M SORRY, I...
I MEAN, WHY DO WE EVEN BOTHER HAVING TWO STRIKERS?

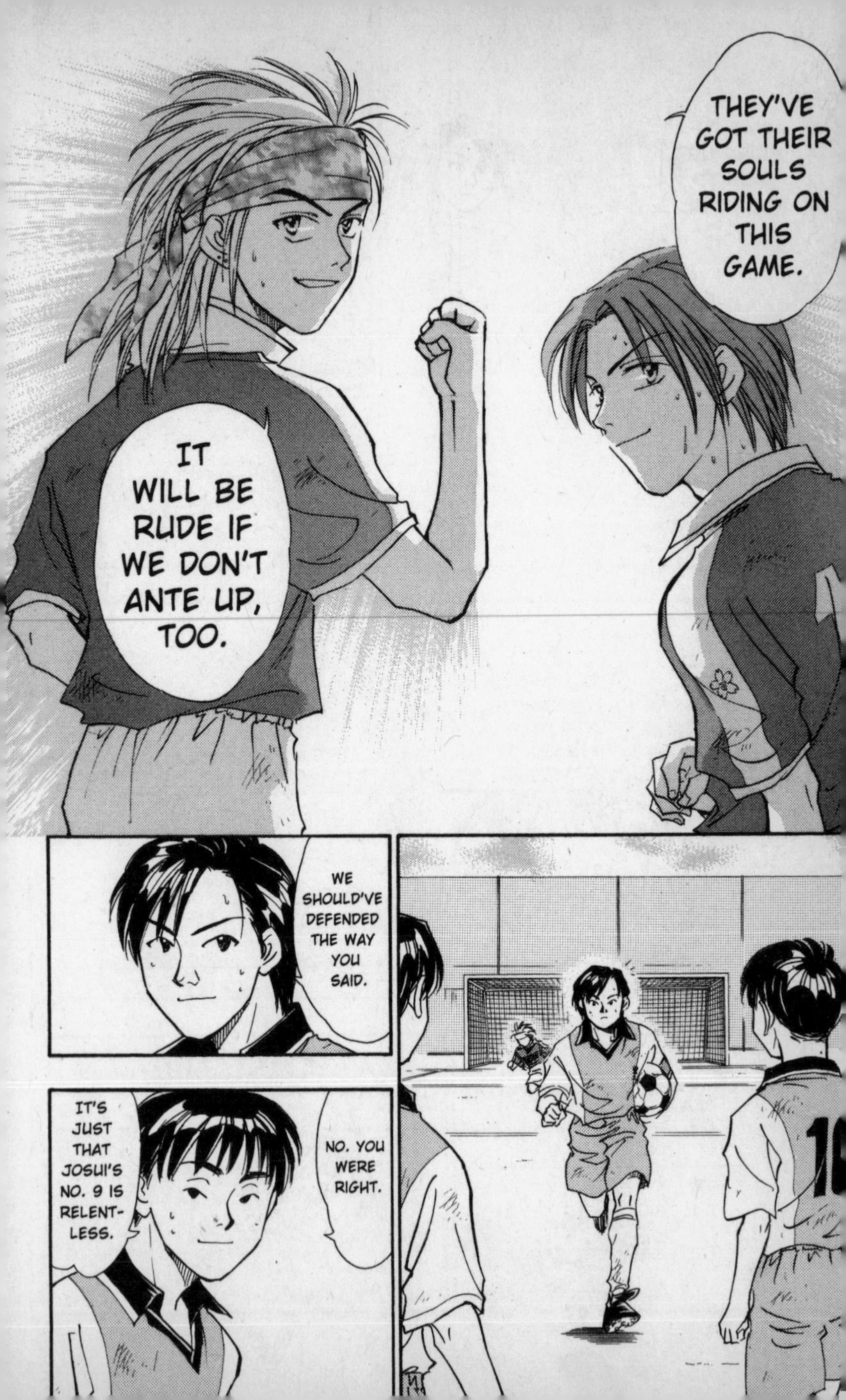
THEY'VE GOT THEIR SOULS RIDING ON THIS GAME.
IT WILL BE RUDE IF WE DON'T ANTE UP, TOO.
WE SHOULD'VE DEFENDED THE WAY YOU SAID.
NO. YOU WERE RIGHT.
IT'S JUST THAT JOSUI'S NO. 9 IS RELENT-LESS.

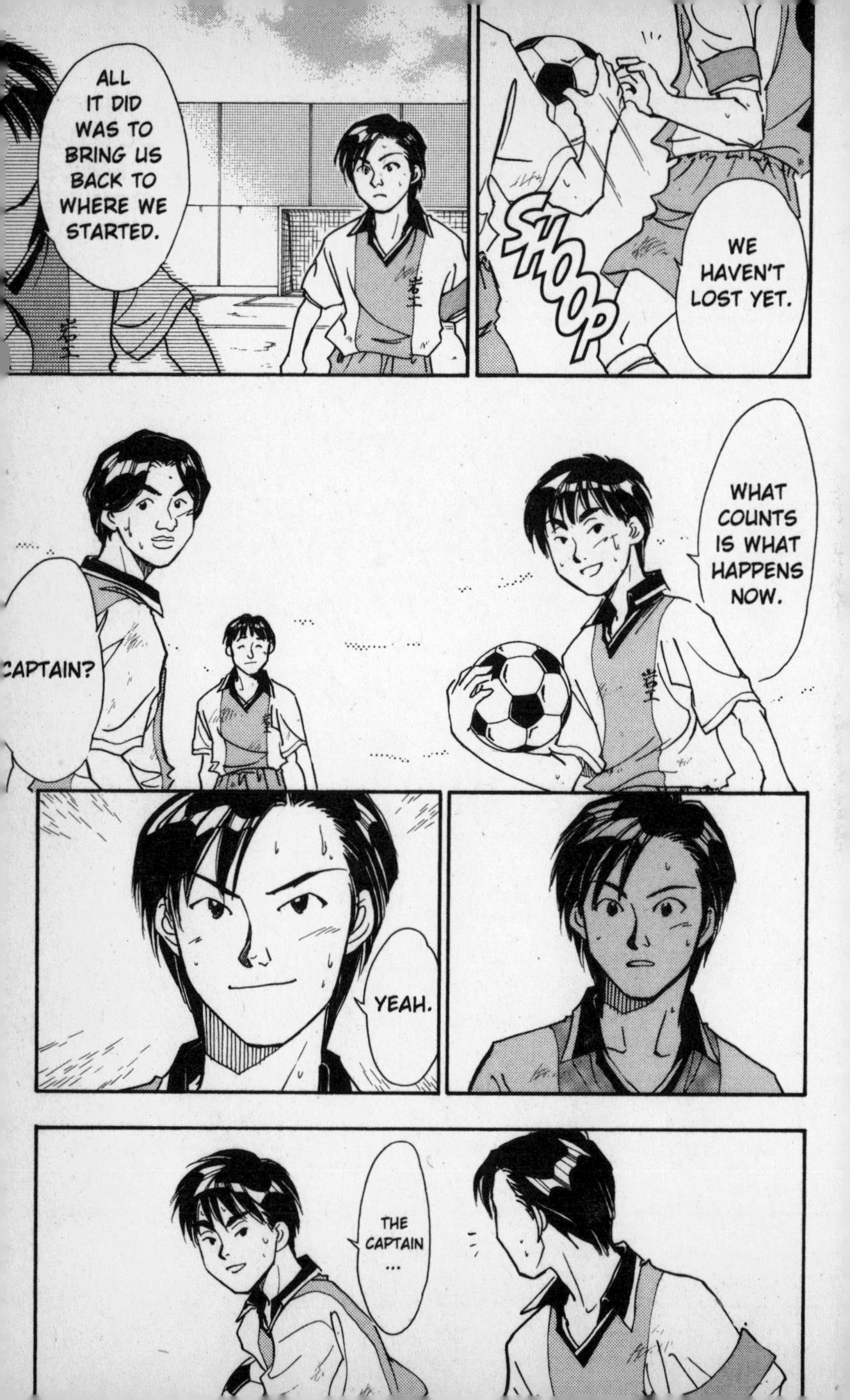
SHOOP
WE HAVEN'T LOST YET.
ALL IT DID WAS TO BRING US BACK TO WHERE WE STARTED.
WHAT COUNTS IS WHAT HAPPENS NOW.
CAPTAIN?
YEAH.
THE CAPTAIN ...

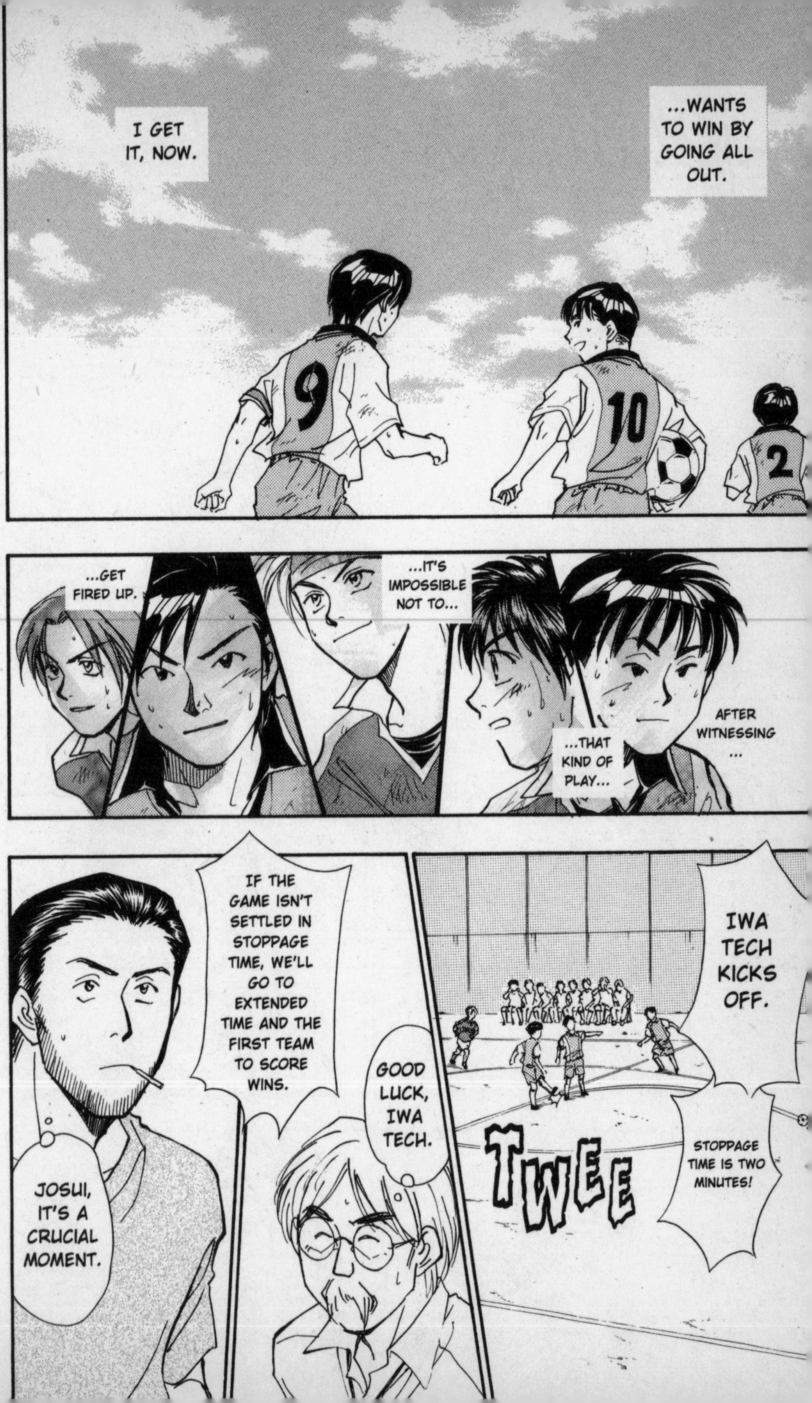
...WANTS TO WIN BY GOING ALL OUT.
I GET IT, NOW.
AFTER WITNESSING...
...THAT KIND OF PLAY...
...IT'S IMPOSSIBLE NOT TO...
...GET FIRED UP.
IWA TECH KICKS OFF.
TWEE
STOPPAGE TIME IS TWO MINUTES!
IF THE GAME ISN'T SETTLED IN STOPPAGE TIME, WE'LL GO TO EXTENDED TIME AND THE FIRST TEAM TO SCORE WINS.
GOOD LUCK, IWA TECH.
JOSUI, IT'S A CRUCIAL MOMENT.

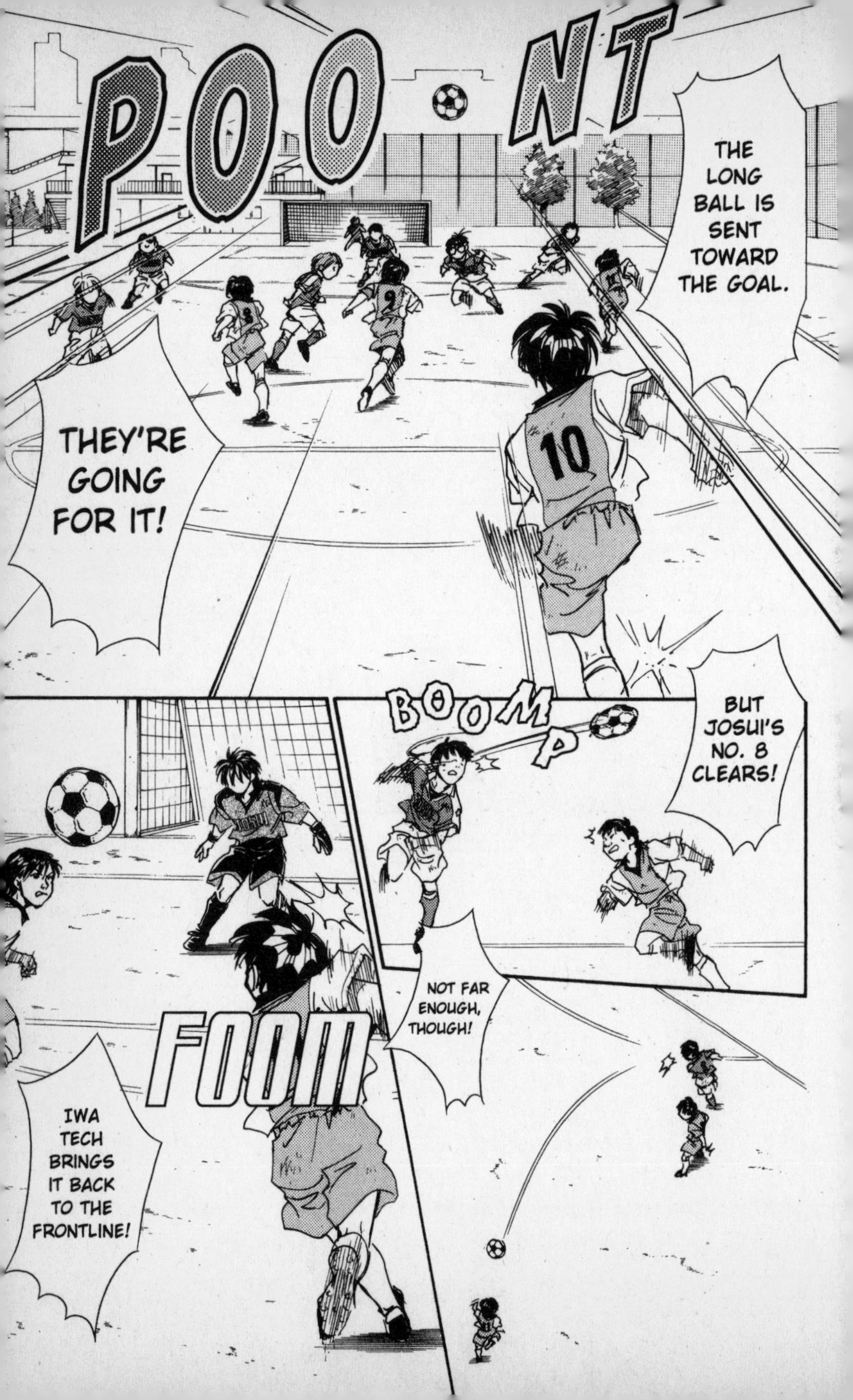
POO-NT
THE LONG BALL IS SENT TOWARD THE GOAL.
THEY'RE GOING FOR IT!
BOOMP
BUT JOSUI'S NO. 8 CLEARS!
NOT FAR ENOUGH, THOUGH!
FOOM
IWA TECH BRINGS IT BACK TO THE FRONTLINE!

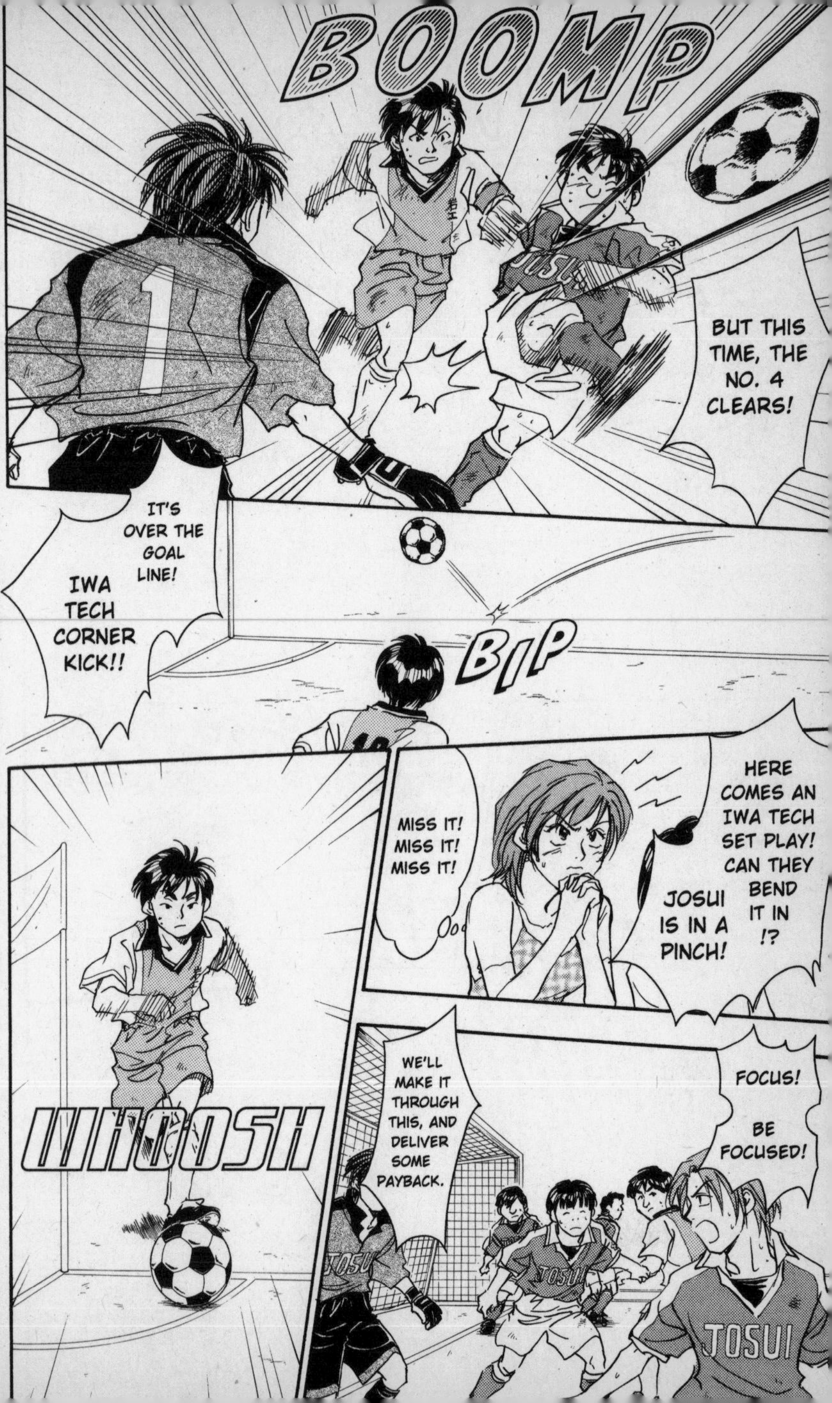
BOOMP
BUT THIS TIME, THE NO. 4 CLEARS!
IT'S OVER THE GOAL LINE! IWA TECH CORNER KICK!!
BIP
HERE COMES AN IWA TECH SET PLAY! CAN THEY BEND IT IN !?
JOSUI IS IN A PINCH!
MISS IT! MISS IT! MISS IT!
FOCUS!
BE FOCUSED!
WE'LL MAKE IT THROUGH THIS, AND DELIVER SOME PAYBACK.
WHOOSH

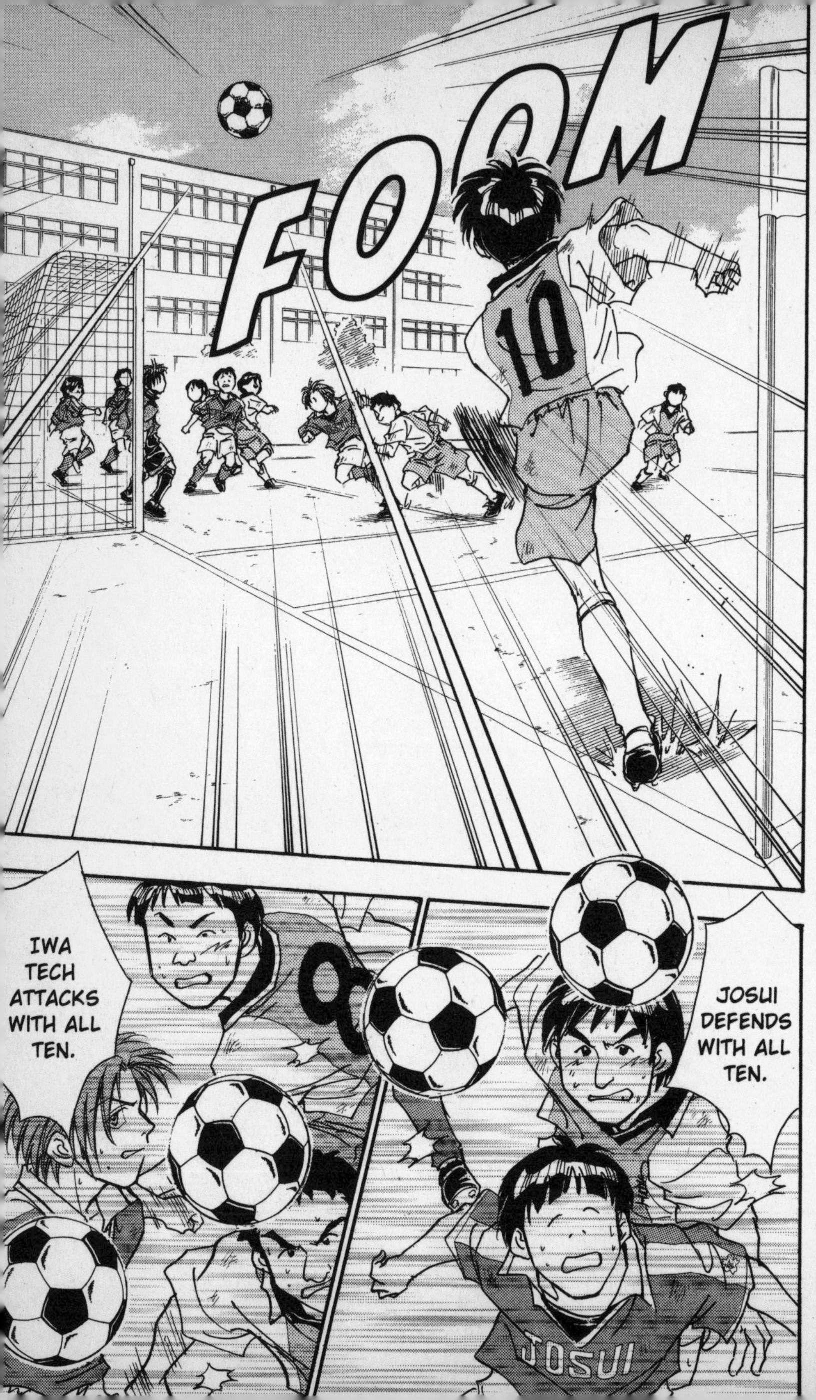
FOOM
JOSUI DEFENDS WITH ALL TEN.
IWA TECH ATTACKS WITH ALL TEN.
JOSUI

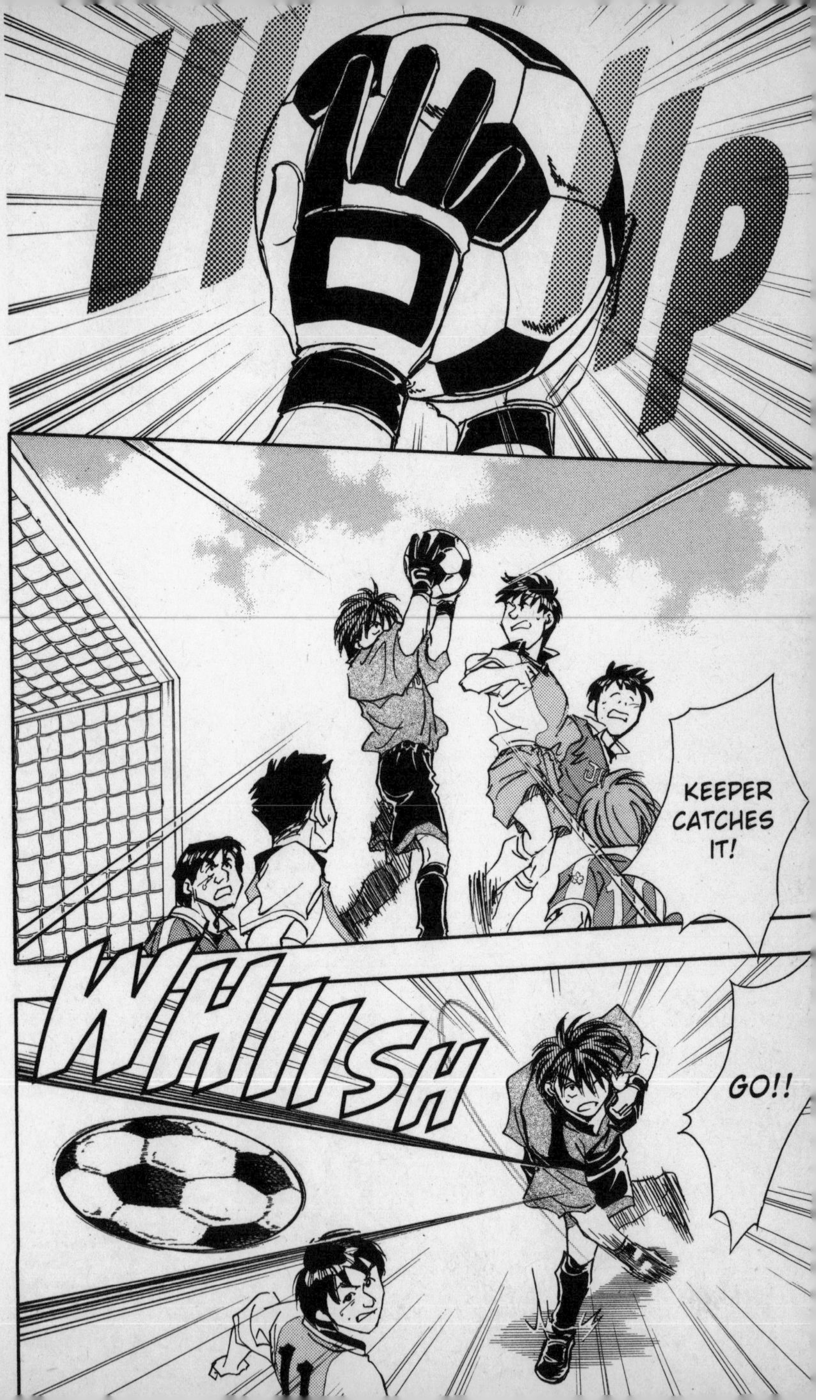
VWHIP
KEEPER CATCHES IT!
WHUSH
GO!!

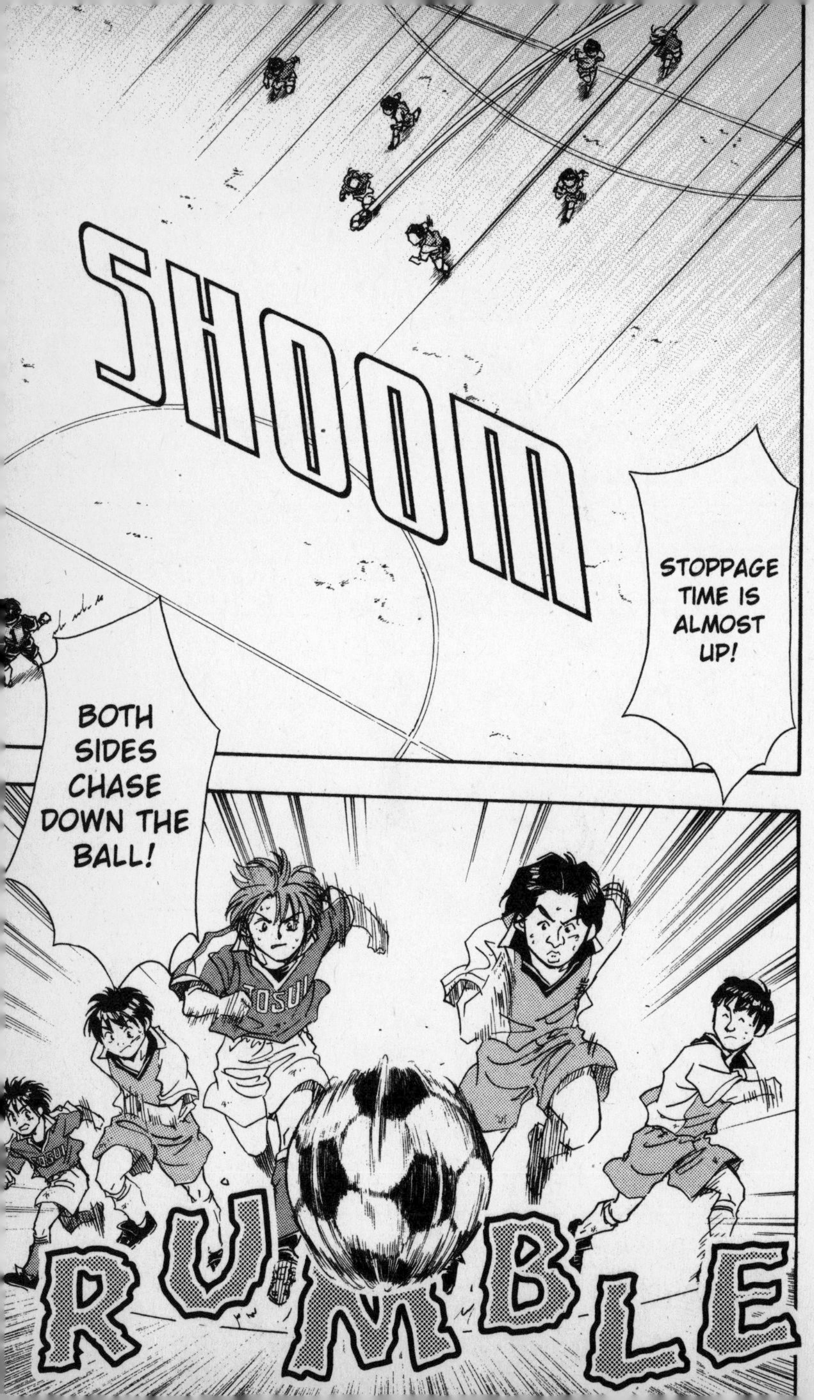
STOPPAGE TIME IS ALMOST UP!
SHOOM
BOTH SIDES CHASE DOWN THE BALL!
RUMBLE

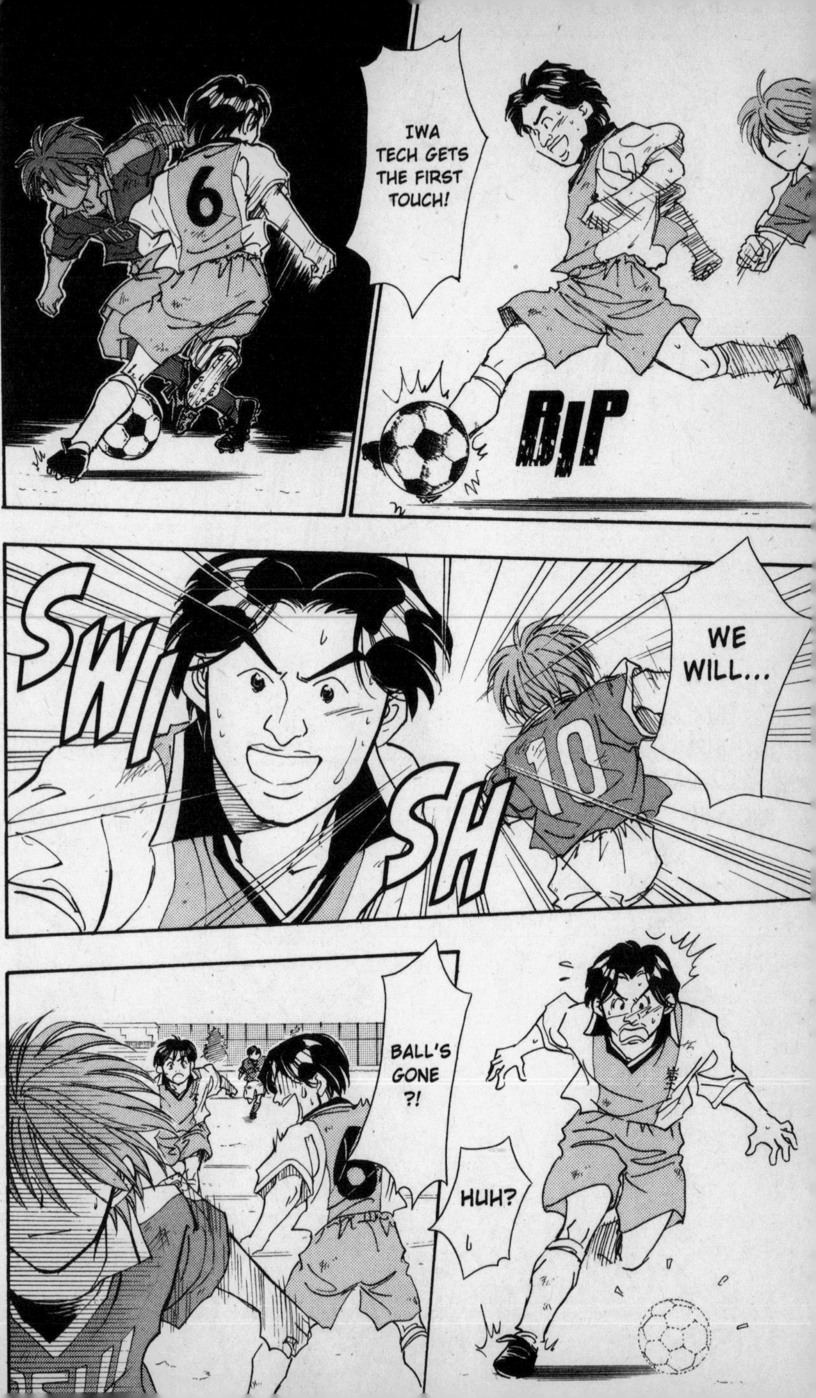
IWA TECH GETS THE FIRST TOUCH!
BIP
WE WILL...
SWISH
BALL'S GONE ?!
HUH?

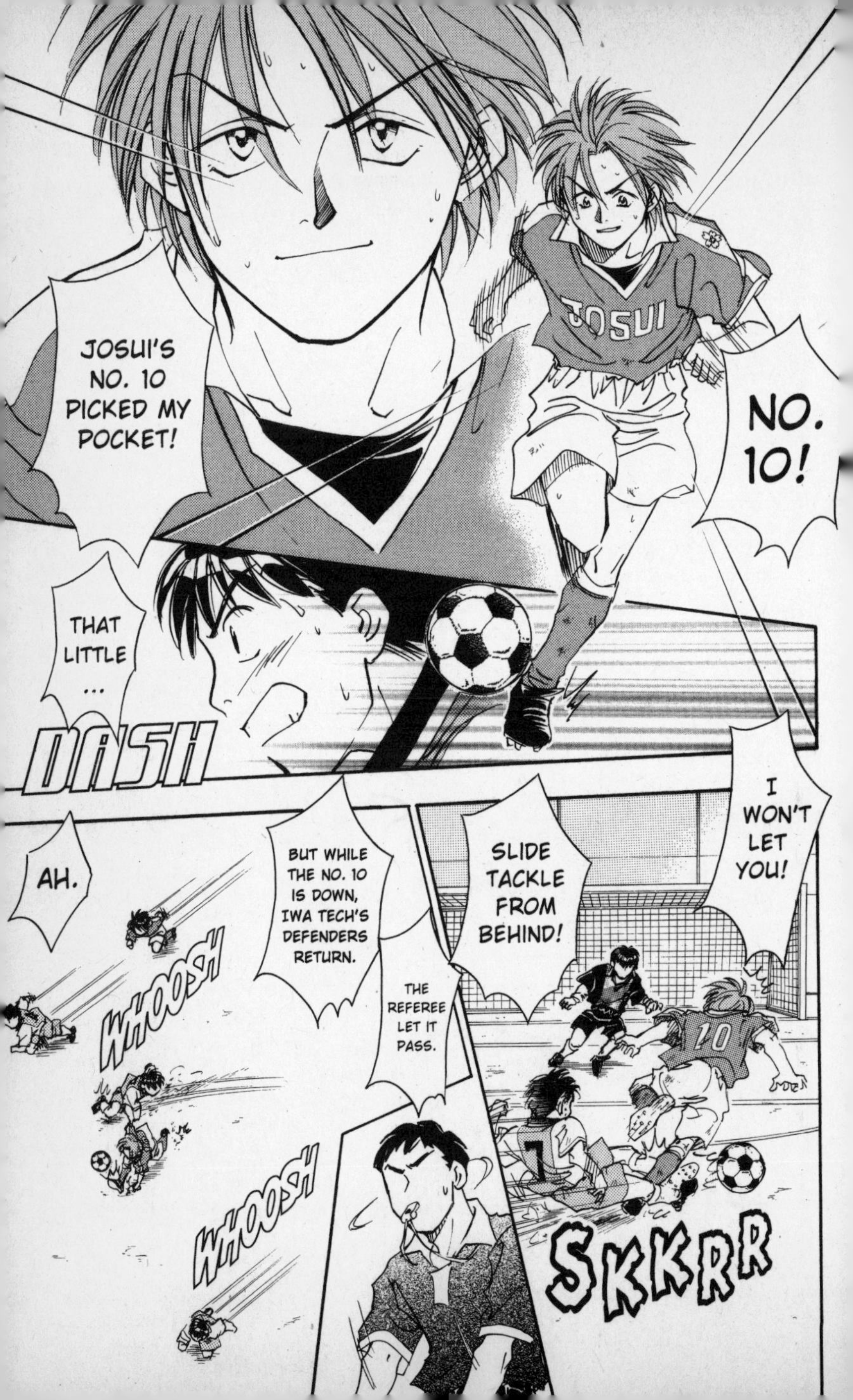
NO. 10!
JOSUI'S NO. 10 PICKED MY POCKET!
JOSUI
THAT LITTLE ...
DASH
I WON'T LET YOU!
SLIDE TACKLE FROM BEHIND!
SKKRR
BUT WHILE THE NO. 10 IS DOWN, IWA TECH'S DEFENDERS RETURN.
THE REFEREE LET IT PASS.
AH.
WHOOSH
WHOOSH

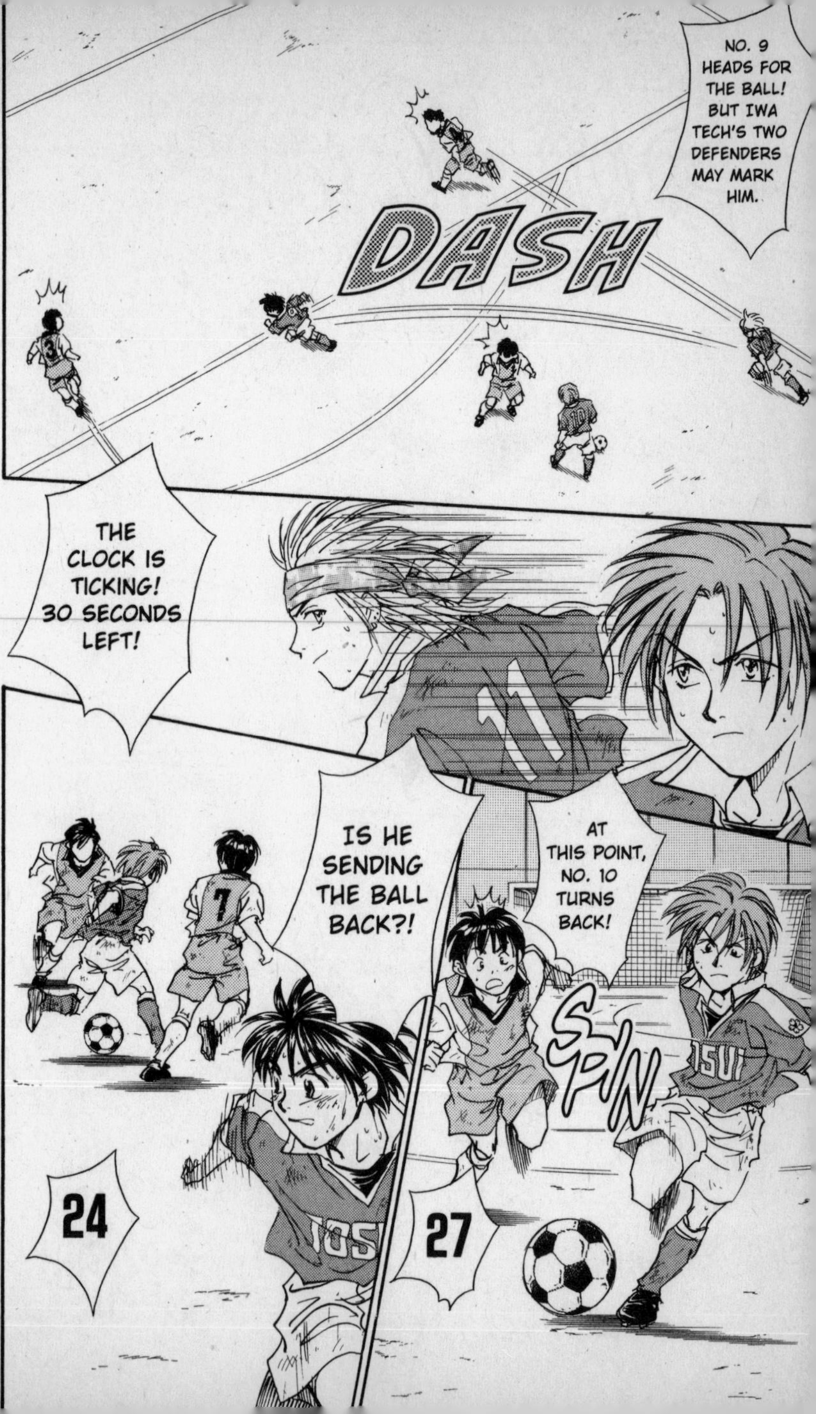
NO. 9 HEADS FOR THE BALL! BUT IWA TECH'S TWO DEFENDERS MAY MARK HIM.
DASH
THE CLOCK IS TICKING! 30 SECONDS LEFT!
AT THIS POINT, NO. 10 TURNS BACK!
SPIN
27
IS HE SENDING THE BALL BACK?!
24

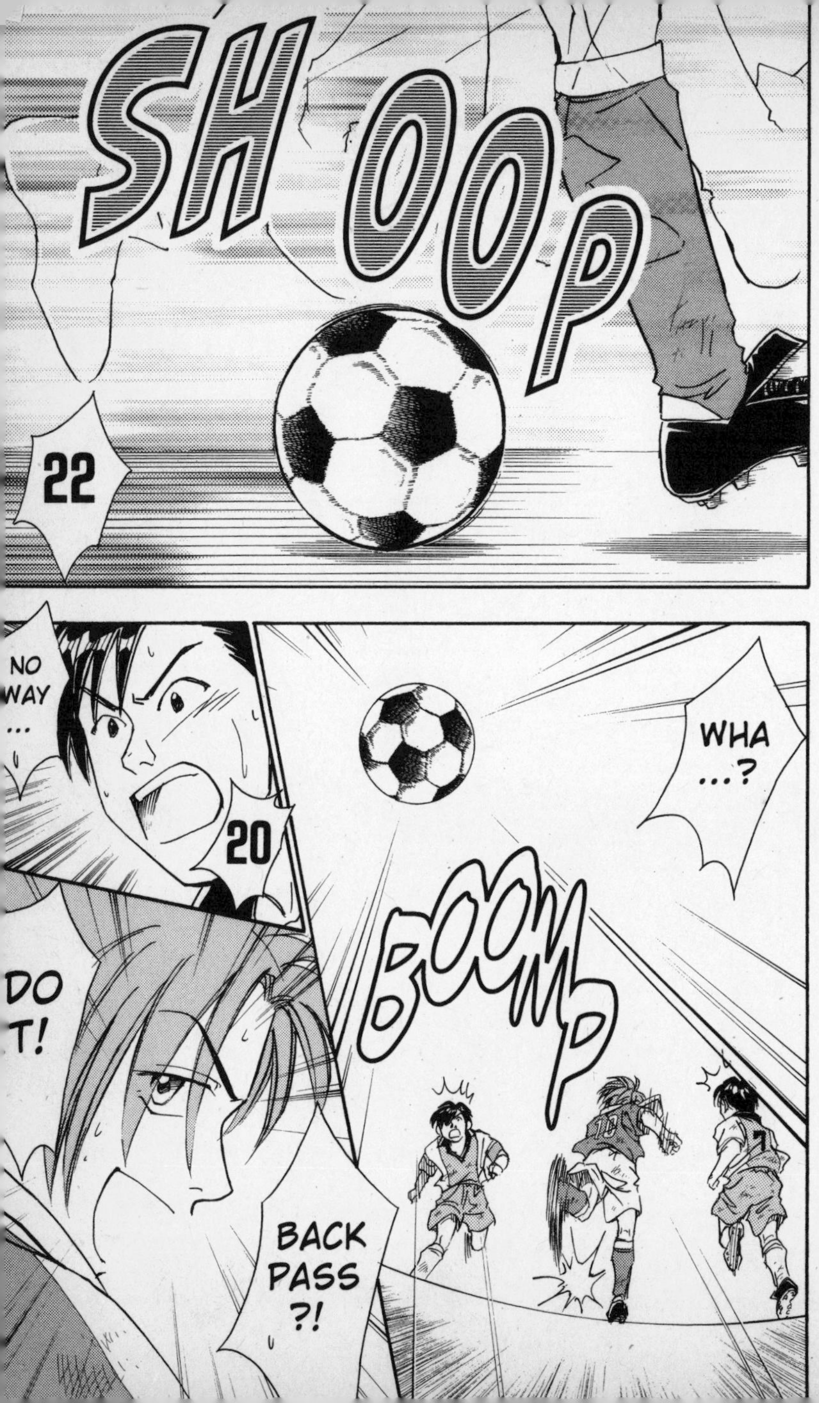
SHOOOP
22
WHA ...?
BOOMP
NO WAY ...
20
DO T!
BACK PASS ?!

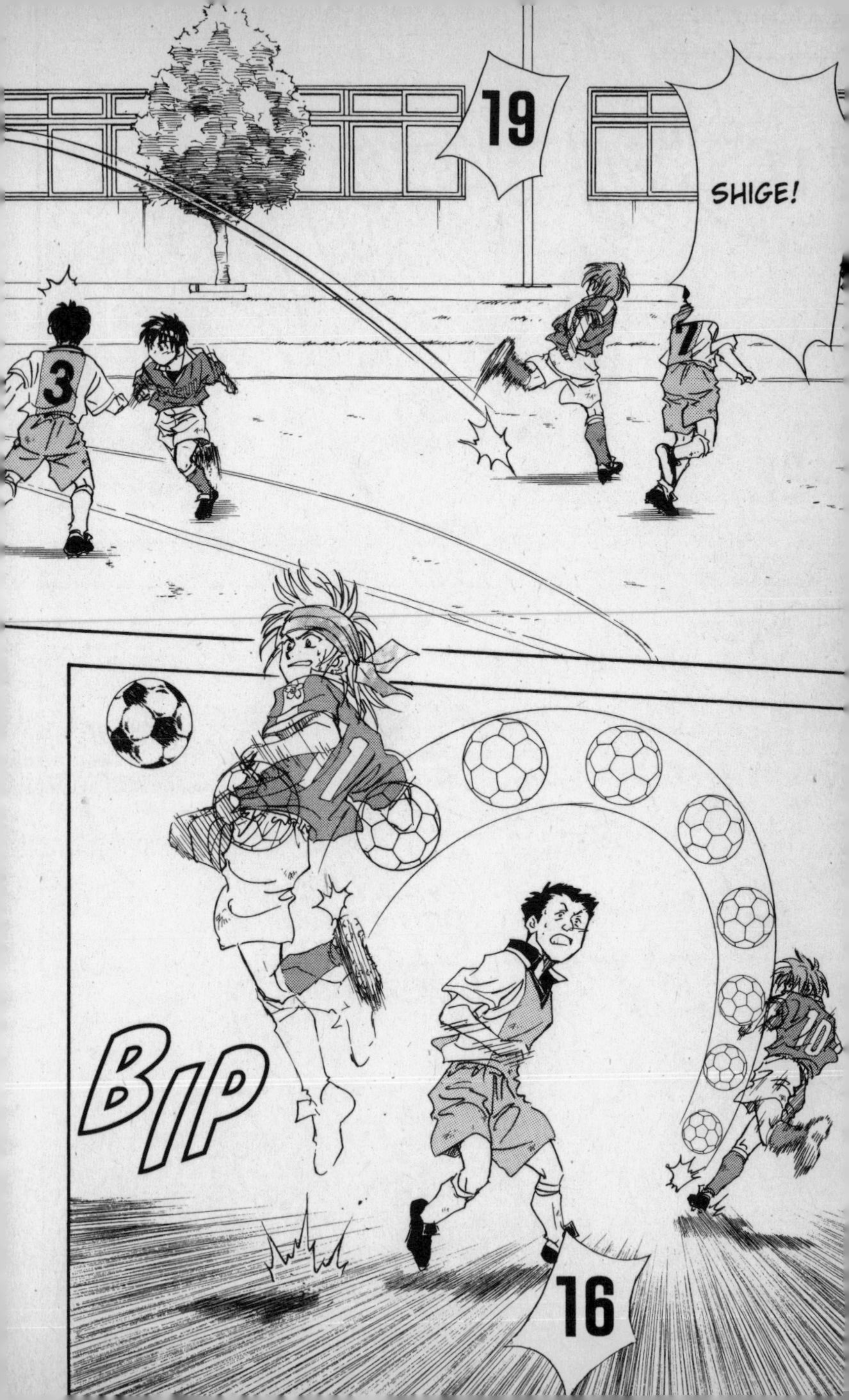
SHIGE!
19
BIP
16

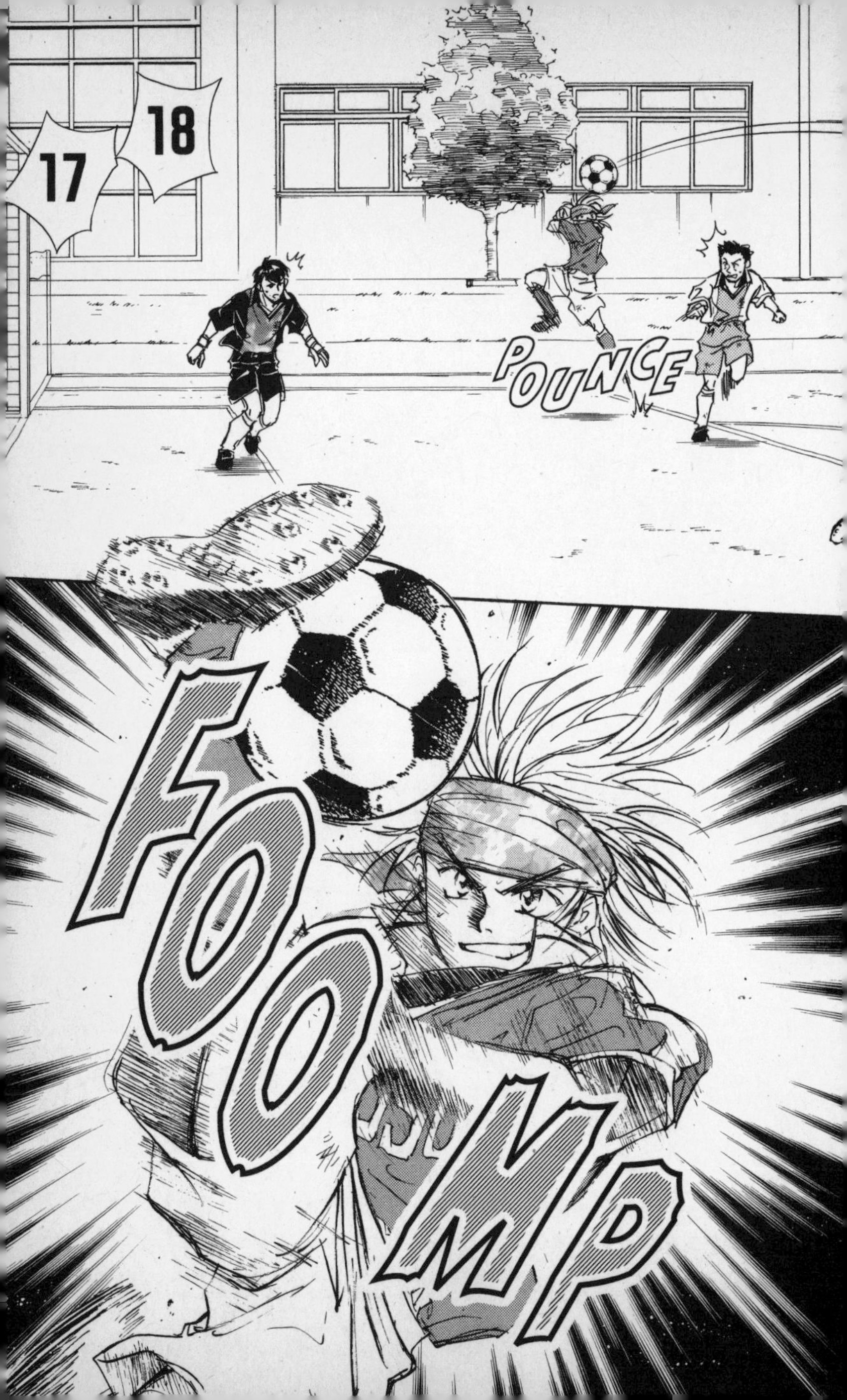
18
17
POUNCE
FOOMP

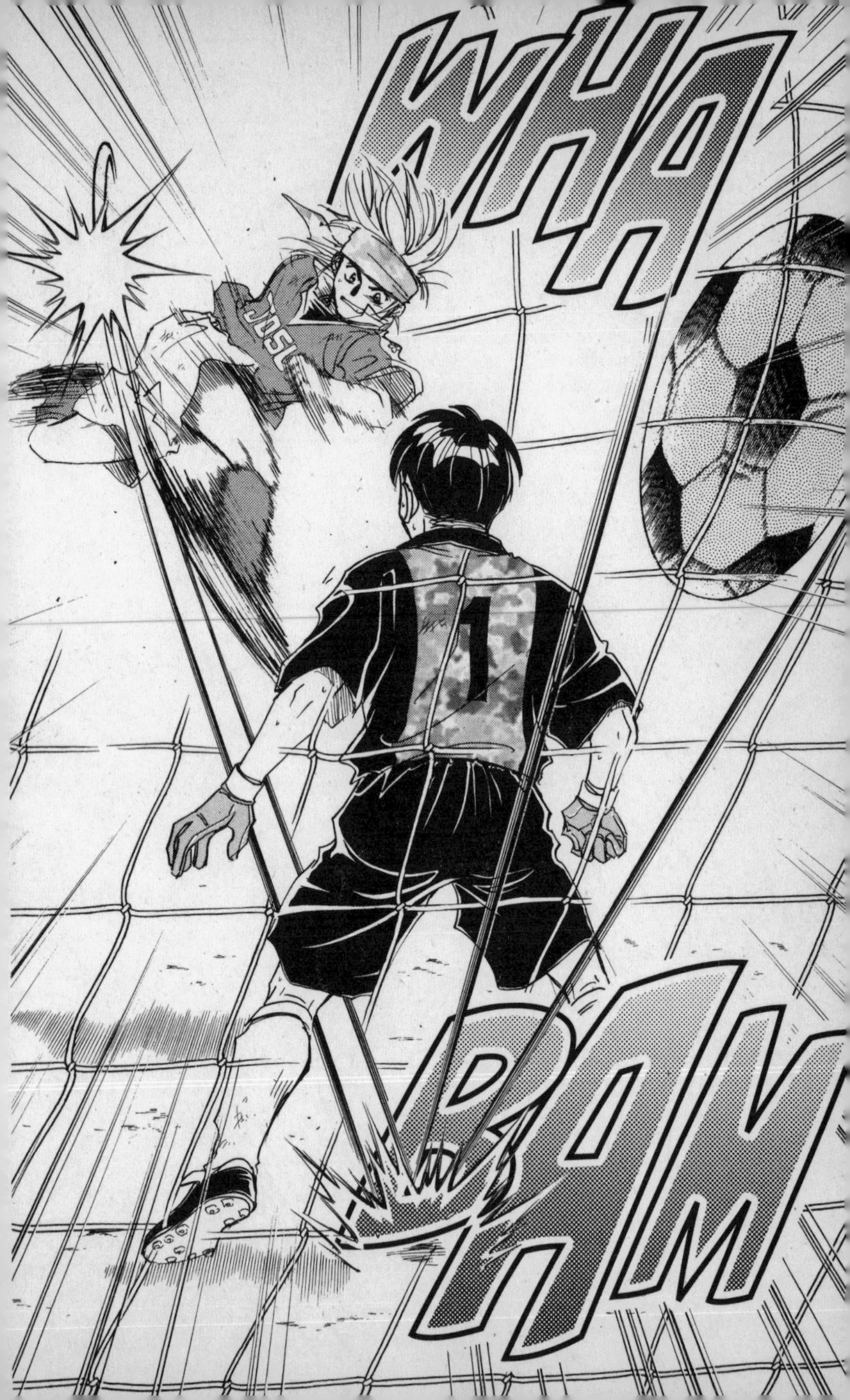
WHA
BAM

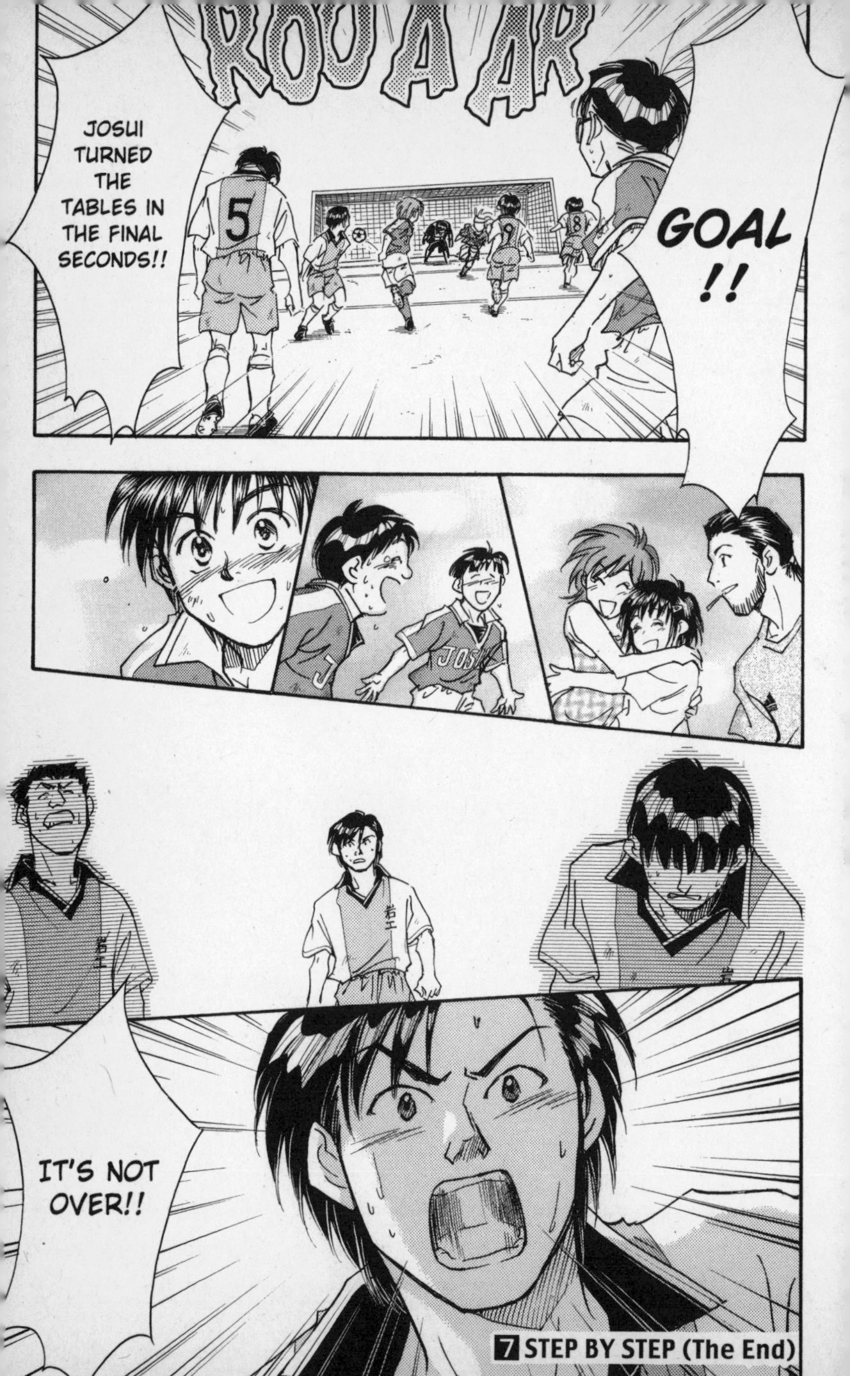
ROU A AR
GOAL !!
JOSUI TURNED THE TABLES IN THE FINAL SECONDS!!
IT'S NOT OVER!!

7 STEP BY STEP (The End)

First Round
Results of Character Popularity Votes

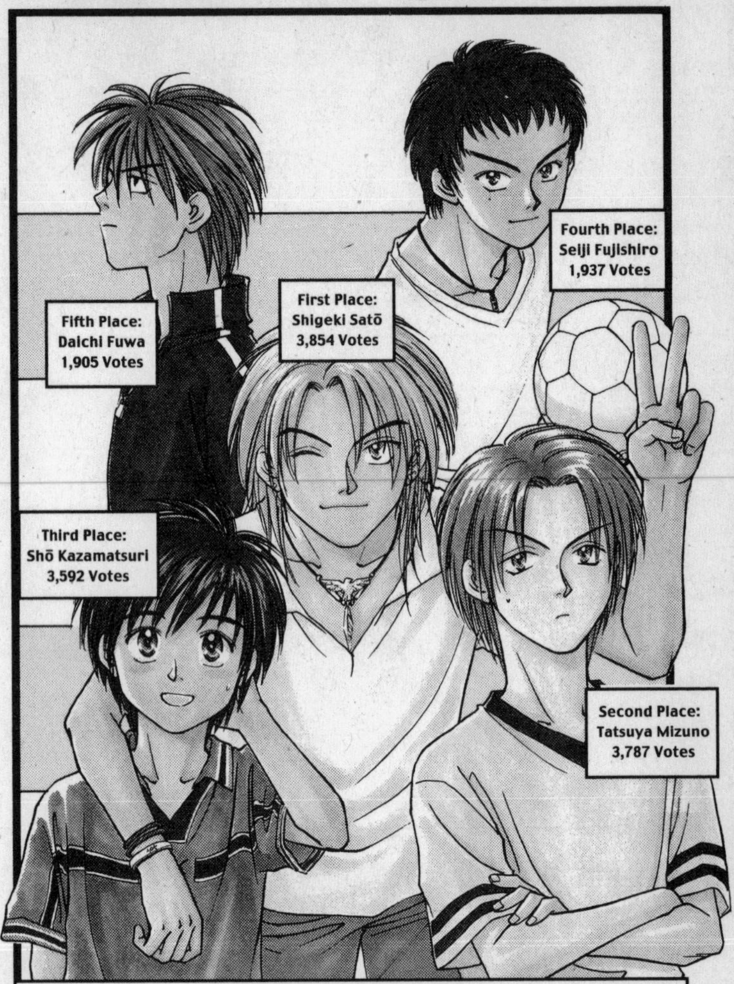

Fourth Place:
Seiji Fujishiro
1,937 Votes
First Place:
Shigeki Satō
3,854 Votes
Fifth Place:
Daichi Fuwa
1,905 Votes
Third Place:
Shō Kazamatsuri
3,592 Votes
Second Place:
Tatsuya Mizuno
3,787 Votes

Well, on behalf of my characters, I would like to express my gratitude.

ALTHOUGH WE HAVE NOT NOTIFIED RESPONDENTS IN DETAIL, THANK YOU FOR VOTING FOR VARIOUS CHARACTERS IN THOUGHTFUL POSTCARDS. COUNTING MALE VOTES ONLY, SHŌ TAKES FIRST PLACE, BUT WHEN WE INCLUDE FEMALE VOTES, HIS OVERALL SCORE GOES DOWN TO THIRD PLACE, WHICH IS INTERESTING. THAT'S VERY MUCH LIKE *WHISTLE!* I WAS GLAD THAT RYOICHI, WHOM I THOUGHT WAS DESPISED, GOT 10TH PLACE AND THAT YUKI AT NINTH PLACE RECEIVED A LOT OF FEMALE SUPPORT. I HEARD SHŌ MIGHT (OR MIGHT NOT) TRY TO GET FIRST PLACE IN THE NEXT ROUND...ANYWAY, BEST WISHES, AS ALWAYS!!

This author's comment was included when the results were released in Weekly Shonen Jump. (It's a bonus!)

HEY AMERICAN WHISTLE! FANS!
THIS POPULARITY CONTEST SURVEYED JAPANESE READERS.
WHO IS YOUR FAVORITE ***WHISTLE!*** CHARACTER? LET US KNOW AT:

***WHISTLE!* C/O SHONEN JUMP**
P.O. BOX 77010
SAN FRANCISCO, CA 94107

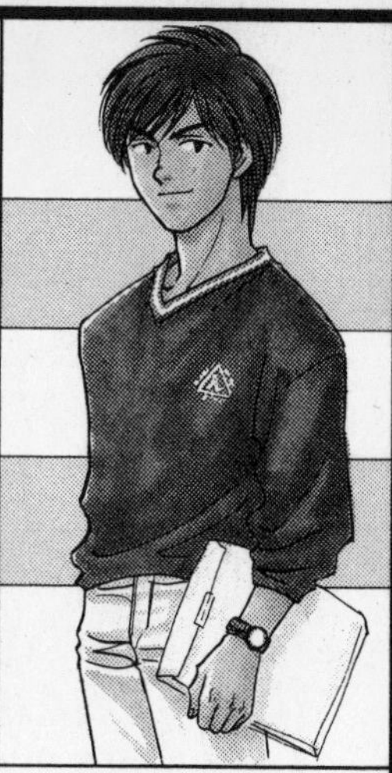

Sixth Place:
Katsurō Shibusawa
1,331 Votes

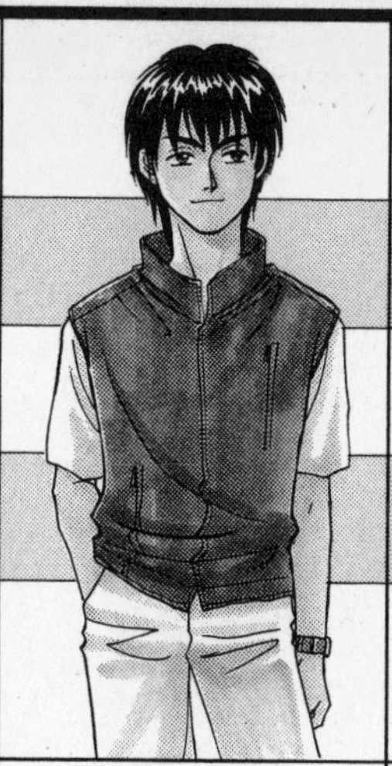

Seventh Place:
Akira Mikami
330 Votes

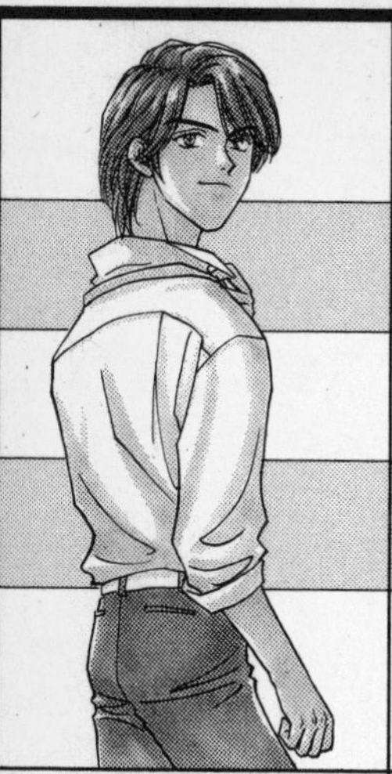

Eighth Place:
Kō Kazamatsuri
303 Votes

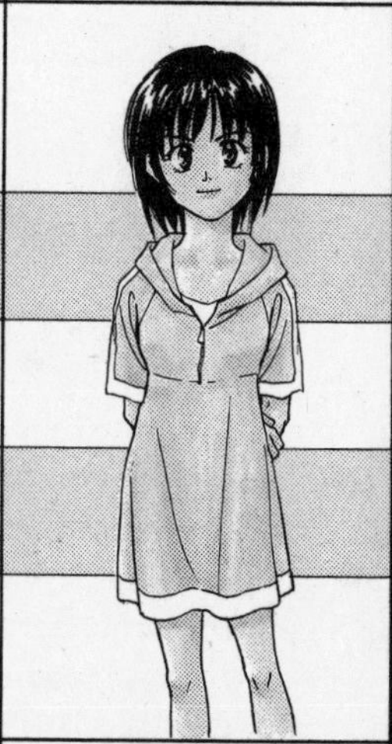

Ninth Place:
Yuki Kojima
301 Votes

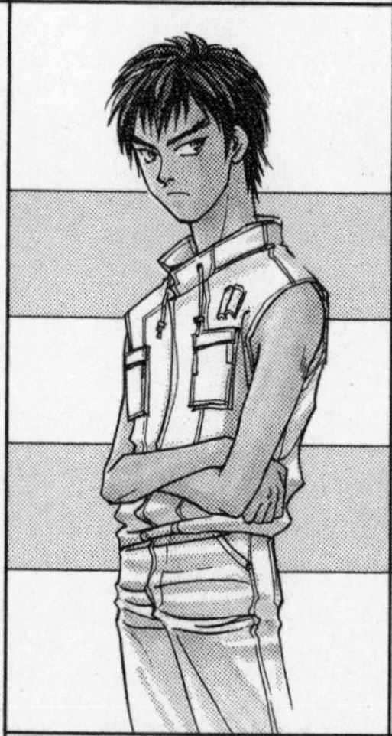

Tenth Place:
Ryoichi Tenjo
264 Votes

The rest are:

11th Place: Takumi Sakai
12th Place: Yūsuke Morinaga
13th Place: Soujū Matsushita
14th Place: Tōgo Amamiya
15th Place: Yūko Katori
16th Place: Imai-kun of
Kokubu Second Junior High
17th Place: Yasuto Negishi
18th Place: Shigeru Mamiya
19th Place: Coach Kirihara
Ex-captain Honma
21st Place: Sakamoto of
Kokubu Second
Junior High
22nd Place: Masato Takai
23rd Place: Hiroyoshi
Noro Oyassan
25th Place: Tomoyuki
Yamakawa
Ryōhei Tatsumi
Captain of Kokubu Second
Junior High
28th Place: Seiya Amano
29th Place: Kazue
Miyuki Sakurai

WE ALSO RECEIVED VOTES FOR EVEN THE MINOR CHARACTERS LIKE "GANGS OF KUZU HIGH," "MADAM IN THE FIRST EPISODE," AND "SOCCER RICE BALL." THANK YOU VERY MUCH.

Next in Whistle!

RAIN CATS AND DOGS

Shô finds out a secret about Tatsuya's family that not even Tatsuya knows about! Soon the conflict of interest turns into a conflict on the field. Matching the stormy moods on the team, the weather takes a turn for the worse, and Josui's players must overcome muddy fields and bad attitudes if they hope to achieve victory in the most important game of the district tournament!

Available November 2005!

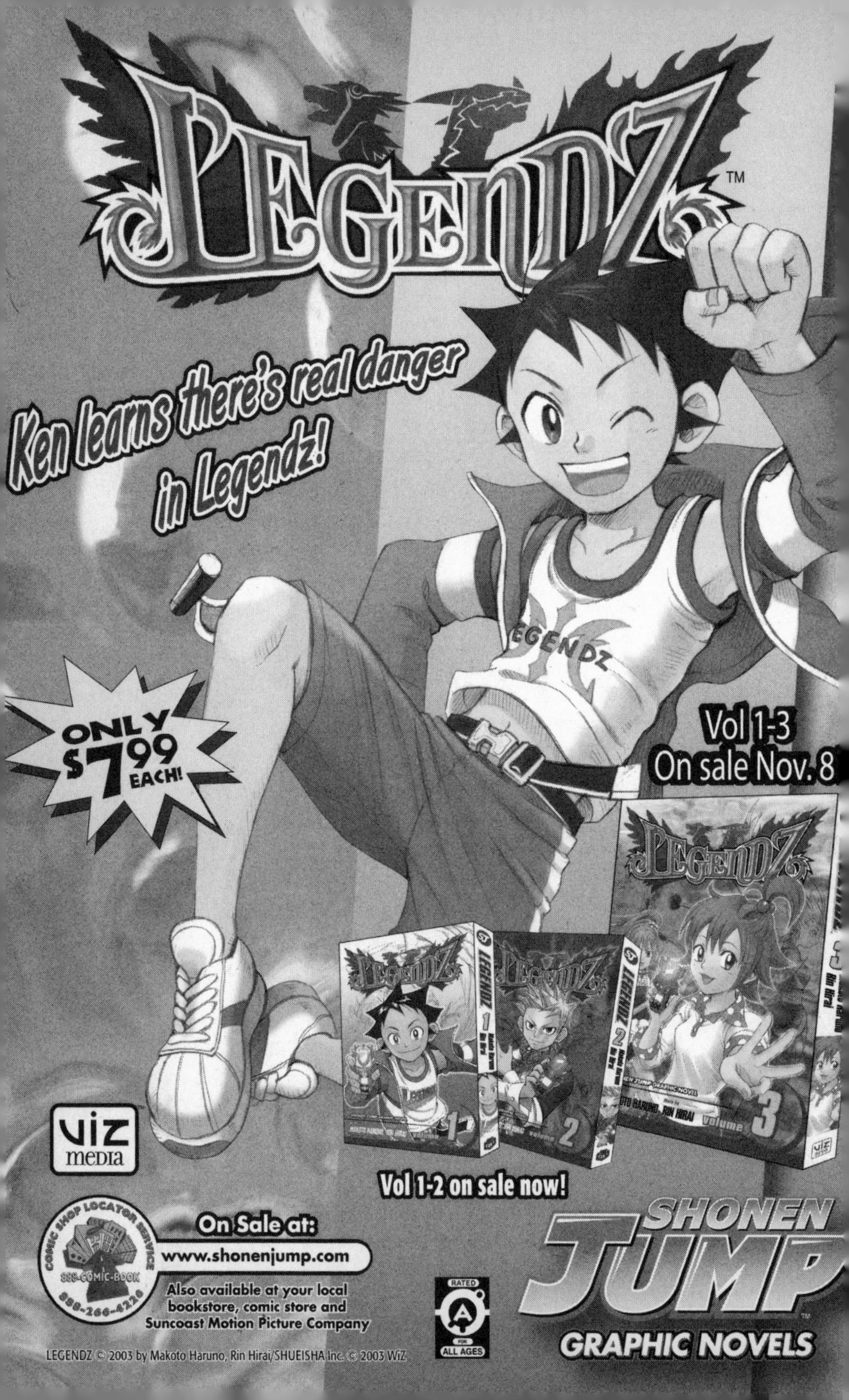

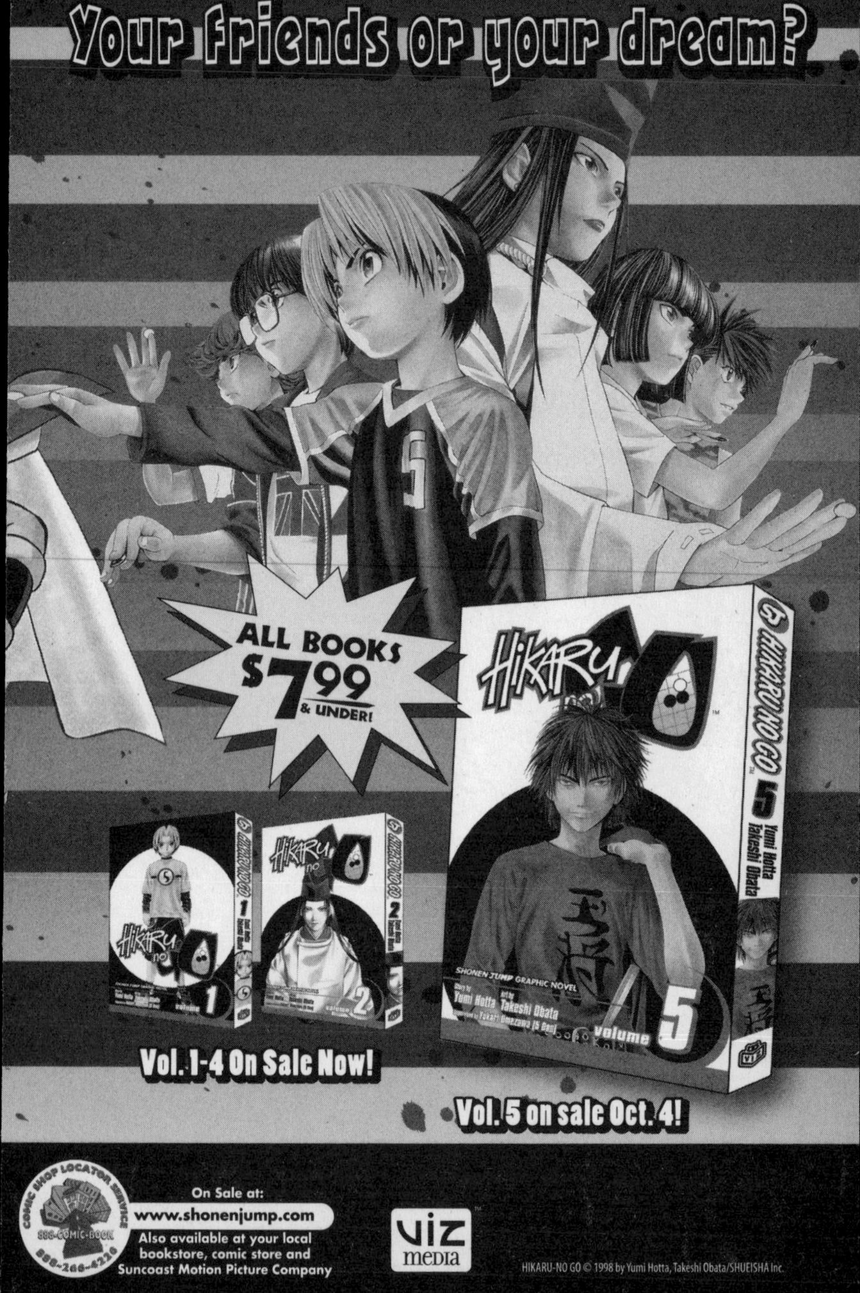

Your friends or your dream?
ALL BOOKS $7.99 & UNDER!
HIKARU NO GO
HIKARU NO GO 5 Yumi Hotta Takeshi Obata
SHONEN JUMP GRAPHIC NOVEL
Yumi Hotta Takeshi Obata
volume 5
Vol. 1-4 On Sale Now!
Vol. 5 on sale Oct. 4!
COMIC SHOP LOCATOR SERVICE
888-COMIC-BOOK
888-266-4226
On Sale at:
www.shonenjump.com
Also available at your local bookstore, comic store and Suncoast Motion Picture Company
VIZ media
HIKARU-NO GO © 1998 by Yumi Hotta, Takeshi Obata/SHUEISHA Inc.

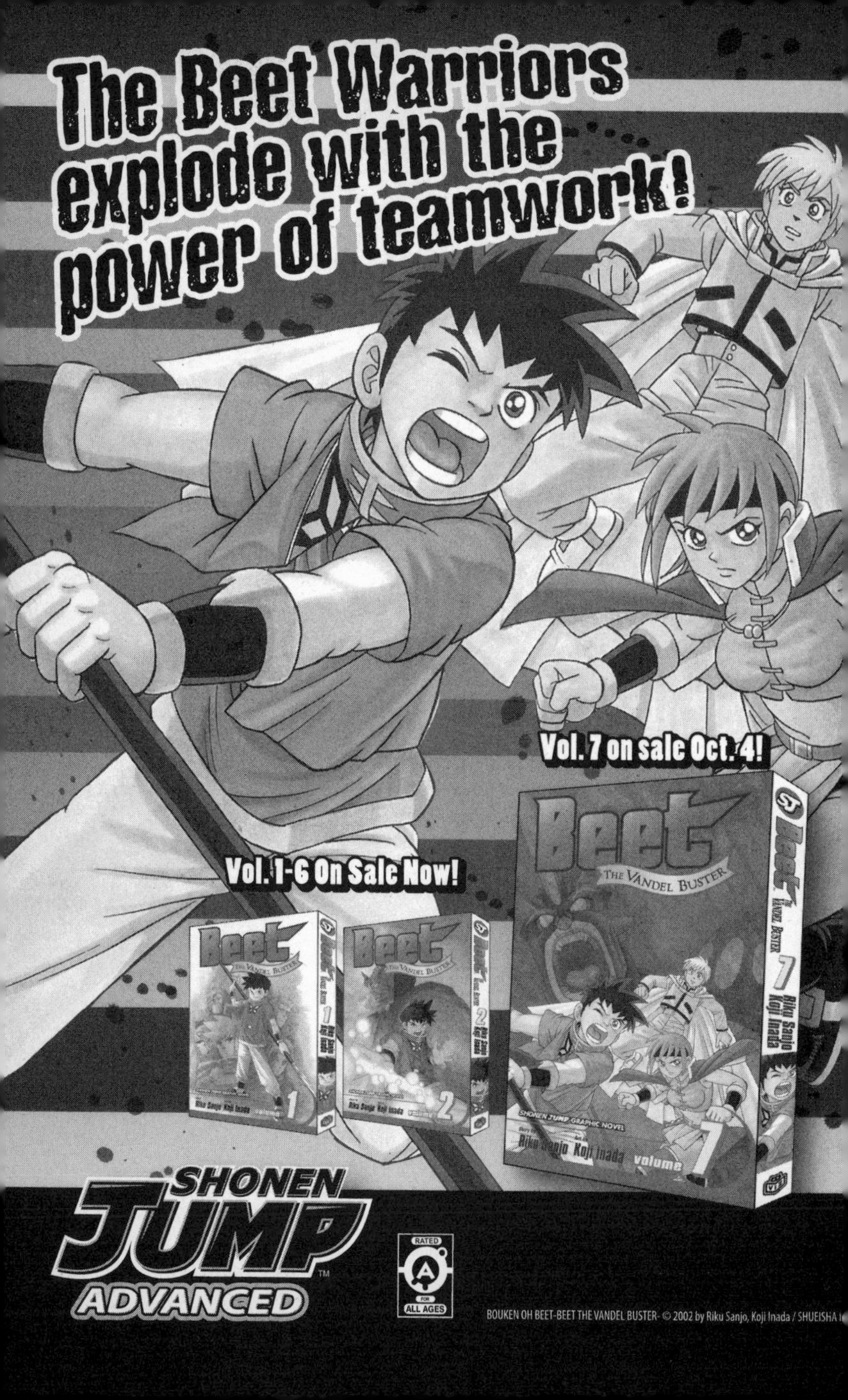
The Beet Warriors explode with the power of teamwork!
Vol. 7 on sale Oct. 4!
Vol. 1-6 On Sale Now!
Beet THE VANDEL BUSTER
SHONEN JUMP ADVANCED
RATED A FOR ALL AGES
BOUKEN OH BEET-BEET THE VANDEL BUSTER- © 2002 by Riku Sanjo, Koji Inada / SHUEISHA Inc.

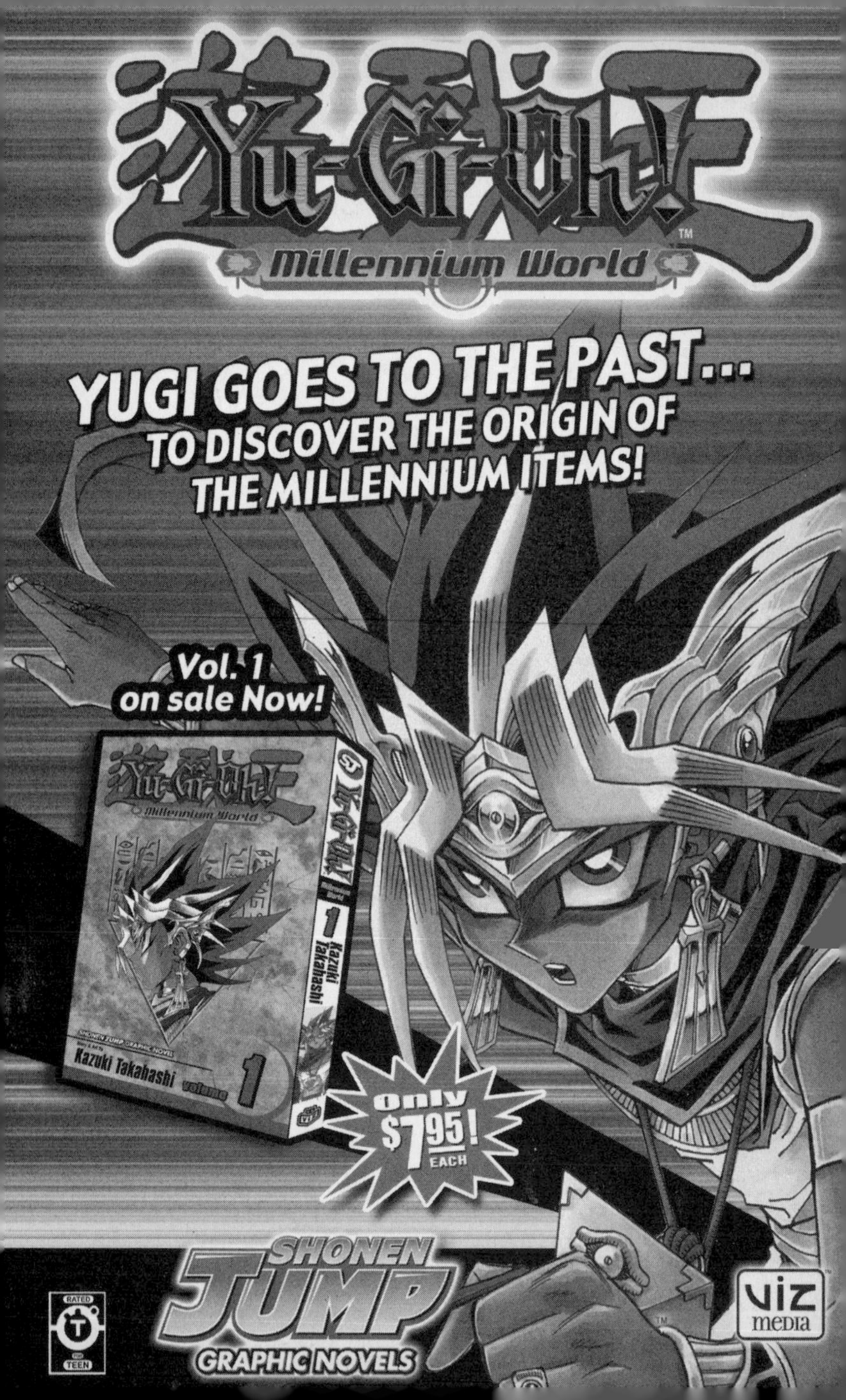
Yu-Gi-Oh!
Millennium World
YUGI GOES TO THE PAST...
TO DISCOVER THE ORIGIN OF THE MILLENNIUM ITEMS!
Vol. 1 on sale Now!
Kazuki Takahashi
volume 1
Only $7.95! EACH
SHONEN JUMP GRAPHIC NOVELS
RATED T TEEN
VIZ media

Check us out on the web!

www.shonenjump.com

COMPLETE OUR SURVEY AND LET US KNOW WHAT YOU THINK!

☐ Please do NOT send me information about VIZ and SHONEN JUMP products, news and events, special offers, or other information.

☐ Please do NOT send me information from VIZ's trusted business partners.

Name: _____

Address: _____

City: _____ **State:** _____ **Zip:** _____

E-mail: _____

☐ Male ☐ Female **Date of Birth** (mm/dd/yyyy): ___ / ___ / ___ (Under 13? Parental consent required)

❶ Do you purchase SHONEN JUMP Magazine?

☐ Yes ☐ No (if no, skip the next two questions)

If **YES**, do you subscribe?
☐ Yes ☐ No

If **NO**, how often do you purchase SHONEN JUMP Magazine?
☐ 1-3 issues a year
☐ 4-6 issues a year
☐ more than 7 issues a year

❷ Which SHONEN JUMP Graphic Novel did you purchase? (please check one)

☐ Beet the Vandel Buster ☐ Bleach ☐ Dragon Ball
☐ Dragon Ball Z ☐ Dr. Slump ☐ Eyeshield 21
☐ Hikaru no Go ☐ Hunter x Hunter ☐ I"s
☐ Knights of the Zodiac ☐ Legendz ☐ Naruto
☐ One Piece ☐ Rurouni Kenshin ☐ Shaman King
☐ The Prince of Tennis ☐ Ultimate Muscle ☐ Whistle!
☐ Yu-Gi-Oh! ☐ Yu-Gi-Oh!: Duelist ☐ YuYu Hakusho
☐ Other _____

Will you purchase subsequent volumes?
☐ Yes ☐ No

❸ How did you learn about this title? (check all that apply)

☐ Favorite title ☐ Advertisement ☐ Article
☐ Gift ☐ Read excerpt in SHONEN JUMP Magazine
☐ Recommendation ☐ Special offer ☐ Through TV animation
☐ Website ☐ Other _____